An Eye for a Bird

Frontispiece: Galapagos hawk

An Eye for a Bird

The autobiography of a
bird photographer

Eric Hosking
with Frank W. Lane

Foreword by
HRH The Prince Philip,
Duke of Edinburgh KG KT

HUTCHINSON OF LONDON

HUTCHINSON & CO (*Publishers*) LTD
3 Fitzroy Square, London W1

London Melbourne Sydney Auckland
Wellington Johannesburg Cape Town
and agencies throughout the world

First published October 1970
Second impression November 1970
Third impression March 1971
Fourth impression January 1972

Printed in Great Britain by litho on antique wove paper
by Anchor Press, and bound by Wm. Brendon,
both of Tiptree, Essex

ISBN 0 09 104460 x

To Margaret, Robin and David

Acknowledgments

I wish to thank the following for permission to quote from the works mentioned:

B. T. Batsford Ltd., London, for *Wild Birds in Britain* by Seton Gordon. William Collins, Sons & Co. Ltd., for *Triumph in the West* by Arthur Bryant.

The author for *Portrait of a River* by Guy Mountfort (Hutchinson & Co. Ltd.).

The Hamlyn Publishing Group Ltd., London, for *Intimate Sketches from Bird Life* by Cyril Newberry and Eric Hosking (Country Life).

Her Majesty's Stationery Office, London, for *Hansard*.

Contents

Illustrations

Foreword by HRH The Prince Philip,
Duke of Edinburgh KG KT

To Eric Hosking, who took his first bird photograph at the age of eight, I am obviously a very slow developer, as I only started at a rather more mature age. Anyone can see what marvellous pictures he takes and he has amassed a wealth of experience and knowledge, yet no one could be kinder or more encouraging to the beginner and the amateur. At first I rather suspected that his very generous attitude towards my rather halting efforts was perhaps a bit more polite than strictly necessary, but I soon discovered that this cheerful kindliness was absolutely genuine and one of the nicest features of his sunny nature.

Taking photographs of birds may not be the most likely way to make a fortune but as this book shows it is obviously a good way to a full life and a happy one. I know few people who enjoy their work and their life as much as Eric Hosking does, in fact I doubt whether he recognises any distinction between working and living.

Many people probably like the idea of doing something unusual, but when it comes to the moment of decision it is usually easier to play for safety or to do what everyone else is doing. It needs considerable enthusiasm and determination to follow an independent line but it needs real talent to make a success of it.

It is quite evident from this most entertaining book that Eric Hosking is both enthusiastic and determined and the pictures demonstrate his talent but, more than this, it makes it quite plain that he has enjoyed every moment of his unusual way of life.

July 1970

o

Introduction by Frank W. Lane

Bird photography in Great Britain began towards the end of the nineteenth century. An anonymous photograph of a long-eared owl was published in 1868; in 1887 J. C. Mansel-Pleydell photographed mute swans at Abbotsbury, Dorset; in 1892 Cherry Kearton photographed the nest and eggs of a song thrush; and in 1895 R. B. Lodge used a remotely controlled camera to photograph a lapwing on its nest.

The first bird photographers worked with simple but cumbersome plate cameras. Their successors have a large armoury of complicated equipment—photographic, mechanical and electronic—to help them in their craft. More than any other man, Eric Hosking links the two generations. He took his first bird photograph with a Box Brownie when he was eight years old; today he uses some of the most sophisticated apparatus that space-age technology can provide.

The autobiography of anyone whose life spans the photographic generations in this way would be of interest, but Eric Hosking's life-story is more than a bare account of photographic expertise. He has visited every continent except the Antipodes, and 'lived rough' in a dozen countries; spent thirty-two years lecturing throughout the British Isles; co-authored a dozen books and illustrated another 700; has a wide knowledge of British natural history and is one of the most experienced ornithologists alive. He has met nearly all the leading ornithologists and bird photographers of the Western world, and been an intimate of some of the leading public figures of our day. All these interests and experiences are reflected in the story he has to tell.

But there are some things about himself which he cannot be expected to tell, and that is the reason for this introduction, written by one who has known and admired him for more than thirty years.

What is he like? Stocky, with small hands and feet; a dark but bright keen eye; and an outgoing easy manner with an oft-exploded friendly chuckle. He is a Cockney, and proud of it, and has his fair share of that species' thrustfulness, plain-speaking and volubility. He is also a perfectionist, superbly skilled in his chosen craft.

His outstanding qualities are dedication and a buoyant enthusiasm. Bird photography is his life, and he is ruthless with himself—and sometimes with others—in its pursuit. After an arduous ten or twelve hours in the field, he rarely goes to bed without thoroughly cleaning and overhauling his cameras and equipment, often spending a couple of hours on the task.

With this dedication goes a physical and mental toughness, and enormous energy—he has been called The Mighty Atom. In the field, and when he has a rush of work at home, Eric frequently works an eighteen-hour day, and sometimes does thirty hours or so at a stretch. He once stayed thirty-six hours continuously in a hide. And much time can be spent in a hide with very little to show for it. One day he endured nine sweltering hours in a Spanish Imperial eagle's hide for four minutes' photography.

There is a revealing passage in Dorothy Hosking's journal of a sojourn on the Norfolk Broads during the filming of the Two Cities Film, *The Tawny Pipit*, for which Eric was photographic adviser. She notes the surprise they felt at the camera-men's eight-hour day, five-day week. 'It was only natural, of course, but it seemed strange to us who worked all day and often all night as well—and a seven-day week at that!'

Bird photography of the Eric Hosking variety is no job for a weakling, or for the man with no head for heights. In addition to his professional skills he has, at times, combined the rôles of mountaineer, steeplejack, carpenter, construction mechanic, navvy and electrical engineer. His work—sometimes with help, sometimes without—frequently involves tramping across rough country loaded down with half a hundredweight of equipment—cameras, lenses, electronic apparatus, tripod, hide and rucksack—and sitting in a small hide, often under a scorching sun, sometimes in Arctic cold, for six, eight and exceptionally many more hours.

That is the comparatively 'easy' form of bird photography—from a hide on the flat. But much of Eric's work has been done at tree-top level, on wooden or steel pylons—on one occasion sixty-four feet high. And that is not the worst. In Wales he sat in a hide on a two-foot ledge of rock on a rugged cliff-face sixty feet above the sea; and in Norway—and this to me is the most terrifying of all—he had to negotiate a wet and slippery ledge beneath a rock over-hang on an almost perpendicular cliff, with nothing between him and the sea 300 ft. below—*without benefit of a rope*.

In a hide, Eric can freeze into immobility, remaining, if necessary, statue-like for hours. Once a poisonous snake slid into his hide, settled between his boots and went to sleep. The snake moved first! Other, more ordinary mortals, who have shared a hide with him say that it is an unnerving experience. The slightest unnecessary sound or movement is apt to draw forth a glare or growl from this preternaturally still and silent man—in a hide only. Hosking must be one of the very few people who have told Field Marshal Lord Alanbrooke to keep quiet. According to the Hosking standard he was making too much noise near a bird's nest.

Eric Hosking is a *bird* photographer and he is ever careful to keep his priorities right: the bird comes first. He is hurt if he thinks any action of his has caused a bird distress. When 'gardening' (arranging the foliage round a nest to get a clear view for photography) he is careful to see that afterwards the nest is again hidden from prying eyes. Guy Mountfort, leader of many expeditions on which Eric has been the director of photography, told me that the only time he has seen him really angry was when someone was 'gardening' with no thought for the welfare of the bird.

Once Eric literally put a bird's welfare before his own life. The nest of a hobby, one of our rarest birds of prey, was being photographed from a hide atop a sixty-four-foot pylon when the sky darkened into a violent thunderstorm. To stay at the top of a steel tower higher than the surrounding trees while lightning split the clouds overhead was courting death. I asked him why ever he didn't come down. He replied: 'Because I would not risk disturbing the birds'; at that age the young would have died in a few minutes if the adult had left them unprotected from the pelting rain.

It is obvious from this book that Eric Hosking has amassed a vast fund of hard-won knowledge. What is not obvious is his generosity in sharing that knowledge with others. Scores of young, and not so young, bird photographers have asked for help and none has asked in vain. For many years—when he was giving eighty or so lectures a year—he received an average of fifteen letters a day, and all but the lunatic ones received a conscientious reply. And he is prodigal of his time in serving on photographic, ornithological and conservation committees.

John Markham told me that during the war he had a fortnight's summer leave from his air-raid warden duties, and wanted to spend it photographing birds. But he had no time to find nests and erect hides. Eric invited him to join him on the Norfolk Broads, where he was working, and to make free use of all his hides. And Markham is probably Hosking's greatest rival.

Manufacturers of photographic and electronic equipment also benefit from Eric Hosking's work, for he frequently carries out tests

B

in the field. His reports and suggestions for improvements have advanced the cause of photography generally.

The greatest and best influence in Eric Hosking's life is his family. His parents gave him understanding and encouragement in the early days when his need for both was all-important. They lived to see the abundant fulfilment of that early promise.

He was equally fortunate in his marriage, as he is the first to admit. A dedicated bird photographer and lecturer is not every girl's ideal for a husband. Away for two or three months in the summer, he comes home to immure himself in his dark-room for several weeks. In October he is off on the punishing professional lecture circuit, rarely spending more than two or three consecutive nights at home. And always there is the business of sending out and selling the photographs, much of which inevitably devolves on his wife.

As if all that were not sufficient to daunt a girl, she must also be prepared for the conversation to revolve round birds and photographs whenever her husband is present. The plates, the table-mats, the napkins, the pictures on the walls, the decorative china—nearly all have bird motifs in the Hosking household.

Only an exceptional girl would take on and make a success of marriage to such a man. In Dorothy Sleigh, Eric Hosking found that girl. The honeymoon was a trip to wildest Scotland to photograph the golden eagle! She and their three children have given him the priceless blessing of a very happy home. He once said to me: 'I could not have done what I have without Dorothy.'

What he has done is the subject of this book. He is an uncomplicated man, little given to self-examination. Similarly, his autobiography is a plain tale, with no attempt at soul searching. It is the story of a man born with no particular gifts who, by hard work and great determination, and despite the loss of an eye early in his career, became the foremost bird photographer in the world. As long as men are interested in that lovely craft they will salute the name of Eric Hosking.

I | *Beginnings*

My maternal grandfather insisted that he was *not* a butcher. A meat purveyor, yes: a butcher, no. He would sell meat, but he was too fond of animals to kill them, and consequently bought his supplies at Smithfield Market in London. As *his* father was a farmer, I suppose an interest in animals is in my blood.

In spite of a weak heart Grandmother had twelve children and lived to be ninety-five. My mother—Margaret Helen Steggall—was the ninth, born on 7 March 1879.

Despite her small stature, Mother was a woman of great drive and determination, and there is no doubt that, had she been of this generation, she would have been an astute business woman. She took charge of Grandfather's office, often working long hours to balance the books. She was only too pleased to help, as she greatly admired him and the way he provided for their united and happy home.

To her marriage she brought her great ability and resourcefulness. Although money was tight and there was no domestic help, her young family was contented and well fed. She made many of our clothes, often working far into the night making and mending, washing and ironing. However tired, she never lost her temper with us, but she knew how to deliver a severe reprimand! She was the backbone, the heart and soul of our family, and we all loved her dearly.

It might well be that I inherited a love of photography. My mother's family lived at 41 King's Road, Chelsea, next door to William Friese-Greene, one of the pioneers of cinematography. Two of my uncles were keen on photography and they were always 'going next door'. The great man welcomed their visits and, typical of the true enthusiast, shared his knowledge with them and imparted something of his own absorbing interest in the new art.

To pay for his experimental work, Friese-Greene took portraits. We possess a family album of photographs mostly taken by him and they are excellent, still retaining a beautiful quality and range of tone rarely seen today. Although some of them are now more than eighty years old, they show no sign of fading.

Like so many geniuses who have contributed so much to human advancement, Friese-Greene did not have much business acumen and was sometimes in financial difficulties. If there were no portraits to be taken he pawned his cameras while he concentrated on his real work—cinematograph experiments. When a client arrived he rushed round to the Steggalls', borrowed money from my grandfather to redeem his cameras, hurried back, took the portraits, returned the cameras to the pawnshop, repaid Grandfather—and had a little money in hand.

One memorable day in the early nineties there came a furious knocking on the door and the whole family were bidden to come, with the magic cry: 'It's moving! It's moving!' Friese-Greene had successfully filmed a military funeral which was passing his house on its way from Chelsea Barracks to Brompton Cemetery. It may well have been the first news film.

In marked contrast to the happy family life of my mother, Father's early life was hard indeed. At one time Grandfather Hosking was a successful business man in Chelsea, owning a bespoke boot and shoemaker's shop. He must have been successful, for by the time he was thirty he was wealthy enough to own three houses, in one of which the family lived with their six children. But in later years he became an alcoholic, ruining his own life and almost that of his family as well. Although a charming man and fond enough of his family when sober, when drunk he lost all sense of responsibility. Eventually his business failed, two of the houses had to be sold, and finally the household furniture. All that remained was the third house, the family home, which in a fit of remorse he had made over to his wife, my grandmother, whom my mother described as 'a perfect angel'.

My father, the eldest child, did well at school and at the age of twelve was head boy, subsequently winning a scholarship to Westminster School. But his father refused to let him take it, saying that as he was top at his school further studies were pointless! So, when twelve years old, Father became an office boy and at the end of his first week received five shillings. As he left his workplace, he saw his father waiting, managed to avoid him, and ran all the way home. He thrust the five shillings into his mother's hand—then fainted.

Each morning, before he went to his office job, Father was out on a baker's round, delivering hot rolls. For this he was paid sixpence a week, plus a daily pillow-case full of left-over bread, rolls and pastries—three most valuable fringe benefits.

In spite of all the difficulties Father determined to make his way in the world and become an accountant. He pursued his studies at evening classes, and in his bedroom, by candlelight, after his brothers and sisters were asleep. More than once his father pawned his textbooks. Yet, despite everything, in 1907 he gained fifth place in Great Britain in the Final Examination of the Society of Accountants and Auditors.

When Father was twenty-one, Grandfather died, aged forty-six, after spending the last two years of his life in hospital. The sad lessons of his life have greatly influenced me. I have an ardent nature and never do things by halves. Rather than run the slightest risk of becoming addicted to alcohol I resolved never to touch it. Some of my friends have wondered at my staunch teetotalism. Now they know why.

I was born on 2 October 1909 and my survival was touch-and-go. To quote my mother: 'You were a poor little thing—legs like bits of stick.' I was weighed every week at the local chemist's shop, and made painfully slow progress. When I was seven my mother took me to the local school, but no sooner had she departed than I bolted, arriving home only just after she did. Since I suffered badly from bronchitis I did not go to school regularly until I was ten, and then it was to the Stationers' Company's School, Hornsey.

Both Mother and Father were keenly interested in animals and the family were frequently taken to the London Zoo. I was particularly fond of riding on the elephants and feeding the sea lions, and soon made friends with the keepers, who allowed me to go into some of the cages and help feed their charges. It is hardly surprising that my first published photographs were taken at the Zoo.

My sister Dylla was born in August 1915. My brother Gordon was then eight and Stuart nine. Father was away dealing with accounts at a munitions factory, so Mother asked Stuart to send a telegram. The managing director sent for Father. From among a sheaf of telegrams on his desk asking for shells, guns, grenades, rifles and other engines of war, he picked up Stuart's and handed it to Father, saying: 'Here, Hosking, I think this is for you.' It read: 'Jesus has sent us a little sister.'

Very different was the effect of another telegram announcing the death, in June 1918, of my Uncle Frank, Mother's youngest brother, and ten years her junior. She had done much to help bring him up, and she adored him. Uncle was a second lieutenant in the Royal Flying Corps stationed in Egypt. He was due home on furlough and only hours before leaving was asked to test a newly repaired aircraft before it returned to service. He made a perfect take-off, but when only thirty feet up the aircraft stalled and crashed.

Whenever he was home on leave Uncle Frank stayed with us at

55 St. Mary's Road, London, S.E.15, and he was our hero. One of our happiest memories of him concerns a Christmas present of a clockwork railway which my parents had bought for us. As well as lots of rails there were *three* engines—one for each of us. Uncle Frank and a friend stayed up all Christmas Eve and well into Christmas morning assembling it on the playroom floor. Mother says our eyes were 'a real picture' when we went into the room—and reckons that Uncle Frank got as much fun out of the outfit as we did.

Just before going to Egypt, my uncle had given me his old shoulder badges, carefully attached to a white card on which he had written: 'Keep 'em clean, old man.' I still recall my own first sense of personal loss at the news of his death, and my mother's profound grief.

My first camera was given to me by my parents when I was seven or eight. It was a Kodak Box Brownie, costing five shillings, and although I took some photographs with it they were not very good. By the time I was ten I had managed to save sufficient money to buy a better camera. 'Saved' is the operative word, for the highest denominator in the bag of cash which I pushed over the counter was sixpence, in company with scores of halfpennies and farthings.

As a result I now became the proud possessor of a thirty-shilling plate camera complete with three plate-holders taking $4\frac{1}{4}$ in. $\times 3\frac{1}{4}$ in. glass negatives. My father, who accompanied me to the shop, bought me a dozen plates with which to get started.

Immediately I got home, I loaded three plates and hurried to a song thrush's nest I had found and took my first bird 'photograph'. Back home again I persuaded my elder brother Stuart to help me develop it. I was so excited I could hardly wait for the light to be switched on, but as we looked at the negative my heart sank—it was just a misty blur. I had not realised that it was necessary to focus a camera and I had merely rested the lens on the edge of the nest and pressed the shutter release! But this served as a useful lesson; it made me realise that there was more in this photography business than I had imagined.

Natural history, especially birds, now occupied more and more of my time. On walks with the family in the country and at the seaside 'Where's Eric?' was a frequent cry, and I would be found, often hundreds of yards behind, searching about in a hedge or on a beach.

I commandeered anything in the natural history line, and what I found I wanted to keep. One of my earliest remembered sayings, when I was two or three, was: 'Wouldn't it be awfully decent if we could catch some beekles and put them in a mashbox.' It was standard practice for a good many years in the Hosking household to shake a matchbox before opening it. The odds were that instead of matches any given box would contain a snail, slug, caterpillar, moth, earwig, butterfly—or 'beekle'.

Then there was the toad. I brought it home while Mother was out visiting, played with it in the garden until bedtime then, reluctant to part with it, put it under my bed. When Mother came home one of my brothers called out: 'Mum, Eric's got a toad under his bed.' When Mother came to investigate I assured her that it was quite all right as toads lived on insects. To which she indignantly replied: 'And where is it going to find insects in here?' Thereafter the toad spent its nights in the garden.

I was only eight when I started a nature club with some like-minded pals. Members had to write down the name of every wild bird they saw each day—not, to me, an arduous task, as I had kept such a record ever since I could write.

At Stationers' Company's School I joined both the Photographic and the Natural History Societies. The school had a fine four-pound perch in one of its three aquaria, and Dr. Rost, the master in charge, suggested that I might like to help him photograph it. What trouble we took! First we placed a sheet of glass inside the tank to keep the perch near the front, and in focus. The camera was erected on its tripod, care being taken that it was square with the tank. Then we had difficulty with the lamps, for wherever we put them, reflections spoilt the picture. But at last everything seemed right, and as the perch swam to the middle of the tank, Dr. Rost took the picture. In all, six exposures were made and I was allowed to make one of them.

In the dark-room we loaded the six precious plates into a developing tank. The developer and hypo (fixing solution) had been prepared and in the darkness the tank was filled. I acted as timekeeper and after twenty minutes the tank was emptied and the other solution poured in. After another twenty minutes we took the plates out to see the results. A complete blank—not a trace of an image anywhere. It was then that we discovered that we had poured the hypo into the tank before the developer! It was a bitter experience, but I have never made the same mistake again.

When I should have been doing homework I was often looking for birds' nests, or was out late in the local woods listening to owls. When on holiday with the family and friends I would run a competition; every day each person was to try to see—and record—a different bird, mammal and insect. Marks were given and at the end of the holiday a prize was awarded for the highest score.

It was hardly surprising that by the time I was fifteen I wanted to leave school. The headmaster said: 'Hosking, you'll never make anything of your life.' It was obvious that the academic life was not for me and, since I badly needed money for my hobbies, the sooner I could start earning my living the better.

So I left school and in 1925 was apprenticed to Stewart & Arden, the Morris motor-car dealers, then in Pimlico. I rose at 6 a.m. and left home at 6.30 to clock in at 8 a.m. I was rarely home before 7.30 p.m.— usually smothered in oil and grease. After the inevitable bath and change I had supper and was then fit only for bed. My salary for this was ten shillings a week, all of which was spent on travelling.

I eventually left Stewart & Arden when they moved to Acton, and when I was sixteen and a half started at Messrs. George Johnston Ltd., in Shaftesbury Avenue, a firm supplying motor body-building materials. I was part clerk, part junior salesman, and although I never really liked the work, I did learn office routine: filing, record-keeping, book-keeping, salesmanship and how to deal efficiently and promptly with customers' requirements. This training has helped me greatly in running my own photographic business.

While working there I had an accident which affected me permanently. Johnston's back entrance, which was in New Compton Street, was about thirty inches above floor level. A large hydraulic car lift was used, not only to transport goods to floor level, but also down to the basement. One day I was helping to lift a box of hinges weighing two hundredweight on to the lift, which was up at back-entrance level. As I did so my left foot protruded a few inches over the lift-well. Thinking to help, a third person lowered the lift, crushing the front of my foot and breaking three toes.

I was rushed across the road to the French Hospital where a doctor took one look and said that the big toenail would have to be removed completely. I asked if he would give me something to deaden the pain. 'That's of secondary importance,' he said, and promptly wrenched off the nail. Since then it has always been deformed. Nor was that all. Some two years later the bursa, or soft pad, under the same toe had to be removed.

Ever since that accident I have had to wear special footwear, and even now suffer considerable pain whenever I walk over rough ground. My damaged foot was also one of the reasons why I could not enlist during the war.

It was now 1929. My employers went into liquidation and, in company with millions of my fellow countrymen, I lost my job. I was on the dole.

Above left: My maternal grandparents. Taken by William Friese-Greene in 1898
Above right: My mother
Below left: Grandmother Hosking with my six-day-old sister Dylla. Photographer unknown
Below right: My father

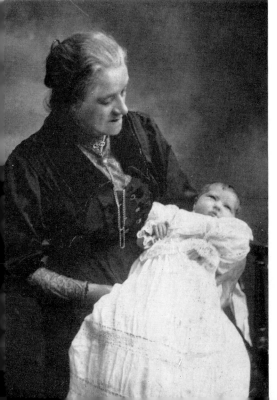

Above: Mary Parkinson and friends: sea elephant and baby alligators
Below left: Dorothy happily cradles a coatimundi
Below right: The first pylon hide, Staverton Park, 1930, with George Boast

EXAMPLES OF CHILD STUDIES

Below right: The secretary is my son David

Their Royal Highnesses Princess Margaret and Princess Elizabeth, photographed watching a Punch and Judy show at Mount Clare, Richmond, Surrey, in July 1935

2 | *Professional*

I was on the dole—during the biggest depression this country had ever known. Every morning I had to sign on at the local Employment Exchange. After that it was round to the library with notebook and pencil to go through the advertisement columns of *The Times* and *Daily Telegraph*, followed by a letter-writing session. But jobs were few and for every vacancy there were hundreds of applicants. Occasionally the Employment Exchange arranged an appointment for me, but my business experience was limited and I was unskilled. The only jobs available were for door-to-door salesmen—commission but no salary. It was the most degrading, depressing period of my life. Yet it also led to the best thing that ever happened to me. I did not know it then, but I had finished with regular employment for ever. Henceforward I was to be my own boss and I am sure I have been more successful—and, what is more important, done better work and been much happier—than if I had continued working in an office. For me, the depression brought release.

It began like this: an old school-friend, Freddie Reekie, then a sub-editor on the *Sunday Dispatch*, telephoned me to say that the London Zoo had just acquired a six-month-old sea elephant and would I go and photograph it, preferably beside a child. This was to indicate its size, because the sea elephant is the largest of the pinnipeds, growing to a maximum length of some twenty feet and a weight of about three tons.

I took along Mary Parkinson—the four-and-a-half-year-old daughter of a friend—and photographed her feeding fish to the young giant. I rushed home, developed the plate and before it was dry made an enlargement which I took to the *Sunday Dispatch*. It appeared the following Sunday, covering half the back page. I was paid two guineas and was delighted. Later a greeting-card firm reproduced it as a post-card. Thus was I launched, at twenty years old, on my career as a professional photographer. Earnings that first year were twenty-three pounds.

About this time I acquired a 1909 quarter-plate Sanderson field camera with a fine mahogany and brass body, double extension bellows and ground-glass focusing screen. I found it on a stall in the old Farringdon Street market in London and managed to knock the price down from ten shillings to seven shillings and sixpence. It had no lens, shutter or plate-holders, but I was able to adapt a lens and shutter I already had, and after a search round second-hand-camera shops obtained six double book-form plate-holders that fitted perfectly. I used this fine old camera regularly for all my serious bird photography until 1947.

My first real field-work and nesting-season photography began in the spring of 1930. I was staying with an aunt at Ipswich who introduced me to George Bird, a well-known Suffolk bird photographer. He, in turn, introduced me to George Boast, the gamekeeper at Staverton Park, a small but thickly wooded area near Woodbridge.

Staverton and the nearby countryside was a wonderful area for birds. Within a radius of a mile there were the sea, salt mud-flats, fields, heathland, a river, a lake—and the thick woods of Staverton itself. In these varied habitats there nested no fewer than eighty species, including such local rarities as stone curlews, water rails, wrynecks, red-backed shrikes, lesser redpolls, Montagu's harriers and hawfinches.

It was arranged that I should stay in a corrugated-iron-roofed hut adjoining George Boast's cottage. It was so hot inside during the summer that it melted the candles—my only source of illumination. I had my meals with George and his daughter Louie—he was then a widower. Times were hard and shops were far away, but rabbits were plentiful. We had rabbit for breakfast, rabbit for lunch, and rabbit for supper! But the next few weeks were the happiest of my young life.

I used to rise before dawn and go round with George as he scattered corn for his pheasants. The forest was alive with a wide variety of birds and I could take my pick from a dozen or so species. I could have had no better guide than George Boast. He could identify a bird by its first note, and a feather or a misplaced tuft of grass were sufficient to guide him unerringly to a hidden nest. The parents had only to begin building for him to tell, from the first few twigs, grasses and moss, which species it was. If we found a dead bird, George would identify it instantly, then say how it had died, or suggest what had killed it.

George later married again and had two more sons who have made excellent gamekeepers. He is now ninety-four and still lives in the same thatched cottage at Staverton Park. His only complaint is that he cannot shoot as well as he used to!

I began by erecting a hide near the nest of bullfinches in a gorse-bush, and thus started the first of my many thousands of vigils, watching and photographing the family life of birds—to me the most fascinating spectacle in the whole world of nature. Never shall I forget the sight of those two birds alighting, one each side of the nest, to feed their family by regurgitation. The cock especially charmed me with his brilliant and elegant colouring of red, black and white.

The meal over, the parents flew away and I prepared for their return in a few minutes with more food. When half an hour had elapsed with no sign of them I wondered if I had frightened them away for good. I decided that the best thing to do was to get away as quickly and quietly as possible. I packed my camera, and was just shutting up the tripod when, taking a last look through the peep-hole, I saw the birds return and, with complete unconcern, begin to feed the young again. It was not until later that I learned that seed-eating birds seldom return to their nests before half an hour has elapsed, and sometimes three-quarters. The parents semi-digest the seeds and it takes that time for them to soften and be ready for regurgitation.

Bird-song has a deep effect on me. It is not surprising, as it combines two of the things which have given me the greatest pleasure in life: birds and music. The most marvellous singing I ever heard was in Staverton Park. I was sitting amid the trees at eleven o'clock during a warm May night when four nightingales started singing against each other. The nearest was not more than ten feet away. The park was still and silent and from the four throbbing throats of those little birds the glorious music poured forth. The tears rolled down my cheeks.

It was at Staverton that I first learnt how utterly unscrupulous some egg-collectors can be. One day, as I was forcing my way through an area planted with Corsican pines about five feet high, by sheer good fortune I saw a goldcrest dive into the top of one of these small trees and when I looked there was its nest *containing a cuckoo's egg*. And the goldcrest is the smallest British bird! This, I thought, made ornithological history and I was bubbling over with excitement.

As soon as I saw George I blurted out my discovery, but both he and another man who was present assured me that I must be mistaken. They said that there was no record of such a thing happening before. If they would not believe me I would show them the nest so that they could judge for themselves. Excitedly I told them that this would make a tremendous series of 'first ever' photographs: this tiny bird feeding a huge young cuckoo. I could already see the enthusiastic reception in the Press! We went to the tree and I proudly showed them the nest and they agreed that I was right. We decided not to go near the site again for several days. Apart from the probability of disturbing the bird, we might trample the undergrowth round the nesting tree and thus make it conspicuous to predators.

About five days later I decided to have another cautious peep. As soon as I got within range I was puzzled. In order to ensure that I could find my way back to the tree I had left guide-marks: a piece of string tied to a twig, a bent branch, a chalk-marked tree, and so on. But now some of these were missing, others had been moved. Fortunately some remained, so I found the tree. And then I got the shock of my young life—both eggs and nest had vanished. I was heart-broken. My dream of double-page spreads in the leading newspapers was shattered. I returned with worried, bitter thoughts. Several years afterwards I was talking to a well-known oologist of the time, Desmond Nethersole-Thompson, and he told me he clearly remembered that at a meeting of the British Oologists' Association a man had shown a great rarity—a clutch of goldcrest's eggs among which was a cuckoo's egg. The exhibitor was George Boast's companion.

Nothing could be done; in those days there was no law prohibiting egg-collecting. I learnt subsequently that this man had obtained the freedom of Staverton Park by a trick. He asked if he could put up nesting boxes and then used this activity as a cover for egg-stealing. Altogether he erected about 150 nesting boxes on the old oaks and holly trees, and in 1931 no fewer than 129 were occupied.

That autumn George and I went round emptying the old nests from these boxes and making the necessary repairs. Inside one box was the skeleton of a bird among a mass of feathers. George, without hesitation, identified this as being from a young cuckoo in the nest of a wren. Presumably the hen cuckoo had projected her egg into the nesting box, the wren had hatched it, and the young cuckoo had been unable to throw out the wren's eggs as these were found broken into tiny pieces. When the cuckoo was fully grown it was, of course, too large to get out of the small entrance hole.

Delighted with the results of my first 'expedition', I was eager to do more natural history photography. I recalled the success of the photograph of the sea elephant and little Mary Parkinson. She was a natural with animals at the Zoo. She was photogenic, completely unafraid, and provided an excellent foil to the animals, so I decided to photograph her with a variety of creatures. I took twenty or so such photographs, including one, of which I was particularly proud, showing Mary with a python draped round her neck. I was delighted with the series and decided that nothing but the world's most famous newspaper should have the honour of giving my photographic masterpieces to the world!

So one morning early in 1932 I arrived with my brief-case at the front door of *The Times*. I approached the doorkeeper and, as far as I can remember across the span of more than thirty-five years, the following dialogue took place:

'I must see the editor, I have some very important pictures.'

'Have you an appointment?'

'No, but it is very important. I must see him personally.'

'I will fetch Mr. Smith.'

'Is Mr. Smith the editor?'

'No.'

'Then I will wait until I can see the editor. I have got something here that will interest him.'

Flourishing my brief-case I sat down. At this the doorkeeper disappeared to summon reinforcements—first a sub-editor, then an art editor, and finally an assistant editor. To each I put the crucial question: 'Are you the editor?' When each enquiry proved negative I refused to open my case. *The Times*' staff were in a quandary; however much they might be inclined to dismiss me, they could not take the risk. I *might* have a photographic scoop which, if they turned me away, *might* go to another newspaper, and then . . .

It was this lingering doubt, I suppose, which eventually persuaded them to allow me into the inner sanctum. Geoffrey Dawson had then been editor for eighteen years and was destined to hold this most famous of all editorial chairs for another ten years.

Having gained my objective, I wasted no time. I opened my brief-case, pulled out a sheaf of glossy whole-plates of Mary and her various animal friends, slapped them down on Dawson's desk and, with all the confidence of my twenty-two years, triumphantly asked: 'What do you think of these?' He was certainly impressed, but he gently pointed out that this type of picture was hardly *Times* material and would stand a much better chance with a popular newspaper such as the *Daily Mirror*.

Well, that was that, but to show that I bore him no ill-will I invited him to join me for a cup of coffee. And that was how the great Geoffrey Dawson came to be sitting in a nearby tea-shop with the youngest, brashest nature photographer ever to storm *The Times* on his first visit.

Hard things have been said of the part Geoffrey Dawson played in national and international affairs, but he was always kindness itself to me. He gave me advice over that cup of coffee which I have never forgotten. He said that he would always be interested to see my photographs, he introduced me to his art editor, U. V. Bogaerde, and followed my subsequent career with interest. Occasionally he telephoned me and, most important, published many of my photographs.

When we returned to his office after that first meeting he telephoned the editor of the *Daily Mirror*, L. D. Brownlee, and I went to see him.

Mary and her friends appeared in the issue for 2 February 1932. Under the heading 'Fearlessness of Youth' it showed Mary patting a cheetah, holding a fox and a young alligator in her arms, and with a python draped round her neck. These four photographs occupied the centre of the two middle pages of the *Mirror* and were flanked by a village and a diamond wedding; three sports pictures; some crime shots; a couple of beauty queens; a man launching a canoe; and other miscellaneous photographs. It must now be many years since the art editor of that lively newspaper crowded twenty-one photographs into his two centre pages.

Mary had helped me break into press photography and the postcard business, now she helped with my first book. In 1933 the Oxford University Press published *Friends at the Zoo*, a slim volume of sixty-four pages of art paper with one page of text facing a picture of Mary with a collection of her animal friends. The book went into a school edition and also a cheap edition. Combined sales were about 50,000.

The book had a side-effect which pleased me very much—it helped to found the Children's Zoo at the Regent's Park Zoo. This is clearly brought out in Ronald Clark's account of the Huxley family (*The Huxleys*), where he refers to the book and says: 'As [Julian] Huxley talked with Hosking, enthused over the prints in front of him, and remembered his recent experiences on the Continent, the idea began to take shape.'

The text of *Friends at the Zoo* was written with the help of Cyril Newberry—the beginning of a life-long friendship and a collaboration in eight books. He is a professional scientist—specialising in mechanical engineering—a good ornithologist and nature photographer, and a fine writer whose prose is sometimes touched with poetry.

Cyril is a quiet man who listens more than he talks, but what he does say is much to the point and often seasoned with a dry humour. He shared all my early enthusiasms, often accompanied me in the field, and was a great help in a variety of ways. He built and installed the lighting equipment for my studio.

Although his business and other commitments have prevented us from collaborating so much in recent years, Cyril is always generous with help and advice whenever I seek them.

One book I was asked to illustrate had nothing to do with natural history. Faber and Faber were publishing a school book about dustmen and their work and Morley Kennerley asked me to take the photographs. This assignment gave me an insight into activities few of us ever consider. I learnt that there are 'totters' who raid dustbins at night for scraps which others consider useless—'where there's muck there's money'. I also formed a wholesome respect for the men who humped such heavy loads, especially when part of it is water which trickles down their necks! Incidentally, there were no dustmen before the seventeenth century; until then refuse was thrown into the streets and left to rot. Kites and ravens were then the scavengers.

The job took several months but presumably Fabers were satisfied because they used many of my photographs in subsequent years, as well as publishing *Birds Fighting* which Stuart Smith and I wrote in 1955.

Another venture started with a telephone call from the advertising agents, Sir Joseph Causton and Sons, who wanted a first-class photograph of a swan. I promised to put it in the post that day, but on looking through my files was dismayed to find that none was suitable. Somehow or other the promise must be kept, so, armed with bread crusts and camera, I cycled to the pond in Waterlow Park near Highgate Hill where there were several swans. With one hand I cast my bread upon the waters and, as the swans approached, worked the shutter of the reflex with the other. As soon as I felt sure that one, at least, of the shots would be suitable I rushed home, developed the negatives, made prints while the plates were still wet, and posted them that evening.

One of these pictures appeared shortly after on hoardings all over the country. A drawing made from my photograph has been the Swan Vesta sign ever since.

In addition I was now being asked to photograph weddings and children. I set up a studio at home. This was good training for later years, especially the child photography. I believe that anyone who wants to be really successful at bird photography should start with child portraiture. It is ten times more difficult to get a really good photograph of a child than of a bird; one is self-conscious, the other not.

The greatest problem in child photography is to overcome shyness. I allowed an hour for each child, telling the mother (fathers seldom came) I would leave them alone in the studio at first. Various toys were scattered about and by the time I came in most children were happily playing. The mother stayed in the room all the time. With particularly shy children I ignored them completely and talked to the mother. Few children like this and soon even the shyest child tried to attract attention.

Next I asked the child to sit on a pouffe in the right position for the portrait. As the dark unwinking camera lens can be upsetting to a child (some Eastern peoples regard it as the evil eye) I had bookcases built all round the camera to hide it as much as possible. When all was ready I brought out the special toy which would usually bring the desired expression to a child's face. This is when a smile is *developing*; taken too soon the photograph is dull, too late and the result is an unphotogenic grin. The toy was a monkey climbing a ladder which, when it reached the top, always balanced precariously before falling down—the high spot of the performance. The toy was manually operated and I controlled it with my left hand, the shutter release with my right.

After the monkey had performed several times the child knew what to expect, and there was a moment—no more than a second or so—when the smile of anticipatory delight was forming, a sparkle coming into the eyes, which was the exact instant to press the shutter.

The photographing of weddings proved to be as hazardous in one respect as photographing birds—both are subject to the vagaries of the weather. Just as sometimes happened when I had waited for weeks for a clutch of eggs to hatch—the climax ruined by rain—so it became near-calamity when, instead of being blessed by sunshine, bride and groom were met with torrents of rain. Sometimes the situation could be saved by using flash, but the general dreariness and greyness took the excitement and glitter from the occasion. Wedding photographs, of course, cannot be repeated, so it is vital to be successful first time. Yet it is necessary to work quickly, especially in winter.

Another sideline was taking photographs of local amateur dramatics. I attended the dress rehearsal in order to have the prints ready for sale on the first night. Flash-bulbs were not yet available so I fired off a mass of magnesium powder for the necessary illumination. Unfortunately, I could take only three or four photographs: after that the stage was blanketed in smoke.

I took any photograph that I thought would sell to the press—accidents, fires, notables. Once I was passing a hospital when a large car drew up and out stepped the Duke of Connaught, Queen Victoria's third son. Before he entered the hospital I photographed him. It was published in the *Daily Mirror* the next day.

Some of my prints were noticed by Marcus Adams, then the leading child photographer. He got in touch with me and explained how we could co-operate. He worked only from his studio; I was willing to go anywhere. Some of his clients wanted their children photographed·in their normal surroundings: Mary galloping round the estate on her favourite pony, Tommy in his model sports car. We arranged that I should go to the various homes and estates of such clients, take the photographs and develop the negatives. These were delivered to Marcus Adams's studio, where his staff made the enlargements and carried out any necessary re-touching.

Now that I was launched on a photographic career I wanted to

Above : Yellowhammer

Below : Golden oriole

Above left : Great black-backed gulls

Above right : Arctic tern

Below left : Puffins in courtship display

Below right : Arctic skua

specialise in birds. My parents were concerned because, as they pointed
out to me, no one before had ever made a livelihood solely by bird
photography. However, this did not deter me.

I soon realised that I could never take enough photographs in and
around the London area and that I would have to make countrywide
expeditions to nesting sites. Since I had already been excited by my
experiences at Staverton Park I returned there in 1935 and 1936, as
well as to nearby Eyke. It was during these two nesting seasons that
I learnt the fundamentals of bird photography, but I realised that if
I were to continue full-time I must not confine myself to birds. So
while in the country and not working specifically on one bird, all
natural history subjects were welcome: mammals, insects, flowers,
trees. Painstakingly I built up my library.

There was a special incentive to make a complete set of tree photographs. The Amalgamated Press were bringing out a weekly series
called *The Outline of Nature* which was designed ultimately to be bound
in two volumes. The work covered a wide field and the great attraction
was the numerous illustrations. For the section on trees, photographs
were wanted showing the different phases throughout the year. I
therefore made many journeys to photograph all the British trees,
showing them in summer and winter and with close-ups of bole, leaf,
flower and fruit. *Pictorial Education* found the series very useful for
teaching in schools, and through working with them I came to know
Miss Russell Cruise, the editor, to whom I supplied many other
photographs through the years.

It was about this time that *Weekly Illustrated* became interested in
some of my work, and I came to know the paper's go-ahead editor, Tom
Hopkinson, and the picture editor, Harry Deverson. They were
always interested in good natural history features and published scores
of my photographs. When they both left to join the staff of *Picture Post*,
I transferred also. I was sorry to see these excellent magazines cease
publication.

The business had increased so much that I found I needed transport,
not only to get around, but to hump my increasing load of equipment.
Since I had no car, I made an arrangement with my eldest brother,
Stuart, who lent me his on condition that I keep it clean and in repair
for his use at weekends.

It was during my stay on the Broads in 1935 that I received my
most exciting assignment so far. It began when I was in a hide photographing a bittern at its nest. When a bittern is walking to its nest over
dried reeds the sound is similar to that made by human footsteps. So
when one morning I heard such a sound I gripped the camera shutter
release and glued my eye to the peep-hole in excited anticipation, but

C

this time it *was* human footsteps, those of Jim Vincent, Lord Desborough's head keeper.

Jim handed me a telegram: 'Can you return London immediately photograph Princesses stop Calkin.' Herbert Calkin was managing director of *Country Life*, and another of those who gave me immense help at the beginning of my career. This was too good a chance to miss, and I left at once.

The Princesses Elizabeth, then nine, and Margaret Rose, not quite five, were going to a hay party at the home of Mr. Lancelot Hugh Smith at Mount Clare, in Richmond, Surrey, and *Country Life* had the exclusive right to photograph inside the grounds. While numerous press photographers milled around outside I, armed with my pass, was taken inside and introduced to the Duchess of York, now the Queen Mother. She gave me a charming smile, which I still recall, and explained that while she would like me to take photographs, she hoped that, as her children were there primarily to enjoy the party, I would try not to make the photography in any way intrusive.

Once in the grounds I began a careful—and unobtrusive—stalk of my royal quarry. Eventually I came upon them tossing hay at each other and, just as Elizabeth was smothering Margaret's face, I raised my camera to get the shot of a lifetime. But at that moment Margaret spotted me and cried: 'There's a beastly old photographer!' I lost the picture.

A little later I saw Elizabeth trying to mount a pony, but she was obviously in difficulties. So I went over and lifted my future sovereign off the ground and on to the saddle.

Yes, I got the photographs. The Princesses were watching a Punch and Judy show and I squatted with my back to the booth, thus facing the audience. The children were soon absorbed and I managed to obtain a number of natural shots, one of which made a full page in *Country Life* for 13 July 1935.

While working at Eyke I met Mrs. Robert Cobbold and she suggested that I might like to photograph on the estate of her mother, Mrs. Gibson Watt, at Doldowlod, in central Wales. One of her husband's ancestors was James Watt, the famous Scottish engineer, and at Doldowlod his study was still kept exactly as he had left it.

I first went to Doldowlod in the spring of 1937, staying at the chauffeur's cottage. Jack Lewis, the local postman, helped me to build a pylon hide on a hillside so that I could photograph some ravens and their three half-grown young. He saw me into the hide and left me to it. But the ravens flew around and refused to return to the nest. I waited for an hour and a half without success, then flew my handkerchief at the back of the hide as a signal to Jack that I wanted to come out. I felt it was necessary to do this because, although the ravens were not on the nest, they were flying around, and if they saw me suddenly emerge they would be frightened and thereafter would be suspicious of the hide.

I wondered why the ravens' behaviour was so different from that of other birds. Usually, if two of us entered the hide and one emerged, the birds returned normally, presumably being unable to count. Then I remembered—ravens are reputed to be able to count up to four or five. Here was a facer. Where could I get half a dozen or so helpers to see me into the hide? Fortunately, there was a school close by, and I persuaded the headmistress to allow a class to join us on a nature ramble. Eventually about thirty children accompanied me to the hide and, sure enough, they had not walked more than a couple of hundred yards homewards, after seeing me inside, when one of the ravens was back on the nest feeding the young.

It was at Doldowlod that, in company with Cyril Newberry, I photographed buzzards. We had been told of a buzzard's nest on a wooded hillside, and we were keen to get some photographs if we could. We approached the nest cautiously, the cock floating on motionless wings high overhead, watching our every movement. As we neared, he suddenly dived close to our heads, uttering a sharp menacing *queeow*. Then the hen joined in with further mock attacks.

In spite of their repeated threats, we climbed to the nest, which was in the crotch of an old oak, about fifteen feet from the ground. It was about two and a half feet across, formed of oak twigs, the centre slightly cupped, and lined with moss, lichen and rabbit fur. We built a pylon hide a little at a time during the next ten days and I began work when the two young were about a fortnight old.

I was greatly impressed by the hen's beauty, her plumage glowing a dappled chestnut brown, and her tail feathers barred with fawn and cinnamon. Her legs and black-tipped bill shone a glistening yellow, and when her piercing brown eyes glared at the hide I felt that she was looking right through me.

Yet for all her fierce expression, she was wonderfully gentle with her young, especially the smaller and weaker one. She tore pieces of meat from the prey, and bending forward with head on one side, she passed the food gently to it.

Some six weeks after we began photography the young were fully fledged and flown. Cyril Newberry thus described our feelings in *Intimate Sketches from Bird Life* (Country Life, 1940).

'In a sense we were sorry to find them gone, for they had been a fascinating study and we had developed a special regard for them, but it was good to know that they had safely passed the helpless nestling stage and could now rely on their own powers of flight. The sky was theirs, and the spread of the hills and valleys, beyond where the eye could see, but even as they entered on this new world, so they came at once to face perils far greater than nature had ordained for them. True it is that the conscience of man is stirring against the needless slaughter of our wild life, but the process is slow, and meantime the buzzard is in grave danger. He is a noble bird, worth preserving if only from an aesthetic point of view, but in point of fact he deserves more adequate protection than he now enjoys, for study reveals him to be economically useful in his preying on rabbits and voles, and his misdeeds, from the farmers' point of view, to be comparatively infrequent.'

Some months after photographing the buzzards we drove to Wales for the family holiday on the day that *The Times* published my photographs. Placards announcing 'Buzzards in Wales Special Pictures' greeted us in towns and villages across the whole country. It was the first time my work had been placarded and I was tremendously thrilled.

For me, no nesting season is complete without photographing owls, and while at Doldowlod I had asked the villagers to tell me the whereabouts of any nests. Some of the children discovered one of a tawny owl containing two young in a copse, in the hole of a tree about eighteen feet above the ground.

With the help of Jack Lewis we obtained from the local sawmills four twenty-five-foot poles and other timber. A hide, twenty feet high, was erected eight feet from the nesting hole. We took a week on the job, working about forty-five minutes at a time, thus giving the owls plenty of time to get used to it.

The hide was completed by 11 May, but I decided to wait another couple of days to ensure that the owls were thoroughly familiar with the new scenery. The 12th was the Coronation Day of King George VI and, as a nearby field was used for the celebrations, many people wandered over to see our weird contraption. Some appeared to think I had built it to live in! Although none of them appreciated its true significance, they succeeded in thoroughly upsetting the owls, one of them whacking a wing across the back of a boy's neck.

During the afternoon of the 13th Cyril and I went to the hide to set up the flashlight apparatus. At 9 p.m. Cyril saw me into the hide and waited in the car near the edge of the copse. I stayed a couple of hours, but the tawnies were disturbed. I decided to finish for the night and signalled with my torch for Cyril.

The night was pitch-black, and so we decided to leave the camera and flashlight apparatus in position. But as we walked across the field to the waiting car we imagined we heard voices coming from the direction of the hide. Poachers? If my flashlight apparatus were stolen

THE TIMES

SATURDAY   AUGUST   27   1938

BUZZARDS IN WALES

SPECIAL PICTURES

THE TIMES

that would be the end of owl photography for that season. Should we go back?

We retraced our steps. I felt my way up the pylon and fumbled with the fastening at the back of the hide. There was not a sound, not even the whisper of a wing. But out of the silent darkness a swift and heavy blow struck my face. There was an agonising stab in my left eye. I could see nothing. The owl, with its night vision, had dive-bombed with deadly accuracy, sinking a claw deep into the centre of my eye.

I almost lost consciousness but somehow managed to clamber down and stagger to the car. Back at our lodgings, our host, Mr. Dyer, a member of St. John Ambulance Brigade, insisted that I see a doctor immediately, even though it was now past midnight. In Llandrindod Wells the doctor announced that it must be Moorfields Eye Hospital in London at once.

The journey to London is a complete blank. I remember virtually nothing from the moment I was struck until I regained consciousness in the hospital. But Cyril told me afterwards that I talked intelligently during the long ride. My mother, to whom I have been particularly close all my life, had a vivid dream that night in which she thought I was calling to her for help.

The hospital had been advised of my accident and within ten minutes of my arrival I was on the operating table. It was hoped to save at least part of the sight of my eye, but about a fortnight later the surgeon, Mr. Alan J. B. Goldsmith, came to my bedside looking very grave. As gently as he could, he told me the stark facts. Despite all they had been able to do, a dangerous eye infection had set in and, by sympathetic action, was threatening the other eye. In those days antibiotic drugs were not available to combat infection. If the eye were not removed there would be more than a fifty–fifty chance that I would go blind. Mr. Goldsmith gave me twenty-four hours to make up my mind.

It was an awful decision to make. In my profession sight is everything. Obviously I could not risk going blind, yet what good would a one-eyed naturalist-photographer be? It looked as if the career I loved so much was to end. I was twenty-seven.

I telephoned my mother and my fiancée, who both strongly advised removal of the eye. Then, in the afternoon, the minister of my church, Dr. Henry Cook, visited me and something he said gave me great comfort. He told me that Walter Higham, a bird photographer whose work I greatly admired, had only one eye. . . . Mr. Goldsmith removed my eye the next day.

By this time I was 'news' and the next day my story was in every national newspaper. My misfortune brought me greater publicity than I have ever known either before or since. I received hundreds of letters;

my photographs were in great demand; the *News Chronicle* asked me for an article and several pages of my photographs appeared on successive Saturdays.

Two days later I left hospital feeling like a pilot after a crash. I must clamber into that hide in Wales just as soon as I could or I would be afraid to photograph owls for the rest of my life. I was there within twenty-four hours of being discharged, *but* my face was covered with a fencing mask.

I found the hide just as it was left. As I entered it I trembled from head to toe and my hair literally stood on end. But the young owls had flown, the nest was empty.

The gamekeepers wanted to shoot the whole owl family, but I implored them not to. The only shooting I wanted was with a camera and the following year I *did* shoot them—on film. That, I thought, was just—an eye for a bird.

3 | *Golden eagle honeymoon*

On my twenty-seventh birthday I became engaged to Dorothy Sleigh. She was a friend of my sister Dylla and all three of us attended Ferme Park Baptist Church. Our first real meeting was when her parents asked me to photograph their 'young daughter'. I was most attracted to her, but she was not then quite sixteen—seven and a half years my junior. As time passed I thought more and more about her, but it was two years before I first took her out.

She was at the Hornsey School of Art, and one day, by careful planning, I 'happened' to be passing in my car just as she emerged from the gates. I took her home and after this had happened several times, knowing that she was interested in natural history, I took her to the London Zoo. I introduced her to some of the keepers who had done so much to help me while I was taking photographs of Mary. In the Reptile House Mr. Budd brought out a seven-foot diamond python and draped it round her. Instead of recoiling she enjoyed it! She kissed the sea lions, went for a walk with a chimpanzee, hand-fed a red panda (a small relation of the famous giant panda), and cuddled a coatimundi. In fact no creature, great or small, held any of the terrors for Dorothy that they do for so many women.

Occasionally, on cold winter mornings, we went to Ken Wood, Hampstead, where Dorothy enticed robins and great tits to take meal-worms from her hand while I photographed them against the frosty background. Although at that time I did not fully appreciate it, it was this mutual love of wild-life which was helping to draw us closer together.

One of Dorothy's subjects was jewellery, so, instead of choosing a ready-made engagement ring, she designed her own, which was later fashioned by a local jeweller—twelve diamonds and a blue zircon set in platinum. It is an unusual ring, and so attractive that when our son Robin became engaged his fiancée, Ann, asked for an almost exact replica.

Above: The best-known swan in the world. A drawing made from this photograph, taken in 1931, has been used ever since as the trade-mark for Swan Vestas
Below: Young buzzard eyes rabbit the hen has just brought. This was one of the series of photographs which appeared in *The Times* on 27 August 1938—the first of many contributed to that newspaper

Left: The tawny owl that robbed me of an eye

Right: The hide I was climbing at night when the owl struck

HONEYMOON MEMORIES
Above left : Atop her huge nest the eagle surveys her domain
Above right : Dorothy negotiates the rocky home of a golden eagle's eyrie.
There was an almost sheer drop of 300 feet below the hide
Below : The opportunist

Above: Robin, David and Margaret to whom this book is dedicated
Below: My study

Dorothy's wedding ring was fashioned from Welsh gold from a mine near where I was photographing at the time. This mine was on a private estate in central Wales, and it was indeed a great privilege to have acquired this very special piece of Great Britain. In this we followed Royal precedent, for the Queen and all the Royal ladies have wedding rings made from Welsh gold.

We were married on 15 April 1939 at Ferme Park Baptist Church, by Dr. Henry Cook, a friend for most of our lives. He was a superb preacher and a real Christian; he died in April 1970 aged eighty-four.

By this time, so deeply had Dorothy become involved in my obsession with birds and the planning of our golden eagle honeymoon, that we both felt we wanted something relevant in our wedding service. We chose J. S. Blackie's hymn 'Angels holy, High and lowly', because of verse 4:

> 'Rock and highland,
> Wood and island,
> Crag, where eagle's pride hath soared;
> Mighty mountains, purple-breasted,
> Peaks cloud-cleaving, snowy-crested,
> Praise ye, praise ye God the Lord!'

As always, I kept an ornithological diary of our expedition, but it was on our honeymoon that Dorothy started to keep a journal which she entitled *I Married a Naturalist*. Here is part of her edited account of that journey which has, I think, freshness and immediacy, and gives something of the woman's point of view of what is, predominantly, a masculine occupation.

On 15 April 1939 we left London by car for Scotland, like many other honeymoon couples had done, though few had the same goal in view. In the weeks that lay ahead my husband hoped to photograph the golden eagle, found in the Highlands of Scotland.

For many months Eric had been making enquiries as to the situation of different eyries. Now the great moment had arrived; not only were we setting out on a new life together, but we were going to visit a new country in search of fresh birds.

As we travelled northwards, the countryside looked bright and fresh in its new green mantle. After an overnight stop at Stamford we left again in bright sunshine and sped comfortably into Yorkshire. We rounded the famous Scotch Corner, and travelled some few hundred yards down the road, when there was a sickening bump and a horrible scraping noise. Our off-side back wheel had come off and careered along the road ahead of us. Eric stopped the car on the wrong side of the road. Fortunately nothing was coming in the opposite direction.

Another car was parked a little farther on, and while we were still discussing what to do two people came back to it. Eric went and spoke to them and they promised to ask the first garage they passed to send a breakdown lorry.

Two very long hours passed before a lorry came down the road, and two men in grimy, oily overalls got out. How well I remember those men. The one in charge had curly red hair, and his mate only one hand, his left, but it was amazing what he could do with it. After about twenty minutes, spent in getting the big towing hook hitched under the back axle of our car, we were towed ignominiously back to Old Catterick.

While the car was being taken in I went in search of a room for the night and some supper. Next door to the garage was a little country inn, the Farmers' Arms, where the lady of the house smiled as she said she could help us. So, wearily, Eric and I turned in.

Much of the next morning was spent in getting into touch with the makers of the car and persuading them of the urgency to despatch the needed spare parts. Late in the afternoon the parts arrived. 'Curly' and his mate went to work and at eight o'clock we waved them goodbye, and by about ten o'clock were at Penrith.

We were off very early next day in an effort to make up for lost time. We were soon across the border and heading for Pitlochry where we stayed with Commander Ferguson who had done much to help Eric in his search for eagles. Then on to Inverness and Dingwall and over the Tain Bonar Bridge to Lairg where we bought tea and two enamel mugs.*

From Lairg we travelled along the road by Loch Shin and I really felt that we had left civilisation behind. Not only was the scenery wild and bleak, but the roads were awful; single track, bad surface, and still under construction nearly all the way. During the very few periods when the road itself did not worry us we were able to look around. Once we saw a black-throated diver on a loch, and later I had the tremendous thrill of seeing a golden eagle soaring over the mountain top. We had a glimpse of highland cattle, looking gaunt and shaggy.

Soon the road needed all our concentration for it was getting worse and the light was going. In one place we stopped to negotiate a step in the reconstruction work between the old surface and the new. Our car was very low-slung and heavily laden, but Eric decided grimly that we must go on at all costs. He bumped the car over the ridge, the undercarriage hitting some stones with a sickening crash and shudder.

* One of these mugs Eric subsequently dropped about 500 ft. from the eagle hide, never to be found again, the other I still use for cooking.

I thought at least the petrol tank was ripped open, but nothing seemed to have happened so on we went. I felt sick and would willingly have got out and walked if that had been possible. In all that forty-mile drive I don't think we saw one human being. The men working on the road had packed up before we got there. Never was I more thankful than to get to the end of that nightmare ride. It was ten-thirty, dark and raining hard when we arrived at Gualinn in Sutherland. Perhaps it was as well it *was* dark or the sight of that bleak wild country which I saw in the morning would have been the last straw to my over-wrought nerves.

In the morning the gillie took us to inspect our first eagle eyrie. A long rough track ascended to a rocky ledge which Eric and the gillie proceeded to climb, but I had had enough and awaited their return huddled in the shelter of a rock. I could see them pulling themselves up and then one crawled out on to a ledge—I could not see which—the other appearing to hold his legs, then they swapped positions. Presently they began to descend. While I waited it began to snow and the wind was very cold, so I was glad when the climbers returned and we started for home. The eyrie I learnt was in an impossible position for photography. On we went to another eyrie and we had a fine view of the two eagles soaring high over the mountain-top. Sadly we turned away—this eyrie was useless too.

Back we tramped to Gualinn, tired and hungry. After a meal we felt rested and refreshed, so we decided to drive down to Scourie on the coast where we had heard of yet another eyrie. Before the light faded we went down on to the shore to see what bird-life was there. We saw three greenshanks, one redshank and some oystercatchers, a barnacle goose flying high overhead and a heron skimming the water.

Our hotel was delightfully unlike so many town hotels. It was used mainly by fishermen and fishing was the main topic of conversation. The sitting-room, one could hardly call it a lounge, had glass-fronted cupboards of stuffed birds and mammals and a real Victorian horse-hair sofa. The next day we clambered to another eyrie on the cliff crags above a loch—again no good for us.

As we had not found the eyrie we had hoped for near Gualinn, and there was nothing else to keep us, we decided to move on to Tongue. On the way we saw four cock teal on Loch Loyal looking more like a child's colourful velvet toys than live birds.

Eric viewed two more eyries near Tongue, but neither was suitable. I went with him and the keeper to see one of these, which was two miles from a shepherd's cottage, situated six miles from the nearest road. The walk in itself was not too bad, as it was level going along the track. The mistake I made was to wear a new pair of climbing boots. The first few miles were reasonably easy but by the time we got to the cottage my heels were feeling decidedly sore. The shepherd and his wife were a young newly married couple, and welcomed us warmly. While Eric went on with the shepherd and the keeper I thankfully went indoors and took off my boots. The shepherd's wife brought me slippers and seemed pleased to see me. I learnt that she had worked in Glasgow until her marriage and I guessed she often felt very lonely in that isolated cottage. She brought out all her new china and insisted on giving me a full tea of Scottish home cooking although it was only noon.

After the men returned tired and hungry, another meal was prepared, and I was expected to eat again! Then Eric and I set out on the return journey. Towards the end I positively hobbled, and an unkind husband insisted on taking a photograph of me. When I got back to the bungalow where we were staying, I found a blister on both heels the size of a half a crown.

One day the keeper, who had accompanied us to the shepherd's cottage, took us to feed the red deer at Kinloch Lodge. Hunger tames many a wild animal, and when winter drives some of the deer down from the mountains the keepers and gillies feed them on small brown cubes about the size of sugar lumps. Deer love these. I was given a bucket of these cubes and immediately the deer saw it they seemed to come at me from all directions. I took a handful at a time and held it out to the animals. On turning round I found one had slyly come up behind me and was feeding straight from the bucket!

At that time of year the Kyle of Tongue was an ideal spot for migrating birds to stop and feed. Each evening after a meal we went out with our binoculars and saw such varied species as wigeons, mallards and shelducks—all brightly coloured against the more sombre eiders, greenshanks, redshanks, whimbrels, ringed plovers, golden plovers, oystercatchers, and black-tailed godwits. To me it was a vast and varied throng, an ornithologist's paradise.

We still had no luck with a suitable eyrie, and I realised what a great element of chance there is in bird photography. It seemed that the eagles in Sutherland were not for us that year, so we had to study the maps and decide what to do. The Spey Valley seemed to hold brighter prospects than most areas, so the next Saturday, just a fortnight after our wedding, we loaded the car and headed south again to Aviemore, where we stayed with Mrs. Graham. She had a motherly air and a strong Scottish accent, her 'Och, come away in, dears' made us feel at home at once. We sat down to a meal such as we had not had since we left home. Our rising hopes went still higher; it all seemed too good to be true.

We were sleepy after our day in the open and retired early. Eric was in bed first, and after putting out the oil lamp I dived in. There was a sickening crash and the sound of breaking china. The spring had slipped off its frame and we were left with our heads on the floor and our feet in the air. We groped our way out of bed and searched for matches and the lamp. By the glimmering light we replaced and remade the bed, and then very gingerly got in again, safely this time.

Next day we went up to Glenmore and saw for the first time Loch Morlich and its beautiful surroundings.

When starting work each year Eric likes to 'get his hand in' on one of the more common birds. So when we found a lapwing and a red-shank's nest in the same field we quickly erected hides at some fair distance from each. After an interval of three days, during which the hides were moved a little nearer each day, Eric went in to try his luck with the redshank. Nothing outstanding came of this, except that I had my first experience of watching a bird from a hide. It was the lapwing I was watching and it seemed wonderful to me to have a wild bird sitting so unconcernedly within six feet of me.

From now on Eric was working in real earnest. Hides were occupied each day, new ones gradually erected and new nests located. One of my chief jobs was to put Eric into and fetch him out of his hides.

Another three days passed in working quietly on the birds near Aviemore. Then, suddenly we got a telegram reporting an eagle site in Argyllshire. A letter followed next day from the bailiff of the estate, giving us details and offering us hospitality. So once again we loaded the car and were off. After presenting ourselves to our host and hostess we immediately sought the gillie who would take us to the eyrie.

I shall not forget that climb, nor were the subsequent ones any easier. I always puff and pant when climbing and never seem to get my second breath. To reach this eyrie we climbed over 1,000 ft. in one and a half miles. Towards the end Eric and the gillie went on ahead and left me to climb at my own slow pace. I got there in the end and found the men in deep discussion as to how a hide could be built. The eyrie was occupied, and was eminently suitable for photography. After all our previous searchings it seemed too good to be true. It was—but more of that later.

Next day Eric was searching for someone to help build his hide. He went to the local timbermills and found two likely helpers, one named Walker and a slip of a lad named Johnnie Cameron. They climbed to the eyrie to make plans and Eric returned very pleased. Walker had promised to build the necessary structure, and as this could only be done gradually so as not to frighten the birds, we felt there was not much point in our staying. They would take about a fortnight and Walker promised to tell the bailiff when the hide was ready and he would let us know. So we went back to Aviemore.

Much was happening in the bird world at this time of the year, and we found plenty waiting to be done. A golden plover was hatching and I was greatly enamoured with the wee chicks which were like little balls of pure gold fluff. They could walk an hour or so after hatching, and had long legs and large feet compared with their bodies. This enabled them to run surprisingly fast. It was amazing how their bodies of speckled fluff harmonised with the ground and so afforded them natural camouflage.

At the end of the week Eric decided to 'phone and find out how the eagle hide was progressing. To his dismay he was told that nothing had been done, and that no one seemed eager to start. After discussing the situation we decided to go back and see for ourselves. Our host, Mr. Graham, who was a plumber, volunteered to come back with us on the following day with two of the lads he employed and make a start on the work. Accordingly next morning we started right early on the 100-mile journey. When we arrived at the foot of the hill we found that poles and planks had been left by the roadside for us. To folks not used to it, carrying a load of wood a mile or more on the straight is tiring enough, but to carry it up the steep, at times almost sheer, mountain was a strain indeed and we had to have many rests. My only contribution was carrying a box of assorted nails. The boys made two journeys, and by the time all the material was up there was no time to start building the hide. So back we went to Aviemore, not having achieved very much.

Eventually Eric and I decided that the only way to build that eagle hide and get any photographs was to go and stay on the spot. Precious time was passing. An eagle chick did not stop growing while we tried to build a hide, and if we could not begin photography soon it would be fully fledged and leave the eyrie before we started. So after a few days in Aviemore, while Eric finished off the work in hand and took down his hides, we headed our car westward once more. We were grimly determined to get something done.

When Eric gets an idea into his head nothing will stop him from carrying it out. He made up his mind to photograph that eagle, and forthwith he set about getting a hide built at all costs. Most of the men he approached proved indifferent to his appeals, but Johnnie Cameron turned up trumps. He was only sixteen, but he worked hard and had no fear of heights. He cheerfully hopped about getting up poles and nailing on crossbars, apparently oblivious to the 300 ft. drop below him. He was a quiet lad and I do not think I heard him utter more than half a dozen words all the time.

After the hide was erected Eric allowed four days to elapse before beginning photography. At last the great day arrived. He agreed that I should go with him. I was very thrilled to be allowed to stay as this was such an important bird to us. The gillie agreed to see us into the hide. We climbed the steep ascent; Eric was beginning to find it easier, but I puffed and panted as much as before. Excitement kept me going this time though, and I was not so far behind the men. We carried a lot of gear with us, for besides photographic apparatus we had food and rugs as we intended to stay for several hours. Eric climbed into the hide and let down a rope on which he hauled up all the equipment. When all was in, he set up his camera, I climbed up too, and we bade goodbye to the gillie. He wished us a cheery good luck and went off promising to return at 7 p.m.

It was about noon when he left us, and as he walked away Eric whispered to me to unwrap the sandwiches. This was not to start eating but so that I should not rustle paper later when the eagle might be near and the least sound or slightest movement might be noticed. We were literally under an eagle eye!

It was a strange experience for me. Although I had sat and watched birds once or twice before, it had only been for a very short period (not more than an hour) and then at ground level. I spent seven hours with Eric that day perched high up on a rocky ledge. The hide was larger than the small portable ones, but this did not mean that I could move about. I knitted for a little while, but after an hour or more that palled. I fidgeted a bit and moved my legs, only to be frowned on by my husband. I developed a profound respect that day for his ability to sit still. He sat on a small stool beside his camera and hardly moved his legs and feet the whole seven hours. I have seen him in hides many times since then and always I marvel at his stillness.

Presently we ate and drank tea from a Thermos flask. Gradually I got used to the situation and learnt to use my ears. We could hear the sea, people's voices far away, a car as it went by on the road below, and deer in the distant valley. Birds called in the distance. To our delight we discovered a wren had built her small nest in the large structure of the eagle's eyrie. This wee bird seemed much more concerned with her family's welfare than the golden eagle was with hers. Back and forth she flew, and sometimes the little cock would sing his sweet shrill song. I always marvel how so small a bird can sing so loudly.

At long last our patience was rewarded. About five-thirty there was a rustle of wings and suddenly the eagle was there. I saw her perch and look at the hide. This was it . . . at long last! I waited for Eric to click the shutter, but nothing happened. I turned to look at him and saw to my horror that he had gone white as a sheet. 'Whatever do I do with a fainting man 1,000 ft. up?' I thought desperately. Fortunately his trauma was only momentary, due to intense excitement, then he started work as the eagle picked up the remains of a rabbit and began to feed the chick. It was only a short meal and in a matter of minutes the parent was off again. Slowly Eric took out a handkerchief and mopped his brow.

'I came over feeling quite dizzy just then,' he said.

'You looked ghastly,' I whispered.

'Still I managed to get about twenty shots of her,' he grinned.

At seven o'clock the gillie returned and we got out of the hide. I did a few leg exercises before venturing down the twenty feet from the hide to the first narrow ledge. Eric lowered all the things down to me then climbed down himself. We were both cold and glad of the descent to get our circulation going, but we were very happy and excited that at last, after so much searching and work, we had photographs of the golden eagle. I felt that in some small way I had helped.

Eric had more spells in the hide, but I did not stay with him again. The chick was growing fast and the parents visited it only twice every twenty-four hours. Then the weather broke, so we dismantled the hide and said farewell to the bird which had been the main reason for our expedition to Scotland.

The morning we left Argyll it had stopped raining for a little while but mist hung heavily on all the hills, the burns were full and swollen, and in many places water rushed down the hillside whether there was a burn or not. It all had a rugged merciless look, but it thrilled us. In Fort William we stopped to buy a small figure of a stag which reminded us very much of the wild country we had just left. Once more we returned to Aviemore and found a very warm welcome awaiting us. More trips, more birds, more photography and in no time it was July and regretfully we came to the conclusion that the nesting season was over and we must return to London.

Little did we think, as we drove southwards, what the future had in store for us.

Opposite: reed warbler

4 | *Home and war*

From my parents I learned the blessing of a united and happy home, and all my life it has meant much to me to be surrounded by an atmosphere of love, understanding and security. In the early days, when trying to start my own business, my parents were always ready to listen to my problems and give what advice and help they could. They encouraged me when things went wrong and sensibly curbed me when I became over-enthusiastic. To them I owe more than I can say for any success I have had.

I have been equally blessed in my own home. Dorothy and I searched for a long time until we found the house we still live in today. Immediately we saw it we knew this was the one for us. It is a square two-storey red-brick Victorian house in North London, and compared with the small modern villas our friends chose it seemed large for just two young people, but it had a character and appeal we could not resist.

After our wedding we went to Scotland for twelve weeks and the house stood empty. On our return in July 1939 we stayed with my parents, who lived nearby, while we cleaned the place and erected the necessary fixtures. Of course we could not furnish it all at once. My study, now full to overflowing, began with three small bookcases and a file of photographs, but our prize possessions were my desk and chair, both over 100 years old. We had already purchased our bedroom furniture and ever since we had been 'going steady' Dorothy had collected everything necessary for the kitchen. But, apart from this, only two other rooms had even the barest necessities.

We moved in and were as happy as two young lovers could be. A month later the country was at war. I volunteered for photographic duties in the RAF. But they had no time for a man with only one eye and one good foot, so I carried out various air-raid precaution duties, particularly fire-watching. I also lectured to the troops, mainly to RAF stations round the coasts of Britain.

D

Opposite: bittern

I had, of course, been lecturing widely for years, but to our dismay all my engagements were cancelled; furthermore, many articles and photographs were returned. The outlook was grim indeed. We had planned to purchase furniture, carpets and a hundred and one other things as the fees arrived for lectures and photographs, but overnight it seemed our prospective income had vanished, and it was obvious that we were going to be desperately short of money. Yet one of the first things we had to do was to provide blackout for the windows. The curtains we had taken so long to find and make were not opaque, so blinds had to be bought and fitted.

With the war came rationing of food and petrol. At first sight the rationing system appeared so complicated that almost unconsciously Dorothy intimated that she wanted me to cope with it. But I was so busy adapting my business to wartime conditions that, tactfully, I ignored her unspoken appeal. She must have got the message, for later the neighbours were seeking her advice on their rationing problems.

Throughout the war our home was a haven for friends passing through London, especially Servicemen. And somehow—in addition to running the house and looking after the business while I was away, sometimes for weeks during the nesting season—Dorothy always found food for them. Sometimes a friend would arrive equipped with a few pats of butter or some sugar lumps. Others, especially Servicemen, brought coupons and such small gifts were very welcome in those bleak days.

As the air raids worsened we decided to sleep in the cellar, and for a time we even entertained our friends there. But after a while we rebelled against such disagreeable conditions and, taking a fatalistic attitude, decided that if we were to die, at least we would do so in comfort.

After the sirens sounded in the evening and the radio was silent (as it was during raids) we derived joy and satisfaction from our gramophone records. The concentration of listening and continually changing the discs—they were the old-fashioned 78's—kept our minds off the appalling din outside. Never have my masters of music—Beethoven, Bach, Grieg, Handel, Mendelssohn and Tchaikovsky—done more for the morale of any man and his friends than they did for us at that time. Records and books were some of the few luxuries of those austere days, and some of our friends still remind us of those evenings.

I well remember a night of a very different kind in 1940 when there was a heavy raid on the Crouch End area in North London. The following morning I had a telephone call from my father who lived about half a mile away. 'We've had rather an exciting night,' he said. 'Do you think you could possibly come down and help with some clearing up because everywhere is covered with dust?' Dorothy and I set off at once, meeting my brother Gordon on the way.

When we walked into the sitting-room it looked as though someone had plucked a chicken and scattered the feathers around. We decided to move the furniture into the garden through the French windows. As we picked up the sofa we saw a round hole in the floor, about twelve inches in diameter. The police were round within minutes, took one look at the hole and said: 'Unexploded bomb.' They shot outside shouting: 'Evacuate the house immediately.'

The bomber had dropped a string of fourteen bombs; thirteen of these went off on contact, the fourteenth was ours. When it fell, Father said, the house seemed to bounce. It went through the roof, three floors and plunged into the foundations. Here it boomeranged and came up underneath the kitchen floor, whence it was eventually dug out. On its way down the bomb passed through the sofa in the sitting-room; that is where the feathers came from. But the amazing thing was that at a casual glance the sofa appeared to be undamaged; somehow the fabric had sprung back covering the hole.

With an unexploded bomb beneath us we needed no urging. Out at the double went what valuables we could lay our hands on. Gordon picked up the big radiogram and carried it straight out to the car. Yet when we got it to our house it took our combined strength to lift it, an example of how crises give special energy.

One other memory of that morning: Mother, with a yellow duster tied round her head to keep out some of the dust, protesting that she could not possibly leave the house then because she had a joint of meat in the oven. . . .

Another recollection of those far-off days was of suddenly hearing the whistle of a nearby bomb. I instinctively flung myself to the ground. But the expected explosion never came. Feeling a bit foolish I got up and looked around. Then I saw a starling and, as I watched, again came that perfect whistle of a bomb—from the starling.

After another bad raid we were told that a tree only 400 yards from our home was harbouring a parachute mine, a weapon even more destructive than ordinary bombs, since it exploded at street level instead of burying itself in the ground. The Bomb Disposal Squad made many attempts to defuse it, but it hung in a particularly awkward and dangerous position and they had to give up.

While my parents and sister and my brother Stuart and his wife were having tea with us one afternoon, there was a loud knock at the front door. I opened it to be confronted by a policeman saying: 'Please evacuate this house. In twenty minutes we're blowing up the mine.'

Never was so much moved so far, so quickly, by so few! My 20,000 glass negatives were shifted from dark-room to cellar; movable furniture was laid underside towards the windows; clocks and ornaments were put on the floor; windows and doors were opened so that they would not resist blast and thus lessen the possibility of breakage; and gas, water and electricity were turned off. Then I drove Stuart and his wife home while the others went for a walk.

On the way back I wondered what damage our home had sustained —would the ceilings have caved in; would the whole place be flattened? As I rounded the last corner, I saw with intense relief that the house was intact. Our precautions had paid off. No damage had been done, yet our next-door neighbours had every front window broken and their front door blasted off its hinges. Indeed, we were the only house in the immediate vicinity with no broken glass.

But 1940 was not all wartime worries. It also saw the publication by Country Life of *Intimate Sketches from Bird Life* written in collaboration with Cyril Newberry. One of the reviewers was Frances Pitt. She praised the book but also said that it was a pity that the authors, in writing about the wood pigeon in London, had said that it was quite tame. She said that this was a common error; it was the so-called feral doves that were tame, not the wood pigeon.

This criticism upset me because it looked as if Cyril Newberry and I had not troubled to check our facts. Yet I knew I was right, having fed wood pigeons in a London park. I wrote to Frances Pitt about it and said that if she would meet me in London I would gladly give her a personal demonstration.

Eventually we met in Trafalgar Square and I took her into nearby St. James's Park. We had not been there for five minutes before a wood pigeon sat on my shoulder. Frances Pitt was magnanimous in her apology, but, unfortunately, too much time had elapsed since the review appeared, and no retraction of the criticism was published.

A much worse instance of misplaced, although understandable, criticism occurred when *Picture Post* published several pages of my photographs. But somehow the captions for two of the pages were transposed, making havoc of the identification of the birds. *Picture Post* received shoals of letters with the general theme that it was a great pity such a good bird photographer knew so little about his subject. Owing to the mechanics of publishing, it was not until six weeks later that *Picture Post* printed a note telling readers what had happened and, of course, absolving me from all blame. But many more people saw the erroneous captions than read the subsequent small corrective note.

However, one good result of my association with *Picture Post* was meeting Macdonald Hastings, who invited me to speak about birds on his radio programme. This was not the first time I had broadcast, but it was the first time without a script, for Mac asked me questions and I answered off the cuff. This was much more congenial than being tied to a script, and I am sure the broadcast gained by our spontaneity.

It is for this reason that I prefer television, which gives freedom from script. I live within a few minutes of Alexandra Palace, and in the early days of television I was often asked to comment on news items about birds.

On 29 November 1942 Julian Huxley and James Fisher called. From my youth I have had the greatest admiration for Huxley, whom I regard as the leading twentieth-century British biologist. This meeting, which had momentous results, was the beginning of a fairly close association which has lasted to this day.

They came to discuss a major publishing project. Collins, in combination with Adprint, proposed a large series of books to cover the whole of British natural history, to be called *The New Naturalist*. The other members of the editorial board were to be John Gilmour and L. Dudley Stamp. Each book was to be copiously illustrated, and colour photographs were to be used extensively; the first time that a series of natural history books had been illustrated in this way. At that time there was a severe shortage of large-size colour film, but Adprint, with government permission, was allowed to import a limited supply from America.

Would I be the photographic editor? In addition to taking a lot of colour photographs myself, I would have to recruit other photographers, and also obtain stock photographs where these were suitable. I accepted and today, over a quarter of a century later, I am still photographic editor. By July 1970, fifty volumes had been published in the main series, and twenty-one monographs.

One of my tasks was recruiting photographers to take colour photographs of the high quality needed for *The New Naturalist*. One of the first of these was John Markham. He was a good amateur photographer but he could spend only a limited amount of time on his hobby as he worked for his father. During the war, however, he was employed as an air-raid warden and had more spare time, often working forty-eight hours on and forty-eight off. I supplied him with colour film and told him what subjects I wanted. He always came back with first-class photographs. I was not at all surprised when after the war he gave up the family business (his father having died) and became a full-time professional photographer. His collection of colour photographs of British mammals is probably the best yet assembled, especially as they have been mostly photographed wild and free.

John has fantastic patience and, like all good natural history photographers, has the knack of staying almost motionless for hours on end.

One story will illustrate this. Several times he saw a wood mouse running under a hedge beside a wood. As this species of mouse had never previously been photographed in colour in the wild he was particularly interested. It was a cold frosty day in March. John focused on a particular spot where the mouse was likely to run and waited, sitting on his heels on the ground. He forgot all sense of time, waiting immovable, his thumb on the shutter. At last the mouse appeared, ran along and came to the pre-selected spot. John sought to press the release. He could not—his hand was numb with cold.

A few days later he went back and repeated the operation; with one difference. He made sure that by slight movements his hand would not be immovable at the crucial moment. He got his photograph.

Another helper was Sam Beaufoy. He was a school-teacher, keen lepidopterist and amateur photographer. Having seen some of his work, I realised that he was the ideal man to help with butterfly, moth, dragonfly and general insect photography. We were not disappointed. Later I persuaded him to publish *Butterfly Lives* (Collins, 1947), which he wrote and illustrated in conjunction with his wife.

For marine subjects I turned to D. P. Wilson, whose book *Life of the Shore and Shallow Sea* (Nicholson and Watson, 1937) had fascinated me by its superb illustrations. Douglas Wilson is a marine biologist who pioneered the use of colour photography in the aquarium, and was probably the first to use high-speed electronic flash in the photomicrography of living marine plankton.

One of the early troubles we had was with processing the large-size Kodachrome. It was made in America, but, owing to wartime difficulties, was not sent back there for processing, but to Kodak's laboratories at Harrow. They were labouring under wartime restrictions and part of their factory had been bombed. Processing this film was difficult: it passed through seventeen baths of chemicals, all of which had to be maintained at exactly the right temperature. Occasionally, with the best will in the world, the results were not up to Kodak's high standards. But somehow the snags were ironed out and the success of *The New Naturalist* series shows that, over-all, text and illustrations were of high quality.

In addition to *The New Naturalist*, another exciting idea was discussed on that November evening. Two Cities Films wanted Bernard Miles to make a film in which the central character would be a star of a different kind from the usual variety, a bird. They discussed it with Julian Huxley and James Fisher and it was decided to choose a British rarity, the tawny pipit, which had allegedly been only once recorded breeding in Great Britain. Would I help with the filming, mainly in nest-finding and erection of hides? Again I accepted, although it was decided that it was quite impossible to contemplate filming an actual tawny pipit; it nests mainly on the Continent where the war was raging.

Again, Dorothy accompanied me—and here I think it best to quote these edited extracts from her journal.

It was decided to photograph a pair of ordinary meadow pipits and keep to shots which showed the back view only; the tawny has a plain breast and the meadow a speckled one, but their back plumage is very similar.

Eric decided that we could not do better than go to Hickling again. It was a familiar spot, and we knew that we were sure of finding what we needed. A camera-man, Eric Cross, and a photographer, Ray Sturgess, were due in May. It was our job to have everything ready for them.

At Hickling we discussed our plans with Jim Vincent. There were plenty of meadow pipits about and next day he promised to find one or two nests. The following day it rained and blew in true Broadland fashion, but on Saturday the weather improved and four nests were found, two in the same field.

When Eric Cross and Ray Sturgess arrived they stayed at the Pleasure Boat inn and, being used to all the amenities of town life, were somewhat appalled at what seemed to their eyes the primitiveness and remoteness of their surroundings. Eric was spending the day with them and the night with a tawny owl, so I saw little of him. After one of his sessions with the owl, he was returning in his car to Hickling in the early hours, when there was the zoom of an aeroplane overhead and the spatter of machine-gun bullets on the road behind him. Eric pulled up and dived for the ditch. When the plane had gone out of earshot he cautiously emerged and so also did another figure. 'Blimey,' said a man's voice, 'he nearly got you that time, mister.'

It intrigued me greatly to see the camera team at work. Each day the hide had to be taken down, the film camera set up and the hide re-erected round it. Eric Cross got the idea of bird photography quite well for a layman, although he said that he found the birds more temperamental than a leading lady. Ray Sturgess on the other hand was rather a restless person, and would pop out of the hide at any odd moment. We then had to shoo him back again and try to explain for the hundredth time that it frightened the birds if someone suddenly appeared out of the hide. He did get the idea in time, but fidgeted and bumped and rustled about inside, so that I was sure the birds were under no illusion that there was no one in the hide.

The meadow pipits were grand on the whole and we obtained some very good shots. Both pairs reared their young, so they could not have been badly frightened. We were sorry that only a little of the birds appeared in the subsequent film, after so many weeks of work.

Eric Cross and Ray worked only from nine till five each day with weekends off when they went off to Norwich to relax after the grim quietness of Hickling. It was only natural, of course, but it seemed strange to us who worked all day and often all night as well—and a seven-day week at that! Our bird season was short and we had to cram in as much as possible. And we had no union to answer to.

Once one of the cameras went wrong and Ray rushed up to London, stayed a night and the next day returned with the camera repaired. Eric Cross had two large lenses, each in its own pigskin case, of which he took great care They had belonged to Flaherty when he was making his *Man of Arran* film. One day we fitted one of them on to Eric's Leica and it was a puzzle to find the camera! But with it he obtained photographs of swallows at Whiteslea boathouse about sixty feet away.

Soon Eric and Ray had finished all the filming they could do so they packed their numerous bags and we saw them off at Norwich station.

A war experience of a totally different kind began when a few days before Christmas 1944 Dorothy and I were driving in Essex. Just when a Canadian despatch-rider overtook us like a rocket—we were doing 50 m.p.h.—we could see in the distance a lorry pulling out from the kerb and, without signalling, start to turn right. We knew an accident was inevitable, yet there was nothing we could do. The despatch-rider had no chance and hit the lorry full tilt.

I sprinted into the nearest house and telephoned for a doctor and an ambulance. Dorothy covered the injured man with a car rug and did everything she could for his comfort, ensuring that no one moved him for fear of causing further internal injury.

Since I was an eyewitness, I was called upon to give evidence before two Canadian army officers who held a tribunal in my study. I took an oath on the Bible, and on being questioned about the whole episode went out of my way to put the entire blame on the lorry-driver, insisting that the accident was unavoidable. When asked to estimate the despatch-rider's speed I said, since he overtook me so quickly, it must have been 65 to 75 m.p.h.

As the officers were leaving I said I hoped that it had been made clear that the motor-cyclist was blameless and expressed the hope that he would get adequate compensation. They replied that despatch-riders have a maximum speed limit of 50 m.p.h. and because this speed had been considerably exceeded the rider was at fault. Thus, quite

The editorial board of the *New Naturalist*, 1943 and 1966. *(L to R in lower picture)* James Fisher, John Gilmour, Sir Julian Huxley, Sir Dudley Stamp and myself

WAR AND PEACE
Above: The fire blitz
on Hornsey,
19 February 1944

Below: Margaret, born
a few days later, shows
her early interest in
birds

Above: The pupil teaches. It was here, in Staverton Park, that George Boast taught me much about field ornithology. Now I pass on some of that knowledge to George's two sons—this time how to find a pheasant's nest
(*Radio Times Hulton Picture Library*)

Below: Camera and high-speed flash lamps (*left*); electronic eye on tripod at right, pointing up to lamp unit, ready to photograph birds in flight a split second after they emerge from tube (standing on box)

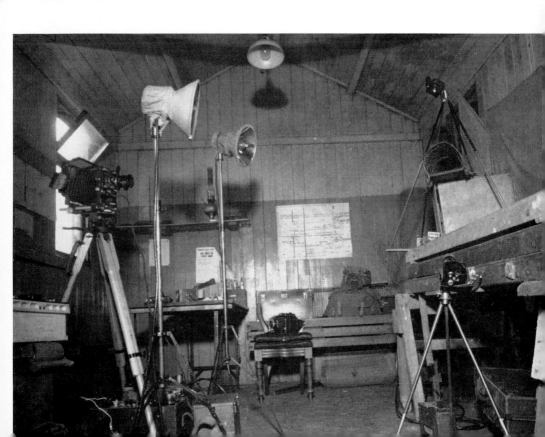

RESULTS OF THE SET-UP SHOWN ON PREVIOUS PLATE
Above: Robin

Below: Great grey shrike

innocently and unintentionally, I may have caused the man to lose his compensation.

Margaret Lucy, our first child, was born in 1944—during the hit-and-run raids and flying-bomb attacks. She was a February child who beat leap year by an hour and ten minutes, and was named after her two grandmothers. When we knew that she was on the way we had a Morrison table shelter erected in our dining-room. The French windows were kept open so that Margaret could be snatched from her pram in the garden and rushed to shelter at the first sound of a raid or flying bomb. The shelter was her bedroom every night we were home until the war ended.

Margaret, now three months old, accompanied us on the 1944 nesting season, which was spent on Gorple Moor, near Halifax, in Yorkshire, *Wuthering Heights* country. I like to think that she acquired her love of birds by hearing the cry of the curlews on those wild Yorkshire moors, where she spent the whole day in her cradle. George Edwards, my companion on many expeditions, came with us.

The moors surrounding the reservoir which supplied Halifax with water attracted a wide variety of birds and George found many nests. Unfortunately, the weather this season was the worst I have ever known, rain continuing for day after day. However, I worked on three pairs of ring ouzels, each nesting in a slightly different habitat; on merlins nesting among bracken; on golden plovers; twites and a few other typical moorland species.

Having a small baby with us meant that Dorothy had plenty of washing, in addition to dealing with our wet clothes, and a daily problem was getting it all dried. We had to rely mainly on a small oil stove. One afternoon Dorothy lit this and then went out shopping. When she returned and opened the door a black snowstorm swirled around her. The stove had smoked and covered everything with soot.

I have sad reason to remember the 1945 nesting season. I was at the top of a tree at Staverton Park examining a sparrow hawk's nest when I became aware of a whistle blowing persistently. Eventually it dawned on me that maybe this was a signal for me, so I shouted and the game-keeper, Willy Bilham, came to the tree. I descended and he handed me a note from Dorothy. It read: 'We have had grave news of your father. Can you come back and telephone home?'

Back at the cottage, Dorothy handed me the telegram from my sister Dylla: 'Father died suddenly this morning.' I had seen him just before we left for Eyke—and he seemed in perfect health. He had died suddenly in the street of a heart attack while waiting for a bus. One of his favourite sayings was 'Sudden death, sudden glory'. He had his wish.

No man had a better father. He was the truest Christian I have ever known. It is no more than the literal truth to say that never once did I hear him utter an angry, cross or unkind word about anyone or to anyone.

Although, contrary to my earlier fears, my business had not suffered too much during the war, we still had to be careful. I was, therefore, very glad when, in 1945, R. T. (Blos) Lewis of the *Daily Mail* asked me to act as nature editor for the *Daily Mail* School-Aid Publications, consisting of booklets and filmstrips. We planned a series on various animals and other nature subjects.

Blos Lewis, an ex-headmaster, had just returned from a visit to the United States, where he had been impressed by the use of visual aids in schools. He particularly liked one on a butterfly's life-history. Why not nature filmstrips in our schools as well? He discussed the idea with me and I arranged with fellow photographers to produce a large series of strips and to supply the commentaries. To help publicise the enterprise, we mounted an exhibition of photographs which went on show in various towns throughout the country, beginning with one in London which was opened by Dr. Julian Huxley.

As with *The New Naturalist*, I enrolled various authors. Frances Pitt wrote *Blackbird and Thrush* and also *Some Garden Birds*. John Armitage wrote *The Skylark*; Stuart Smith *Migration*; Sam Beaufoy *Butterflies*; Frank W. Lane *The Flight of Birds, Bats and Insects*; and Stanley Porter *British Fungi*. Altogether twelve booklets were published.

By the time our elder son Robin arrived in February 1947 we had begun to get used to peaceful conditions again. Dorothy's confinement was to be in Charing Cross Hospital, to which she was taken by ambulance late on a Saturday night. There was deep snow everywhere and the ride seemed to take hours.

Having seen her comfortably settled in at the hospital, I found myself in the street at two-thirty on a perishing cold Sunday morning. How was I to get home? There were no buses or trains at that hour, not a taxi or a vehicle of any sort in sight. Then I spotted a lorry pulling out from Charing Cross station, so I frantically thumbed a lift.

'I'm only going as far as King's Cross,' the lorry-driver said.

'That'll be a help,' I answered, and climbed in. On the way I told him why I was in the middle of London in the middle of the night. All too soon he put me down by King's Cross.

As I trudged along York Way a lorry pulled up beside me and the same cheery voice said: ' 'Op in, mate.' He took me to within a stone's throw of my home and when I tried to press a tip into his hand he said: 'Forget it, chum, I'd like someone to do the same for me in the circumstances. Hope it's a boy.'

It was the advent of our third child, David, in 1955 which enabled me to realise one of my long-standing ambitions—to see the birth of a human baby. And because it was my own son, the miracle of birth was even more wonderful. Our second son was born at home early on a May morning, and it was thrilling to be with Dorothy when he arrived. As dawn came and the sun began to rise, the first swifts of the year screamed past our windows as though sharing our joy.

Now our family was complete. As the children grew, so also did my business. Gradually more sophisticated equipment was acquired and often this needed to be tested before use in the field. Who better than the family to practise on? Thus, using my early experience in child portraiture, I have built up a complete family album. It started when Margaret was only two days old and embraces every phase of the children's development right to the present day. Now it consists of two huge volumes! While we love to look through it, we do not burden our friends with it, as was the habit of the Victorians.

Sometimes I make my tests in the garden on other subjects and our neighbours must think I am a very queer type—grovelling around on hands and knees, or perhaps pointing the camera at an apparently clear blue sky. The truth is that I am trying to photograph insects, flowers and sometimes reptiles. Once our garden housed thirteen young adders and their mother. Dorothy and the children were rounded up, each being responsible for several snakes so that none should be lost during the photography. Although from birth adders have a poisonous bite, Robin allowed them to crawl over his hand as he seemed to know instinctively that if he did not frighten them they would not hurt him.

When some greater horseshoe bats were temporarily in residence we made the attic bat-proof and shut the trap-door. Here they were secure until I had finished my work on them, Dorothy meantime feeding them on maggots industriously extracted from pea pods.

Every spring there are sure to be several visitors bringing wild birds in need of care and attention. Generally they are young birds just out of the nest, unharmed but not old enough to look after themselves. Anxious callers are advised to put these back where they found them, if possible out of the way of cats. The parents will soon hear them calling and will come to feed them. But some, having been caught by a cat or knocked down by a car, are so badly injured that it is kindest to put them out of their misery. Others we attempt to feed and restore to health, but quite often they live only for a short time.

Sometimes, however, we have a success story like Sooty and Blackie. Sooty was a feral pigeon that fell down the chimney, hence his nickname. We cleaned him as best we could and put him in a box in a warm place to get over the shock. Soon he consented to take a little food, and gradually the effects of soot and shock wore off. After a few days he fluttered round the garden but came indoors whenever he was hungry and demanded food. A few more days and he was flying strongly, but he still expected us to feed him and would take food from my hand while he sat on top of Margaret's pram.

Blackie was a very young blackbird when brought to us after being rescued from a cat. He seemed so dazed that we wondered whether he had internal injuries. We kept him quiet in a warm place and after some time he opened his eyes and looked around. Cautiously he stood up and fluffed his feathers. I wondered whether he would take some food, so I dug for worms in the garden, but since this was during a dry period my efforts had little success.

He was force-fed with two small worms as he did not at first get the idea of taking food from my hand. Although he kept them down, a couple of tiny worms did not give much sustenance, so I bought some meal worms which he found very much to his liking. He developed a taste for this delicacy, and as my supply was quickly running out I telephoned my secretary Peggy Hadfield and asked her to call in at a pet shop and buy some more. She arrived holding a bag of worms at arm's length. 'Never before have I done such a revolting bit of shopping!' she exclaimed. She had not realised that the meal worms would be alive and wriggling.

Soon we were able to leave Blackie out in the garden but had to keep an eye open for cats. At night he was put in the garage. He grew sleek and fat and whenever I appeared he flew straight at me demanding food. He seemed to realise that it was much easier to get me to supply his food than to forage for himself. When he seemed to be strong enough to fly well I began to cut his rations so that he had to supplement them himself. Gradually he learned to be self-supporting, but for a long time he would come when called.

Such side-lights make a pleasant relief from my other work which is done from my study. This room has become so much a part of me that, apart from photography, which I can do anywhere, I cannot settle to serious work elsewhere. Over the years I have collected a library of about 7,000 natural history books and we have now reached the stage when they encroach on every room in the house. I have illustrated over 700 books either wholly or in part. These line the walls, and I can lay my hand on any volume at a moment's notice, something often necessary as a result of a telephone enquiry for an illustration.

As one of my conditions for reproducing photographs, I insist that a copy of the book be sent to me. This is essential since I am often asked for a photograph which has appeared in one of the books. My books are always kept in the same place and, while I am glad for my friends to refer to them, I get rather cross when they do not replace them correctly.

From my study walls, above the bookshelves, enlargements of my own photographs look down at me. After taking a fresh series I change the prints, and find these bring back happy memories, as well as spurring me on to do better.

Also in my study is our visitors' book, which we started in 1942 after having distinguished visitors. Not only is this a useful address book, but it also recalls memories of our host of friends, some from such far-away corners as the Falkland Islands, Pakistan, Tristan da Cunha, Australia, Uganda, Florida, Labrador, Singapore, Johannesburg and Buenos Aires.

Even more varied than the entries in our visitors' book is our correspondence. Although no record has been kept, I am sure letters have been received from more than 100 countries. My mail was greatest when I was lecturing, but even today it is formidable. When I returned from four weeks in Switzerland in 1969 I replied to 137 letters in seven days and there was still a pile of unanswered ones on my desk.

These were some of the subjects dealt with: a schoolboy asked to borrow some transparencies to illustrate a talk on birds—he had tried to take them himself but after five months had succeeded in obtaining only nine results and the birds were so small in the picture that he could not see what they were; another boy said that he had a passion for owls and asked 'Where can I find their nests?'; a third boy was making an attempt at photographing badgers and wanted to know whether I thought it was possible to sink a shaft into the ground by the holt so that he could watch them in their home; a polio victim who loved flowers wanted some colour transparencies just to look at; a youth who had recently left school asked if he could accompany me on an expedition and assist me but, as he had no money, it would be necessary for me to pay his expenses, although he would not expect any wages; a lad who was going to the Scottish Highlands intended to photograph wild cats and wanted to know if he should use flash (no one has yet photographed this intractable feline in the wild, with or without flash!); three correspondents asked if I knew where jobs were available in natural history; several others asked if I could identify birds seen; and there were the usual ones about the best camera and lens to use for bird photography. This last question is difficult to answer because the writers rarely give a clue as to how much they can afford to pay, whether they intend to use the camera mainly for the photography of birds at the nest or for stalking, and whether they have practical experience of photography, etc. With new models coming on to the market each week I find it impossible to keep up to date with them all.

To deal with such a volume of correspondence obviously takes a good deal of time, but it is a pleasure to help those who share my enthusiasms. I have been helped by many in my life; the best way to show my thanks is to aid those who now look to me for similar help.

Ever since I can remember, my mother has had a Christmas party. After Dorothy and I were married we felt that we could save her work by giving it at our house. However, owing to wartime travelling difficulties, the party developed into two days of festivities, with camp-beds and sleeping-bags for those who lived at a distance.

Such a large party also, of course, created food difficulties. Poultry was not rationed, but we seldom saw any in our local shops. So Mother and Dorothy, who had the same butcher, pooled the family rations for two weeks and bought a leg of pork. Dorothy would consult the other women of the family and eventually we had all the makings of a traditional Christmas. As rations were so restricted—a weekly two ounces of butter and half a pound of sugar each—we stock-piled a little each week for months beforehand, and thus we fared well when wartime Christmases came.

This family party has continued throughout our married life, as it is the only occasion in the year when the whole family can be together. Over the years the numbers have increased; although there are now fewer aunts and uncles, there are more grandchildren and great-grandchildren.

This is the one time of the whole year when my study is turned upside down, because our usual dining-room cannot seat the twenty or twenty-five people at the party. So out go my desk, chair, papers and other workaday objects, and in come two long tables and many chairs. This family gathering entails much preparation and even more clearing up afterwards, but the happiness it gives to my ninety-one-year-old mother is ample reward.

In this party, each year, the wheel travels full circle, for my home is the hub of my life. To it through the years have come many changes of fortune, and many visitors. All have helped to weave the tapestry of events that have made my life and have given my home the warmth and atmosphere that it has today. Wartime shook it, childish laughter cheered it, love and friendship mellowed and warmed it. From it I shall draw my strength—always.

5 | *In search of birds*

As the swallow's urge to migrate drives it to fly thousands of miles, so, each spring, a restless urgency stirs within me and I must migrate from London. Every year brings its hopes and its disappointments but also its unexpected thrills and successes. In this chapter I would like to recall some of the highlights of my search for birds.

Many of these have been experienced in Staverton Park and the surrounding countryside. Here, in 1932, I met Willy Bilham, on the estate at Eyke, adjoining Staverton Park. Willy, like his father, is a gamekeeper and knows every trick of his trade and is completely dedicated to his job, gladly working a seven-day week and often most of the night as well. As he walks by a hedgerow he can tell exactly where a partridge is nesting—where the hedgerow is neither too thick nor too thin. Similarly, he can go direct to a pheasant's nest.

He told me that partridges nearly always feed at the same time each day during the breeding season. The hen alone incubates the eggs. The cock calls her at, say, 8.30 a.m., and they go off together to feed. Afterwards he brings her back, sees her on the nest and flies away, returning four and a half hours later for the next feed. And this time-interval—within a few minutes—is rigidly adhered to throughout the nesting season.

Gamekeepers usually guard their charges jealously and do not like bird photographers interfering with the nests. So I was delighted when Willy allowed me to erect a hide by the nest of a partridge containing thirteen eggs. I decided, however, not to start photography until the eggs were 'sprung', a change which develops about twenty-four hours before hatching. Willy could tell within a few hours when an egg would hatch. If he gently shook it and there was a hollow sound, hatching was not far off; if he could feel slight roughness on the surface, hatching was nearer still. Why? Because the roughness indicated that the egg-tooth was beginning to mark the shell where it would finally break and release the chick.

Before breakfast on the day he said that the eggs would hatch, I was in the hide. The hen returned and incubated for the next three hours. Then suddenly she left, ran a few yards and flew away. I quickly got out of the hide to examine the eggs and found that one of the young was pushing its way out.

Hurriedly I re-entered the hide and was hardly settled before I heard a scurrying in the oats at the back of the hide. Then the hen appeared, closely followed by the cock. He looked into the nest, saw his first-born and seemed to go wild with excitement. He rushed frantically about, banged himself against a tree and then came back to have another look. Seven times he repeated these actions before he calmed down and let the hen settle to brood.

Once hatching starts the young emerge fairly quickly, one after another. The hen kept pushing her head under her body and seemed to be helping the young break out. She called and the cock came to sit by her side. A moment later I saw one of the young appear from under the hen and stagger across to the sheltering warmth of the cock. A few minutes later another appeared, then another, until about half the brood were under the cock. It was a never-to-be-forgotten incident.

Witnessing such a scene made me realise why Willy had such little sympathy with vermin, and that included virtually everything that threatened his chicks. If a stoat was around at nesting time he would forget everything, including food and sleep, until he shot or trapped it. In the spring, when bucks are searching for does, Willy would kill a doe, hang her up so that the bucks would scent her, and then set traps all round.

Once, while out with him on his rounds, we found a sparrow hawk's nest and Willy agreed to my photographing it but said that when my camera was finished his gun would take over. I had to erect a pylon hide and spent a long time watching and taking photographs, and got to know the family intimately. I did all I could to stave off the day of execution, making every possible excuse.

At last Willy would wait no longer and told me that he was going to shoot the old bird. I went with him feeling very depressed. The nest was in a dense forest of pines. Willy took position where he had a clear view of the nest and where he could rest his gun in a fork of a tree, pointing it towards the nest. I sat a few yards away. After about an hour the sparrow hawk flew low through the wood, *and alighted on the barrel of the gun!* This softened Willy's heart and he let it go.

On many of my visits to Eyke and Staverton I was accompanied by George Edwards, who also came with me on many other trips. George

Above: Guillemots *(above)* and kittiwakes festoon the Pinnacles in the Farne Islands off the Northumberland coast

Below: Spaced with almost mathematical precision, part of a colony of 5,000 gannets nest on a cliff-top on Grassholm off the Pembrokeshire coast

Above: Rockall—the westernmost part of the British Isles, 160 miles west of St. Kilda

Below: In this aerial shot from a Sunderland flying boat, a rainbow lightens the dark skies behind Fair Isle

is a Yorkshireman, and is well endowed with down-to-earth common sense, humour and imperturbability. He is a friendly man who is at home in any company. Short and wiry, he can cope with the longest and most arduous day in the field, and then pour out a fund of anecdotes, puns and jokes till midnight—and after.

He is a first-rate field ornithologist and an expert nest-finder, in which capacity he has been of immense help to me. And George's skill with tools has often been called on in the various carpentering jobs which bird photography sometimes entails.

George is also an artist and his sketches of people and incidents in the field, complete with homespun poetical commentary, have often delighted his many friends. In latter years his skill as a cine-photographer has been used by some of the television companies, for whom he has travelled far—including the Antarctic—in search of birds.

George was with me once at Staverton Park when there was one of the shelduck 'processions'. The majority of these ducks in Staverton nest in ancient hollow oak trees and when the young hatch they clamber up the inside to an opening, jump out and just float down and land unharmed. On one occasion we watched as the parents kept going in and out of the hole encouraging the young and then, when all were out, led them through the dense undergrowth, across George Boast's garden and on to the road. Just before reaching the village of Butley the procession turned off into ploughed fields, and eventually reached a stream which leads to tidal waters—a walking distance of about a mile. We watched fascinated and, as the birds reached the road, David, one of George Boast's sons, said: 'Isn't it marvellous—left-hand side of the road, too!'

It was in 1945 that I met Charles P. Rose of Mistley, Essex, and we have been friends ever since. Charles is a master builder and also a very keen bird photographer, famous throughout East Anglia for his lectures, illustrated with his own 16 mm colour films. I approached him about filming a rookery. John Matthias, of Countryman Films, was making a film, *Birds of the Village*, which he had planned with the help and guidance of James Fisher. He asked me to be technical adviser, which involved finding the rookeries, arranging for the erection of the hides and giving general advice on the work. Charles built two excellent wooden pylon hides, each sixty feet tall, and these were erected at two rookeries in Suffolk, one at Wickham Market, the other at Elmsett.

When all was ready I telegraphed the official cameraman. He arrived next day and I took him to the site. He took one look at the towering hide and said: 'I've no head for heights,' and refused to climb the pylon. So I did all the filming. While I did not have much sympathy for the cameraman at the time, I have now. Since I have had to wear bi-

E

focal spectacles I have developed a fear of heights and know what a paralysing emotion it can be.

During the summer of 1946 I made my first visit to the Orkneys, taking George Edwards with me. On the ship from Aberdeen we were amused to read this notice: 'The poop deck contains 828 sq. ft. and is certified for ninety-two first-class passengers when not occupied by cattle, animals, cargo or other incumbrance.' Could 'other incumbrance' possibly mean the mound of equipment which, as usual, accompanied us?

We were surprised at the remarkable tameness of some of the birds. Curlews and lapwings, usually nervous birds, came to within a few yards of where we stood. Golden plovers and redshanks allowed us to approach quite near, and even a drake long-tailed duck remained on a small loch as we watched it. Red-breasted mergansers were still displaying on 4 June. At night it was almost impossible to sleep because of the craking of the corncrakes; eight pairs were within earshot of our lodgings.

We had an example of how individual birds of the same species vary. Normally hen harriers are comparatively tame and, provided normal care is taken, present no problem to the photographer. However, we found the nest of an especially nervous pair which would not tolerate a hide twenty yards away, so we had to remove it and find another pair. And these were as tame as barnyard fowls and we filmed and photographed to our hearts' content!

To photograph some of the birds it was necessary to visit several of the smaller islands. We were transported by George Arthur, the warden for the Royal Society for the Protection of Birds in the Orkneys. He was a baker by trade, watch-mender by inclination and bird-lover all the time, utterly devoted to their welfare. As far as he was able, he would see that they lived out their bright lives without interference from mankind. He hated the mere sight of an egg-collector, or anybody else whose activities might upset the welfare of his beloved birds.

George even had serious misgivings about bird-ringing, despite its proved value in ornithology. I was at Spurn Head with him during the remarkable robin invasion of October 1952 (see page 66). Of course, many of them were ringed, much to George's indignation. He maintained that the robins had already been delayed and upset by adverse weather conditions before leaving Scandinavia. Trapping and ringing would cause them to use up nervous energy when it was most needed, thus endangering their chance of survival.

To me, and I believe to most other bird photographers, he was kindness itself, but not to the man who put his photography before the welfare of his subject. He always maintained that there were two types

—the bird photographer and the photographer of birds. The first always gave precedence to the bird, whereas the other put photography first and did not really care much what happened to the birds. I remember how vitriolic he was about a well-known photographer erecting a hide within nine feet of the nest of a red-throated diver and not checking to see whether the bird had accepted it or not. The bird deserted. George never forgave him and the transgressor never did any more bird photography in the Orkneys.

George has left an enduring mark on the ornithology of the Orkneys, and it may not be too much to say that he saved the hen harrier as a British breeding bird. It was a sad day for the birds when he died in December 1952.

The next year (1947) it was the Scottish Highlands for nine weeks, again with George Edwards. Although it was May when we drove north, near Braemar it was snowing hard and on the hill at Blairgowrie there were snowbanks five feet high. The weather was icy at times, and we had no luck with the golden eagles I had hoped to photograph. We saw several, but found no eyrie suitable for photography. It was a fortnight before I even unpacked my cameras.

But as the season developed it got better and better. We met Desmond Nethersole-Thompson, a brilliant field ornithologist who had made a particular study of the greenshank. (See *The Greenshank*, published as a monograph in *The New Naturalist* series in 1951.) He suggested that we might like to accompany him as he searched for a nest—one of the most difficult to find, particularly in the early days when the eggs are being laid. Tommy, as we called him, had already watched a pair for three days and after following various clues had an idea where they might be nesting.

We hid among the branches of a winter-stricken tree on the moors near Loch Morlich, watching the cock display and listening to him singing beautifully from the top of an old gnarled tree bole. Tommy saw the hen trip daintily through ruts and tussocks and then lost sight of her. Half an hour later we walked to the place where she had vanished and flushed her from the nest containing two eggs. Two more were laid subsequently.

A hide was erected and gradually worked into position, and then left, as I wanted to confine the photography to the period of the hatch. One evening we found the eggs chipping and could hear the young piping inside the shells: they would hatch within forty-eight hours. Then, during the night, a tremendous storm broke. Near-hurricane winds scoured the forest, snapping many trees, uprooting others. Heavy rain fell and in the morning we found the hen brooding amid pools of water. Three young were hatched and two egg-shells lay in the nest-cup. The light was still bad and photography impossible, so I just sat and watched.

The hen was brooding when the cock suddenly flew down, snatched one of the empty egg-shells and flew away with it. An hour later he removed the second shell, returning shortly afterwards to relieve the hen. What a delightful series of pictures of greenshank family life ... if only the light had been good enough.

Young greenshanks are lovely creatures, with striped down, large dark eyes, and long, greenish, stilt-like legs. Usually they leave the nest the same day as they hatch. As they make their way towards the nearest loch the parents are obviously nervous. They seem to suspect every bird, and almost every blade of grass, as they fly or run noisily to and fro, urging their brood forward. The young may well have a mile or more to walk, so every now and again the hen calls a halt to brood and warm them. Sometimes she has to dry them after the journey through the jungle of wet grass and heather.

It was Tommy who also found a crossbill's nest. I had long wanted to photograph these strange birds, which seem to live in the tops of pine trees, and have specially adapted crossed bills to enable them to extract the seeds from the pine cones. There is a legend, however, that their bills really became crossed after one of the birds had struggled to pluck a nail from the hand of our Lord as He hung on the cross.

Usually the crossbill is an early breeder, building its nest in March or April, which was before I could get away. But in 1947, owing probably to the exceptionally bad winter, the Scottish crossbills nested late. Indeed it was not until 27 May that we found a nest. It was thirty feet up in a Scots pine and contained three eggs. The hen took no notice while we erected a pylon hide. Two of the eggs hatched on 5 June, the third mysteriously disappeared.

The olive-green hen remained brooding while the splendid red cock gathered food. While flying to the nest he uttered a distinctive 'chipping' note. When he arrived the hen stood up, rapidly quivered her wings and begged, with open bill, to be fed—exactly like a chick. The cock regurgitated softened pine seed into her bill and then similarly fed the young. As the cock left, the hen tidied the nest and attended to the sanitation of the young. Several times she prodded them to produce a faecal sac (a tiny cellophane-like bag containing excrement) which she then swallowed, before settling to brood and sleep.

In June the British Ornithologists' Union held their first conference since the war in Edinburgh, and quite a large number of foreign ornithologists attended. After the meeting a number of excursions were arranged, one of which was to Aviemore, Inverness-shire, where

George Edwards and I were staying. One day a large party, including representatives from fourteen European countries, descended upon us for a field outing. We took them around and displayed such comparative British rarities as crossbills, crested tits and greenshanks. The visitors, however, seemed quite unimpressed; they had seen all the birds we showed them in their own countries. Somewhat deflated we took them to tea at the Aviemore Hotel, and during the meal someone noticed a male pied wagtail on the lawn. At once tea-cups were hastily put down, and a concerted rush was made to the windows to view the wagtail—a 'lifer' for most of them!

My search for birds has taken me to many lovely places. One was the grounds of Balmoral Castle. But the first time I went there I was disconcerted to be told on introducing myself: 'You're not Eric Hosking.' I assured them I most certainly was and eventually they told me this story. A man who had impersonated me had been shown around and a golden eagle's eyrie pointed out to him. He was then given permission to wander about on his own. After he had gone the keepers discovered that he had stolen the eggs.

A similar incident occurred during the war, also in Scotland. I saw a man photographing a ringed plover's nest and, thinking that here was a kindred soul, I introduced myself. Again I was greeted with: 'You're not Eric Hosking.' This chap took a lot of convincing, and it was only when I produced my identity card that he finally accepted me. His disbelief arose from an incident at an exhibition of the Royal Photographic Society some years before, when a man pointed to one of my photographs and said: 'I took that.' Naturally he was taken at his word, and that is why my companion took so much convincing. He was John Markham, and that was the beginning of a life-long friendship.

The year 1947 was also notable for my first attempt at aerial reconnaissance photography on a flight organised by my old friend James Fisher. The objective was Rockall, a small outcrop of rock 160 miles west of St. Kilda, to find out whether any birds were breeding there and whether it had any vegetation. The party comprised Sir Frederick Whyte, distinguished public servant and author with a special interest in Rockall; Dr. Brian Roberts and Christopher Lewis who, with James, were to devote their energies to observing birds throughout the flight; and Robert Atkinson and I who were to take the photographs.

We were airborne from Stranraer in a Sunderland flying boat at 11.30 a.m. on 30 July. The weather was brilliant and the sea perfectly calm. In less than three-quarters of an hour we were over the Mull of

Kintyre, flying between 500 and 800 ft., and coming in as near as possible to the cliffs to observe the birds. James was particularly interested in discovering breeding colonies of fulmars, so we kept a special watch for them and found our first over Islay. At Barra Head large numbers were either flying near to the cliff-faces or sitting on the cliffs.

While I preferred my 35 mm camera, I was asked to take as many photographs as possible with the big 5 in × 5 in. Williamson air camera —a machine I had never seen before and did not know how to operate. And none of the air crew knew either. Fortunately, it did not take me long to find out—on a survey flight there is an urgency about everything; an aircraft does not stand still while one tries to puzzle out how to release the shutter or wind on the film.

Just after one-thirty we flew over St. Kilda, an island that had excited me since, as a lad, I read *With Nature and a Camera* (Cassell, 1911) by Richard Kearton. Here then was where Finlay Gillies caught puffins in a noose, and where a girl had her petticoats ballooned by a sudden squall of wind and was lifted right over the cliff; she falling 180 ft. on to an earth-covered ledge, her petticoats forming a parachute that saved her life. These and many other incidents came to life for me as I gazed at the spectacular cliffs. At 1,000 ft. we actually looked up at the top of the great Conachair which rises 1,392 ft. from the sea, the highest cliff in the British Isles, and then we rose to 1,500 ft. to get a better view. Down again and closer in to look at Stac Lee, Boreray and Stac an Armin with the huge colonies of pure white gannets—a marvellous sight. Finally we flew between Boreray and Stac an Armin, a breathtaking experience, but with so much to photograph I had no time to marvel at it all but just banged away with the camera as fast as I could. As James said over the intercom: 'There's surely nothing like these cliffs anywhere in the world.'

At 2 p.m. we headed due west for the open Atlantic. Now I had a respite from my non-stop two-hour stint of photography. My arms ached and my eye felt as if it were being pulled out of its socket, but I had been so absorbed in the photography that I had not realised the discomfort.

It was interesting to watch the radar operator. Tiny blips on his screen were ships thirty miles away, until soon after three o'clock when a slightly different blip appeared—Rockall. As we closed, a little cheer rang through the aircraft, partly perhaps a tribute to the navigator who had brought us direct to this spot of land in a vast ocean. We dipped and went in at about 100 ft., making ten runs in all, some with the flaps down so that we were flying as slowly as possible. We studied Rockall and photographed the rock from every angle.

When we arrived some eighty kittiwakes took wing at our approach, although some had returned by the time we flew over the rock again. We saw four great shearwaters and five fulmars gliding over the sea. About a dozen guillemots were on or near the rock. James gave instructions that on three of the runs I was to put my camera down and join the others in watching carefully to see whether there was a sign of any young birds, but none was seen. It was obvious that many pelagic birds used Rockall as a perching and resting place but nothing more.

Rockall has always been notoriously difficult to land on because of the almost perpetual swell, but as we looked down we could see how calm it was. James, an experienced rock climber, said that the climb looked easy but I must confess that to me it looked pretty grim.

After twenty minutes (how much one crams into a small space of time when there is so much to do) we turned back and within three and a half hours were again over St. Kilda, then the Flannans and on to Lewis, where we followed the coast. James was in his element, calling out: 'Fulmars to starboard—small breeding colony, no more than about ten pairs,' or: 'I say, chaps, can you see those fulmars on the port side—must be a new colony as there's no record of them breeding here before.' James has an infectious enthusiasm especially where his beloved fulmars are concerned. We flew over Sula Sgeir and North Rona, then south-east to Cape Wrath and photographed the lighthouse and the cliffs on the west coast of Sutherland. Then on to Handa, The Shiants, Fladdachuain Islands, Treshnish, Iona, Oronsay and finally Ailsa Craig, where I used up the last four exposures. We landed at Stranraer at 8.45 p.m. after an unforgettable day. Our pilot said that this was the first flight he had ever known in which there had not been a single bump. We were airborne for nine hours, covered 1,534 statute miles and took 300 photographs.

Incidentally, when the Royal Navy annexed Rockall to the British Isles on 18 September 1955, James landed by helicopter and obtained specimens of Rockallite, a piece of which he gave me as a memento of our flight.

My next aerial reconnaissance—again organised by James—was on 28 September. My colleagues on this flight were E. M. Nicholson, Chairman of the British Trust for Ornithology; Stephen (Lifemanship) Potter, a BBC producer; Keith Piercy, Chairman of the Bedfordshire Natural History Society; Dr. Brian Roberts of the Foreign Office Research Department; Ronald Lockley, Chairman of the West Wales Field Society; Dr. Bruce Campbell, naturalist; and J. L. Davies, mammalogist.

The object of this trip was to make a census of the grey seal breeding population on Welsh and Scottish islands. We were airborne about nine o'clock and soon after were flying over Skokholm, Skomer and

Grassholm. My job was to take photographs of every seal colony that we could find, but this was not easy. New-born seal calves have white coats but within a few days they moult and are then an indefinite colour. Although we flew mainly at about 500 ft. and quite slowly, it was difficult to distinguish calves from driftwood and rocks.

Unlike the Rockall flight, this one was decidedly rough—bumps nearly all the time—and at one time all the civilian observers except James, Stephen and myself were air-sick. I was so busy photographing that I did not have time to worry about sickness. Every now and again someone shouted over the intercom: 'Calf on the shore to port'—or starboard. Often, however, by the time I had it in view we had flown too far away to obtain a clear enough photograph. But as the day went on we all became more expert at our tasks.

We flew over Island Farm at Dinas Cross in Pembrokeshire, where Ronald Lockley's family all waved to us, and then northwards over Holyhead and out to the Isle of Man, the Mull of Galloway, Ailsa Craig and then across the Scottish lowlands to the Bass Rock. At two-thirty we landed at Invergordon where we spent the night.

The following morning we were airborne before eight and for me it was another of those days that I shall remember for the rest of my life. Dr. F. Fraser Darling,* the Scottish naturalist, had now joined us and within half an hour, as he craned his neck out of the hatch, the air-stream whipped off his cap! Soon we were over the Orkney Islands and although we could find no seals, around South Ronaldsay we saw many gannets. Over North Ronaldsay we thought there were seals but closer inspection showed that the animals were seaweed-eating sheep. Our next call was Fair Isle, another island that has always interested me because of the numbers of rare migrant birds that have first been recorded there, and where at the beginning of this century William Eagle Clarke did so much of his work on migration. Just then the present observation station was lit by a rainbow and I made an exposure. It proved to be the best photograph of the whole flight (see plate facing page 47).

Lighting conditions became progressively worse as we flew over Sumburgh Head, the southernmost tip of the Shetlands. James urged me to do my best, but the pilot said: 'Only a bloody fool would attempt to do photography in these conditions.' Here was a dilemma. Such an opportunity was unlikely to recur, but was I just wasting material? I decided to carry on and try to overcome the flat lighting by using an extra contrasty developer. This would exaggerate the grain—but it worked.

I was surprised how quickly the weather changed. One minute

* Now Sir Frank Fraser Darling.

cloud seemed to be almost at ground level, the next overhead. Then suddenly there were shafts of sunlight that changed everything.

We looked at the islands of Mousa and Noss, the Outer Skerries, Yell and Fetlar, on to Unst and round Muckle Flugga, the northern-most part of the British Isles. Then we turned south coming down the west side of Yell and over Ramna Stacks to the main Shetland island, then out to Foula with its sheer cliff-face of over 1,000 ft. Twenty minutes later we were over the Orkneys again and then on to North Rona, where Fraser Darling once lived. We estimated the seal popula-tion here as approximately 250 adults and 160 calves. I shall never forget seeing Fraser Darling, who was terribly air-sick, forcing himself to look out of a port-hole at the island he knew so well and then sink back into his bunk. We flew on to the Flannan Isles and over to St. Kilda. While flying over the village bay we had the biggest air bump I have ever experienced; we must have dropped 200 ft. before levelling off. I thought we were going to crash.

We flew to Cape Wrath, then along the north coast of Scotland and finally back to Invergordon. We were nine and a half hours in the air and it would be impossible to praise too highly the skill of the air crew.

Although the weather had been so indifferent, I was very pleased that the photographs came out as well as they did. We did not see as many seals as we wished but made one interesting discovery—the large seal colony on Gasker, west of the Outer Hebrides. There had been rumours that it was a breeding ground, but there had been only one visit by a scientist in fifty years. When we flew over the island, we could see at least ninety adults and 150 calves.

Thus ended a most eventful season. James Fisher, who helped to make it so interesting, died just before this book was published.

We spent the spring of 1948 at Staverton Park, and took so much equipment—besides the family, George Edwards and our belongings—that I had to make two journeys. We stayed in Shepherd's Cottage, a small thatched-roof bungalow in the middle of the forest. Conditions were primitive: water came from a well and had to be boiled before use; paraffin lamps were the only source of light; there was an earth closet but no bathroom.

When it rained and we came home soaking our clothes had to be dried before the open smoky fire in the living-room, and both we and our clothes usually ended up slightly kippered.

But there were sunny afternoons when we had friends and work was forgotten. Then we picnicked outdoors and afterwards played cricket—with no lack of fielders!

It was a season of high-speed flash and experiments. Philip Henry had designed and built the photo-electric shutter release (see Chapter

1 2), and he was anxious to be with me when this was tried out in the field. We started off by working at a great tit's nest in the hole of a tree about two feet above the ground. The high-speed flash and the automatic shutter release were all erected and tested, and I marvelled at the way they worked. To test, Philip passed his hand rapidly across a beam of light shining on to the photo-electric cell, thus causing it to activate the solenoid that released the camera shutter, firing the two flash-lamps. All I had to do was to sit in the hide and wait for the great tit to fly back to the nest and take her own photograph.

Unless disturbed, a bird usually returns to its nest along the same flight-path. By watching carefully we noted this, and erected the photo-electric shutter release so that the bird would cut across the beam about two feet from the nesting hole with its image approximately in the centre of the photographic plate. The time lapse between cutting the light-beam and the lamps firing was only a hundredth of a second. Everything worked beautifully. The first time the bird returned and took its own photograph it swerved to one side, alighting on a nearby branch, apparently perplexed at what had taken place when there was no sign of anyone about. Subsequently it accepted the flash as some sort of natural phenomenon.

On each visit to the nest food was brought and the bird entered the hole to feed the young. Before leaving, it usually waited to see if any of the young would produce a faecal sac for it to take away. The slight delay enabled us to get everything ready for another flash. Immediately the bird dived into the hole I had to change plates and quickly reset the shutter. The apparatus took only nine seconds to recharge and thus be ready for the next flash. As great tits feed their young every two or three minutes it was not long before several dozen plates had been exposed, and I was naturally eager to see the results.

Back at the cottage I loaded the plates into developing tanks, having to do this in a changing bag as there was no means of making any place really dark during the middle of the day. As the plates developed I was trembling with excitement. I was thrilled with the results. Some showed the bird with its wings vertical, others with them down, some showing the braking movement, others showed the insect food they carried so clearly that we could easily identify gnats, flies, small moths, caterpillars, spiders—in fact a pretty comprehensive collection of all the invertebrates found in the forest!

Spurred on by the success at the great tit's nest, similar series of photographs were taken of several other species. We found an attractive wheatear's nest built in a hole in a fallen tree-trunk and both cock and hen took their own photographs as they flew to and fro. A coal tit nesting in an old petrol can produced some fascinating results. Whinchats used to perch on an old stump before flying down to their nest, and this led to spectacular depictions of wing attitudes a fraction of a second before touching down. Swallows nesting in a shed arrived with mouths crammed with flies caught on the wing and, as they slowed down immediately before alighting, were caught in some delightful poses. These photographs revealed, probably for the first time, the swallow's perfect streamlining. At first sight they appeared to have no legs or feet, until it was realised that these were tucked under the stomach feathers, thus reducing wind resistance.

It was at this time that I took what is, I suppose, my most famous photograph, a barn owl in flight, wings spread, vole in bill (between pages 150 and 151). It has been reproduced hundreds of times throughout the world—in 106 countries to my certain knowledge. It even greeted me in a photographic shop in Amman, Jordan, where it illustrated a Kodak advertisement.

During this season Dr. Stuart Smith stayed a fortnight with us and it was then that we carried out much of the work recounted in Chapter 13. During the evenings in that old cottage we had many stimulating discussions, and laid our plans for the next season.

All his life birds had fascinated Stuart. As a schoolboy he made notes on bird behaviour, but it was a chance meeting, when he was thirteen, with the great Richard Kearton that gave him the inspiration and guidance he needed. Despite the disparity in ages a close friendship developed between them and they corresponded regularly. Stuart wanted to make the study of birds his career but Richard Kearton was strongly against this, advising him that he should qualify in a career that would give him financial independence yet allow him enough leisure to follow his hobby. (How often I have given similar advice to young people who write to me!) Stuart followed this advice. He took a degree in physics at Leeds University, and thereafter spent the whole of his working life with the British Cotton Research Association in Didsbury, Manchester.

I first met Stuart in the spring of 1940 on the shores of Loch Morlich in Inverness-shire while we were both looking at birds. I was immediately captivated by his infectious enthusiasm. This overflowed into everything he did and said, whether at his work, in his home or with his beloved birds. He had a dynamic personality which somehow swept others along with him when he was pursuing an idea.

Soon after we met we arranged to spend some time together during the following spring, and thereafter Stuart usually came every year to join us during the nesting season. He had a lively stimulating mind, disciplined by his scientific training and work. He was widely read, was an excellent observer, and knew how to make the most of both book learning and first-hand knowledge. He was an excellent photographer and derived great pleasure from it. Whenever I was faced with a knotty problem he always seemed to know the answer.

Unfortunately he did not enjoy really good health and his untimely death in 1963, when only fifty-six, left a gap in my life which no one else can ever fill.

The whole of the 1948 season was wonderfully happy, especially as Dorothy and the family were with me, and we enjoyed such excellent company. I therefore decided to spend the following season in the same area. Unfortunately we were unable to stay at Shepherd's Cottage because the owner was in residence, but there was a wonderful old Tudor mansion at nearby Tangham, owned by the Forestry Commission and leased to Mrs. Monica Fearon.

While we were here, Dorothy brought the children down for a week—and they nearly cost me a small fortune. Mrs. Fearon had an antique shop in nearby Woodbridge and occasionally brought home furniture that needed renovation. On this occasion, two Chippendale chairs were awaiting repolishing. Margaret and Robin thought they would help by giving them a coat of green paint. What a mess! They splashed it everywhere and it took George Edwards, who once worked in a furniture shop, three days to get it off.

George's principal job, apart from helping me in and out of hides, was to find nests. Only a small proportion of nests are suitable for photography, either because of their situation or because the young are too large to be disturbed, which causes them to leave their nest before they are ready, thus reducing their chance of survival. Consequently I always like to have a choice of nests. One day George found a little owl's nest in an excellent position—in the hole of a tree about four feet above the ground. We could not see into the hole to find out how many young there were but this did not really matter—what was important was the fact that there were young. We erected a hide a safe distance away, and moved it daily towards the nest until it was within five feet. Dummy flash reflectors were fixed into position twenty-four hours before I started photography. These reflectors are polished aluminium and sometimes birds take a little while to get used to them.

It is difficult to describe the uncanny feeling of sitting in a hide in pitch darkness half expecting the owl to return to its nest, cut the beam and fire off the flash—but never knowing the exact moment. Owls are absolutely silent fliers and give no clue, no warning whatever, and then somehow when it is least expected there is an almighty flash. Each time it went off I nearly hit the roof! After six flashes in fairly quick succession it seemed certain that something was wrong with the photo-electric cell and it was tripping itself, so in disgust I gave up and went back to Tangham and decided to develop the negatives before going to bed. The results showed that high-speed photography is full of surprises. The first photograph showed an oak leaf in mid-air. But in all the others the little owl was in full flight with the prey clearly defined —a field mouse, an earth-worm, a dor beetle, and cockchafers twice. Even insects as small as ants could be identified—but surely an ant could not be much of a meal for a young owl?

The 1950 season was spent at Minsmere, but as I have done so much of my work there, and because it is my favourite resort, I have made it the subject of a separate chapter.

The following year, 1951, was what might be called a hotch-potch, because I did not stay anywhere for long. I went first with George Edwards to Walthamstow Reservoir, within five miles of my home. These reservoirs were completed in 1897 and consist of twelve separate but interconnected stretches of water, the majority of which have two or more small tree-covered islands, and it was on one of these that a heronry was established in 1914. This island was no more than 100 yards in diameter and was a jungle of small elder and hawthorn bushes, between which grew sycamores and willow trees and mature haw-thorns, some thirty feet high, which contained part of the heronry.

It seemed ideal for photography. The Metropolitan Water Board kindly gave us permission to erect a pylon hide and allowed us to use a rowing boat to get to and from the island, which lay about 200 yards from the shore. Because of the number of boys who trespassed, the boat was kept locked up, which resulted in its drying out and springing several leaks. When contrary winds were blowing George rowed as hard as he could while I baled furiously. Once we had to battle against a real gale and had visions of being shipwrecked almost in the centre of London!

The erection of the pylon hide took a week, as we thought it would be unwise to work for more than an hour each day while some of the nests still contained eggs. But the slow building paid off; by the time it was completed the herons apparently looked upon it as part of the scenery and ignored it.

After seeing me into the hide George rowed back to shore, and before he landed most of the herons were back on their nests. The herons with eggs quickly settled down to incubate, but at other nests the chicks started squawking for food at the first sign of an adult's approach. The feeding process is a free-for-all. The young try to grab hold of the parent's bill and tug it down to the nest. The adult then starts to retch, which makes the young even more excited at the antici-pation of a meal. Finally, the parent disgorges the meal and the young seize it, swallowing whole anything they can grab. Not until they are certain that the adult has no more to deliver do the young give up, and settle down to sleep.

At this period I confined myself to taking stills, mainly in black and white but also some in colour. George made a film, and so did Lord Alanbrooke, a keen bird photographer (see Chapter 9). Parts of both films were shown on BBC-TV.

While we were rowing to and from the heronry we noticed a pair of kingfishers on another of the islands. To our joy, we found that there was a nest. It was at the end of a tunnel at least four feet long so we could not see what it contained, but George kept a watch and one day saw the kingfishers carry fish into the hole, obviously to feed the young. Although it was no simple matter to put up a hide, as the ground was far from level, we built a wooden platform, one edge of which rested on the island, the other in the water four feet deep.

Here was a wonderful opportunity for flight photography of Britain's most colourful bird. We noticed that having caught a fish, the kingfishers flew direct into the tunnel. The flight path was carefully studied and the photo-electric beam aligned so that the bird would take its own photograph when eighteen inches from the hole. The results were very pleasing, in fact I think they are the most successful colour photographs I have so far taken.

One day in April 1951 Lord Alanbrooke telephoned to say that Lord Portal (Chief of the Air Staff during the war), an ardent falconer, had invited him to go to Cocking, near Midhurst in Sussex, to see the nest of a pair of goshawks and he wondered if I would like to accompany them. I did not even know that there were any goshawks nesting anywhere in Great Britain, so the news excited me and I enthusiastically accepted the invitation.

As we walked through the wood I wondered whether the nest would be in a position where we could take photographs. Most of the trees were enormous beeches, some standing more than eighty feet high, and almost at the top of one of these was the nest. A forester climbed the tree to find what the nest contained, and as he swarmed up I kept a careful watch on the nest as I particularly wanted to see the bird leave. The climber had almost reached the nest before the bird suddenly leapt off, and as she flew through the young, fresh, green leaves I could clearly see that she trailed jesses.

Lord Portal told us that most of the hawks and falcons trained for falconry eventually escape and it was obvious that a pair of goshawks had come together.

Most of the thrill of photography was lost for me by knowing they were escapees, but apart from this the nest was in such a difficult position I do not think that it would have been possible to erect a hide.

The nest contained three eggs all of which hatched and the young were reared. I still have a feather the forester brought down for me.

About this time I was asked by E. R. (John) Parrinder to take a series of photographs of the little ringed plover. What owls are to me, this plover is to John. He was intrigued by the way this bird was extending its geographical range, and he had noticed that during the years in which the mile-long Girling Reservoir at Chingford was being constructed, the plovers nested in the man-made shingle beds. In 1951 the work was nearly completed and soon the reservoir would be flooded, covering the plovers' breeding grounds.

George and I went with John to Chingford several times to find a nest. But finding the rudimentary nest containing four eggs that closely harmonised with the background was not easy. There were five pairs: two already had young, another pair were courting and gave us excellent views of their displays. We felt sure that the remaining two pairs must have eggs. After a great deal of concentrated watching and searching John eventually found a nest, but bulldozers were still working all round it. When we pointed out the nest to the workmen they seemed almost as interested as we were and volunteered to erect a fence round the area until the eggs hatched.

A hide was erected and worked up in stages until it was only six feet away. Fortunately the young hatched during a Sunday morning while I was occupying the hide. The cock was incubating the eggs but rather restlessly, rarely sitting still for more than a few moments at a time. Then, when he half raised his body, I saw the first chick wriggling out of its shell. The cock was agitated and called, all the while gently raising and lowering himself on the nest. The chick whistled and the cock replied. He picked up the top piece of the egg-shell, held it in his bill, dropped it, picked it up again, moved away from the nest, turned round and came back with it still in his bill. This went on for about five minutes before the hen arrived, when the cock flew away, taking the shell with him. The hen picked up the other piece and ran away with it, dropping it fully twenty yards away, and then hurried back.

Similar behaviour took place at the hatching of the remaining three eggs but the point that interested me most was that the cock was in attendance each time. I have watched the hatch at the nest of several other species of wader and nearly always the cock has been at the nest at the critical moment. Is there any significance in this?

This was not the first time I have been impressed with the way workmen have protected nesting birds. I once found that over an Easter holiday, a blackbird had built its nest on the axle of a goods truck. When I pointed this out to the railwaymen they shunted the truck into a siding and left it there until the young had flown.

On another occasion pied wagtails made a nest in a crane on a building site and, despite the deafening noise, refused to leave. During lunchtime the men used to leave scraps of their sandwiches for the birds, and they became so fond of them that they would cheerfully have murdered anyone who dared to harm them.

In 1951 I also photographed a bird in London which was there largely because the blitz provided ideal nesting sites—the black redstart. It nested in the Palace of Engineering during the Wembley Exhibition in 1924. Subsequently there were several other attempts at nests within the London area, but it was the havoc wrought by the bombing of large towns that seemed to provide the ideal nesting conditions for the black redstart: a ruined building with a nearby food supply, namely the insects which bred on the plants growing on ground exposed by bombing. N. J. P. Wadley studied the redstarts' spread and it was he who showed me a nest in a bombed office site near St. Paul's Cathedral. It was probably one of twelve or more pairs nesting within the sound of Bow Bells.

The nest was between the ceiling of a second-floor room and the floor of the room above, and a small pylon hide was necessary for photography. The black redstart is a rare breeding bird in this country so obviously the fewer people who knew what we were doing the better. The doors of the building had been destroyed, so there was no means of keeping people out, and if we were seen we might attract unwanted attention. The City is, of course, packed with people every weekday but on Saturday afternoons and all day Sunday it is relatively deserted. I therefore hired a lorry to transport the materials so that they arrived soon after midday one Saturday. We felt rather like burglars, keeping a careful watch for the local policeman to pass by, although later we took him into our confidence. He and his colleagues took a great interest in what we were doing, quite apart from keeping a special watch on the building, the nest and our hide.

Fortunately, black redstarts are very tame birds and they took little notice of us as we erected the hide. Whenever we saw them approaching we stopped, remaining still until they had fed the young and left. We noticed that the hen caught most of the prey among the Oxford ragwort that was growing profusely on the ground exposed by the air raids. Cinnabar moths and their caterpillars feed on this plant and they formed a large part of the diet. Apart from these, the redstarts found crane-flies, small beetles, several different species of ants, aphids, moths and gnats. Now that the City has largely been rebuilt the black redstart breeds there much less frequently.

Only a small proportion of the young black redstarts bred in London survived. When they first fluttered down from the nest many

Above: As this little owl takes off from its nest in a tree, it breaks the electronic beam thus firing the flash lamps and triggering the camera shutter. The 1/5,000th second exposure 'freezes' all movement

Below: On a two-foot wide cliff edge on Skomer, 60 feet above the sea, a peregrine falcon gazes at her downy eyas

Above: This little ringed plover made its nest on a man-made shingle bed that was later covered by the mile-long Girling Reservoir at Chingford, Essex

Below: Her brood complete, this hen greenshank clears the nest of the remaining egg shell

were killed by traffic; the numerous feral cats that inhabit the city are always on the look-out for such succulent and easy prey; and at night the tawny owls are on the hunt.

This season was based at home and I photographed a wide variety of species in different localities. I was intrigued when Drs. John Ash and Kenneth Rooke told me that two rare British nesting birds—the Dartford warbler and the cirl bunting—were breeding in Hampshire. So in June I drove down with George to find that the Dartford warblers were nesting on a heath about three-quarters of a mile from the nearest car-parking spot. The flash equipment I was then using weighed a hundredweight and was in five different units. In addition, of course, there were the cameras, hide, tripods, seat, etc. It was too much for us to carry in one load, so we each took as much as possible, humped that halfway, piled it on the ground, returned for the remainder, took that all the way to the nest and then went back for the other pile. By the time this manœuvre had been repeated in reverse and everything was back in the car, we realised that heavy manual labour was an intrinsic part of this form of bird photography.

This was the first time the opportunity had presented itself of photographing the Dartford warbler. It is a lovely little bird, especially the male with his dark brown upper parts, slate-grey head and light brown underparts. Both male and female have a bright reddish-orange eye. The Dartford is the only one of our warblers which does not migrate.

I was surprised to notice that the cock was feeding the young about six times to the hen's once. Why? Then I saw the hen collecting material nearby and it seemed that she was already constructing a new nest in preparation for another brood. The cock had evidently been left to look after the young.

When George came to relieve me he whispered that an adder was only three feet from the nest. He lifted it with a small stick and released it well out of reach of the nest. Adders do feed on young birds but I am loth to kill them as they also have their place in nature.

On our return from the Dartford warblers I saw that the car was surrounded by cows. Through my binoculars I was alarmed to see that they were scraping their horns against the paintwork, and when we finally reached the car it was a mess. One side was a mass of scratches—a file could not have done a more thorough job—and all the windows were smeared by the cows' tongues.

There were no such complications about photographing the other rarity: the cirl bunting's nest was in a roadside hedge. The chicks had only recently hatched and, while the hen was in almost constant attendance, the cock brought all the food. It was a moving experience

F

to watch, only five feet away, the delicate way in which the cock passed food to the hen and she, in turn, to her young. I know it is important to be scientifically objective about such things, but it certainly *seemed* to me that these birds showed a care transcending the mere fulfilling of a biological urge.

It is partly, I suppose, because I have watched so closely the family lives of so many birds, that I just cannot subscribe to the view that all their actions can be explained in purely physical terms—innate behaviour patterns, etc. I believe there exists a bond of attachment between a pair of birds hatching and rearing a new family into the world. I have already referred to this in the partridge family I observed at Eyke.

Some birds, such as bullfinches, apparently pair for life, staying together summer and winter and sharing all the family chores in the breeding season—the cock even incubating at times. When the young hatch, the cock collects the food, regurgitates it directly into the hen's mouth and she passes it to them. When the young no longer need brooding, cock and hen forage together, return to the nest together, and seem to want to be continually in each other's company.

Once at Staverton I was photographing a bullfinch family when the cock was killed. For thirty-six hours the hen hung around, plaintively calling for her lost mate. Then she disappeared, and her young were left to die in the nest. Just innate mechanical behaviour?

About this time, with George Edwards, I visited Morton Valence in Gloucestershire at the invitation of Philip Brown, then Secretary of the Royal Society for the Protection of Birds. There were numerous marsh warblers' nests, one of which contained a cuckoo's egg. This was unusual and, as far as I knew, had never before been photographed. Hides were erected at this nest and one other.

At the second nest the hen did nearly all the feeding. Why wasn't the cock helping? Then I discovered that an unmated cock was singing continuously only a few yards from the nest. So the mated cock stayed on his territory, ready to attack the moment the intruder passed the invisible territorial line. Incidentally, once the hen had to defend the nest; a common shrew several times climbed one of the stems supporting the nest, each time being driven off by the hen's furious attacks.

We had to leave the area for a while, but when I returned the cuckoo in the other nest was about ten days old. It had already ejected the young and was now so large that it seemed to overflow the nest. The foster parents were working overtime trying to keep pace with its insatiable appetite; moths and damsel-flies seemed to be the favourite fare. Some of the insects were so large that the cuckoo had difficulty in swallowing them. The food was withdrawn and reinserted, but I noticed that the wings were not removed as had been done with the larger insects given to the young in the other marsh warblers' nest.

When the cuckoo was about a fortnight old it was so heavy that the nest was collapsing and the bird was in imminent danger of falling out. George therefore secured the nest with thread, thus undoubtedly saving the young cuckoo's life. By this time it was so large that I had the impression that the foster parents took their lives in their bills every time they fed it. As the enormous, orange-red cavern of a mouth opened, the parent plunged in its head and neck, and pushed the food right down the youngster's throat.

As a finale to this nesting season, George and I accepted the invitation of Alec Robertson to use the hide he had erected at a corn bunting's nest at Lakenham, Suffolk. The cocks are considered to be polygamous, spending much of their time singing their wheezy song from a high vantage point, such as the top of a telegraph pole. Apart from displaying to their various hens, they take little part in family affairs, preferring to guard their harem from the advances of other amorously inclined cocks. Thus the high singing perch: it enables them to keep a large area under observation.

So I had been taught by the textbooks. But the cock at Lakenham was a model husband. His perch was on telegraph wires above the nest and during the eight hours I was in the hide he fed the young thirteen times. As far as I could ascertain he had only this one family. Some corn buntings have had seven hens: was it a lean year at Lakenham, or was this an exceptional cock that was satisfied with one hen?

This year was also memorable for an exciting sojourn at one of the bird observatories. These are situated at various places round the coast of Britain and are manned principally by volunteers whose main interest is the study and recording of bird migration. Here birds are caught, and to one leg is affixed a small metal ring marked 'Inform British Museum London S.W.7', followed by a serial number. The birds' vital statistics are recorded and then they are released.

A small percentage of birds are later retrapped, either at the same observatory or elsewhere, and from the details already known it is possible to deduce various facts. It was from ringing that we discovered that swallows bred in this country fly some 8,000 miles to overwinter in South Africa, return the following spring, and often home to the same nesting site from which they flew.

Various types of trap are used at these observatories. The largest is the Heligoland, so called because it was first used on the island of that name. Many of these traps are thirty feet wide and ten feet high at the entrance, narrowing to a small collecting box from which the birds are taken to be ringed. The smallest is the Potter trap. The bird takes food from this, and in doing so releases a small door which closes behind it. What are called 'mist nets' are also used. These are erected between two poles and, since they are made from extremely fine nylon, are almost invisible.

Once in a while comes a lucky break—you are in the right place at the right time. Such was my good fortune at the beginning of October 1952 when I went with a party of ornithologists to stay at Spurn Head Bird Observatory. George Ainsworth, who has done so much to establish this observatory, suggested that I might obtain some interesting photographs of the birds as they were trapped, ringed, weighed, measured and finally released from the ringing hut.

For some time the weather had been unfavourable for birds migrating from Scandinavia, so we were far from hopeful. But an anticyclone had been intensifying, producing fine settled conditions, and overnight tens of thousands of birds took off. Associated with the fine weather were strong easterly winds which drifted them across the North Sea to Britain, from the Shetlands right down to North Norfolk —a front of 400 miles.

Our first intimation of anything unusual came during the morning of 1 October, when a robin attracted our attention by the intensity of its song. We found that it was a local resident trying to defend its territory against a horde of robins which seemed to have descended on its domain from nowhere. Robins are largely nocturnal migrants and these 'intruders' had left Scandinavia during darkness, arriving at Spurn Head in mid-morning.

The hedges seethed with birds. We went into action immediately, driving as many as we could into the Heligoland trap. While these were being ringed, others arrived, and so it went on incessantly throughout the day. By nightfall we had ringed 189 birds, 152 of which were robins.

The next day was my birthday and what a birthday present I had! The whole of the three-mile peninsula was alive with birds, principally robins. They crowded on to the bushes and hedges, on the marram grass and on the sand dunes. Some were so tired that they just stayed where they had flopped on the ground. It seemed almost too much effort for them even to flutter out of our way. Others landed on the beach, only to be drowned by the next wave. Many of these exhausted birds were rescued but the same tragedy was probably happening for miles along the east coast, and thousands must have perished.

After dark three of us walked around with a powerful torch. Groups of birds were roosting side by side in the bushes; so tired that most of them failed even to stir as we passed.

Thousands more arrived next day but by the 4th the numbers began to decrease. In three days we had ringed over 500 robins, and about 200 birds of twenty-five other species. Normally far fewer than 500 robins are ringed in a whole year at this observatory, and the large number we had ringed on this occasion was but a fraction of this invasion.

This was my first visit to a bird observatory yet I had enjoyed the incredible good fortune of witnessing a spectacle denied to many ornithologists who spend most of their spare time at observatories.

But I was not only an observer: I was also a photographer, and we devised a method whereby the birds photographed themselves as they left the ringing hut. We arranged a cardboard tube about thirty inches long and seven inches in diameter through which the birds flew to the open door. The camera stood on a tripod at right angles to the cylinder and focused on the spot where the bird would cut a beam of light thrown on to a photo-electric cell, care being taken that the end of the tube did not appear in the picture. Thus, when it was halfway between the tube and the door, the bird took its own photograph.

I had taken with me on this trip what I thought would be ample film stock, but never in my wildest dreams did I think that during those few fantastic days I should expose no fewer than 700 plates. One day alone we photographed six species of thrush—blackbird, ring ouzel, song and mistle thrush, redwing and fieldfare.

However, we consistently failed to trap one bird which we had quite frequently seen—the great grey shrike, a bird I had not photographed before and one that normally passes through this country on migration, only rarely staying as a winter resident. This bird spent most of its time perched on telegraph wires watching for suitable prey. It was almost as if it were mocking our attempts to entice it down, then, without warning, it capitulated. We had been using a double-compartment automatic drop trap. A robin had flown into one compartment and the shrike, in circling the trap trying to get at the robin, entered the second compartment. No harm came to the robin, and when we released the shrike it took a beautiful photograph of itself in flight.

Several of the birds we ringed were recovered, the most interesting being a robin found dead six weeks later 1,000 miles away at Livorno in Italy.

The 1952 season was spent in Holland (see Chapter 7) but spring 1953 found George and me on home territory again, this time at Skomer, an island off the Pembrokeshire coast. We broke our car journey at Llanthony, in Monmouthshire, staying in a curious hotel. The building was originally a twelfth-century abbey and much of it remained unchanged. A spiral staircase led to a dungeon-like room with bare stone walls and tiny windows near the ceiling. Here we slept in four-poster beds, half-expecting to see a knight in armour walk through our room with his head tucked underneath his arm.

Next day we drove to Martin's Haven, some twenty miles from Haverfordwest, where we met Reuben Codd, who looked after Skomer and was in charge of the boat which took visitors across. Reuben had married the daughter of a previous owner of the island, and for a time he farmed there. In 1950 Skomer was bought by Leonard Lee, a Midlands industrialist, and Reuben moved to the mainland. However, the new owner asked him to keep a watch on the island. In 1959 Skomer was bought by the Nature Conservancy.

One of the greatest snags about visiting small islands round the British coast is that wind and sea are the masters. They kept us waiting for three dreary days, while we watched rain lashing against the windows of Reuben's house. One unexpected event, however, gave us some cheer. The weather cleared for a little while one day and, although a gale-force wind still blew, we walked up to Wooltack Point, sheltering on the lee side. We were watching a whimbrel feeding along the edge of the tide when suddenly a peregrine stooped and knocked it over. The peregrine then made an almost vertical climb before turning to stoop again. At that moment it was mobbed by two carrion crows and, while the falcon took avoiding action, the whimbrel escaped.

Then the weather cleared and we loaded Reuben's small boat with all our gear and pushed off. The crossing took only half an hour but we could see by the tide race through Jack Sound how treacherous it could be, for in places the sea was like a whirlpool. Fortunately, the southerly wind made our landing in North Haven easy, but it was not so easy manhandling all our equipment—hides, apparatus, bedding, stores, paraffin, etc.—the three-quarters of a mile, mostly uphill, to where we were going to live.

It was late in the afternoon before we settled in and had a chance to survey the island. Our first impression was of the large population of great black-backed gulls, most of them already nesting. There are no trees on Skomer so we found that the carrion crows built their nests on rock outcrops. But the other birds nested in a vast bed of bluebells which seemed to cover most of the island in a gorgeous blue haze.

We lived in huts erected near the derelict farmhouse, but since much of its massive walls and great beams still stood with the roof intact, we stored some of our gear in it.

Skomer is renowned for its colony of Manx shearwaters, and we were warned that at night they make such an infernal, blood-curdling din that it can scare the unwary. That this is no exaggeration had been tragically proved some years previously when a workman, who had been unable to leave the island because of a sudden increase in wind force, had to spend the night among the Manxies. Reuben told us that no one had warned him what to expect, and it is thought that when he was awakened by this diabolical chorus he went mad and committed suicide.

George and I decided to stay awake the first night so that we could hear these ghostly cries. But the day had been so tiring and heavy that, when nothing had happened by one o'clock, we decided to go to bed.

I immediately fell into a deep sleep. At two-thirty I suddenly sat upright, awakened by the most appalling din I have ever heard—as if Satan and all his devils were on the rampage! The air seemed to be filled with the half-strangled sobs of people being cruelly done to death, and the fact that the sounds were coming from under the floor-boards immediately below my bed, made matters worse. The Manxies' dormitory was directly below me.

We went outside in the darkness and the air seemed full of flying shearwaters which whizzed past within inches of our faces. They are not truly nocturnal birds and their eyes are not accommodated for night vision. On very dark nights, therefore, they cannot see at all well —unlike owls which can see on the darkest nights.

How, therefore, do they avoid hitting objects in the darkness?— their wings span nearly a yard. If they had collisions we should occa-sionally have found injured ones, or those with broken necks. Is it that Manxies born and bred on the island have an instinctive knowledge of the terrain?

Every now and again we heard one flop on to the ground, pre-sumably somewhere near its underground nesting hole where its mate was incubating the single egg. Both birds incubate, each doing a continuous stint of several days, occasionally as long as six. All this time, of course, one bird fasts, while its mate flies—sometimes up to 500 miles—to gorge itself on sea food, rich in fat. So the routine continues until the egg hatches and the chick is old enough to be left on its own. And if this 1,000-mile return journey seems spectacular, it is nothing for a Manx shearwater. In 1965 one flew 5,700 miles to Brazil in fifteen days.

On its arrival, the homecoming bird starts calling to its mate, who replies from the fastness of its burrow. It is then that this eerie, blood-curdling tumult occurs. It goes on and on while darkness lasts, and when the two meet underground it reaches the unnerving crescendo that awakened us.

The bird that now leaves the nest to fly south must scramble in darkness to a take-off point on high ground. Like some other birds with a very wide wing-span, such as the albatross, a shearwater cannot lift-off from level ground—it must be able to launch itself into the air from a vantage point.

The change-over is timed to take place in darkness, not in moonlight, for if a Manx shearwater is grounded when dawn breaks, it is quickly killed by great black-backed gulls which can locate one even in dim light. Even so the mortality among the Manxies is high. In an area of about 100 yards square George counted the remains of forty-three adults, all killed by these predatory gulls. We knew that they had been the assassins by the condition of the corpses: the gulls pull the shearwaters' skins inside out and eat the flesh. A final macabre touch: several of the gulls' nests were lined with shearwater corpses.

The whole of Skomer appeared to be honeycombed with rabbit holes and, in addition to the shearwaters, countless numbers of puffins lived in these warrens. The cliffs provided homes for thousands of guillemots and razorbills. Various gulls bred on the more level ground and a few storm petrels nested in the old ruined walls. We noticed several fulmars sitting in places that seemed ideal for nesting, but although we disturbed some of them we did not discover a single egg. But fulmars often occupy new ground for several years before starting to breed.

One bird I was especially keen to photograph was the peregrine falcon at its nest, but the eyries are usually in the most dangerous places on cliffs and I had never succeeded in finding a suitable site. George and I had already seen peregrines at two different places on the island and one of these was part way down the sheer face of the highest cliff. It was an impossible site for me, but by good fortune some keen rock climbers arrived for a few days' stay. I pointed out the eyrie and the falcon sitting tight. One of the climbers agreed to go down and examine the nest. As his friends lowered him on ropes, we kept our binoculars on the bird, and were surprised that she showed no sign of alarm, even when the climber landed on the ledge containing the nest. The cragsman inched his way along until he was no more than six feet away, but still the falcon did not move. She was dead! The peregrine falcon had actually died on the nest, her head half raised and leaning against a rock. She was egg-bound—dying in labour. She could not have been dead very long, for the tiercel was still attending the nest and a fresh puffin lay by her side.

This was a great disappointment and we had almost given up hope of another nest when, a few days later, a tiercel starting 'cacking' at us near some cliffs on another part of the island. This almost certainly indicated that an eyrie was nearby. A friend, Gerald Sutton, had now joined us, so George volunteered to be lowered on ropes held by us. The falcon did not take kindly to this and several times came hurtling down at him. Each time, however, the head-long stoop deliberately missed him, although he felt a buffet of wind as this magnificent bird swept by.

It was difficult to find a spot for a hide on the rugged cliff-face, but eventually we decided that one could be erected on a ledge no more than two feet wide. Some days later I had my first experience of being lowered over a sheer cliff—on ropes which would have held a battleship.

Part of the hide hung over the edge and the narrow ledge was crammed with tripod and camera, ruck-sack, photographic paraphernalia, stool—and me. Within minutes of George and Gerald leaving the cliff above, both tiercel and falcon quietened down and then, suddenly, the falcon landed, not on the nest but behind the hide. She then tried to push her way between the cliff-face and the hide but there was not sufficient space. She flew up and landed on the roof and I saw one sharp claw penetrate the canvas within six inches of my head. She jumped down to the side of the eyrie, straddled the chick and brooded.

Nothing more happened until, nearly two hours later, the tiercel flew by, calling, and in one movement the falcon stood up and took wing, calling as she went. In less than a minute she was back at the eyrie with a puffin in her talons, presumably passed to her by the tiercel. Immediately she began to feed the chick, and continued for the next seventeen minutes, feeding herself meantime, chiefly with the feathers and bones. Eventually the chick became so satiated that it did not even lift its head, and the falcon then leapt from the nest carrying the carcase. After a few minutes she returned and began brooding again.

When George and Gerald called for me the falcon continued to brood, looking up fiercely at the sound of their voices. But it was not until they shouted and clapped their hands that she left, leaping into the air with great suddenness, in common with her other movements. It was a fascinating session.

Supported by the ropes, I started the ascent and was about halfway up when my foot slipped and the rope tangled. Never have I been so frightened. I was dangling on the end of a rope with waves crashing against the cliff sixty feet below. My feet slithered off the slippery rock in my efforts to regain a foothold. I yelled to George and Gerald, who immediately realised my difficulties and hauled me up—a dead-weight like a sack of potatoes. I have never felt such relief in my life as when I lay down once more on solid earth.

We returned briefly to London as I had promised my family that I would be home to watch the Coronation on television. From Haverfordwest we took the night train and from Paddington we caught the first Tube train at 5.30 a.m. We expected the train to be empty, but no sooner had it drawn in than hundreds of 'Mrs. Mopps' emerged carrying buckets and brooms—the army of office cleaners who do their day's work before the white collar commuters take over.

On our return to Wales we asked Reuben if it would be possible for him to take us to Grassholm Island (owned by the Royal Society for the Protection of Birds) some nine miles out, but he said that his boat was so small that it required three days of calm weather for the sea swell to die down sufficiently for it to be safe. Nor was that all. Grassholm has no landing place and jumping from a small boat is a tricky business. If we did not jump at precisely the right moment, we and the cameras were likely to end up in the sea.

We were almost at the end of our stay when Reuben arrived and announced: 'Today's the day.' He had been unable to warn us beforehand as there was no communication between the island and the mainland, although we had arranged that in a real emergency we would light a bonfire at night on the highest point of the island. Hastily we collected our gear and took off for Grassholm in ideal conditions—a flat calm sea and the sun shining brilliantly from a clear sky. As we landed successfully Reuben looked at the sky and said: 'There's a blow coming. Half an hour, that's all you've got.' With that he pulled away to avoid the boat being damaged by scraping against the rasp-like rocks in the uneasy swell.

We set off immediately for the enormous gannetry, which was the purpose of our visit. Some 5,000 gannets were breeding in an area a few hundred yards square; they nest so close together that they sit almost within bill distance of each other. Whenever a bird returned to take over incubation from its mate it ran the gauntlet of a forest of pointed, viciously stabbing bills. Then the process was repeated as the relieved bird made its way in the opposite direction to the perimeter of the colony, where alone there was enough runway to enable it—with its six-foot wing-span—to become airborne.

George and I worked furiously, trying to get cine-film and stills in colour as well as black and white. All too soon we realised that the time was up, and we must hurry back to the boat. Reuben's forecast was right, the wind was getting up and the sea was choppy. We got back safely, but only just, for that night it blew a full gale.

After a few days at home, during which I spent most of the time developing the negatives of the photographs taken on Skomer and Grassholm, George and I drove to Seahouses on the Northumberland coast. Here we stayed with Dr. and Mrs. Eric Ennion in their beachside house once inhabited by monks, hence its name 'Monk's House'. It is believed to have been a smugglers' hide-out at one time.

Eric was a general practitioner for nearly twenty years but eventually relinquished medicine for his other interests: nature and art.

For some years he was warden of the Flatford Mill Field Study Centre but in 1950 became director of the Monk's House Bird Observatory. He has also found time to give frequent broadcasts, write several books and many articles, and exhibit his bird drawings and paintings. This is a bald summary of his achievements, but no mention of Eric Ennion would be complete without referring to his love for, and interest in, young people. He is never happier than when sharing his wide knowledge of natural history, or the art of sketching birds, surrounded by enthusiastic youngsters.

Soon after arriving we were joined by Stuart Smith and Edward Bradbury. The main reason for our visit was to cross to the Farne Islands to photograph the enormous breeding colonies of sea birds. The nearest of the islands is less than two miles from Monk's House, the farthest nearly five.

Although we were so close we did not even see the islands for the first three days of our stay since they were shrouded in mist. But on the fourth day the weather cleared sufficiently for us to hire a boat and make a reconnaissance. Immense numbers of guillemots were flying about, but it was the sight of them massed on the Pinnacles that was most impressive. This rock stands vertically out of the sea off Staple Island, and its summit was so closely packed with guillemots that it seemed impossible for even one more to crowd in. Down the sides on every ledge, however narrow, a kittiwake had its nest. And the air was full of their lovely mewing as they flew overhead. We landed on Staple Island and walked to the highest point where we could photograph the guillemots across the narrow channel to the Pinnacles.

Birds were everywhere and were remarkably tame. Across one fissure of rock, no more than six feet wide, kittiwakes were sitting on their nests, and in the middle a pair of shags attended their young. In the updraught of wind along this gully kittiwakes hung in the air, hardly moving for seconds at a time, thus giving superb opportunities for photography.

After the Staples, the boat next took us to the Inner Farne. On landing we first went to pay homage to St. Cuthbert at the little chapel and there, sitting right beside it, was a St. Cuthbert's duck, or eider, incubating her eggs. The saint gave these ducks his blessing and is said to have provided them with safe nesting places, and even fixed the times of their comings and goings. No wonder they are the most famous birds of these islands. As they sit on their nests you can stroke them, but once the young are hatched and the duck has taken them down to the sea, they quickly lose their tameness.

Although many of the islands are colonised by Arctic terns we found that the most suitable, from a photographic point of view, were those on the Inner Farne. So we walked towards the huge colony to find an attractive nest at which we could erect a hide. Stuart, who was just behind me, suddenly yelled out in pain—an Arctic tern had struck him with its bill across the crown of his head and drawn blood. After that we walked with a stick held vertically over our heads. Stuart maintained that it is easy to tell the difference between the common and Arctic terns, which look very alike, because while both will strike, only the Arctic draws blood!

On one of our trips a crowd of visitors ambled along the path through the middle of the colony, and found themselves being dive-bombed. After one particularly vicious attack an American lady shook her fist at a bird and cried: 'Do that just once more and I'll wallop you with my umbrella!'

While taking photographs from the hide I became aware of a quite different call among the harsh cries of the Arctic terns. It was a heron-like *frank frank* and although difficult to locate, I eventually tracked it down. It was another tern with a black crown like the Arctic, but I noticed that its bill was black, not red, that it had longer tail-streamers and a flush of pale pink on its breast and underparts. It was a roseate tern, then the rarest of the regular British breeding terns, and a pair were nesting among the other birds.

Whenever there was a 'dread'—an expression used when, often for no apparent reason, all the birds in a flock leap into the air in panic—I noticed that the roseates were always the last to return to the nest. The other terns appeared to regard the pair as aliens and several fights took place by the nest, real fierce affairs when bills, wings and feet were all in action. Although the sexes are alike, it was soon possible to identify the cock by his displays, when he strutted round the hen with his head and long tail pointing skywards. Although the hen seemed to do nearly all the incubation, the cock stayed by to deal with trespassers.

Later we found several more pairs of roseates on the Longstone. This is the island made famous by Grace Darling—her father was the lighthouse keeper—at the time of the sinking of the *Forfarshire* on 7 September 1838, when she played such a gallant part in rescuing some of the survivors.

On days when weather conditions made it impossible to go to the islands, we searched for birds along the coast. Fulmars nested on the ledges of Bamburgh Castle, which must have appeared to them very like the sheer cliffs on which they normally breed. In the other direction is Embleton, where we found twenty-seven nests of house martins built on to the cliffs. I had never seen their nests before in their 'natural' surroundings, and had become used to their 'civilised' nesting sites under the eaves of houses.

At St. Abb's Head we discovered fifteen newly dead guillemots floating in the sea and managed to get five of them ashore. They all had their wings cut off, and we assumed that they had been caught in fishing nets while diving, had drowned, and that the fishermen had cut off the wings while freeing them from the nets.

As I had not spent a nesting season in central Wales since 1938, I suggested to George Edwards and Stuart Smith that we should go there in 1954 and stay at Doldowlod. The area contains a wealth of species because the Upper Wye Valley has such a wide variety of habitats. In the floor of the valley, where the river runs between wide pastures, there are dippers, common sandpipers and kingfishers, and many other species are found among the woodland on the hill slopes.

We had just crossed a tiny trickle of a stream and were going up the opposite bank when we saw a small pale yellow bird fly up and disappear into the tree canopy. At first we thought it was either an escaped canary or budgerigar. Presently it reappeared accompanied by its mate, whose song, with its final drawn-out shivering trill, showed that they were wood warblers. Observation through binoculars revealed the remarkable fact that not only was the female wood warbler a most unusually plumaged bird, but that the male bird, too, was abnormal. The female soon flew down and disappeared close to the spot where we first saw her. She was easily flushed from a typical wood warbler's nest containing six eggs just about to hatch.

We left the young for several days before attempting any photography, but then a violent thunderstorm ushered in four days of torrential rain. The Wye rose seven feet in less than twenty-four hours, and the tiny spring beside the nest became a torrent. When next we visited the site the herbage was flattened and sodden, the day-old young drowned. Our hopes for some unique photographs had been dashed. There was no sign of the adult birds but we still hoped they might attempt to breed again.

Just over a fortnight later we returned to the wood and as we walked down the same dingle I had the great satisfaction of flushing the pale female from her replacement nest, not fifty yards from the original site. It contained five eggs.

This time the Fates were kinder, and by careful stages we managed to work the hide to within five feet of the nest where close-range observation and photography were possible.

The variant hen was very remarkable. She had pure white underparts and two white outer tail feathers. Her head and back were a beautiful primrose yellow, and there were splashes of darker yellow on her shoulders and lower back. The cock had the normal coloration of a wood warbler except for his head. This had a pale straw-coloured cap running backwards to the nape.

The birds were feeding the young mainly on pale green caterpillars collected from oak trees, and small two-winged flies (Diptera). There was no obvious variation in the downy covering of the young, but unfortunately we were unable to remain in the area long enough to see if they had inherited any of their parents' abnormal coloration.

The type of variation we had seen in this pair of wood warblers is known as 'xanthochroism' and is extremely rare in wild birds. It is caused by an abnormal retention of yellow pigment in the feathers, combined with loss of dark pigment, and is quite different from the 'albinism' that produces a true albino. But what was so remarkable was that of all the wood warblers in the area, the two that were abnormal should have mated *together*.

It was here that I had my first—and vivid—experience of the tragic effect of pesticides. In the walled-in area of the kitchen garden to Doldowlod House we had hides erected at six nests, one at a particularly attractive goldfinch's nest. But when I went to photograph them all the young were dead. We then visited the other five nests, as well as several others we knew, but it was the same story—every chick was dead. In a grey wagtail's nest built in the wall, the hen was also dead. It had been a very bad year for slugs and all the young cabbages had been eaten by them. To combat this a large quantity of slug-killer had been put down and the efficiency of this was only too obvious. Weed-killer had also been used with similar effect. Presumably adult birds had been collecting the dead and dying slugs and a variety of insects, all of which had been contaminated. These, together with poisoned seeds, had been fed to their young with disastrous results.

After working in Wales in 1954 I went in the opposite direction, to Minsmere in East Anglia, during 1955.

Although I did not realise it at the time, when I returned home after that 1955 season it was the end of an era for me. I was not to work in the countryside of Britain during the spring months for another twelve years. My journeyings were to take me far and wide but, again like the swallow's urge to come back from its winter sojourn, I always returned to the land of my birth.

6 | *Lecturing*

The first lecture I ever gave was in 1925 at the age of sixteen—to an audience of teenagers at the Campsbourne Baptist Church in North London. Of course, the subject was natural history, but at that time I had no slides of my own. However, a firm which specialised in hand-painted slides of natural history subjects supplied me with fifteen mammal studies. I did my 'homework' by thoroughly learning about the subjects of the slides, zoo animals such as lions, tigers, cheetahs and chimpanzees.

The projector worked by acetylene gas and the screen was a sheet. I was very nervous. I had notes but forgot to take a reading lamp; fortunately I had memorised the order of the slides and somehow managed to spin out the lecture to thirty minutes. At the end of what had seemed like thirty hours, several questions were asked which I managed to answer. When it was all over I felt utterly exhausted, but rapidly revived when several people told me how much they had enjoyed it.

This was to be the first of a series of some 1,500 lectures, spread over a professional career of thirty-two years. I have lectured in every county and every major town in the British Isles—and hundreds of smaller ones—and spoken to nearly 400,000 people in audiences ranging from three in a small room, to 3,000 in London's Royal Festival Hall.

It was about six years after my début before the Baptist Hall audience that I decided to try professional lecturing. As my series of photographs of *Mary at the Zoo* had been so successful I used them as the basis for my lecture, making 120 3¼ in. square monochrome slides, and tried them on various small local audiences. It seemed to go down well, so I went to see the most famous lecture agent of the day, Gerald Christy. He was interested, but told me that he never put a lecturer on his list until he had heard him himself. Would I be lecturing in London in the near future?

Since I was shortly due to lecture on *Mary at the Zoo* to the Royal Photographic Society at their then headquarters in Russell Square, Christy said that he would be there. I certainly prepared for that lecture! On the night I anxiously scanned the audience for the great man. He was not there. When the lights went up I again looked carefully to see if perhaps he had slipped in after the lecture had started. No; obviously he had not come. So much for my attempts to become a professional lecturer.

Then, a few days later, I received a letter from Christy. He *had* been there, listened to my lecture with interest and thought I had distinct possibilities. But I was young and had a lot to learn about lecturing. He advised me to give as many lectures as I could to gain experience. Then he would like to hear me again. He added a useful tip: always begin a lecture with the second-best slide, end with the best. He added that when he went to an auditioning lecture he usually made a point of going in late and leaving early. (So if I had followed his advice he would have missed my two best slides!) Before the lecture he was loth, by his known presence, to add to a young lecturer's already strained nerves, and afterwards he preferred not to discuss the outcome of the lecture within earshot of others.

During the next twelve months I lectured to any audience that would have me—Methodist Guilds, Church Fellowships, Photographic Societies, Boy Scouts and Girl Guides. All this was before Youth Clubs or else there would have been an epidemic of natural history among the teenagers of Crouch End.

At last I thought I was ready for another audition, so I arranged to lecture to the North Middlesex Photographic Society and again invited Christy to come. This time he came before the lecture. I was glad; knowing he was there stimulated me and at the finish I felt that, whatever the verdict, I had given my best. When the lights went up, contrary to what he had told me, Christy was still there. What did this mean? As soon as I left the platform he came up to me, shook my hand warmly and said: 'Hosking, you have improved beyond measure. I shall be delighted to have you on my books.'

Gerald Christy was the most successful British lecture impresario of all time. He will have no successor: the heyday of the popular lecturer is past. Radio, the cinema and, above all, television have seen to that. But Christy should be remembered. For over a half a century he was the means of bringing entertainment and pleasantly absorbed education to millions.

Information about him is scanty; he kept in the background while his lecturers enjoyed the limelight. He was born in 1864 near Chelmsford. His parents were Quakers and he was a life-long member of the

Above: Roseate tern, a summer visitor to the Inner Farne off the Northumberland coast

Below: Havoc wrought by the bombing raids on London provided the ideal nesting conditions for the black redstart. This one nested in a bombed office site near St. Paul's Cathedral

NORWAY

Above: Silhouetted against the sky off a west coast fjord, this white-tailed eagle clearly shows why it is so named

Below: To photograph the eagle at her nest it was necessary to negotiate a dangerous cliff face and build a hide overhanging a 300-foot drop

Chelmsford Meeting. He had the calm quiet bearing that seems characteristic of many members of the Society of Friends.

As a young man he went on a world tour. Possibly as a result of this he became interested in the possibilities of the lecture platform; he was especially successful with explorers and travellers. There was already in existence a Lecture Agency, founded by G. W. Appleton in 1879, and Christy took this over about 1890 and ran it from offices in the Outer Temple, London.

He had a flair both for gauging public taste in lectures and also for persuading popular figures to meet it. His annual list of lecturers read like an illustrated *Who's Who*. Jerome K. Jerome, Hilaire Belloc, G. K. Chesterton, John Masefield, J. B. Priestley, Sir Arthur Conan Doyle—explorers such as Scott, Peary, Nansen, Amundsen and Shackleton—together with a host of literary, religious, political, theatrical and other public figures, all appeared at one time or another under Christy's auspices. In 1934 he could proudly claim 'A Hundred Thousand Lectures'.

The most illustrious name to appear on Christy's list was Sir Winston Churchill. When he returned from South Africa after his spectacular escape from the Boers he received several offers to lecture. Although he was not keen to do so, he badly needed money. In a letter to his mother he wrote: 'You must remember how much money means to me and how much I need it for political expense and other purposes.'

It was Christy who arranged a short but highly profitable lecture tour in Britain. Between 30 October and 30 November 1900 Churchill gave twenty-nine lectures for which he received, after Christy's commission, £3,782 15s. 5d.

My lectures for Christy, in chronological order, were:

> *Mary at the Zoo*
> *Nature in the Wild*
> *Wild Nature's Charm*
> *With a Camera in Birdland*
> *Two Eyes and a Camera in the Countryside*
> *Wildlife through the Eye of a Camera*
> *Wild Wings*
> *The Call of the Wild*
> *Birds in Action*
> (illustrated by photographs taken by
> high-speed flash)

Mary at the Zoo was in my repertoire for more than twenty years. One girl heard it at school, and many years afterwards asked a headmistress to invite me so that her daughter could also hear it.

G

In thirty-two years and 1,500 lectures I missed only three: once I had laryngitis, once fog stopped me travelling, and once my train was cancelled.

All these lectures were illustrated with slides only; never fewer than 100, usually about 120. Each lecture lasted one and a quarter hours, which I consider the ideal time. This meant that each slide was on the screen for an average of forty seconds. I worked hard on the preparation of each lecture so that I not only knew it thoroughly, but could time it to a matter of seconds. This was important, especially when lecturing to schools, as to overrun might upset their time-table or cause children to miss the bus home.

It took me several weeks to prepare a new lecture and it took a severe toll of my nervous energy. At times my family suffered. I was told I was 'like a bear with a sore head', and 'Eric's preparing a new lecture' became an ominous slogan.

Like an actor, I learned my commentary by heart, which helped to get maximum response from the audience. I endeavoured by my words to capture the audience, and transport them into the world of nature portrayed by the slides or films. I knew when they were held and then I could easily sway their moods.

Before every lecture I examined each slide, cleaned it and, just before leaving either home or hotel, warmed it, for the combination of a cold slide and a warm projector results in condensation and a misty picture. I sometimes wished that the projectionists who handled my precious slides had taken a fraction of this trouble. I have had slides dropped, cracked, over-heated, jammed, put in out of focus, before I was ready, *after* I was ready, upside down, sideways and back to front. There are eight ways in which a slide can be put into a projector, only one of which is correct. Some of the operators seemed to go through the lot before they got it right! Yet the correct way is clearly marked by a white strip along the top of the slide.

Some societies went to great trouble to arrange their lectures, which were given in an excellent hall. A large audience assembled, but then everything was spoiled by a poor projector, which gave such a bad picture that even I had to look twice to see what it was. At one society not only was the lantern an antique but the screen was no more than a badly worn double bed-sheet. Fortunately, I had my own lantern and screen in the car and we used these. So often the lecturer gets the blame for producing bad-quality slides when it is the projector and screen that are at fault.

On one occasion a lecture had to be abandoned because a fuse blew, putting all the lights out, and nobody knew where the fuse-box was. The audience had to file out in the darkness.

It is a curious fact, endorsed by virtually every public speaker, that practice never overcomes nervousness. No matter how many times the lecture had been given, however well I knew the audience, I always suffered from nerves, in a general way for about an hour beforehand, then acutely just before speaking. In the last few minutes I sometimes felt like running away. But reaction being equal and opposite, once I was on my feet and speaking, nerves went and I felt exhilarated.

Audiences differed immensely. I wonder if those who attend public meetings, whether it be concert, poetry reading, sermon, address or lecture, realise just how much *their* attitude and response contributes to the success or failure of the function. A responsive friendly audience calls out the best in a speaker. There is a psychic fusion which somehow adds up to more than the sum of the parts—as the musician who 'from three sounds makes not a fourth sound but a star'.

The reverse is also true. Many an audience which has gone away blaming the speaker shares that blame. Not always, of course. I have heard some speakers who would bore to death the finest audience ever assembled. In passing, it is much easier to talk to a full house than one that is half-empty.

I gave only one film lecture, *Wild Spain*, which dealt with the two Guy Mountfort expeditions to the Coto Doñana. That was by far the most difficult lecture to prepare, not because of the subject-matter but because of timing. I reckoned to keep my commentary two to three seconds ahead of what was showing on the screen, but at least once I had to time to within one second. Such timing meant that I had not only to commit the whole one-and-a-quarter-hour lecture to memory but also keep the narration at the right speed. Nor was that all. I had to gauge where *and how long* the audience was likely to laugh and thus drown anything I might say. So learning my lines involved considerably more than committing words to memory.

There was a sequence where a great grey shrike brought to the nest a lizard which was four times the length of any of the young. That sounds so extraordinary that in my commentary I said to the image of the shrike on the screen: 'Go on, hold the thing up to show how long it is!' And as I said 'it is' the bird did just that.

When the lizard was given to the chick it was swallowed in five seconds. I counted the seconds aloud and as I said 'five' the lizard's tail disappeared into the chick's mouth.

I have lectured to many boys' and girls' schools and almost invariably found boys more difficult to talk to than girls. Somehow boys are more reserved and take longer to respond and laugh than girls. Christy used to say, and I believe him, that the most difficult audience of all is a boys' public school, for if the boys can get a laugh *at* the speaker that, to them, is the best part of the performance.

Laughs, of course, are essential to any successful lecture, but they must come at the speaker's bidding. The unexpected laugh at the wrong moment can be disastrous. Some are impossible to avoid, simply because the audience knows something the lecturer does not and cannot know. At St. James's Girls' School at Malvern two of the mistresses were sisters called Partridge. Part of my lecture was on these birds and each time 'partridge' was mentioned a ripple of laughter ran through the audience. It was more than a ripple when I referred to partridges hatching, and rose to a roar which stopped the show when I spoke of 'a couple of young partridges crawling across to the cock'.

It was the same when I lectured to Bromsgrove Boys' School when it was evacuated to Llanwrtyd Wells in Breconshire. I was talking about buzzards and each time I said the word there was a titter, but when I once referred to 'the old buzzard sitting on the nest' the audience rocked in helpless laughter. Unknown to me 'The Old Buzzard' was the headmaster's nickname.

An unfortunate choice of words can also bring gales of unforeseen laughter. I once had the unusual job of lecturing to a house-party in one of the stately homes that was sometimes opened to the public. I thought it would be gracious to refer to this. So, in opening, I said that although I had lectured in most public schools, in the Festival Hall and many other public halls, this was the first time I had lectured in a public house . . .

Only once have I had a lecture so interrupted by hilarity that the laughter-maker had to be removed before the lecture could proceed. It happened at a mental hospital in York. There was no sign of anything untoward until I signalled for the first slide to be changed. A patient in the front row giggled. When the next slide changed he giggled a bit louder. The next change was greeted by a hearty laugh, and thereafter each slide-change was the signal for a growing crescendo of laughter from this man, who, by now, was infecting the whole audience. It became obvious that either the lecture would have to be abandoned or the over-hilarious patient removed. He was led away, but I shall never know what he found so funny in mere slide-changing.

Every public speaker has experienced unhelpful chairmen at times. I was flabbergasted by one man who began by praising my navigational skill in piloting a small boat halfway round the world, and said how much they were all looking forward to the thrilling account of my epic voyage. He had got his dates mixed up and was introducing me as the next week's lecturer—the yachtsman Eric Hiscock!

Then there was the fellow at Lytham St. Annes who turned his chairman's remarks into a twenty-minute lecturette about the local Roman wall, which apparently the Council intended to demolish. The chairman bitterly opposed this as sacrilege. After this tirade he called on me to speak, and just as I rose he said: 'You will back me up on this wall, won't you?'

My reception at lecture halls varied greatly. Once, on asking for a reading-lamp, I received the reply: 'What! Do you call yourself a lecturer!'

To which I countered: 'No lamp, no lecture.' What my impolite critic did not know was that I had 120 miscellaneous slides to show and it was impossible to remember the order—they did not run in an obvious sequence. Moreover, the lecturer has his back to the screen and if he turns round to see the picture his voice fades away, and he momentarily breaks contact with the audience. So I had passport-sized photographs of each slide stuck on sheets of paper and thus knew exactly what was to be shown on the screen.

Some societies regard a lecture as a purely business transaction with no social frills whatever. The lecturer arrives at the hall, goes on to the platform quite alone (no chairman or introduction), walks off when it is over (no vote of thanks) and goes home (no refreshments).

How different are the really big societies. Whenever I lectured at the Caird Hall, Dundee, I was met at the station by a member of the committee and taken by car to my hotel. I was asked if I preferred to rest in my room or whether I would welcome company. Later, the chairman and I dined together, during which we discussed how he should introduce me, and I asked him anything I wanted to know.

Then we drove to the great Caird Hall which seats some 3,000 people. It is so large that the projectionist uses a pair of binoculars to make sure he has critical focus. The committee met us on arrival. Would I like water or milk to refresh myself while lecturing? I was introduced to the projectionist, then the chairman led the way to the platform. He introduced me with a few well-chosen words, made a light quip to mellow the audience, and they were all mine. There were three microphones on the platform, which gave me freedom to move about. (This was before the days of neck microphones.) The slides were, of course, shown superbly and at the instant I wanted them. Is it surprising that in such circumstances a lecturer is challenged to give of his best?

Afterwards I took a bow and walked off. The committee considered a vote of thanks to be an anticlimax, and I agreed. Often one man has proposed a vote of thanks, another has seconded it, it has been carried by acclamation, and then I have had to reply! A lecturer knows well enough by the applause if he has pleased his audience, and there is intense satisfaction in hearing the spontaneous ovation from a crowded hall after a lecture you know has gone well. Before being driven back to my hotel I was given a much-needed cup of tea, and next morning was taken to the station.

There is a saying that people do not appreciate what they get for nothing. In my experience this was never more true than with free lectures. For many years I helped friends or causes I believed in, but eventually after numerous frustrating experiences I had to decline further invitations. Here are two examples of the sort of thing that happened.

I received a letter saying that it was hoped to form a natural history society in a part of Gloucester and, to raise funds, would I be good enough to give a lecture? I agreed to go on the Saturday before Christmas. Three weeks before the day another letter arrived saying that as the hall held only 100, and as it was expected that people would be travelling from outlying districts, would I please give two lectures, one at three o'clock, another at seven-thirty. One more thing, as they had no equipment, would I please bring a projector, a screen and, if I wanted one, a pointer. I agreed.

Came the day: I arrived at two-fifteen to find the hall locked. At two-thirty the secretary arrived with the keys and together we fitted up the screen and projector. By the advertised time two adults and one child had arrived. I and three officials discussed the situation. No doubt, being so near Christmas, many who would otherwise have come were out shopping, but have no fear, I was assured, the hall would be packed in the evening. I suggested that it was best to cancel the afternoon lecture, only to discover that the little girl was unable to come in the evening and would be bitterly disappointed. I gave the lecture. And the evening? An audience of seventeen appeared, three of them officials who had been at the afternoon performance.

The other disappointment occurred at a church near Lewisham. A friend asked me to lecture there to raise funds to redecorate the church and I agreed. Again I was asked to provide projector and screen—no pointer this time. I arranged to arrive thirty to forty minutes before the time of the lecture so that there would be ample time to erect the screen and test the projector. When I arrived the hall was deserted and in darkness. Was it the right place? It was a bitterly cold night, and as I hung about I began to regret agreeing to come at all.

Twenty minutes before the lecture was due to start the minister arrived. He unlocked the door and we went into the hall—a great barn of a place. No chairs had been arranged for the audience. Nobody had thought to turn on the heating and, if anything, it seemed even colder than in the freezing street. Solid ice had formed in a wash-basin.

With the minister's help, by seven-fifty we had the screen and projector ready, and together we arranged the chairs for the audience. At eight o'clock eleven of them were occupied. Nobody, apparently, had thought about a projectionist and eventually a member of the audience was persuaded to try his hand. By the time he had been shown what to do, someone else had arrived, so we still had eleven in the audience. This was the only time that I have lectured in an overcoat. Yes, they took a collection—the whole purpose of the exercise—and the church funds profited by eighteen shillings and elevenpence. I would cheerfully have given a pound not to have gone!

Let me make it quite clear—especially as a member of a Baptist church myself—that I am in no way knocking at churches. The vast majority where I have lectured have received me very well. At a church in Bolton I lectured from the pulpit to an audience packed to the doors. After five minutes I had to stop while the people sitting in the aisles were moved to conform to fire regulations.

Before the war I used to lecture in the City Temple in Holborn Viaduct. When it was blitzed the congregation moved to the Marylebone Presbyterian Church near Marble Arch, where I lectured several times. The minister, Dr. Leslie Weatherhead, was an excellent chairman, saying just the right few words to get the audience in a receptive mood. There were always over 1,000 in the audience, some of them standing.

Probably my most unusual experience was as a cabaret star—and top of the bill, too. It happened like this. Before the war there was a celebrated restaurant off Piccadilly called the Trocadero. (It is now Tiffany's and The Golden Nugget.) Herbert Calkin of *Country Life* often lunched and dined there, and was on friendly terms with the management. One day he suggested that perhaps an interesting and unusual item for the cabaret would be a turn by a young bird photographer he knew. Ornithology was certainly a new idea for such a sophisticated show, but after seeing some of my slides it was decided to bill me for a week in November 1938.

My usual nervousness before a lecture was intensified before my début in cabaret. The Trocadero served a first-class dinner—including partridge and pheasant, two of my subjects—between eight-thirty and nine-thirty, then a versatile comedian opened the proceedings. Singing, conjuring and other typical cabaret acts followed so that by ten-thirty the audience, already well dined and wined, were in that mellow and convivial mood when I thought they would be far more ready to laugh at a comedian's crack or admire birds of a different plumage than those I was about to show. How did it go? I cannot do better than quote a few press reports of the time.

'TROCABARET'

THE LATE DINNER SHOW

ERIC HOSKING

GALI - GALI

SENATOR MURPHY

EVE BECKE

MONSEWER EDDIE GRAY

ADAM
and the Trocadero Orchestra

Tables booked from 8.30.p.m.

TROCADERO

'Phone : Gerr. 6920.

w/c 21st November, 1938

The Star

A big screen is brought forward, out go the lights and we might be back in the days when one of the delights of life was to brave the winter wind to enter a draughty hall and to sit huddled together while a lecturer showed us slides and talked entertainingly about them.

Now one has a good dinner first, takes one's ease, listens to a few turns, to be finally introduced to bird pictures that take one's breath away and make one envious in the knowledge that Mr. Hosking has had the real entertainment getting them, and that he is merely telling the rest of us about it.

He shows us the hides in which he squatted with his camera to take a series of pictures of a partridge hatching out its young; wonderful pictures of kingfishers; and almost incredibly lovely pictures of the barn owl taken by flashlight.

The Field

It cannot be easy to talk about birds to a crowded room of diners who probably know nothing about birds: it must be very difficult to do so when that talk is limited to ten minutes and fitted in between a beautiful young lady singing love songs to rhythm and an oriental conjurer who produces live chickens from nowhere. Mr. Hosking, I submit, is an extremely brave man.

Applause greeted his first picture. His talk was punctuated throughout by applause, which was pronounced when he showed kingfishers and which was enthusiastic when he finished. He was, beyond doubt, a success.

The Daily Telegraph

With the recent revival of Edwardian hair styles and Récamier gowns, the old-fashioned magic lantern comes to the West End. This week's cabaret at the Trocadero features Mr. Eric Hosking, the young nature photographer, with his slides showing wild birds as no one ever sees them.

This modern Peeping Tom who spies on British birds with lens and flashlight brings a new thrill to cabaret. His shot of a barn owl dangling a still live rat in its mouth is a masterpiece of patience and skill.

Country Life

This 'turn' is a new departure in a cabaret, and the audience were at first a little taken by surprise at finding instruction being thus blended with their amusement; but, when once they had grasped what was happening to them, they were, we are told, both pleased and interested. To break entirely fresh ground in any form of entertainment is always an adventure.

In the summer of 1939 I had 127 lectures booked for the forth-coming season. With the outbreak of war every one was cancelled. Later a few bookings were made, but it was obvious that for the duration lecturing was to be a minor activity for me.

In 1940 I was asked to lecture to RAF stations on the east coast. There were two reasons for this request. The most obvious was the general interest, boredom-relieving angle, but there was another idea. The main job of airmen at these stations was to give advance warnings of approaching enemy aircraft, for, despite echo-location (as radar was called in those days), binoculars and the human eye were still necessary. But it is not easy quickly to pick up fast-moving objects in the sky, especially when they are intermittently obscured by clouds. What better practice than to spot birds in flight? And having learned to differentiate the various species by their diagnostic features, to apply the same principles to aeroplanes. It was thus an important part of my job to kindle the necessary interest in birds, their identification and the quick use of binoculars.

After a lecture in Scotland I was taken to the officers' quarters where I was to spend the night. It was bitingly cold. There was no heating in the bedroom and icicles hung from the ceiling. The total covering for the bed was one blanket. I slept in every scrap of clothing I could muster.

Only once did I have to abandon a lecture because of bombing—at the Kodak Photographic Society at Harrow when, soon after I had started, the sirens sounded and we all trooped down to the shelter. The raid went on too long for it to be worth while to start again.

On several occasions I continued to lecture while the guns fired and the bombs whistled down. Once a bomb fell so close to the lecture hall that I felt the platform shake.

After giving a lecture at St. Mary's School, Calne, Wiltshire, in November 1940, the headmistress, Miss E. M. Matthews, asked me whether I would help her to start a School Natural History Society. The idea was for me to stay in the neighbourhood for three or four days, give a lecture each evening and during the day take parties of girls round the nearby Bowood Grounds, showing them what to look for and what to collect. I readily agreed and arrangements were made for Dorothy and me to stay there in March 1941. During our first outing with some forty girls we found nests of a mistle thrush and a long-tailed tit, and noticed that herons were hard at work building their nests on the tops of trees on the island in the middle of the pond. We found several owl pellets and took them back to the school where we carefully took them to pieces and identified the contents.

The girls were very enthusiastic and I believe three-quarters of them joined the Society, of which I was made Patron. Miss Aubrey, the biology mistress, was in charge and her keenness showed in the frequent letters I received from the girls. Nest-boxes were put up and careful records kept of the occupants and what happened to them. But in 1945 Miss Matthews died and fairly soon afterwards Miss Aubrey left for another post and I lost touch with the school.

A master who had a great influence over his pupils was Dr. Kenneth Fisher, headmaster of Oundle and James Fisher's father. After I had lectured there in February 1941 he asked me whether I would drive Keith Shackleton, then a lad of eighteen, back with me to London to have lunch with Herbert Calkin, Frances Pitt and Keith's father and mother. I still remember how enthusiastic he was about birds and painting. He never stopped talking all the way to London. Although only eighteen he was already a skilled painter, and *Country Life*, always on the look-out for new talent, were considering publishing an article and some of his paintings. They did; it was the start of Keith's career and now he has become one of the great wild-life artists of the day, as well as a television personality. *Country Life* had already launched Peter Scott, who, incidentally, was also educated at Oundle—what a wonderful natural history tradition this school has!

A lecturer must never forget the responsibility he has because he never knows what effect his subject, and the way he presents it, may have on someone in the audience. A chance remark, or perhaps the appeal of a slide or cine sequence, can set a boy or girl on a path that will affect the rest of their lives. As a boy I hero-worshipped Richard Kearton and whenever he lectured in North London I was there if possible. Indeed, I heard one of his lectures so often that I think I could have given it for him.

When David Attenborough opened the Exhibition of Natural History Photographs at the Royal Photographic Society he mentioned that he remembered my giving a lecture at his school, and said that it made him consider whether he could devote his life to natural history. The result we all know.

I ceased to lecture in 1963 for two reasons—financial and personal. Taking into consideration travelling expenses and hotel bills, taxis and tips, meals and commission, all in all I could earn more at my desk and in my dark-room.

It is true that lecturing itself is pleasant and interesting, but the necessary journeyings often are not. The stimulus of travelling the length and breadth of the country in wintry conditions, and the experience of staying in hotels, palled many years ago. Sometimes I was booked for lectures in nearby towns, and found it difficult to occupy the twenty-four hours between one lecture and the next, especially when home and other interests were calling. During and just after the war conditions in some hotels were really grim: no heating in the bedrooms and sometimes insufficient bedclothes, so that life was spent almost continually in an overcoat in an attempt to keep warm.

Train services were so uncertain that I always had to allow for a train being late. Saturday was often the most popular night for school lectures, which meant travelling home on a Sunday—the day British Rail reserve for repairing tracks, so that trains were usually at least an hour late, often two or three. This meant that coming home even from a place like Exeter or Manchester sometimes took the whole day.

I hated to be away so much. During some years, between October and the following March, I rarely had more than two consecutive days at home. In those days I received an average of fifteen letters a day, which meant that after being away for three or four days I came back to a pile of between forty-five and sixty letters, and almost before these were dealt with I was off again. All this meant that I was neglecting my family; even when I was home they saw very little of me. By the end of the lecture season I was often in a poor condition, both physically and mentally, and then I had to prepare for the nesting season or for an expedition. At the most important period of the year I was at my worst when I ought to have been at my best.

It was the expedition to Bulgaria which really showed me the red light. I was tired out and exhausted before we started and just not 'with it'. I fear the result showed in my photographs. There could be no half-measures: either I would be a professional lecturer or I would give up lecturing altogether. I gave it up.

So I put away my slides and films. I'd had a good innings—thirty-two years. I experienced many times the heady thrill of holding a great audience, and enjoying their spontaneous applause.

Times change. This generation is more familiar with television stars than with the personalities of the lecture platform. But to me no image on a screen can ever replace the satisfaction of seeing and hearing a fine speaker hold sway over an audience in a packed lecture hall.

7 | *Holland, Finland and Norway*

HOLLAND By 1952 I had travelled a great deal in the British Isles and had photographed most of our breeding birds. Unfortunately I was often asked for those I had not photographed, and I felt it was important to take some of these. So George Edwards, Stuart Smith and I planned our first overseas expedition—to Holland. It was to be a wonderful new experience for me.

Because of the large amount of equipment we decided to take my car. We drove to Harwich and with some anxiety watched the car being craned on board, wondering if the excessive weight would break its back.

The calm sea and warm sun made the crossing perfect. Apart from gulls following the ship, we saw few birds until we neared the Hook of Holland. Then, among the crowds of black-headed gulls, we saw a smaller bird, white with a jet-black head—a little gull, a rarity to us. This was a happy augury and, as we docked, our excitement mounted.

Like every British motorist on his first trip abroad, I found driving on the right side of the road needed all my concentration. To make matters worse, we drove into Rotterdam during the middle of the rush hour. Never had I seen so many bicycles, none of which took the least notice of cars. There seemed to be no right of way; cyclists came at me from every direction. My nerve was rapidly cracking when a barrier dropped, barring further progress. A bridge, crossing one of the innumerable canals, then swung in a semi-circle to allow a ship to pass. After a short wait the bridge swung back, the barrier lifted and we drove towards the narrow one-way bridge, but hundreds of cyclists beat me to it. I stopped to weigh up the situation, but scores of angry car hooters behind me quickly made me drive on regardless. With half a dozen cyclists hanging on to the car, I kept the hooter blaring continuously and forced a way across the bridge. This motorists' night-

mare did not end until we reached our destination, on the other side of
Rotterdam—I had been initiated into Continental driving.

We received a warm welcome from Jo and Truus den Haring, who
were to be our hosts for the six weeks of our stay. Jo is a first-class
botanist and also has an excellent knowledge of Dutch birds. We plied
him with questions, especially about the whereabouts of nests of
black-tailed godwits, Kentish plovers, golden orioles, little bitterns,
black terns and avocets. We decided to spend a few days driving round
to likely places and to obtain necessary permits.

I shall never forget my first view of the great sandwich tern colony
at De Beer, opposite the Hook of Holland. There were about 8,000
pairs and the rasping noise, as we approached, was deafening. The
nests were so densely packed and the eggs so beautifully harmonised
with their surroundings that it was difficult to walk without treading
on them. We erected a hide and soon after George saw me in the birds
were back on their nests. There was much bickering and fighting, the
birds stabbing viciously at each other with dagger-like bills. But little
harm was done. Conditions were ideal and I soon had all the photographs I wanted.

On our return journey to Rotterdam we saw two Dutch boys with
opera glasses round their necks, leaning on bicycles, obviously bird-
watching. We stopped and tried to speak to them, but they had little
English, we no Dutch. But an illustrated bird book is a universal
language and as we pointed to the colour plates of the birds we especially wished to see—ruffs, black terns, Kentish plovers and avocets—
the boys grinned and set off, beckoning us to follow.

After about two miles we came to the Vondelingenplaat, a large
area of soft mud near the River Maas. We crept up an earth embank-
ment and peeped over the top. I gasped with astonishment. There were
at least fifty pairs of avocets with their nests spaced out over the mud;
black terns rose from pools surrounded by reeds; and ruffs displayed
their multi-coloured neck feathers from their jousting-grounds, working themselves into a frenzy whenever a reeve nonchalantly passed by.
On the drier ground Kentish plovers ran and piped before settling
down to incubate their eggs; and gloriously coloured blue-headed
wagtails skipped and danced around, catching insects and for ever
calling *tsip-tsip-tsipsi*. As we walked towards an avocet's nest the hen
displayed, then limped away lamely flapping her wings, and giving the
impression that she was mortally injured. When we knelt by the nest
she ran back, stood over the eggs and pecked George's hand.

This was a birds' paradise and we spent several days securing
valuable photographs. Unfortunately, soon after we left builders
moved in and today there is a gigantic oil refinery where once so many

birds first saw the light of day. It is sad that so much ideal ground for birds is being swallowed up by man's appetite for extending his acres of bricks and mortar.

One bird I particularly wanted to photograph was the golden oriole, the cock being one of the most beautiful birds I have seen. About the size of a blackbird, it is brilliant yellow with black wings and tail. That bald statement conveys little of its gorgeous appearance; ornithologists are apt to become lyrical when describing it. Ludwig Koch saw a pair displaying in the early-morning sun and likened them to a 'see-saw of golden balls'. To W. H. Hudson the sight of this oriole among more sombre-coloured birds was as a 'gleaming topaz in a necklace of little brown and green freckled stones'.

We found the delicately made nest slung between the small twin branches of an alder in a public park and erected a small pylon hide which was completely hidden among the surrounding foliage. Our work attracted much interest: even the local Burgomaster and his officials came to inspect our operations and requested me to send them some of the photographs. Probably because of the large number of people who walked through the park, the golden orioles were remarkably tame, thus enabling me to secure some lovely photographs. Prints were sent to the Burgomaster, who had one framed and hung in his parlour.

Jo took us to a place called Reeuwijk, not far from Gouda, famous for its cheese, and introduced us to Cor van de Starre, an expert on the little bittern, who showed us two nests, each containing six young. As we approached one nest the hen climbed to the top of some reeds before flying off. We left a hide which Cor promised to work into position.

We returned in a few days and within fifteen minutes of my being left in the hide, the cock arrived and stood like a statue immediately behind the nest. His camouflage was so perfect that after looking away I had difficulty in finding him again. He came on to the nest and, as the young stroked his bill, he regurgitated food which they quickly gobbled up. He settled to brood, but not for long, because a movement to one side of the nest attracted his attention—the return of the hen. To my astonishment the cock started to 'blush', his normally pale yellow bill turning to a brilliant blood red. For a while the two were together, then slowly the cock moved away, his bill gradually returning to its normal colour.

During the next few weeks I was able to photograph most of the birds I wanted, plus several extras. My bag included Kentish plovers, which pleased me very much, as in 1925 I had found a nest on the beach at Dungeness in Kent (it was exterminated as a British breeding species in 1956); ruffs performing their ecstatic displays; black terns at their floating nest on a narrow dyke; reed warblers feeding a young cuckoo twice their size; hoopoes, when my flash set blew up (see Chapter 12); and icterine warblers with their fantastically varied song—vehement and intense, shrieking and warbling, chuckling and grunting, discordant and musical, mellow and jarring—which it seemed impossible could come from the same throat.

A remarkable coincidence occurred during this expedition. It started because I particularly wished to photograph the black-tailed godwit. Jo thought that the most likely place would be the bird sanctuary near Vlaardingen, about sixteen miles from the Hook. To get there we had to drive about a mile down a very bumpy torn-up cart-track between dykes which drained the polders, low-lying re-claimed land. It was not until our third visit that we found a suitable nest; a godwit sprang from a tussock almost at Stuart's feet, and there, hidden in the dense rough grass, lay four eggs. We erected a hide at a distance.

During the evening of the fifth day the hide was moved to within six feet of the nest. The eggs were then chipped—slightly cracked at the larger end where the chick was hammering at the shell with its egg-tooth. The next evening one chick had emerged and the remaining eggs looked as though they would hatch within twelve hours. The godwit family was nearly ready for photography.

In high spirits we set off for Rotterdam, determined that we would be back there soon after dawn next morning. Halfway along the rough track we heard a sharp crack; just a stone hitting the underside of the car, I thought. But another, much louder crack followed, and immediately the front near-side tyre scraped ominously against the wing. We stopped to investigate. Several leaves of the near-side spring had broken; the axle was now supported by only a single leaf—a strip of metal a quarter of an inch thick.

It was a black moment. Our only course was somehow to get the car to Rotterdam for repairs. But since it was now 9.30 p.m. the chances of finding a garage which could tackle the job in time were slight.

We drove at about 5 m.p.h.; a faster speed caused the tyre to bump and scrape against the wing and threaten the remaining leaf. We crawled on to the main highway to Rotterdam, and crept along looking for a garage. The first one was open only for petrol, others were either closed or had no mechanic on duty. It was the same all the way back. As we rang the bell a distant clock chimed midnight. The normal half-hour journey had lasted two and a half hours. Our hopes of photographing the godwits were about nil. How could we possibly get a new

HOLLAND

Above : A black-tailed godwit flies overhead in the Vlaardingen bird sanctuary

Below : Comparatively rare in England, avocets are abundant in Holland. Here one adopts threatening pose as George Edwards extends an exploratory hand

NORWAY
Above: Female lemming and young. Every few years lemmings greatly increase in numbers and millions migrate towards the sea. Some drown, hence the stories of mass suicides

Below: Cranes are among Europe's shyest and rarest birds, yet this pair was found nesting only 200 yards from a main road

Above: The red-spotted bluethroat is only a passage-migrant in England, but in parts of Norway it is so abundant that it appears to have replaced the robin

Below: The Terek sandpiper is one of the rarest European breeding birds. This photograph was taken on a small island in the Gulf of Bothnia

Above left: The cock little bittern's bill flushes red as he arrives at the nest and approaches the hen
Above right: Hen yellow-breasted bunting disposing of faecal sac, while the cock waits to feed the young
Below: Chris Booth, James Ferguson-Lees and Nils Fritzen searching for the yellow-breasted bunting's nest in Finland

spring fitted in the morning and be back at the nest before the hen led the young away?

Truus welcomed us. 'Have you had trouble? You are so late.'

'Yes, we have,' I replied. 'Is Jo at home?'

It was a Saturday night and he was out playing chess with his friend, Mr. Klip. Truus kindly fetched him, and his friend came too. Not realising the urgency of the situation, Jo followed the niceties of Dutch etiquette.

He bowed to each of us, saying: 'Meet my good friend Mr. Klip.' He spoke no English, so after shaking hands I said to Jo: 'Please tell him we are delighted to meet him. Is he also a gardener like yourself?'

Jo shook his head: 'No, Mr. Klip has a small factory where he makes springs for motor-cars.'

Before I realised what was happening the car was round at the works and by 1.30 a.m. on Sunday the car had a new spring. After a few hours' sleep I was in the hide taking photographs of the black-tailed godwit with her four young.

FINLAND Six years after my visit to Holland I went to Finland, but this time I decided not to take my car. The country roads were reputedly in poor condition and I might not have such good fortune if another spring collapsed. I therefore shipped my apparatus to Helsinki, and James Ferguson-Lees and I left Harwich on 28 May 1958, on board the *Fredericka*, crossing the North Sea and landing at Esbjerg in Denmark next day. From there we travelled by train to Nyborg, on the ferry to Korsör, train to Copenhagen, ferry across to Malmö in Sweden, then by overnight train to Stockholm. We completed the journey to Helsinki on the steamship *Bore II* and never was I more glad to land: my berth seemed to be within a few feet of the propellers. The noise and vibration made sleep almost impossible. We docked on 31 May after three days of almost continuous travel—the aircraft on the return journey took little more than three and a half hours!

We were attending the XIIth International Ornithological Congress at Helsinki, and then spending some weeks bird-watching and photographing in this land of 60,000 lakes and some 84,000 square miles of forest—about two-thirds of the country. I had been invited by the Secretary-General of the Congress, Baron Lars von Haartman, to exhibit a selection of my photographs. Kodak kindly helped me to make the 40 in. ×30 in. prints which were prominently displayed, and

H

I should be less than human if I had not relished the many kind remarks or the numerous demands for my autograph.

By the time the Congress opened on 5 June over 450 people had gathered from many parts of the world, including about 100 from Great Britain. It is at times like these that I miss a lot by not knowing a foreign language. Most of the delegates, of course, understood English, but quite a number spoke only German or French, and it was frustrating not being able to communicate with them. Dr. J. Berlioz gave the Presidential address in French and several of the lectures I would have liked to attend were not in English.

One of the most enjoyable things about such gatherings is the social side and the opportunity to discuss various ornithological problems with fellow workers. It is also, of course, a great pleasure to meet the famous ornithologists of the world, people who have been only names before: Dr. Alexander Wetmore, one of the world's greatest systematists; Dr. Salim Ali, the outstanding Indian ornithologist; Dr. Erwin Stresemann, the doyen of German ornithologists; Dr. G. P. Dementiev, who held a similar position among the Russians until his death in 1969; and Dr. Y. Yamashina, so well known for his work on Japanese birds. I also met Dr. Kai Curry-Lindahl of Sweden, several of whose books I have helped to illustrate; Dr. Finnur Gudmundsson of Iceland, one of the largest men I have ever met; and Loke Wan Tho of Singapore, a fellow bird photographer, so tragically killed in an air crash in Formosa in June 1964.

I was sorry when the Congress ended, but looked forward keenly to doing some bird photography in a new land. By now, George Shannon and John and Eileen Parrinder had joined James and me. I hired a large car, complete with radio, roof-rack and, most important, a boot so enormous that I clambered inside to help load the luggage. We left the University on 12 June and drove over 400 miles to Oulu at the northern end of the Gulf of Bothnia. We soon realised that the Finnish roads lived up to their reputation; there was little clearance under the car and with our heavy load it kept banging and bumping on the axles. In Britain such roads would be classed as impassable; there was certainly little traffic and we managed to average 25 m.p.h., eventually arriving at Oulu at 2 a.m. after seventeen hours on the road.

As we unpacked the car a reporter arrived and asked me my first impression of Oulu. 'It stinks,' I replied. This was literally true, as a cellulose factory on the outskirts of the town was belching out evil-smelling black smoke.

A few hours later the local newspaper headed its interview with me: 'Bird man says Oulu stinks'. Apparently the local people had become so used to the smell that they did not notice it.

Later that morning some seventy members from the Congress arrived and we all went on an excursion to see the local birds. The first of importance was a yellow-breasted bunting, a 'lifer' for most of us, as Finland and northern Russia are the only areas where it breeds. We stopped to watch ruffs on their jousting areas, and a few minutes later James found a reeve's nest with three eggs and George one with four. A hen harrier's nest with three eggs came next, followed by a pintail's with eleven and a lapwing's with four. Obviously there was going to be more than enough to keep me busy with the camera.

Back at the hotel we met Nils Fritzen, a Finnish naturalist, who had come to collect plants and to study the hen harrier and the Terek sandpiper. The latter was of great interest to me as its only European breeding grounds are Russia and—rarely—Finland.

When we mentioned to Nils that the hotel was expensive he offered to try to find us private accommodation. He did—in the school at Tupos, a few miles from Oulu and in excellent bird country. The children have three months' holiday in the summer to help with the farming and as a consequence have only a few days at Christmas and two at Easter. We were shown into a classroom which was *completely* empty, just floor, ceiling and walls. This was to be home for our stay here. I quickly unpacked the stove and Eileen Parrinder brewed the best cup of tea that I had drunk since leaving home.

We wondered about sleeping arrangements. James, Nils and I had sleeping-bags, but what about the others? The caretaker said that he would find a bed for John and Eileen but we roared with laughter when it appeared—a wooden box so short that John's head overlapped one end, his feet the other. Eventually they and George stayed at an hotel fifteen miles away.

Before going to bed, James and I had a sauna bath, a new experience for both of us. In a small hut, some eight feet by six feet, a wood-burning stove was roaring in one corner and on the opposite side were some benches so high that when sitting on them our heads were within a few inches of the ceiling. We stripped and sat on the benches, then James threw some water on to the stove and immediately we were enveloped in steam which almost scalded us and made us perspire profusely. More water, more steam, more sweat and just to encourage the perspiration we beat ourselves with thin leaf-covered branches. As a grand finale, and to show how tough you are, you are supposed to jump into an ice-cold river. We found that a bucket of cold water was more than sufficient.

Arrangements had been made for members of the Congress to visit other areas, so we decided to go on one to the Arctic, leaving some of our gear at the school, planning to return in five days.

It was, of course, light all through the night and when we dressed at four-thirty it was broad daylight. We called for George, Eileen and John and started on a 350-mile drive to Karigasniemi, near the Norwegian border, and 200 miles north of the Arctic Circle. We had to drive slowly because of the poor road, but this had the advantage of giving us a better opportunity of seeing birds. The Arctic Circle was reached at 4 p.m.; I was grasping a biscuit with one hand and holding binoculars in the other watching the courtship feeding of a pair of waxwings. We had a good view of a pair of willow grouse, the cock calling: *go back, go back, back back back*. A cock merlin flashed past with food in his talons. No sooner were we on our way again than James slammed on the brakes and we all leapt out of the car to see a Siberian jay, a fine bird with chestnut-red wing and outer tail feathers, brown head and grey back and underparts.

We stopped to eat at 8 p.m. the first real meal since our very early breakfast: reindeer meat from a tin, washed down with tea brewed on my portable gas stove. There was another stop at Kaunispää, where we had our first view of Russia. Snow still covered much of the ground so we were all surprised when Eileen calmly told us that she had found a shore lark's nest with four eggs. Then I surprised myself by stumbling across a mealy redpoll's nest also with four eggs. We had hardly started again when we were stopped by a herd of reindeer crossing the road—the first time in my life that I was able to take photographs at midnight without the aid of flash.

Eventually we arrived at our hotel at 6.45 a.m., having been on the road for twenty-five hours. I had three hours' sleep in two nights, but it seemed a waste of time to stay in bed when the weather and light were so good for twenty-four hours a day.

George found a red-spotted bluethroat's nest with six eggs and, as the bird seemed fairly tame, I fitted a 400 mm Kilfitt lens to my Contax camera and took a series of photographs of the cock displaying. We watched a red-throated pipit carrying a green caterpillar and hoped that it would take this to its nest, but it seemed to know that we were watching and did not do so. While finding the nest of a red-necked phalarope, George broke through an ice-covered bog and went in up to his waist. No sooner had we hauled him out than James found a nest of a Lapland bunting with six eggs. Then he fell in a bog!

That night I dropped into bed at 10 p.m. and knew nothing until eight o'clock the next morning. It was dull and drizzling with a bitter wind. I would quite happily have stayed indoors but was very glad I went with the others. Mauri Rautkeri, an excellent Finnish ornithologist, took us for a fascinating walk. Space will not permit me to go into detail but here are just a few of the highlights: a magnificent view of a cock pine grosbeak with its lovely rose-coloured head and body, and almost black wings with their white wing-bars; a pair of Arctic ringed plovers at their nest containing two eggs; a golden eagle that dived from a considerable height to within a few feet of the ground; a long-tailed skua that put on a superb injury-feigning display as we stood by its nest, and even in flight gave the appearance of having difficulty in keeping air-borne as it flapped its wings vigorously to gain height, then lamely flopped to the ground, repeating the performance time and again; a broad-billed sandpiper that kept us guessing whether it had a nest; a cock Temminck's stint that enchanted us with a lovely display as he stood on a rock, quivering his wings up and down, trilling all the time; a bar-tailed godwit that stayed by her nest of three eggs apparently because she feared a pair of nearby long-tailed skuas more than us; a dotterel that sat on his nest and allowed us to stroke him (the cock does all the incubating while the hen joins others of her sex) and perhaps most exciting of all was the finding of a spotted redshank's nest, a bird I knew well in Britain in its grey winter plumage, but had never seen before on its breeding ground in full breeding adornment of pure black with white spots on the back.

What a day! I had walked fifteen miles in thigh boots and worn through the whole of the heels of two pairs of socks.

We were told that if we did not climb to the top of Ailigas, the Lapp Holy Mountain, all kinds of misadventures would befall us and our loved ones, so the following day saw us on another long walk. We were some 200 miles north of the Arctic Circle and although it was Midsummer Day it was bitterly cold. I never wear a hat but that day I pulled up the hood from my windcheater, almost completely obscuring my face, and was promptly called Edmund Hillary! We reached the summit of the mountain and to placate the gods placed a stone on the cairn. We had hoped for a wonderful panoramic view but visibility was down to 100 yards. However, to compensate for this, we found a snow bunting's nest, containing four eggs, hidden among some rocks. On our way down we found among some pine trees the nesting hole of a three-toed woodpecker and soon after, not forty inches above the ground, the nest of a Siberian tit in a disused woodpecker's hole. The tits were so tame that I was able to take all the photographs I wanted.

Instead of going to bed we started on the long drive back to Tupos, each taking a turn at the wheel to give the others an opportunity to sleep. I still could not get used to the lack of darkness as the night wore on; in place of moonlight and starlight we had sunlight from a clear sky. The sun, of course, was low in the sky, which caused the brightest light to shine almost horizontally. Somehow this seemed to add a dimension of loveliness to already enchanting scenery. This is what I wrote to Dorothy:

'It turned into a most lovely night, the sun came out giving the most gorgeous reflections, with truly wonderful colours, all gloriously shown in the mirror-like surface of the waters in the many lakes we passed. As the midnight sun dipped behind cloud, almost on the horizon, the effect was that of a prolonged sunset, turning from a delicate pastel pink into a deep rose-red. Only between eleven and midnight did the light dull off just a little but even then it was good enough for photography.'

We had three punctures on the way and then, thirty miles from our destination, and only a few hours before John, Eileen and George had to catch the train for Helsinki, a tyre burst. But then, on what appeared to be a completely deserted road, some foresters appeared on bicycles. They spoke no English but somehow we conveyed to them the urgency and need for a taxi to get three people to Oulu. But apparently the only taxi in the whole region was already in Oulu!

One of the men cycled off and shortly after a lorry arrived with a couple of men. Expertly they repaired the damage. John, Eileen and George were barely in time to catch the train, whose engine was named 'Stephenson', and burnt wood and belched black smoke.

Back at Tupos, Chris Booth joined us and I prepared for a fortnight's bird photography. Nils had been searching for nests while we had been away, and suggested that we should go to a little island in the Gulf of Bothnia where two pairs of Terek sandpipers were breeding. This really was exciting. At first glance the Terek looks rather like a common sandpiper, but has an upturned bill and yellow legs. It is on the British list as a rare vagrant.

Leaving the car, James rowed us to the island in a leaky boat, although 'rowed' is hardly the word—the water was so shallow in places he got out and towed us while we baled in an effort to keep our equipment dry.

In the first Terek's nest one egg was well chipped, another beginning, which meant that the young would soon be hatching. The temperature inside the hide rose to 87°F and the humidity was very high. The hen Terek sandpiper fell asleep and it was all I could do to stay awake after so many short nights, as there was little to photograph. Suddenly I saw the cock running towards our hides, calling softly to the hen. He ran past Nils's hide, less than five feet away, then stood by the side of the hen. I photographed the pair together and listened, waiting for Nils to expose before attempting to change plates, for fear I made a noise and disturbed them. Then I heard a sound—a snore! Nils was even more exhausted than I.

The photographs we took are believed to be the first ever of this great rarity taken at its nest.

This islet was remarkable for its bird-life. While Nils and I were taking photographs of the Terek sandpiper, James and Chris went bird-nesting and I could hardly believe my ears when they told me what they had seen. Here is a complete list:

Pintail	1 pair	Dunlin	1 pair
Shoveler	1 ,,	Temminck's stint	5 ,,
Scaup	2 ,,	Herring gull	1 ,,
Tufted duck	6 ,,	Common gull	4 ,,
Velvet scoter	1 ,,	Black-headed gull	6 ,,
Red-breasted merganser	2 ,,	Common tern	4 ,,
Oystercatcher	3 ,,	Arctic tern	10 ,,
Turnstone	6 ,,	Skylark	2 ,,
Ringed plover	18 ,,	Sand martin	6 ,,
Ruff	5 ,,	Wheatear	3 ,,
Redshank	11 ,,	White wagtail	3 ,,
Terek sandpiper	2 ,,		

The small colony of sand martins had dug their nesting holes in a little hollow only ten inches deep. Never have I heard of such a variety of breeding birds in so small an area—103 pairs of twenty-three species in about ten acres.

Soon after we had arrived in Oulu we had seen a yellow-breasted bunting, a bird I particularly wanted to photograph. After a long search James and Chris discovered a nest with six eggs. Alas, four days later the nest was empty. James had returned to England so there seemed little hope of finding another.

I was depressed because the chances of my visiting Finland again during a nesting season were remote. But I had reckoned without Chris. He spent nearly a whole night watching and searching, and eventually located a nest with four eggs. It was deep in dense herbage and when Chris showed it to me the hen remained sitting until I almost touched her. Probably the reason for her sitting so tight was that the eggs were hatching. The nest may have been difficult to find but the cock and hen presented no problems; they continued to feed their young without taking any notice of the hide.

Although I was unable to work on all the species I wanted on this expedition I photographed fourteen, eleven of them for the first time.

NORWAY Again another six years elapsed before I revisited Scandinavia, this time going to Norway. My object was to photograph

Europe's largest, wildest and most spectacular members of the eagle and owl families, as well as the bird that has been described as its shyest—the crane. I thought this expedition would be the toughest yet; I was right.

For some months I had been corresponding with Dr. Johan Willgohs, the Norwegian authority on both the white-tailed or sea eagle, and the eagle owl, and he promised every assistance. Both these birds can be found on the west coast of Norway but the crane nests inland. Thus it was necessary to plan the adventure in two parts.

My companions on the first part were George Shannon, Sdeuard Bisserôt, and John Wightman, who knew Norway well. We left in the spring of 1964 and stayed on an island off the west coast. Because both the sea eagle and the eagle owl are rapidly declining in numbers I have been asked not to mention the names of the islands where these birds were breeding.

To reach the island we boarded a coastal steamer at Bergen and, after calling at several islands en route, drew alongside the quay at 8 a.m. in pouring rain. As we disembarked, Dr. Johan Willgohs gazed in astonishment at our twelve cameras, telephoto lenses, tripods, flash equipment, hides, tents, sleeping-bags, ruck-sacks, typewriter, sound-recording apparatus and other impedimenta as they were regurgitated from the ship's hold.

Johan took us in his motor-cruiser for a conducted tour of some of the islands and it was not long before a white-tailed eagle soared overhead, clearly displaying the short, white, wedge-shaped tail, tawny head, huge yellow bill and enormously broad wings—a magnificent sight. Ashore, we were amazed at the size of their nests, one of which must have weighed several hundredweights.

As I had already photographed five of Europe's nine species of eagle, naturally I was keen to add this new species to the list. And there, as we landed on another island and looked across a forty-foot gully, was the perfect eyrie. For months I had been thinking, reading, writing, talking, dreaming sea eagles, and here I was standing on a spot from which I should be able to film and photograph to my heart's content. My hopes were shortlived. Johan inspected the nest and found that it contained two infertile eggs. Such is the lot of a bird photographer.

But we had better luck on another island. While I stayed below—I had hurt my back and found it almost impossible to bend—the others climbed to an eyrie which could be photographed from a ravine 120 ft. away. So George and the others erected a hide and he, as was only fair, went in first. He was delighted with his session and then it was my turn. But had I known the conditions I doubt whether I should have gone. Since I have been wearing bi-focal spectacles I have developed a fear of heights and this, coupled with an aching back, made some of the more precipitous parts of the roundabout climb to the hide utterly terrifying. The climax came when we reached an overhang, and without a rope I had to inch round on a narrow ledge of wet slippery rock with nothing between me and the sea 300 ft. below.

I was trembling by the time we arrived. And what a hide! It had to be on the very edge of a shelf of rock as otherwise we could not obtain an unobstructed view across the ravine. Yet, in a way I cannot explain, just being in that hide gave me a strong sense of security. Only a frail cloth refuge on a sheer and dangerous cliff-face, yet once within it, I forgot everything but the job in hand—the photography of the sea eagle.

Whatever terrors the cliff held for me, it was a playground for Johan. He was an expert rock-climber, having visited a number of sea eagles' nests on the west coast of Norway, and he came directly up that 'unclimbable' precipice!

The eyrie contained two eaglets, one several days older than the other, and to judge by the appearance of its bulging crop the elder had recently eaten a hearty meal. After a wait of one and a half hours I heard a whoosh of powerful wings and the hen arrived. It was a wonderful experience to see this magnificent eagle at close range. Gently she fed the younger chick with small pieces of fish, but the elder eaglet remained fast asleep. Now and then the eagle's fierce, yellow eyes glared at the hide or down at the sea.

The meal completed she preened herself and removed fish scales and other debris from the chicks' down. Then the cock flew over yelping loudly and the hen leapt from the nest. Within half an hour she was back with a lumpsucker (fish) clutched in her talons. This was fed to the young, the larger one, who was now wide awake, taking his share. But both were satiated before the fish was finished so the hen carried the remains away. As she was back on the eyrie again within two minutes I wondered whether she had dumped the fish or left it at a feeding place.

Soon hen and young were fast asleep; only the noise of the engine of the returning boat disturbed their slumbers. As I relaxed and made ready to leave I was surprised to find that I had been in the hide for eight hours. I was terribly stiff and found the descent even more nerve-racking than the ascent. Never was I more thankful than when I stepped aboard the boat. Nothing would induce me to make that perilous climb again. But I was delighted to have made it once to photograph such a superb bird.

On the way back to our base we saw a great black-backed gull feeding on a lumpsucker at least two feet long. Johan told us that to catch such a fish the gull swims immediately behind, steers it towards the shore and then hauls it out!

Thus for Europe's largest eagle, now for Europe's largest owl, the two-and-a-half-foot-long eagle owl. Johan showed us a nest in a rock fissure which, compared with the sea eagle site, was a very easy position. On our first visit the hen waited until we were almost at the nest before she took off, her wing-tips almost brushing my shoulder, her enormous orange eyes glaring into mine.

In the nest were two owlets, about eight and ten days old, and surrounding them was a feast: the corpses of oystercatchers, hooded crows, common gulls, eiders, mallards, long-tailed ducks, mergansers and blackbirds.

Most owls are nocturnal and feed their young at night, but here, at this time of year, there is continuous daylight. How would this affect their habits? The little which has been published on the breeding biology of Scandinavian owls did not answer the question and I wanted to find out. Our time was short and obviously a complete answer would mean an intensive study of several pairs. But I could at least make a start.

After erection of the hide we left it for two days, before I entered it at noon on a fine sunny day. The adult owls were sitting on crags near the highest point of the island and became agitated while we were by the nest. Herons, hooded crows and gulls had mobbed them but all became quiet once I was left on my own. Nothing happened until 6.15 p.m. when blackbirds became very noisy mobbing something I could not see. Then, in the distance, hooded crows began croaking, the sound increasing rapidly in volume as they flew towards the hide. Suddenly an eagle owl alighted by the young, dropping a small bird it had carried in its bill. The larger chick picked it up and swallowed it whole. The adult gazed down at the chick and for a moment their bills touched and rubbed against each other. Rarely have I been so wildly elated, seeing this great owl only ten feet away.

The adult flew off after several minutes but returned an hour later, carrying more food in its bill, and this time held it in front of the smaller chick. The adult murmured and tried to persuade it to feed but, before the youngster got a grip, the larger owlet leaned forward and swallowed the prey whole. A third visit was made just before 9 p.m. and once again the larger chick grabbed the food. My companions came for me at 11 p.m. They brought a fish, part of which we fed to the baby owl.

The following morning I was in the hide by ten-thirty, prepared for a twelve-hour stay. The larger owlet had almost a full crop but the baby looked nearly dead. While I warmed it, Sdeuard and John cut up and fed it with the remains of the fish and it rapidly revived. The parents made no visits to the nest until the evening. At seven o'clock I noticed one of them perched on the pinnacle of a crag a hundred yards away. Presently it left and in one long dive came straight towards me at such a speed that I thought it would crash into my hide. Instinctively I threw up my arms to protect my face, but at the last split second it jinked away and made a perfect landing at the nest. It started to tear up an immature blackbird it had brought but the larger chick snatched it away and, with two or three hefty gulps, swallowed it whole, feathers and all.

No other visit was made to the nest while I was in the hide. We fed the baby again but wondered whether it would survive. Whereas the larger one was able to swallow prey whole, the baby still required it to be torn to pieces and usually, before this was done, big brother had snatched it.

As we hurried down to the boat just before 11 p.m. we witnessed a scene that happens regularly but is rarely observed. An eagle owl was being mobbed by at least twelve hooded crows, one of which ventured just a fraction too close. A flurry of feathers marked his fate.

It was a pity that we could not stay longer among these enchanting islands but we had to leave for our next objective, the Fokstumyra bird sanctuary near the centre of southern Norway. Terrain and bird-life were, of course, entirely different from the island-dotted west coast. This was the summer home of the crane, four feet tall, exceptionally shy and rare, whose usual nesting site is in the middle of a featureless bog.

By now Jimmy Hancock and Charles and Sarah Rose had joined us and we all searched for two days before we even saw a crane. Then Jimmy, ever alert and with extremely good eyesight, glimpsed something in his binoculars. He signalled to the rest of us and we all trained our glasses on the spot where he was looking. Yes. No. Yes. It *was* a crane, sitting on a nest only 200 yards from a main road!

Led by Jimmy, we sloshed our way through the bog—is there anything more difficult to traverse? We collected small reservoirs of water in our rubber boots. But we had seen the crane run low from her nest before flying away and this spurred us on. The nest contained two large eggs, and the final stroke of luck was the finding of a stand of birch scrub, within 160 ft. of the nest, where we could erect an inconspicuous hide.

A few days later I started photography. Although it was 2 June snow had fallen and formed the floor of the hide, but the sun shone so warmly that I had the strange experience of freezing feet and baking head. Within minutes of my entering the hide the crane walked un-suspiciously to the nest and settled down gently to incubate the eggs, but I waited a full half-hour before taking the first photograph. As the shutter clicked, I was relieved to find that she gave no sign of being disturbed.

Once or twice she stood up to turn the eggs but little else took place until the male arrived two hours later. She rose at his approach, picked up small bits of vegetation and cast them to one side. Then the birds changed stations. The cock was not so relaxed, constantly fidgeting, and he seemed pleased to be relieved when the hen returned. The same change-over ritual took place, as it usually does with these birds. Few people are fortunate enough to see such intimate behaviour of such rare and shy birds.

After ten hours in the hide I was well satisfied and looked forward keenly to my next visit, especially to being present when the eggs hatched. I never occupied the hide again. An egg-collector apparently stole the eggs. This was on a sanctuary, but what is that to a determined and unscrupulous egg-collector? But I had better luck at other nests, including fieldfares; redwings; bramblings; wrynecks, now almost extinct as a breeding species in Britain; and the northern form of the golden plover, with jet-black face, breast and stomach, and more handsome colouring than the bird we know.

We also found two willow grouse nests in open country. At both the hen sat so tightly that no hide was necessary. By walking slowly towards her, I took all the photographs I wanted. They obviously had complete confidence in their camouflage. I was even more fortunate to be able to photograph the cock. While driving with Charles we spotted him creeping away from the edge of the road. We stopped, so did the cock. Carefully lowering the car window I pushed out the telephoto lens, focused and made an exposure before he continued on his way and was lost in the vegetation.

One other bird I was particularly pleased to photograph was the red-spotted bluethroat; only a passage-migrant in England, but so common here that it appears to take the place of the robin. Nests were exceedingly difficult to find. They are well concealed, and when leaving the eggs the hen creeps through thick undergrowth for a little distance before flying away. But, strangely, as soon as the eggs hatch the behaviour changes, both cock and hen flying directly to and from the nest.

Two days before we were due to leave, John, who had searched for many hours on several days, eventually found a red-spotted blue-throat's nest containing nearly full-grown young in the bank of a stream. We erected a hide on the opposite bank and got to work. The cock, especially, is a beautiful bird: splendidly iridescent blue throat starred with the characteristic red spot, dark brown back, light brown underparts, russet-red tail. Both birds were surprisingly tame, visiting the nest and feeding the young while John and I were standing only eighteen feet away.

Our seven-week expedition was an unqualified success. I had never really expected, even in my most optimistic moments, that I should succeed in photographing white-tailed eagles, eagle owls and cranes all in one season. It was a tremendous challenge and the result gave me a feeling of great satisfaction.

8 | *Hickling*

For the greater part of my life I have known and loved the Norfolk Broads. In the early 1930's I had short holidays at Potter Heigham, staying in a tiny bungalow belonging to an aunt. Often Cyril Newberry was with me, and it was he who taught me how to sail a boat and drive a car. The first time I went solo in an old two-seater bull-nosed Morris I met some cows in a narrow lane and, taken completely by surprise, pushed my foot down hard—on the accelerator instead of the brake! The car shot down the lane like a rocket, the cows leaping the hedges on either side of the road with surprising agility. I did not stop to listen to the flow of Norfolk vituperation that came from the lips of the cowman.

From Potter Heigham, Cyril and I went on to visit Hickling, famed throughout Europe for its bird-life. During the period between the two world wars no one visiting Hickling failed sooner or later to meet Jim Vincent. As a boy Jim had been so keen and learnt so much about birds that at the age of nineteen he was engaged by the late Lord Lucas to organise and supervise a bird sanctuary on Hickling Broad. Later, when I met him, he was head keeper for Lord Desborough's Whiteslea estate at Hickling, and there he remained for the rest of his life.

He was a lean, lithe man of medium height, strong as a horse, with piercing blue eyes, which could identify an unusual bird at long range without binoculars. He was an expert nest-finder and understood the behaviour of Broadland birds better than anyone else. Jim was the complete Broadsman: he had a good knowledge of boats, was a first-class angler, brilliant shot and an excellent gardener.

About this time I read in a book by Oliver Pike, a pioneer of nature photography, that the best lens for bird photography was the seventeen-inch Dallmeyer Dallon telephoto. After considerable sacrifices I managed to buy one and fitted it with a Compur shutter to my camera. When Cyril and I first met Jim he asked us what birds we would like to photograph, and with all the assurance of youth we said bearded tits and Montagu's harriers, two of the rarest British breeding birds. Jim in his kindly way suggested that we would be wiser to start with a more common bird, and as he knew of a lapwing's nest in a suitable position, he suggested that we photograph it. We erected a hide thirty feet from the nest.

I proudly showed my new lens to Ian Thomson, a friend of Jim's and an excellent bird photographer, who was on the Broads at the time. I expected him to be impressed. Instead, he regarded it gravely, turned to me and said: 'You know what you want to do? Borrow Jim's punt, go out to the middle of the Broad—and drop it overboard.' I was dumbfounded.

Ian explained that with such a long focus lens I should get very little depth of field in my photographs, and anyway it was always preferable to work close to a nest. The results of our work with the lapwing proved how right he was. This, of course, is no criticism of the lens itself, which is excellent for most long-distance work. Ian was a Harley Street dental surgeon whose absorbing hobby was bird photography, and after that first encounter became my friend, adviser—and dentist.

When I got home I called on Dallmeyer's who kindly changed the offending lens for an 8½ in. Serrac. This worked well for me for many years, enabling me to take photographs that are still being published. One of these was the bittern, a bird that had been extinct in Britain as a breeding species for many years. But in 1911 Jim, with Miss E. L. Turner, found a nest, and from then onwards he did everything in his power to help and protect them while they were re-establishing themselves.

His biggest problem was egg-collectors and he told me how he had once saved a nest. From a high observation point he spotted an unnatural movement in a reed bed where he knew a bittern was breeding. He punted over and came upon the intruder right beside the nest, and threatened him with violence if he did not leave the Broads immediately.

One day Jim and I were listening to the cock bittern's weird boom which sounds rather like a fog-horn, and in favourable conditions can be heard a couple of miles away. The boom was coming from a dense reed-bed and Jim astonished me by suddenly saying: 'Would you like me to catch him?'

'Yes', I replied, thinking that he was pulling my leg.

Jim had a wonderful ear and unhesitatingly went through the thick reeds to within a few yards of where the bittern had been calling. He walked right round it, keeping within a distance of about six yards, took off his jacket, walked towards the bird and threw the jacket over it. Grasping the dagger-like bill, which can easily stab out an eye, he triumphantly showed me his prize before setting it free.

Why the preliminary circling? If bitterns are as easy to catch as that, why did not Jim go straight to it? He explained that by walking round out of sight, he caused the bird to become confused. And when a bittern is confused it always behaves in the same way—it stretches its neck upwards to its fullest extent, points its bill skywards and stays absolutely still. Its wonderful protective coloration makes it one with the surrounding reeds—except to Jim's keen eye.

Jim had introduced me to Major Anthony Buxton who owned the adjoining estate at Horsey. He, too, was keen on taking photographs of birds and had already erected a hide in shallow water beside a water rail's nest in a sedge-bed. We were having trouble with the 'gardening'; as soon as we tied one piece of sedge back another collapsed. We therefore decided to remove the nine young for a few minutes while we completed the job. Major Buxton was wearing an old deer-stalker's hat, so we put the young in this about three feet to one side of the nest and carried on with our work.

Just then the hen returned. She acted as though we were not there. She went to the hat, grabbed a chick by its neck and planted it back in the nest. Then another one, and another, and so on until the whole family was back home. She then settled to brood, while the Major and I stood helplessly by. I entered the hide, although it was obvious I did not need one for this bird. After a while the water rail left, so I took photographs of the young. The bottom of the hide was just clear of the water and shortly after I had started I heard a slight noise behind me and was amazed to see the water rail making her way under the hide, over my boots, out the other side and so on to her nest!

When we had finished photography for the day we released the sedge around the nest.

Back at Hickling Jim found another water rail's nest. During a spell of very dry weather the ground had become so hard that we could walk dryshod over what was usually marshy ground. The rail's nest *appeared* to be in a most unusual situation. One day we noticed that the birds were busily engaged raising the level of the nest cup. As one bird incubated the eggs the other gathered pieces of sedge which were pushed under the eggs. Work continued throughout that day and the next. Why were they doing this? That night violent thunderstorms burst over the Broads. The torrential rains flooded the marshes but when we were able to visit the water rail's nest we found that it was undamaged.

HICKLING

Above: Foster parents to a young marsh harrier

Right: The magnificent spread of the cock marsh harrier's wings contrast with those of the down-clad young

Left: This photograph of a Montagu's harrier alighting at its nest was used as the crest for 193 Squadron of the RAF (*Crown copyright 1970*)

Below right: Jim Vincent, famous Norfolk naturalist, holds two young marsh harriers at Hickling, June 1943. He died the following year

I came to know both Hickling and Jim very well during three consecutive war years when, each spring, Dorothy and I stayed there for many weeks. Because of the war my aunt was now occupying her bungalow at Potter Heigham, so we had to find alternative accommodation. Ted Piggin, Jim's assistant, offered us a bedroom and sitting-room, and the use of the kitchen in his cottage which stood at the end of the cinder track leading to Whiteslea Lodge, Lord Desborough's residence. From our bedroom window we had a wonderful view over the marshes to the Broad. Often at night we heard enemy planes, and the surrounding countryside was so flat that we could clearly see any air raid on Norwich—like a diabolical firework display.

Jim was a great conservationist and was especially interested in the marsh harrier, at that time our rarest breeding bird. Often we would watch them and in 1942 noticed that while there were three hens there was only one cock. One of the hens nested at Horsey and laid six eggs, but they were all infertile.

Halfway through April Jim found the second nest when only the preliminary pieces of sedge had been placed in position. It was deep in very thick, rank sedge marsh, standing in several inches of water. He first showed me the nest when it was ready for eggs and during the next ten days a full clutch of five was laid. The first egg hatched on 7 June, the second on the 9th, the third on the 12th, the fourth on the 14th, and the fifth on the 17th.

Ian Thomson and I decided to photograph this pair and we erected a hide some seventy yards from the nest. On subsequent days we moved it nearer and nearer, still without causing any alarm although the cock was usually calling as he circled overhead. It was only when we finally erected the hide twelve feet from the nest that the hen left. We watched her from a dyke wall a short distance away. She first flew from sight, but within half an hour returned with food in her talons. As she neared the breeding marsh the cock flew towards her, also carrying food, and it appeared that he was trying to pass this to her, but could not as her talons were already full. Both marsh harriers then circled before the cock dropped to the nest, followed immediately by the hen. For some seconds they were both at the nest, then the cock flew away.

Two days later Jim and I made an interesting discovery. We saw the cock fly in and circle, whereupon the hen flew up to receive the food which she immediately took back to the nest. The cock continued hunting and we watched him quartering the ground. He dropped to rise a minute later with food dangling from his talons. With this he flew to a spot on another marsh about 300 yards away from the nest under observation and, after circling, was met by a

I

second hen which received the food from him. For some time we had suspected that the two hens were both mated to this cock, but this was the first definite proof we had, and the incident provided what was, I believe, the first known case of a polygamous cock marsh harrier. In my opinion this was probably an example of enforced polygamy, as had there been two cocks it is probable that both would have taken a single hen.

We also obtained evidence of polygamy in the Montagu's harrier. For the first time since the floods of 1938, this harrier nested in this area of the Broads, two hens and one cock arriving late in the season—they had probably been disturbed from another breeding ground. The cock mated with both hens, who each built a nest not more than 300 yards apart, and both reared young. The cock fed these hens more or less alternately. Polygamy in this species has been recorded several times.

We were gratified at our success in building our hiding place without disturbing the marsh harriers, and were looking forward to spending many hours watching them from close quarters. We were to be disappointed, however, for there occurred a disastrous incident which showed how easily marsh harriers will desert. Sunday, 21 June, was a delightfully hot day, and many of the local children swam, fished and played games near the broad dyke which flowed within a few yards of the nests.

This activity was too much for the harriers. The second nest was deserted altogether, and the three small chicks perished. The nest at which we were attempting photography was not entirely abandoned, but from that day the parents merely dropped food into the nest, then left immediately. As the young were far too feeble to pull the food to pieces and feed themselves they would undoubtedly have died if left to themselves. When Dorothy and I arrived at the nest that evening we found them cold and hungry and we decided to attempt to feed them. I pulled a young pheasant to pieces and the young took morsels of this from me without hesitation. I fed them until they would take no more.

Early next morning we paid another visit. The smallest chick was dead, and the others were stiff with cold. While Dorothy warmed them I prepared three newly fledged meadow pipits, which the adults had dropped since the previous evening. As the young were warmed and fed, life seemed to surge into them, and they became very active.

During this visit there was no sign of the hen but the cock had circled over our heads, calling continuously. We now realised that if these young were to be reared at all we should have to take on the rôle of foster parents, and accordingly we visited the nest regularly two or three times each day. Unfortunately, food alone was insufficient to preserve the spark of life, and the cold nights on the marshes proved fatal to two more of our charges. Yet another unaccountably disappeared from the nest, so that eventually only one remained.

On 23 June we saw the cock fly towards the hen, perched on a dead tree-stump, and mate with her. The hen crouched very low, almost in a horizontal position, and the cock slowly flapped his wings. On two other occasions mating was seen, and each time the hen was perched on the same tree-stump, although we seldom saw her there at other times. Had this stump a special significance for them? Since the parents continued to provide food for the sole surviving chick, and the hide was still in position, we tried to obtain records of the parents' visits, spending many days in concealment for this purpose. On our arrival at 9 a.m. on 24 June we found the surviving chick stiff with cold—the previous night had been bitter—and it was first necessary to provide warmth and food. Since our visit the night before, the adults had left a young rat, two day-old partridges and a fledged meadow pipit lying on the rim of the nest, and from these we fed the chick.

At 9.30 a.m. I was left in the hide, and within a quarter of an hour I heard the cock calling *quek, quek, quek,* softly but rapidly repeated, and a few seconds later he alighted on the nest. He dropped the food and within five seconds was gone. The chick called encouragingly but the cock made no attempt to feed it. Just over an hour later I heard lapwings and redshanks calling, and presently I could see them mobbing the hen, diving furiously to drive her away. She paid little regard, however, and came straight for the nest, over which she hovered, dropping as the chick called excitedly. The chick snatched the food from her talons and, as it tried to tear it, she watched for a few moments, then flew off. The chick's efforts were unavailing and as the food was too big to be swallowed whole, it finally abandoned the struggle. We obviously had to continue feeding it for some time yet.

Another visit was made by the hen later in the morning and as usual she was accompanied to the nest by the mobbing lapwings and redshanks. One of these probably had good reason for its hostility as the prey was a half-grown lapwing. During the afternoon several more visits were made by both parents and they brought parts of rabbits.

Early in the evening I had a fine view of a food-pass. The cock first called over the nest, then flew towards some bushes where apparently the hen was perched. As she flew up to meet him she turned over on her back and took the prey from his talons. Usually, of course, the food is dropped by the cock and caught by the hen in the air. I left the hide at 8.30 p.m. after an eleven-hour watch.

When the chick was eighteen days old the greyish-white down took on a distinct pinkish hue, while the head remained the same colour with a circle of white on the nape. At this age it fed itself for the first time. The cock brought in a day-old partridge and, after a struggle, the chick swallowed it, although for some time the legs protruded from its bill. Larger prey was tackled, but unsuccessfully. The chick held the food down with its talons—it could not stand, so rested along the length of the tarsus—and gave sharp upward pulls with its bill, but only small bits of fur or feather were pulled away, and eventually it gave up. When twenty days old the first trace of feathers—very dark brown, almost black—appeared along the outside edges of the wings.

On the 27th we watched the marsh harriers from a nearby dyke wall. We first noticed the birds circling at a great height and saw the cock pass food to the hen in the normal way. Both birds then descended, not in a direct line, but by wheeling in great circles, until they were about fifty feet above the ground. The cock remained at a higher altitude than the hen, but when immediately above the nest she swung upwards again, rose above the cock, and called, whereupon the cock turned on to his back and took the food from her. On the 29th Jim and I saw a similar performance. Neither of us had witnessed a hen bird pass food to a cock before, nor had we heard of it happening with any of the other harriers.

On 4 July, while watching from this same place at 3 p.m., I saw the cock circling higher and higher, in a manner similar to a buzzard. As I watched, another harrier appeared, and together they circled each other until they were mere dots in the sky, when they began to descend, still wheeling. The higher bird, which I afterwards identified as the hen from the deserted nest, dropped something from her talons, and the cock turned over to catch it, but missed. The food went hurtling towards the ground, and the cock dropped like a stone after it. He failed to overtake it, however, and I heard it hit the ground.

On the 29th when the chick was twenty-four days old, I saw it tackle a young partridge. It still could not stand, but it pulled until eventually the partridge split open. Then pieces were torn off and swallowed, until there was nothing left. I noticed that it had inherited the adult method of dealing with food, particularly the sharp upward twist of the head and bill as it endeavoured to tear open the prey.

It is astonishing how quickly a young bird develops at this stage. Feathers were now visible along the edges of both wings and tail, whereas four days previously the first traces could be seen only on the wings. The white fluff was falling out on the throat and breast, leaving bare spots.

These harriers usually carried the food in the left talon—a habit practised similarly by the golden eagle, buzzard, kestrel and sparrow hawk, and each of our five native owls. I have never seen the talons of both feet used at once. Generally the food is passed from the talons to the bill a moment before alighting in order to leave both feet free to clutch the perch. I have also witnessed and photographed both cock and hen marsh harriers carrying food in their bills, sometimes while flying at a considerable height.

On 1 July the parents made a record number of visits; eight in two hours. The cock came three times in seven minutes, each time bringing food.

On 5 July, Jim and I saw a remarkable display flight. The cock began by circling very high, then dropping swiftly to within a few feet of the ground, rose again, and circled with slowly flapping wings until he became a mere speck in the sky. Then, on closed wings, he fell through the air, spiralling in small circles until it appeared that he must crash. He straightened out just in time and repeated the performance. Evidently he was displaying to one of the two hens, as we later saw a hen rise to meet him, followed in similar fashion by the second hen. Jim told me that this was the first time he had seen a cock marsh harrier displaying in July, or after the young had hatched.

No doubt owing to the parents' neglect, the chick relied on us for food; it certainly paid more attention to us than to its parents. On 9 July I visited the nest as usual, but there was no trace of the chick. I called and it replied immediately, running towards me from a point some twelve yards from the nest along a track in the sedge. As I knelt beside the nest cutting up the food, it jumped on my shoulder, and then on to my knee where I was able to feed it.

For some days men had been clearing vegetation from the dyke, and on 14 July they began working within fifty yards of the nest. This activity kept the adults away altogether and we had to supply the food. Normally this might have been difficult, but I was then studying a pair of barn owls and fortunately they were providing their young liberally with voles, often eight or nine being in the nest at one time. We took some of these to our chick. When the men finished their work on the dyke and left the vicinity, the cock resumed his visits, and continued each day until the chick could fly. The hen, however, lost all interest and deserted the nest entirely.

We had hoped to stay long enough to see the chick on the wing, when we felt sure that it would join the cock. Unfortunately, it was impracticable to do this and, shortly before leaving, we made arrangements with a local resident who volunteered to feed the chick as long as necessary. We paid our last visit to the chick on 21 July and as we neared the nest the cock flew over our heads, calling. Possibly because of this warning—or the presence of a stranger—the chick jumped into the air and took its first flight of about five yards. It was then forty-five days old.

Three weeks later Jim reported that he had seen the bird flying strongly. We felt amply rewarded for our trouble. In addition to securing a unique series of photographs, we were able to help rear to adolescence what was in all probability the only marsh harrier chick in the British Isles that season.

Rearing the young marsh harrier took a great deal of time but, occasionally, we managed to get a few hours off. One night Dorothy and I went 'babbing' for eels with Eddie Piggin, Ted's son. Many eels are caught in the Broads, sometimes in nets similar to those used for decoying ducks, which have a wide opening at one end and taper to a trap at the other. But the method used by many of the local residents was that known as 'babbing' which has to take place at night, because only then are eels active and feeding. At nightfall the three of us rowed out to 'Miss Turner's Island', so named because this famous Norfolk naturalist had a hut there, and anchoring close to the reeds dropped two heavy weights overboard, one at each end of the boat.

The babs were yard-long lines of worsted on which worms were threaded lengthwise. These lines were looped together and tied to a short length of fishing line attached to a small rod. A lead weight sank the bait. When we were all ready, Eddie sat at one end of the boat, Dorothy at the other and I in the middle. We cast the babs and waited, gently moving them up and down to attract the eels, and as darkness fell we could feel them biting. The art was to draw them out in one smooth quick movement before they had a chance to disentangle their small fine teeth from the worsted. At first they often escaped, but as our skill improved we landed more and more. Once they touched the bottom boards they released the bab and it was ready for use again.

When the eels were biting well I found myself in the worst position. First Eddie would catch me a smack on one side of my face with a slimy wet eel and, as I was mopping myself and recovering from this, Dorothy's would hit the other side. By the time we turned for home at 3.30 a.m. I was feeling like a jellied eel myself. It was a good catch—107 eels weighing eighteen and a half pounds.

Next morning Dorothy was initiated into the intricacies of eel-cookery. She skinned them, chopped them into two-inch chunks, sprinkled them with salt and—the whole lot jumped out of the pan. She nearly had a fit! Apparently the nerve ends of freshly caught eels remain active for some time after death.

One wet July day we were in Jim's hut at the edge of his black-currant field when we saw a strange-looking bird perched on an electricity cable. It was very erect, with a long tail, light throat and breast and a conspicuous head crest. As we watched it flew down among the bushes and back to the cable. This was repeated several times and we presumed that it was catching insects. Jim crept out of the hut and carefully stalked it by keeping a row of blackcurrant bushes between himself and the bird. He was within eight to ten yards before it flew away. It was a great spotted cuckoo—only the second time this bird has been recorded in Norfolk, and only the sixth record for the whole of the British Isles. The next time I saw one was in Spain fifteen years later.

An osprey had spent the whole of the spring and early summer at Hickling catching fish from the Broad. Its regular perch was a pole used to indicate the position of the deep channel. It sat there so long and so frequently that whenever there were ornithological visitors we could almost guarantee them a view of it. I made plans to secure photographs by building a hide on a boat anchored within range. But there was so much else to photograph that I did not do it until, one evening, I arranged with Jim to borrow a rowing boat. It was too late to take it out immediately so we left everything in readiness for the next morning. But the Army arrived even earlier than we did and spent the day hammering in hundreds of poles all over the Broad to prevent an enemy landing. Consequently with so many excellent observation points from which to fish, the osprey used whichever happened to be most convenient. I never did get its photograph.

Whenever I had a lecture engagement in Norfolk I would stay a day or two in Hickling, and in February 1942 I took Jim out for a short run in the car. As we drove slowly along between Waxham and Horsey, Jim gripped my arm and told me to stop. He pointed to something pure white perched on the top of a pole set in the sand-dunes. It was a snowy owl—the first I had seen in the wild, and through binoculars it looked beautiful. We would have loved to stalk it to get a closer view, but all the sand-dunes and beach were mined. A few minutes later we were vividly reminded of this when there was an explosion not 100 yards from where we were parked. A dog chasing a rabbit had trodden on a mine.

In May 1943 Lord Desborough, then eighty years of age, paid his last visit to Whiteslea Lodge. He came alone and Jim was to stay with him. I think Jim was worried at the thought of being on his own with the old man at night with no means of contacting anyone else in an emergency. So he invited Dorothy and me to sleep at the Lodge. This was a really pleasant interlude, and it was delightful to meet Lord Desborough, who took an immense interest in my work.

Soon after dawn there would be a knock on our bedroom window and there was Jim with a cup of tea. I quickly dressed and out we went.

These early mornings were glorious; the thick mist rising from the reed beds as in a Japanese print. We would go bird-nesting and I was amazed at Jim's ability to find them. Standing in the punt he would mark a bird down and then go unerringly to its nest. One morning he found no fewer than seven bearded tits' nests before breakfast, surely an all-time record.

Jim had a special liking for bearded tits and he had a theory about their breeding habitat. He maintained that they preferred to nest in reed-beds that were five years old. Before then the reeds were too thin, after that they were too thick and rank. So he used to burn the reeds in rotation, thus ensuring that every year at least one bed would be suitable. He certainly proved his point to me. Several times he told me that most of the bearded tits would breed on this marsh this year, and that marsh the following year. And he was always right.

We came to love Whiteslea Lodge, a bungalow made of white painted wood with a fine thatched roof. Outside a flight of steps led to a little platform at roof-level where we could look across the Broads. It is a fair-sized bungalow with four bedrooms, a bathroom, dining- and sitting-rooms, as well as the servants' quarters. To us I think the most striking feature is the bird pictures in every room. Framed reproductions from Gould's *Birds of Great Britain*, published in 1873, hang everywhere two rows deep, even in the bathroom and passages.

Pictures of birds most likely to be seen on the Broads hang in the most prominent positions. I spent hours gazing at them, learning, for example, the subtle difference between the different species of terns and warblers. The drawing-room had a most unusual frieze depicting the surrounding scenery, exquisitely painted by Roland Green. The scene outside is faithfully reproduced in this frieze, but beautifully inter-woven into it are the birds of the Broad—the harriers, bitterns, short-eared owls, ospreys, bearded tits, ducks and swans.

The first week in June of that year was memorable for the number of ornithological friends who forgathered at Hickling. The first to arrive was John Markham. Later that day Dorothy and I drove to Norwich to meet Harry Witherby. He was a tall thin man with a slight stoop, very quiet but with a commanding voice which demanded your attention. In return he always listened patiently. Witherby did more for British scientific ornithology than any other man of his time. Research worker and life-long field ornithologist, he was the founder and editor of *British Birds*, organiser of the ringing scheme run in connection with that journal, as well as editor and chief author of *The Handbook of British Birds*, which, although published between 1938 and 1941, is still regarded as the standard work on ornithology in this country.

The next day we returned to Norwich to meet Stuart Smith and

Cyril Newberry. And then George Edwards and his friend Vernon Crapnell arrived. It had taken all my persuasive powers to get lodgings for them all.

The Broads were new ground to nearly all our friends and I had a busy but enjoyable time making sure everyone had facilities for observing, studying and photographing. Jim was at first slightly taken aback to see such a large party, but he was soon enjoying himself displaying the rare and lovely birds which he had done so much to establish. He was a great showman and raconteur and everyone loved him. One evening we all gathered at his home and he read poetry to us. It was, of course, concerned with birds, some of the poems having been written by Arthur Whitaker, an authority on eggs, who was also staying at Hickling.

During this week Harry Witherby received a parcel containing one badly crushed small, white egg. In a letter the sender wrote that the egg was one of thirty-three found in a loosely constructed nest on a branch near the ground. He was completely mystified and wondered if Witherby could identify the egg. The great man was obviously puzzled. Could several birds have laid in the same nest, as sometimes happened with pheasants and partridges? We were discussing this, each putting forward his own theory, when Arthur Whitaker wandered in. 'Who's sent you a sand martin's egg?' he asked. Witherby showed him the letter, which indicated that the egg could not have come from a sand martin's burrow. Whitaker was quite unmoved; and he was right. It subsequently transpired that the village lads had raided the local sand martin colony, piled the thirty-three eggs into one nest and then boasted of their find!

Harry Witherby also received a letter from W. S. Gunton informing him that he had found the nest of a black-tailed godwit containing four eggs in Lincolnshire. Gunton had found a nest in 1940 but prior to this there had been no records of breeding in Great Britain for well over 100 years. Witherby was therefore anxious to check this observation for himself and he asked me if I could find sufficient petrol to take him, together with Jim Vincent and Dr. B. B. Riviere (author of *A History of the Birds of Norfolk*, 1930). We drove there on 5 July and, after meeting Gunton, went to the breeding area. Almost immediately a black-tailed godwit flew towards us, calling vehemently and making mock attacks. After a considerable search Gunton found one of the half-grown young crouched in dense grass. As Jim held it in his hand for me to photograph, the adults became hysterical and came so close that I was able to take several flight shots of them.

But black-tailed godwits did not breed regularly until 1952, when a nest was found, not in Lincolnshire, but on the Ouse Washes on the

Cambridge–Norfolk border. Since then their numbers have steadily increased until, by 1968, thirty-four pairs were breeding on land now owned by the RSPB and the Cambridgeshire and Isle of Ely Naturalists' Trust.

Harry Witherby had partially retired from the family publishing business in 1936, but the war forced him to return and there is little doubt that the additional work, added to his ornithological pursuits, overtaxed his strength. I am glad that I was with him at Hickling on his last day's bird-watching.

George Edwards's Yorkshire wit reduced him to helpless laughter, until at last he begged him to stop his banter. We had certainly seen this rather austere man in a different light. Shortly before his death he sent me the first twenty-four volumes of *British Birds* to make my set complete. I was proud to have been of service to him and was touched by his generosity.

As petrol was rationed we had taken our bicycles with us, and they were excellent for getting around the flat countryside. When George and Vernon Crapnell joined us they helped transport much of the equipment. One morning the three of us were pedalling down the cinder track towards Whiteslea Lodge, laden as usual, George having wedged one of my hides on his cross-bar. It slipped, causing George to swerve. He slammed on the brakes but, since only the front ones worked, he went head first over the handle-bars into the dyke with his camera and binoculars still round his neck. But my hide was safe and dry! George crawled out covered in black evil-smelling mud.

It was a grand time filled with bird study, photography, discussion and fun. After it was over and we were back home, George recaptured some of our enjoyment by sending us a caricature study of each person with a cryptic verse by the side. Here are four of them.

'Remember that first week in June
Listening to the bitterns boom,
Mixed with Spitfire and Typhoon,
At Hickling.

Dorothy we all adore,
Must be patient to the core,
Knitting hide tents by the score,
At Hickling.

Who left Markham in a hide
Surrounded by a Broadland tide?
Three more weeks, and he'd have died,
At Hickling.

Pray for Edwards on his byke,
Turned to watch a red-backed shrike,
Discovered depth of nearest dyke,
At Hickling.'

I like to think that Jim, too, enjoyed that week. He had not much longer to live, but he had no idea that death was near. As he lay dying his thoughts still turned to his favourite birds. One of the last things he said to his old friend Anthony Buxton was: 'Look after the beardeds.' He died in 1944 at the age of sixty-two, and he left a big gap in the ranks of ornithologists. So it was with pride that in 1946 Cyril Newberry and I dedicated to him our book *More Birds of the Day* (Collins). It was Jim who had made it possible for me to obtain many of the photographs that illustrate it.

9 | *Hilbre*

Some of the most interesting experiences of my life have centred on the Hilbre group of small islands in the Dee Estuary a mile off West Kirby in Cheshire. Hilbre itself occupies about twelve acres, Middle Hilbre three, and the Little Eye half an acre. In earlier times the three islands formed a single reef and even today, at low tide, they are still connected by sandstone reefs.

When the tide is out, fifty square miles of the sea-bed are firm enough to walk on. But when the waters of the Irish Sea roll in, the whole area is submerged beneath many feet of water—except for these three islands.

Long before Hilbre became famous for its natural history, it had made its mark on British history. Sheep and goat bones have been unearthed, indicating that early Britons kept domesticated animals on the island. Relics of Roman pottery have also been found, and the discovery on Middle Hilbre of a bronze axe testifies to the extreme antiquity of the human occupation of these little islands.

Hilbre also has its place in military history. In the reign of Queen Elizabeth I, about 4,000 soldiers encamped there on their way to Ireland. When the Armada threatened, Hilbre was garrisoned against attack by the Spaniards. In the Second World War a machine-gun crew was stationed there to repel any attempted landings, either from the sea or from the air. Later, Middle Hilbre was turned into a giant decoy: it was set ablaze with great oil fires to mislead the German bombers aiming for the docks at Liverpool and Birkenhead.

But whatever history's claims, Hilbre is overwhelmingly a *natural* history paradise, especially for ornithologists. In the autumn, bird migrants from the far north—many from within the Arctic Circle—having nested and reared their young, fly south; ducks and geese by the hundred, waders by the tens of thousands. At low tide in the Dee Estuary some of these migrants find a rich feeding ground: miles of

Hilbre Island: drawing by Alfred K. Wiffen

sand and mud in which the probing bills of the waders find crabs, molluscs, worms and other marine fare. Norman Ellison, in *The Wirral Peninsula* (Robert Hale, 1966), lists 204 species which have been seen on or around the islands, including three species of owl and swan, five of geese, and sixteen of duck.

The tide here has an enormous range; frequently there is a difference of thirty feet between low and high tide when everything is submerged save the three islands. Here the multitudes of birds, which have previously been widely dispersed, seek refuge from the sea, waiting until the tide recedes after replenishing their feeding ground with the sea's bounty.

As may be imagined, the water sweeps in at a dangerous pace— 10 m.p.h. at times—and men, women and children have been drowned when caught in the landward-rushing seas. Here lay the scene of Charles Kingsley's poem *The Sands of Dee* where Mary went to 'call the cattle home'.

> 'The western tide crept up along the sand,
>   And o'er and o'er the sand,
>   And round and round the sand,
>   As far as eye could see.
> The rolling mist came down and hid the land:
>   And never home came she.
>   . . . .
> But still the boatmen hear her call the cattle home,
>   Across the sands of Dee.'

I first learned about Hilbre and its surrounding bird-life in October 1945 when lecturing at West Kirby. Two authorities on the area, Bill Wilson and Norman Ellison—the BBC naturalist, Nomad—having aroused my interest, invited me to explore its ornithological and photographic possibilities. I eagerly agreed but because of other commitments a full year went by before I could go. However, I have since made up for my tardiness: I have now been to Hilbre over twenty times.

At low tide it is quite easy to walk the mile from the mainland to Hilbre across sea-sculptured sand. But with my mass of equipment plus food, water and fuel, transport was essential. In October 1946 this was not easy to find, but my resourceful hosts quickly supplied a horse and trap, although when this was loaded with the gear there was no room for passengers! So, like the benevolent magician that he was, Bill Wilson produced a second pony and trap and we made the journey in convoy.

I looked eagerly for the tens of thousands of birds that had been promised. At most there were thirty in half an hour or so. I began to wonder.

At least I could not complain of the accommodation. There would be no question of roughing it. There was a house, outbuildings and a delightful bungalow occupied by Dr. and Mrs. Lewis McAfee, where we stayed. What the members of the various Hilbre parties owe to this charming couple is known only to those who have enjoyed their hospitality.

Here I must again refer to Bill Wilson, now alas no longer with us. He was the largest man I have ever known, standing six feet four inches, extremely broad in proportion, and weighing over twenty stone.

Nothing was ever too much trouble for Bill, as I discovered on my first morning at Hilbre. I was to photograph on the Little Eye, a soggy mile away across soft-yielding mud, water-filled gullies and slippery rocks. I had visions of a bird photographer, his weight doubled with equipment, disappearing without trace in a quicksand in the Dee Estuary. I had reckoned without Big Bill. He tied two hides together and slung them over one shoulder; a third hide, tripods and seats went over the other and each huge hand carried several cameras. Then it was Norman Ellison's turn. By the time we had finished with him he was festooned like a Christmas tree, decorated with hammers, chisels, guy-ropes, staking irons and other impedimenta.

I brought up the rear with a ruck-sack containing, among other things, the all-important sandwiches and tea flask. Bird photography, especially of the Hilbre variety, is thirsty work.

It took the three of us forty-five minutes to walk to the Little Eye. I slithered and sloshed along and, although carrying the lightest load, I had difficulty in keeping up with Bill and Norman.

When we arrived the tide—and the birds—were far out; the Little Eye was a tiny oasis of eroded red sandstone in a vast expanse of mud and sand. But, unless we were very unfortunate, as the tide encroached we should be surrounded by a great multitude of birds. The problem was where to put the hides. If beyond the highest reach of the tide we should see the birds only in the distance, if too near the tide-line we, and the precious cameras, would get soaked—if nothing worse. If high tide were fairly constant there would be no problem, but the Hilbre tides are variable. There can be a range of several feet between one tide and the next owing to differences in strength and direction of the wind, and in barometric pressure. The problem was complicated for me because I was then using a quarter-plate camera with an eight-and-a-half-inch lens, which meant that birds nearest to the camera should come within six to eight feet of the hide.

Bill was the expert on tides and he advised us where to place the three hides. Red sandstone is fairly soft but it took nearly an hour to chisel out the holes for the supports. By the time these were erected and secured to rocks with ropes to prevent the canvas flapping in the wind, one and a half hours had elapsed and the tide was coming in rapidly.

Then for the first unforgettable time I witnessed the 'build-up'. The swift incoming tide inexorably drives the birds from their vast feeding grounds towards the islands, the only dry land before the distant thickly populated coast. If nothing scares them, thousands upon thousands converge on the Little Eye, which seems to be the most favoured spot. Rocky fingers extend from the island and the birds first settle on these. As the rising tide gradually submerges these rocky outcrops the birds farthest out leap-frog over their companions, the great concourse of birds slowly converging on the island. This is the build-up, and the higher the water rises, the more excited do the birds become. They are torn between the desire to continue feeding on the fast shrinking strip of sand, and the need to shelter on the island from the rapidly encroaching tide. They are never still, never quiet. They quarrel continuously. Nothing must disturb them now, or they will immediately fly away.

Occasionally I have witnessed what Niko Tinbergen calls 'a dread', a sudden panic that flashes through the vast flocks which then spontaneously erupt in an explosion of wings. The sudden sight of a man, the stoop of a peregrine falcon, a loud noise, sometimes for no apparent reason at all, and the flocks will panic away.

But on my first day, no 'dread' dispersed the birds. What had sounded like a high-pitched hum in the distance slowly became a deafening cacophony as the birds reached the island. Every bird seemed to be calling at the top of its voice. The noise was so great that I could have shouted and not been heard. Almost before I realised it our hides had become three small islands in this sea of birds. So close were they that some of them actually pressed against the hide. Some 15,000 birds were standing on half an acre of rock.

Almost all were waders—dunlins, knots, sanderlings and redshanks were nearest, while on the perimeter were turnstones, oystercatchers and curlews.

The birds were so closely packed that it seemed impossible for another bird to squeeze in, yet first five bar-tailed godwits alighted, and then a large pack of knots tumbled out of the sky like a flurry of autumn leaves. The rock was already so jam-packed with knots that many of the new arrivals had to stand on the backs of other birds until they could fight and shove their way to the ground. For the first time

Above: The Hickling party, June 1943. *Left to right:* John Markham, Cyril Newberry, Arthur Whitaker, Jim Vincent, Harry Witherby (sitting), Vernon Crapnell, E. H., Dr. Stuart Smith, and George Edwards. Dorothy took the picture

Below: For two days water rails nesting in a Hickling reed bed were seen pushing sedge under the nest cup until it was raised some twelve inches. The following night torrential rain flooded the marshes—but this nest was undamaged

Above: When I first visited Hilbre in 1946 this was how we travelled from West Kirby

Left: The first Hilbre party—with Bill Wilson and Norman Ellison

Below: Shelling shrimps. *Left to right:* Dr. Grant McAfee, Bill Wilson, Jerry Jamieson (half hidden), Dr. Lewis McAfee, Norman Ellison, Ronnie Pryor, Joe Wells and Lord Alanbrooke

I realised why the noun of assembly for knots is 'pack'. The birds near me were so crowded that it would have been impossible to slip a sheet of paper between one bird and the next. It is said that occasionally a single pack of knots in the Dee Estuary has numbered 50,000. I believe it.

Never in a quarter of a century's bird photography had I seen anything to equal this spectacle. I was *so* excited that perspiration trickled down my forehead and into my eye—I could hardly see to focus. I went trigger-happy. Before realising it I had exposed all my plates. It was only then that I noticed a dramatic change had come over the birds. They were all silent, fast asleep, bill tucked into the scapular feathers. I could have heard a pin drop—if there had been room enough to drop one. It was as if the birds knew that the tide would rise no farther and they were safe. There was little fear of a 'dread' now. I could talk, move about, drop things—provided I stayed in the hide the birds took no notice.

Philosophers talk of the relativity of time; I experienced it then. I had been so absorbed that time meant nothing, and was surprised to find that four hours had passed. Never had I known time pass so quickly.

But the spectacle was not over yet. The tide was now ebbing and the birds began to wake and run to the water's edge to bathe and feed. I prepared to take the final photographs which were to be of the birds in flight. For flight shots I was using a 35 mm Contax fitted with a 135 mm telephoto lens and, fortunately, there was still film for this camera.

When all was set I crawled out of the hide and stood up, camera at the ready. There was a tremendous roar as many thousands of birds rose simultaneously into the air. A few resettled after a short flight but the smaller waders—knots, dunlins and sanderlings—flew out to sea and gave a wonderful display. One moment they appeared as an undulating snake-like cloud thirty feet deep, the lowest birds but a few feet above the surface of the sea, the next, the flock flashed silver as the birds turned and wheeled. Then they dipped, and so great was their mass and weight that the birds at the bottom were forced beneath the water. As the flock rose again these sprang up, shook themselves and rejoined the rest. The final shots of these aerobatics completed my photographic bag for the day. Hilbre had lived up to its reputation.

There was an interesting confirmation that I did not exaggerate the numbers of birds on the Little Eye. From the negative of a tightly packed mass of waders I made an outsize enlargement and gave it to a friend. He spent an afternoon counting—there were 1,500 birds in the

K

photograph. And that was of only a fraction of the flock. We estimated that at the time the photograph was taken there were at least 15,000 birds on the island.

Since then I have been back to Hilbre many times and do not know which has given me the most enjoyment: the birds, the photography or the comradeship. For after that first visit there sprang up what came to be known as the Hilbre Party, strictly all-male. The party consisted of Bill and Norman (naturalists), Ronald Pryor and Joe Wells (engineers), Grant McAfee (doctor), John Craggs (physicist) and Alfred Wiffen (art master).

After we had been going regularly each spring and autumn for three years we thought of inviting some celebrities to join us, men for whom birding was a relaxation in their busy lives. Talking round the fire one evening in October 1949 Bill suddenly said: 'You know Lord Alanbrooke. He is keen on birds, isn't he, and loves filming them? Why don't you invite him to come to Hilbre?' Actually, the idea had already occurred to me—but, well, he *was* a Field Marshal, Churchill's chief military adviser during the war and Chief of the Imperial General Staff, the man of whom Lord Montgomery said: 'He was the greatest soldier, sailor or airman produced by any country taking part in the last war.' But how would he fit in? I pointed out that while living conditions on Hilbre were comfortable, no one could call them luxurious. We did all our own cooking and washing-up, and made our own somewhat hard beds. But Bill quite rightly declared that Lord Alanbrooke was a soldier and was certainly used to hard conditions. 'I bet he has known darned harder beds and poorer food than he will get here.'

So on my return to London I wrote to Lord Alanbrooke, inviting him to join the Hilbre party in April 1950. By return post came an enthusiastic acceptance. We met at Waterloo station and drove the 200 miles to West Kirby. I wish there had been a tape-recorder in the car. The Field Marshal was a remarkably interesting and amusing conversationalist and, to quote *The Times* obituary notice, 'when relaxed he was no respecter of persons or indeed of reputations'. Despite his immense and well-earned reputation he was a most modest man and rarely spoke about himself.

The morning after Lord Alanbrooke's arrival I was up early and was dismayed to find that a full gale was blowing. Under such conditions a journey to the Little Eye was impossible. Fortunately, we had foreseen this possibility and erected a hide at the foot of a cliff on the lee side of Hilbre. We installed our guest, then the rest of us walked round the island, driving the birds, mostly turnstones and purple sandpipers, towards him. This was not as easy as it sounds, for the wind was really terrific, at times almost blowing us off our feet.

We realised that under the exceptional conditions the tide would rise higher than usual on the lee side of the island, and unless we did something about it quickly there was a distinct possibility of Lord Alanbrooke drowning—there would be water on three sides of him, a steep cliff behind. We had uneasy visions of the history books recording how one of Britain's greatest soldiers met an inglorious death by drowning in a tent on a beach through the carelessness of a bunch of amateur ornithologists.

Bill went into action. Since the shore was now submerged, it was impossible to reach the hide except by lowering a ladder down the twenty-foot-high cliff. I climbed down, to find the Field Marshal quite unperturbed, although the sea was already lapping against his hide. As there was still half an hour to go before high tide our fears were obviously justified. After we had clambered up the cliff to safety we suggested that he might like a drink and a rest, but he said that he would rather stalk the waders with his cine-camera before the tide went out.

So ended Lord Alanbrooke's first day's filming at Hilbre and I am afraid conditions during the rest of his six-day stay were not much better. I was, therefore, both surprised and relieved to receive a letter from him on his return in which, among other kindly things, he said:

'I do not know how to thank you enough for that wonderful trip to Hilbre Island. I have seldom enjoyed six days more and am most grateful to you for all your kindness and hospitality which made this trip possible. I shall never forget the sight of all those birds, it was quite beautiful. I am looking forward to our next trip.'

The letter was so typical of Lord Alanbrooke. Nothing that was done for him, however trivial, went unappreciated. I have never forgotten a little incident that happened when we were in the Savoy Hotel. He wanted to go up in the lift and the attendant opened the doors, stepped out and ushered us in. As we reached our floor the liftman opened the doors and I prepared to walk out. But Lord Alanbrooke stopped, looked the man straight in the eyes and said: 'Thank you very much.' Similarly, whenever he returned after a trip to Hilbre, he wrote as soon as he got home and thanked me. He often dropped into my house for a cup of tea, and always the visit was followed by a thank-you note.

Altogether Lord Alanbrooke joined the Hilbre party seven times, the last being in October 1955.

It would be pleasant to recapture something of those long evenings when, gathered round the fire in the living-room, Lord Alanbrooke regaled us with stories from his long adventurous life. With the Irish brogue he could affect at will, his gift of mimicry and a vast fund of anecdote, he was wonderful company. Yes, if only there had been a tape-recorder . . .

We had great fun together. Many who saw the Field Marshal only on official occasions thought that he was haughty and forbidding. That was not the man I knew, and I was his friend for twenty years, sometimes spending weeks with him on expeditions in remote areas where you really get to know a man. Certainly at Hilbre he behaved like a high-spirited boy at times.

There was an amusing incident when he arrived one day at the island, just after he had been appointed Constable of the Tower of London. We decided to give him a welcome appropriate to his new status. First a tattered flag was broken on a miniature flag-pole. An ancient bugle sounded the general salute, and then one of the 'natives' walked up to the Field Marshal bearing a moth-eaten cushion on which reposed the key of the bungalow. We also tried to fire a salute on an ancient naval cannon, but the home-made charge just fizzled out.

The Master Gunner later got his own back. After we had jokingly complained about the advantages lords enjoyed over commoners he said: 'I will soon cure that. Kneel down, Hosking.' He then took a battered bayonet that we used for poking the fire, dubbed me on the shoulders, and said: 'Rise, Lord Hilbre.' Yes, it was childish but it was darned good fun.

I never think of Hilbre now without recalling two men who helped to make my trips so memorable: Lord Alanbrooke and Bill Wilson. Both are now gone but, for me, their friendly shades still walk the sands of Dee.

On a memorable Hilbre party in October 1952 we had both Lord Alanbrooke, to my mind the world's greatest soldier, and Dr. Roger Tory Peterson, to me the world's greatest ornithologist. It was Roger who invented the identification key whereby the distinguishing features of a bird are arrowed in the illustrations. This system has been used in the successful series of Field Guides to the birds of various countries.

Never have I known a more dedicated bird man than Roger—and I have known scores in a dozen countries. He just lives, thinks, reads, talks, paints, films and photographs birds, and is so utterly devoted to ornithology that, apart from his family, he appears to be interested in little else.

Roger's one-track mind was amusingly demonstrated one evening as we sat chatting and reminiscing after a day with the waders. Roger had been completely surrounded by a large flock of oystercatchers. He was painting the plates for *A Field Guide to the Birds of Britain and Europe* (Collins, 1967), written in collaboration with Guy Mountfort and Phil Hollom, and on this occasion he was working on the plate which included the oystercatcher. He had revelled in the experience and for a time all the talk was about these birds.

But somehow, as is the way with conversations, the talk gradually broadened and in a short time we were with Alanbrooke, Churchill and Stalin in the Kremlin during a tense scene in the war. We were enthralled. Alanbrooke vividly described the night before the British delegation was to fly home. He, Churchill and Stalin, with an interpreter, were sitting round a table sipping vodka when, suddenly, Stalin shook his fist at Churchill, swore, and demanded to know when the British were going to start fighting.

The effect on Churchill was explosive. He crashed his fist on the table and lit into Stalin with a burst of impassioned oratory. Stalin listened for a minute or two, then, with a broad grin on his face, stood up, stopped Churchill's interpreter, and through his own said: 'I do not understand what you are saying, but by God I like your sentiment!'

While the rest of us hung on his words I happened to glance across at Roger and there seemed to be a glazed look about his eyes. He was not with us at all; he was still with his beloved oystercatchers. When Alanbrooke's wonderful story was done, and there was a slight pause, Roger spoke—'Y'know, I guess these oystercatchers eat most any mollusc.'

But Roger, unlike some other single-minded individuals, is far from a bore. Quite the reverse. He shares his vast knowledge and experience of birds with an infectious enthusiasm which I, at any rate, find utterly absorbing. To anyone interested in birds there is never a dull moment in Roger's company, and I would gladly listen to him for hours.

During one washing-up session Roger and Lord Alanbrooke were talking together and General Eisenhower was mentioned. And thereby hangs a story.

A rather mysterious rumour circulated during the war that on one occasion General Eisenhower had issued orders that a certain bird book was to be procured in America and air-mailed to him immediately. Was the General as interested in birds as that—and in the middle of the most fearsome war in history? Roger had heard this rumour and he thought Alanbrooke might be able to enlighten him. Hence the conversation.

The Field Marshal told Roger that he did not think General Eisenhower was particularly interested in birds, but he recalled that during the North African campaign Eisenhower had presented him with the National Geographic Society's two-volume *Book of Birds*.

This was the clue Roger wanted. Back in New York he was at luncheon with Gilbert Grosvenor, then President of the National Geographic Society, and from him Roger heard the other end of the story. During the African campaign Eisenhower and Alanbrooke were in close professional accord, but, while their personal relations were friendly enough, there was a touch of formality about them. Then one day Alanbrooke happened to mention to Eisenhower that he had tried to get the *Book of Birds* but had been told it was out of print. That was enough for the General—hence the order that started the rumour.

Within two days a copy of the book had been located in the States, flown across the Atlantic, and delivered to Alanbrooke with Eisenhower's compliments. That was the end of any trace of formality between these two great soldiers; from then on it was 'Brookie' and 'Ike'.

Incidentally, when *Birds of the Day* (Collins, 1944), which Cyril Newberry and I wrote, was published, Lord Montgomery sent a copy to Lord Alanbrooke inscribed: 'To Brookie with very best wishes from Monty'. I wonder where that book is now? I would love to lay my hands on it.

Another veteran of the war who found relaxation at Hilbre was Admiral Sir William Tennant. Although always pleasant, he spent much time alone, seemingly content just to watch the teeming bird-life of the islands. He was a silent man—at least compared with Lord Alanbrooke—and we never really knew him. It was not until I read his obituary notice in *The Times* that I realised he was a leading figure in the greatest naval tragedy of the last war. Sir William commanded the battle-cruiser *Repulse* when, with the battleship *Prince of Wales*, she was sunk in the Pacific by Japanese air attack on 10 December 1941.

Undoubtedly our most famous visitor was Prince Philip. But first I must go back a little. When Prince Philip's book *Birds from Britannia* was published I was asked to speak about it on television. He saw the programme and was interested in some of my remarks.

A few days later I was in my dark-room when the telephone rang. There is a strict rule in our household that when Eric is developing or printing he is not to be disturbed for anyone. So Dorothy answered.

'This is the Duke of Edinburgh's office,' said a voice. 'Prince Philip's equerry would like to speak to Mr. Hosking.'

The rule was broken—I spoke. As a meeting had been cancelled, the Prince had a few hours to spare and would like to see me.

I was in no sartorial state to meet Royalty—I wear my oldest clothes in the dark-room because of acid developers—but I said yes and changed immediately. As my Rolls* (at least I had the right car!) drew up outside Buckingham Palace the police saluted. Surely I was not so well known as that? No, they had been given the number of my car. I was taken straight to the Prince's equerry, Squadron Leader David Checketts. We talked for a few minutes, then I was shown into the Prince's book-lined study.

The Prince and I talked bird photography for just over an hour and before leaving I suggested that, to learn some of the finer points of the art, the best plan would be for him to spend some time with me in the field. He was eager to do this and it was left to me to arrange a trip.

A few months later at a Hilbre party Joe Wells said to me: 'You have brought quite a few famous people to Hilbre, who will you bring next?'

For a bit of fun I replied: 'Prince Philip, if you like.' I never thought I would be taken seriously, but the point was pressed home. So on my return I wrote to David Checketts.

Arrangements were made for Prince Philip to join the party from 10 to 13 October 1965, but then we wondered if we had taken on more than we could manage. There were three important conditions for success: absolute secrecy, fine weather, and plenty of birds, none of which we could control.

How do you keep a Royal visit secret? 'The fierce light that beats upon a throne' extends to the Queen's Consort, and protocol must be observed. Obviously the fewer people who knew about it the better, but whenever Royalty visits a county the Lord Lieutenant has to be notified, and he in turn notifies other officials and the police, so that eventually about twenty people are in the secret.

Prince Philip would have to leave the island by helicopter at midday on 13 October, as he had to open the British Trades Fair in Milan that evening, and was to join the aircraft of the Queen's Flight at Hawarden aerodrome. The pilot of the vivid red Royal helicopter wished to make a trial landing on the island ten days beforehand—would it be spotted by the local people or press? If so, they would want to know what it was all about. We could only hope for the best. The trouble was that the Little Eye, where we wanted Prince Philip to occupy a hide, was so small that even one intruder would keep all the birds away and ruin the chances of photography.

The final plans were made. Prince Philip was driving from Balmoral, and we arranged that we should meet at 7.30 p.m. by the 30 m.p.h. speed-limit sign leading into West Kirby on the Chester side. Lewis McAfee and I would sit in our car while David Checketts and Detective

* Incidentally, I have had only two cars in thirty-four years: the Rolls and a Rover, in which I travelled 300,000 miles in eighteen years.

Inspector Ivor Thorning, who would arrive from London a little earlier, would wait in their car a hundred yards farther up the road. As the Royal car passed them they would signal with their headlights and we would then pull away as Prince Philip reached us. This would save any introductions in the road and minimise the risk of the Royal car being recognised.

All was going well. The weather and forecast were good. There were lots of birds about. No one seemed to have spotted the Royal helicopter during its trial landing. The fact that we had erected two hides on the Little Eye had apparently not been noticed.

At 7.15 p.m. we were in position. We did not really expect His Royal Highness to arrive by seven-thirty, but when there was still no sign by seven-forty-five and then eight I was worried. The last possible moment for crossing to Hilbre was 9 p.m., after that the tide would be too high. What were we going to do if Prince Philip did not arrive until after that? Even a Royal car can have a breakdown. Accommodation would have to be found not only for the Duke but for Checketts, Thorning, the chauffeur and myself. But Lewis did not seem to be the least bit worried—beds for everyone had been prepared at his house.

I was getting more and more worried when there was a sudden flashing of lights and almost immediately the Royal car slowed down behind us. Lewis and I started off and the rest followed in convoy. It was eight-twenty, still time to get across to Hilbre.

Lewis had thought out every detail and had arranged for two Land Rovers to be available, one for luggage, one for passengers. This also covered a possible emergency—if one car got bogged down the other would be able to pack in passengers as well as luggage.

A full moon shone from a cloudless sky. As soon as we left the foreshore and got on to the sand all car lights were switched off, for lights heading towards Hilbre at night might arouse suspicion. As we drove across the sand and shingle by moonlight I think Prince Philip wondered what he had let himself in for. But he was in excellent form and wanted to know what the prospects were for bird photography next day.

It was quite late before we finally turned in. The next morning I took Prince Philip a cup of tea at seven-forty-five and by nine-thirty we had breakfasted and were off in a Land Rover to the Little Eye. It was a glorious day—fine, calm and quite mild with only a few patches of cloud scattered in a clear blue sky. The secrecy and the weather were OK—but would the birds realise the importance of the occasion?

The Duke went into the hide covering the best position. The Land Rover left and we were on our own. I reflected that I, who had once had the rare experience of lifting my future sovereign off the ground

Prince Philip on the Little Eye

Above: The start of the build-up. A pack of knots fly in to join their companions alongside dunlins, redshanks, bar-tailed godwits and a curlew

Below: A flock of oystercatchers come within camera range of the hide

Above: Part of the 5,000 knots, plus two oystercatchers *(top left)* waiting for the tide to turn on the Little Eye. Not surprisingly, the noun of assembly for knots is 'pack'

Below: The pack in full flight. 'They appeared as an undulating snake-like cloud thirty feet deep, the lowest birds but a few feet above the surface of the sea.'

Above: Roger Tory Peterson at work at Hilbre. This painting was subsequently reproduced in *A Field Guide to the Birds of Britain and Europe*

Below: Writing home

on to a horse, now had the equally rare experience of spending six hours alone with her husband on an uninhabited island.

The tide was coming in, and although the sea was still distant, we could see that the oystercatchers were disturbed. Soon the birds began to congregate at the end of the strip of land on the north-west of the island. The 'build-up' increased and now the oystercatchers were jostling each other and moving nearer. A flock of about seventy bar-tailed godwits alighted; the most I had seen in front of a hide. Knots and dunlins and over 200 redshanks stood about in the shallows, and a sprinkling of sanderlings looked lovely in their white winter plumage. In deeper water, stalking on their long legs, were about 150 curlews.

The high barometric pressure prevented the tide from coming in as much as usual so the birds were rather far from the hides, but a constant clicking indicated that Prince Philip was busy. He told me afterwards that he had had a wonderful time and that there had been so many birds to photograph he hardly knew where to start.

After being cramped in the hides for so long we decided to walk back to Hilbre; the Land Rover would transport our equipment. I shall never forget the Prince's tremendous enthusiasm. No sooner had we reached the main island than he was off in the motor-boat with Lewis McAfee on a shrimping expedition. This was done by trailing a net behind a motor-boat driven very slowly. Every time the net is hauled in over the stern the shrimps are riddled to sort out the small ones, which fall back into the water. Prince Philip riddled away with the best of them. When the shrimps are boiled they are then shelled. Here Prince Philip thought a little time-and-motion study was called for, and was full of ideas on how the process could be done more efficiently. But we noticed that when things went wrong, and the 'improved' technique resulted in a broken shrimp, this was quickly popped into his mouth.

In the evening we showed some of the Field Marshal's Hilbre films, kindly lent by Lady Alanbrooke, and also some by Ronnie Pryor.

The next day followed a similar pattern, and then, all too quickly, another Hilbre party came to an end. (But Prince Philip enjoyed it so much that he came again in 1967 and 1970—and I hope he will continue to come.) He was due in Milan on the evening of the 13th and at twelve-ten the red helicopter that was to take him to Hawarden aerodrome arrived. The final goodbyes were said, the Prince climbed into the pilot's seat, and he was away.

As the helicopter flew off I thought of the three conditions necessary for the success of the visit: secrecy, weather, birds. All were fulfilled—just. An alert *Liverpool Daily Post* reporter, noticing unusual police activity on the mainland, risked his life to beat the tide and come out to Hilbre—eight hours after the Prince had left. His story began: 'It was Merseyside's best-kept secret of the year.' The weather had been perfect, the best I had known on Hilbre. And the birds had put on a show fitting for one who, probably more than any previous member of the Royal family, has shown such interest and concern for their welfare.

10 | *Minsmere*

The old car ground to a halt by the beach at Sizewell on the Suffolk coast. Cyril and I had driven from Staverton Park in June 1933 to see if we could locate nests of some little terns that George Bird had told us nested on this strip of coastline. Leaving the car, we walked northwards along the foreshore watching the birds carefully through our binoculars. Although we saw several pairs of little terns we had gone nearly three miles before we located a nest, and then being near Minsmere cliffs we decided to see the view from this higher level.

Little did we think as we surveyed the surroundings that the agricultural and pasture land to the south of us would one day become the most famous bird sanctuary in the British Isles. Curiously, had it not been for the war, it might never have become a sanctuary at all. In June 1940, as part of the coastal defences, the area was flooded, and it was not until five years later that the sluices, which had been kept closed, returned to normal operation. In the meantime, a large reedmarsh had grown, providing a new habitat for marshland birds. Then, in 1948, Minsmere was leased from Captain Stuart Ogilvie to the Royal Society for the Protection of Birds, and Dick Wolfendale became the first warden.

Apart from the marshes the Minsmere reserve comprises three other main types of habitat—shore, heath and woodland. Altogether they support a wealth and variety of bird-life that is unequalled by any other area of its size in the country. No fewer than ninety-eight bird species breed here annually and over 210 species are recorded each year.

In 1950 the Society allowed George Edwards and me to photograph birds in the sanctuary. We stayed in Westleton, two miles away. Our first evening stroll gave us a clue to what we might expect. We heard a bittern boom, the squealing of a water rail, and along a path between two reed-beds watched bearded tits. Quartering the ground, just above the tops of the tall reeds, was a marsh harrier, while perched on the top of a dead tree on the edge of the woods was a peregrine falcon. We saw or heard all these within half an hour of our first visit.

But although I delight to see and hear such rarities, I am equally fond of watching and listening to the common species. South Wood was alive with song—at least five pairs of nightingales were singing against each other, stimulating garden warblers, song and mistle thrushes, blackbirds, willow warblers and blackcaps to join the chorus. And just outside the narrow belt of woods the sweet song of the wood lark completed the symphony.

It took only a few days to locate the nests of some of the birds we wanted to photograph. Sitting on the hill to the north of the marsh we watched a bittern drop into the reeds and, as I directed him, George went almost straight to the nest, which contained three young looking like ginger golliwogs. Some bearded tits had young already on the wing but George managed to locate a nest with five eggs—these tits sometimes have three broods in a season. We also found nests of little grebes, sedge warblers, coots and reed buntings.

On the heath we watched a stone curlew creep from its two eggs and a wheatear carry food into a rabbit hole. We found that the wood lark, whose song had so attracted us, had four well-grown young in a carefully concealed nest. Other nests of particular interest to us were those of stonechats, nightingales, red-backed shrikes, yellow wagtails and reed warblers. We erected hides at many and gradually worked them into position. It is well worth while erecting a large number of hides when working on a reserve like this—the birds regard them as part of the landscape and behave quite naturally.

One of the first hides I occupied was at a bearded tit's nest containing five young. The adults were bringing bills-full of black flies every few minutes. After an intensive feeding period of about an hour, both adults took time off and presumably went to feed themselves. During one such interval a chick squealed and I saw the head of a rat pushing its snout through the rear of the nest. Its body was completely hidden but I could see it had seized the leg of one of the young. I bawled out as loud as I could, at the same time trying to unfasten the back of the hide which George had securely closed. I struggled frantically as the chick continued to squeal. Eventually I got out and the rat shot off, leaving the young behind. I thought it would come back and not only kill this chick, but the others also. I waited in the hide for an hour, armed with a stout stick, but it did not return.

Then I hurried over to the warden's hut and asked Dick Wolfendale to keep watch while I found the gamekeeper, from whom I borrowed a trap. It was a delicate job setting this in a position where it would catch the rat but not the bearded tits. The next morning three of the

young had gone but the rat was dead in the trap. The remaining chicks
were safely reared.

We noticed that large parties of sand martins—about 500 altogether
—were on an island of reeds on one of the meres and decided to
photograph them. We built a platform and secured it in position,
several times sinking into the mud until our waders were filled with
black water.

While the sun was hidden behind the clouds, the martins rested on
the reeds. But when the sun appeared nearly all took flight. Why?
Then I saw; as soon as the sun came out myriads of flies rose in
clouds from the reeds and the martins made the most of this banquet.

About this time Charles Tunnicliffe, one of our finest bird artists,
came to stay and he showed me a portrait of a bittern he was painting.
He seemed to know that something was wrong and asked my opinion.
I said that the position of the eyes was inaccurate. He had used the skin
of a bittern as a basis for his sketches and this, of course, did not show
the eyes, which are not right on the sides of its head but slightly forward
of that position—the bird is a trifle boss-eyed. As I had a hide at a
bittern's nest I suggested to Charles that he should use it.

When I returned for him a couple of hours later he was as excited
as a schoolboy. Never before had he seen a bittern at such close range.
Jokingly I told him that would cost him a small painting, say about
postcard size. He readily agreed. When he heard that I had a hide at a
stone curlew's nest he hinted that he would like to watch from this
also, and again he was thrilled. We decided the painting would now
have to be a little larger, and so it went on until by the time Charles
left Minsmere the promised painting had grown to something like
6 ft. × 4 ft.!

Obviously I intended all this purely as a joke and had almost
forgotten the incident when, about two months later, a large parcel
arrived containing a superb painting of a long-eared owl—not
6 ft. × 4 ft., it is true, but a good deal larger than postcard size. It
remains one of my most treasured possessions.

Once when I was in the bittern hide the hen seemed to be dozing
off, when she suddenly became alert and looked intently into the reeds
behind the nest. She softly called *ik-ik-ik*, frequently repeating it with
partly opened bill. From somewhere in the reeds came a reply which
I can only describe as a grunt. The hen brought forward her mantle,
like a ruff, and quivered her feathers with a distinct rustling sound.

Then I noticed another bittern, no more than six feet away, only
just visible in the reeds and harmonising perfectly with them. As it took
a step towards the nest the hen rose and adopted a full aggressive pose,
fluffing out her feathers until she looked twice her normal size. The

intruder, which I feel sure was a cock, turned and moved away. The hen relaxed and resumed brooding. For once in my lifetime I was so fascinated by this extraordinary performance that I completely forgot to use the camera!

Ludwig Koch visited us to make recordings of a water rail. We ran out about 100 yards of cable, and placed the microphone in a reed-bed near the spot where we had last heard the bird call. This was before the days of parabolic reflectors, which, of course, concentrate the sound. Ludwig said that he would give us a signal to come away when he was ready to record, but while we were waiting the rail began to call, and Ludwig became so excited that he forgot to signal and began recording. Unfortunately, he also recorded our voices, including such remarks as however much longer was the silly old so-and-so going to take—we, of course, thinking he was still adjusting his apparatus.

The microphone was extremely sensitive: one recording had been spoilt by the noise of pebbles running down a far-distant beach. Now, every time our boots crunched the reeds a few feet from the microphone, the sound produced at Ludwig's end was like gunfire. He, of course, failed to understand why we did not come away and, dancing with rage, shouted: 'Why do zey not shut up ven zer water rail she is sinking.' Ludwig's English, original at any time, tends to incoherence when he is excited.

Another scarce species we photographed was the grasshopper warbler. This was more of an achievement than it sounds, for in my experience it is more difficult to find one of these nests than that of any other passerine. It builds in dense rank vegetation where it is easy to pass within inches of the nest and not see it. It plays every trick in the book. A skylark's nest is easy to find; watch where the bird rises and there, generally quite near, is the nest. Watch where a reed warbler carries nesting materials and there will be the nest among the reed stalks. Watch where a redstart with food disappears inside the hole in a tree and there is its nest. Not so the grasshopper warbler. Before feeding its young, not only does it alight some distance away from the nest but having fed them it moves several feet before taking off.

Once the nest is found, the grasshopper warblers are usually very tame. George lay down within a few inches of the nest and the birds still fed the young, one of them even pecking at his finger when he put it too near the nest. Subsequently he stroked an adult's breast feathers as it attended the young.

In 1947, after an absence of about a hundred years as a regular breeding species, avocets returned to this country to nest. Four pairs settled at Minsmere, while another four went to Havergate Island a few miles to the south. They all reared young and returned the following year. Unfortunately the water conditions, on which they depend for their food, had become unsuitable at Minsmere so all the avocets went to Havergate. Here the breeding colony steadily increased in numbers, although one year rats played havoc and destroyed most of the nests. In 1950 discussions took place with Philip Brown, then Secretary of the RSPB, and permission was given to Tom Fowler, Alec Robertson, George Edwards and me to take a series of photographs and a film, and for Ludwig Koch to make sound recordings. Obviously the welfare of the birds must come first, yet a film and a series of attractive photographs of these waders nesting on one of the Society's reserves would be excellent publicity.

We waited for a fine warm day so that even if the birds left while we were erecting the hide, the eggs would not become chilled. Every detail was worked out with almost military precision. The nest we were going to photograph was pin-pointed, the place where we would first erect the hide fifty yards from the nest was selected. The route we were to take was carefully worked out; the deep dykes made it impossible to walk in a direct line and we had to skirt these. Our plans were made as we sat in the observation hut which had been built by the RSPB for visitors to be able to watch the nineteen pairs of avocets. To reduce disturbance to a minimum it was decided that George and I would erect the hide on our own. Philip allowed us twenty minutes from the time of leaving the hut to the time we returned. We took seventeen minutes and before we got back the avocets were all again on their nests.

On subsequent days we had to drive from Minsmere to Orford, meet Reg Partridge—the RSPB Warden for Havergate—who ferried us in his boat to the island, move up the hide a few yards and hurry away again. Now that we had been given permission we felt that bird photographers were on their mettle and if anything went wrong we should bring disrepute on all our clan.

At last the day came when everything was in readiness for photography and George and I set out for the hide. We were loaded down with photographic equipment, which made the journey somewhat difficult as the whole area was covered with mud, slippery as ice in places, and there were holes of assorted sizes where bombs had been dropped during the war.

Once in the hide the camera was fitted up as quickly as possible but somehow the excitement of the occasion made this more difficult than usual. My heart seemed to beat at twice its normal rate, perspiration blinded me; I found it hard to focus accurately and I was generally fumble-fisted. No sooner had George left me than I began to worry. Would I make a complete hash of it? Then suddenly a black, upcurved bill came into view, followed by a lovely black and white head and body on two beautiful slate-blue legs. When close to the nest the bird hesitated—and my heart seemed to stop beating. Was she nervous? But after a second's hesitation she was incubating the eggs.

In all I spent most of nine days in that hide, taking as complete a series of photographs of the avocets' family life as I could. A careful check was kept on the eggs so that photographs could be taken of the hatch, which took place on 24 June. It was thrilling and beautiful to watch. It is easy to become sentimental and anthropomorphic, but I am sure that no father could have been more excited than the cock. He was on the nest and as he raised his body I saw the first chick push the top off the shell. At this the cock called wildly and kept jerking his head up and down. The hen arrived and the two birds stood side by side surveying their offspring.

It was now late in the nesting season and young birds were to be seen everywhere. During the past few weeks starlings had been congregating at Minsmere, and towards dusk thousands made spectacular roosting flights and noisily assembled in one of the thick reed-beds. As they fell asleep, all was quiet on the marshes.

In 1959, after Dick Wolfendale retired, Bert Axell became warden at Minsmere. Thousands of people now visit it every year, many more read about it, and see it on film. Its fame has reached far beyond these islands and the RSPB are justly proud of it. Many people have met the man who has done more than anyone else to make this reserve what it is today—but how many people really *know* him? The tall, smiling, tanned, cultured man who greets you so heartily will talk about any aspect of ornithology by the hour, if you both have the time, but is reluctant to tell you anything about himself. After a fine war record, followed by four years with the Postal Services Department in London, he went through a period of ill-health and doctors warned him that he should work in the open air.

The GPO's loss was the RSPB's gain and in 1952 Bert began by re-creating their reserve at Dungeness in Kent. This was his home ground, he knew the birds and their habits, and he put all his expertise and effort into it.* Outside the breeding season his spare time was devoted to the establishment of Dungeness Bird Observatory in adjacent ground close to the Point, where large numbers of migrant birds are trapped and ringed. When Minsmere needed a new warden there was no man better qualified for the job than Bert Axell. Since then his vision, patience and hard work have overcome almost insuperable difficulties to make the reserve the bird paradise that visitors

* I was delighted Bert received recognition in the 1965 New Year Honours List when he was appointed an MBE.

FOUR FRIENDS AT MINSMERE

Left: Charles Tunnicliffe concentrates on the drawing of a bittern

Centre: E.H. with Roger Tory Peterson and Bert Axell

Below: Ludwig Koch before the days of transistors

Left: A rare visitor photographed through the windscreen of the car on a Suffolk road. In November 1962 a Houbara bustard frequented East Anglia

Below: In 1947 avocets were photographed for the first time on their breeding grounds in the British Isles on Havergate Island

MINSMERE

Above: Wood sandpiper intent on finding a meal

Below: Grey plover strolls past the hide

Left: Often called locally the Prince Charming of the reed beds, the bearded tit is confined almost entirely to East Anglia

Below: Typical hide at Minsmere for photographing waders

see today. Bert seems to be able to put himself in the place of the bird and knows the type of habitat it requires for breeding purposes. Then he sets to work to make an area suitable for a specific bird or birds to breed in.

One of the first things Bert noticed was that there was some dead ground, an unproductive area which lay close to the sea, which, properly prepared, would provide a much needed new breeding site for terns and waders. A bulldozer cleared the ground, which was then flooded with a few inches of sea-water. In the centre a small shingle-covered island was made. A pair of common terns bred on this small island, the first to do so within the sanctuary since 1950. During the next few winters the area was enlarged to twenty-four acres and sluices were made so that the height of the water could be carefully controlled.

The result of all this imaginative labour has been remarkable; on twenty islands there now breed some 500 pairs of common terns, 700 pairs of Sandwich terns (which in 1967 fledged no fewer than 1,000 young), a few pairs of little terns, 200 pairs of black-headed gulls, eight pairs of ringed plovers and, what to me is so exciting, seven pairs of avocets. The Scrape, as it is called, also provides food for many thousands of migrants who stop here to refresh themselves before carrying on farther south in autumn, or north in spring. It is a show-place of active conservation. Bert says that conservation must not only be done, but seen to be done—so he built two hides for the free use of the public.

It is this man-made habitat that has been so attractive to me—a bird photographer. At a strategic site Bert and his assistant, Peter Makepeace, built another wooden hide to permit visitors fine close views of many of the birds. It was from this Scrape hide that I photographed for the first time gadwall, drake and duck swimming within a few feet, feeding as they went. Spotted redshanks and ruffs can be photographed in breeding plumage in the spring and in winter plumage in the autumn. Snipe probe their long bills into the soft mud as they feed quite unconcernedly within ten feet of an observer. Dunlins, knots, curlews, sandpipers, little ringed plovers, greenshanks, avocets, and black-tailed godwits and many more species often come within range.

To list all that can be seen would be tedious. Occasionally there is a rarity. Once a white-rumped sandpiper settled by the hide but did not stay long enough to let me photograph it. The fascination of sitting in one of the large hides is that almost anything may turn up.

Towards the end of November 1962 Bert telephoned me to say that an Houbara bustard was living in a field not far from the reserve. It was a cold frosty morning when I drove down to see a bird which is associated with the heat of deserts, and one which I was hoping to see during the forthcoming Jordan Expedition. (Incidentally, we did not see one in Jordan on the first two expeditions and the photograph I took in Suffolk was the one that was used in Guy Mountfort's book *Portrait of a Desert*.)

The Houbara was feeding in a field of mustard, which the farmer had generously refrained from ploughing-in while the bird was there. I met Bert and arranged for him to drive my car across the frozen field while I attempted to photograph the bird from the car window, using a 400 mm Novoflex lens with the Contarex camera. Unfortunately the light was bad and it was raining, but the next day the weather had improved so we decided to make another attempt. But it was a Sunday and news travels fast—no fewer than eighteen cars were parked by the edge of the field and hordes of bird-watchers with every possible size and shape of binocular and telescope were observing the bustard's every movement. Obviously photography was out of the question.

We made another attempt on Monday. A hide was erected along the edge of the field most favoured by the bird and I was just about to go into it when a press photographer arrived from London. He hadn't a clue about bird photography and imagined that he could just walk up, take his pictures and rush back to London. I could not convince him that he would get nothing with the apparatus he had unless he concealed himself in some way. But he was too old a hand to take any advice from an amateur like me and set off across the field. Before he got within 200 yards of the bird it leapt into the air and was away. Sheepishly he came back full of apologies, realising for the first time that he had spoilt my chances of photography as well as his own. As I had a spare hide with me I suggested that this should be erected by the side of mine and that he should sit in it and keep absolutely quiet until the bird returned, not attempting to take any photographs until it was well within range of our cameras.

I think he must have suffered from St. Vitus's dance or something because there was hardly a moment when I could not hear him moving—striking matches to light cigarettes (he was a chain-smoker), making the wooden box on which he sat creak, playing with his camera, etc. After about an hour I saw the Houbara alight by the far edge of the field and start to walk slowly in our direction.

As so much noise was coming from the other hide I whispered: 'The bird's coming.'

'What did you say?' answered a loud voice.

'The bustard is approaching your hide, from the left,' I replied.

'Where? I can't see it,' he shouted.

'For goodness' sake keep quiet!'

There were a few seconds of silence and by now the Houbara was within five yards of our hides but at such a sharp angle to me that I decided to wait until it came by the front of the hide. Not so my impatient friend. In trying to turn his camera lens round sufficiently to focus on to the bird, the wooden box collapsed with a crash and the Houbara took off!

The press photographer returned to London without getting a single picture and I was beginning to think that I would be equally unlucky. But as Bert and I drove along the narrow country lane we could hardly believe our eyes—there was the Houbara in the road walking steadily towards us! We pulled up. I focused the camera through the windscreen, and fired the shutter when the bird came to within eighteen feet. The result was published in *The Sunday Times* on 16 December 1962.

This chapter would not be complete without mention of two remarkable migration experiences. Early one morning in September 1961 Bert and I went by tractor to the south-east corner of the reserve known as The Sluice. As we neared the last reed-bed we heard bearded tits 'chipping' in the reeds. From the high viewpoint of the tractor we saw that some of the tits seemed to be excited. A party of about twenty leapt into the air, rose almost vertically, then flew towards the south along the sand dunes. We watched them through binoculars until they were mere specks. Then some turned back, then a few more, until finally all were back in the reed-bed. During the next three-quarters of an hour this performance was repeated several times. Had the urge to migrate been superseded by the desire to stay?

Some days after I had returned home, Bert saw several parties of these tits leave the same area and not return. I had always thought that the bearded tit was sedentary and that, while it could withstand a normal winter, any prolonged period of extremely cold weather had a devastating effect. After the exceptionally cold winter of 1947 it was difficult to find a pair of these tits anywhere in the country, but since then their numbers have steadily increased until today they are more numerous than for at least the past 100 years. As far as I know, no one had observed any eruptions of these birds until the autumn of 1959, but since then such movements have been recorded every year.

The other migration experience was in 1965 when Minsmere had the biggest fall of birds in its history. A depression, which had flooded Italy with rain, moved north-west and was over the southern North Sea on 3 September, reaching East Anglia by midday. Everywhere was flooded. It was impossible to do anything, so Bert and I stayed in his bungalow and talked birds. Suddenly Bert remarked that the wind had veered to the south-east and very shortly after we saw wheatears and redstarts appear in the bungalow yard and on the outbuildings.

Bert realised that something unusual was happening and so we hurried to the observation hut that overlooks the marsh. Birds were everywhere, the place was alive with them, not only small passerines but a variety of waders as well. The mud round The Scrape was packed—ruffs, grey and golden plovers, dunlins, various species of sandpipers, redshanks and greenshanks, a score or more of stints and a large flock of lapwings. Four of us set off to make a census, each going in a different direction. In all, between 1.15 p.m. and dusk, we recorded fifty-two species along a three-quarter-mile front. Here is a selection of them: 4,000 wheatears, 750 whinchats, 7,000 redstarts, 400 robins, 2,000 garden warblers, 200 whitethroats, 500 willow warblers, 300 spotted flycatchers, 1,500 pied flycatchers, 150 tree pipits.

The following day we recorded these rarities: 3 dotterels, 25 wrynecks, 3 ring ouzels, 25 bluethroats, 2 icterine warblers and 1 tawny pipit. During one week in July 1969 no fewer than 29 species of waders were seen at one time on The Scrape.

In 1970, by which time The Scrape had been increased to thirty acres with fifty islands, fifteen pairs of avocets bred and reared thirty-five young. For two or three days at the end of May two pairs of adult spoonbills went through all the actions of courtship behaviour, including the gathering of nesting material that was taken to one site. Unfortunately their breeding activities never progressed beyond this and shortly after they left. Perhaps one day The Scrape will see a breeding colony of spoonbills.

Thus although many species of birds are declining in Britain, it is good to know that others are returning, some after a century or more.

This then is Minsmere, the sanctuary that might never have been but for the tragedy of war.

11 | *Hides*

To see without being seen is the best way to observe wild-life. To photograph birds successfully you must either stalk them or work from a hide. There are three main ways of using a hide: near the nest, near bait put out to attract birds, or 'wait and see' when a hide is erected near a place where birds are likely to come to feed or rest.

In the early days of bird photography it was thought that, however crudely, the hide must represent something within the birds' previous experience. Thus the Kearton brothers produced a 'cow' or 'sheep' in whose hollow interior one of them would ensconce himself—the birds did not seem to notice that the mammal had six legs, the two human ones appearing from its middle. Another pioneer photographer similarly used a 'haystack'. Later the Keartons discovered that anything that prevents a bird from seeing the photographer is adequate, provided only that it is stable—loose or flapping parts defeat the object. In this chapter I shall describe some of the more unusual hides and memorable incidents which have occurred to me in my rôle as a bird photographer.

But first I will explain how the standard hide I normally use is constructed. It is really a small square tent. The frame consists of four poles, five and a half to six feet long, the pointed ends of which are driven into the ground to form a three-foot square. The upper ends of the poles, which may be jointed for ease in carrying, are joined together by stiff wire.

The covering of the hide consists of two pieces of opaque material, thirty-six inches wide and five yards long. These are laid over each other to form a cross, the double thickness forming the roof. The material must be firmly stretched. Three arms of the cross are sewn together to form three sides, the fourth is left open from about a foot from the top and forms the 'door' of the hide. When the photographer is installed it can be secured with safety-pins.

It is useful to have shallow pockets on the outer bottom edge of the hide as these can be filled with stones or sand to provide extra anchorage —very useful in a strong wind. Sometimes guy-ropes are needed, and tabs should be stitched to each top corner of the hide so that the ropes can be attached.

The opening for the camera lens is a hole about nine inches across cut in the front of the hide. A sleeve is stitched to this and the free end should have elastic through it so that it will slip neatly over the camera lens hood. The sleeve gives mobility for the camera and prevents vibration if the hide is shaken by a strong wind.

At least four peep-holes, about one inch square, should be cut, one in each of the sides. They should have small flaps, which can be closed with safety-pins when not in use. Large pockets sewn inside the hide hold notebooks, etc.

These hides are portable, simple in construction and can be quickly and easily erected and dismantled. It is vitally important after erecting them to get away from the site as quickly as possible, because the more time spent there the more frightened and nervous will the birds become. Incidentally, I have found that large, stainless steel safety-pins are best for closing a hide and pulling it tight so that it does not flap. I always have a plentiful supply as they have a remarkable habit of disappearing. On one Spanish expedition every safety-pin vanished. Soon afterwards all the small children had bright new safety-pins to keep their nappies on!

Once in the hide I quickly erect the camera and focus on the nest, then sit quietly for the bird to return. I make no attempt to take a photograph at first but watch the bird carefully, noting exactly where it perches. Immediately it flies away I check the focus—the spot where the bird perched must be critically sharp. Usually a bird perches in almost exactly the same place each time it arrives at the nest to feed the young, but hen and cock often select different spots, sometimes on opposite sides of the nest. When this happens I focus on the spot nearest to the camera, then stop down the lens aperture until the farther spot is also sharp.

When the bird again visits the nest the shutter is operated only while the young are being fed so that the sound is muffled by the noise of the young. Usually the bird is so preoccupied that it takes no notice, so on the next visit a photograph is taken after the young have been fed and settled down. Generally the adult bird is alert at once, sometimes even flying away. However, on the fourth or fifth visit the bird's reactions will be less noticeable and after that, so long as care is taken, the bird rapidly gets used to the clicks and other sounds coming from the hide. It is always necessary, however, to repeat this routine separately for both cock and hen.

During the height of the nesting season I often have as many as ten hides ready for use. This may seem a lot but if really natural photographs are to be obtained the bird must be thoroughly relaxed, which means it must be accustomed to the hide. I therefore spend several days, sometimes even a week or more, moving the hide closer until it is in its final position. I hope I may be forgiven for quoting here an extract about one of my photographs from *Wild Birds in Britain* by Seton Gordon (Batsford, 1938), one of our great bird photographers.

'I should like the reader to notice especially the magnificent study of a pair of stone curlews at the nest. This photograph, the work of Mr. Eric Hosking, is to my mind one of the finest nature photographs ever taken. Note the happy expressions of these very wary and un-approachable birds, and contrast them with the hunted look of birds which have been photographed by cruder methods and are so nervous that they are torn between mother-love and the fear of man and all his contrivances.'

In an article about the Coto Doñana Expedition for *The National Geographic Magazine* Roger Tory Peterson made this remark about my hides:

'Eric Hosking had brought with him nine of his fine gabardine photographic hides, but I felt that my own blind of burlap was better suited to the Spanish heat. I must admit that Eric's were fancier; they had everything but H. & C. running water.'

The hide's peep-hole is a window on the birds' world, giving an unparalleled view of their private lives—and loves. Although the standard hide was planned for use at ordinary ground-level, it can easily be adapted for use in tree-tops or on water. At Hickling I erected a hide near the nest of a great-crested grebe but, as the nest floated on water some six feet deep, I had to build a platform on which to fix it. This was made with four poles in a three-foot square hammered down into the mud until they were firmly fixed and about six inches above water-level. A wooden platform was fitted to these and the standard hide fixed on top.

As is my usual practice, the hide was then left for several days. On my return I was amazed to find that it had been appropriated by a female water vole, who had built her nest inside. I carefully entered the hide, and took particular care not to let any of the tripod legs touch the nest. I kept well clear of the vole's nest because they have a keen sense of smell—had I even touched it she would probably have deserted.

I concentrated on the grebes and forgot about the voles, except that I heard plops and scratchings as the female either dived into the water or scrambled out of it. Then, as I happened to glance downwards through the peep-hole, I saw the water vole swimming away carrying one of its young by the scruff of its neck. She returned and repeated the operation—then repeated it again. She evidently decided that with me in the hide as well, her quarters had become too cramped for comfort and thus removed her family to a better home.

Again on the Broads, at Horsey, my hide acquired a lodger—a pied wagtail. I had intended to photograph a sedge warbler's nest, but on returning a few days after the hide had been erected, I found that the wagtail had completed its nest inside. This time I gave the wagtail best —and forfeited photography of the warbler as well.

Wasps once built their nest in a hide which I had fixed up at a whinchat's nest in the Scottish Highlands. On this occasion I left it to them and was unable to retrieve it before I returned south. Several weeks afterwards a friend dismantled the hide and sent it to me not very much the worse for this hymenopterous invasion.

But perhaps the most delightful incident was when a pair of partridges used my hide as a shelter for their brood of day-old young during a torrential downpour. For all the notice they took of me I might have been part of the scenery!

I always dislike building a hide in a tree because it *never* seems to be possible to make it really rigid, and the branches seem to be in the wrong places for constructing a flat platform. In 1936 when I was staying with Willy Bilham at Eyke, we found a green woodpecker's nesting hole about twenty-three feet above ground. That evening we discussed what would be the best way to build a hide when the thought occurred to me that a pylon would be the answer. So far as I was aware no one had constructed a pylon-type hide before, so we had nothing to guide us. Our first problem was to locate and then cut down four moderately straight trees, each twenty-eight feet long. This length was necessary to sink them well into the ground, and also have two feet projecting above the level of the nest so that we could lash the hide poles to them. The platform was built at the level of the nest.

Although we did find four such poles and cut them down I had no idea how heavy they would be. They were no more than five or six inches in diameter at the base, but they were all that Willy, his assistant and I could carry. We fixed one pole into position each day, nailing climbing-steps on the back, about three feet apart. Finally we joined the hide to the nesting tree—which was six feet away—with a pole, so that when tree and pylon swayed in the wind they would remain the same distance apart, thus preventing the nesting hole going in and out of focus.

Almost all the time we were building the pylon the green wood-pecker remained inside her nesting hole brooding her small young. Whenever the cock had collected sufficient food to bring back to the

Above: Sandwich terns on the man-made islands in The Scrape, created for their use by Bert Axell at the RSPB Reserve at Minsmere

Below: Duck and drake gadwall photographed from the wooden hide in The Scrape shown above. This is one of the few photographs of wild gadwall taken in this country

This high-speed flash shot of a barn owl in heraldic pose, grasping a vole, is the
most widely published of all my photographs, having appeared in 106 countries

MINSMERE
Above: Turtle dove, feet coated with mud, pauses for a moment by the hide
Below: Spotted redshank in winter plumage, shows threat display

nest he called with his happy yaffle, and we quietly moved away. When he departed we moved in again.

As the young grew they clambered up to the mouth of the hole and called, becoming more and more excited as they heard the adults answering as they returned to the nest. There were frequent squabbles as each fought to be in the most favourable position when the adult actually arrived. The young continued to call even when food was being forced down their throats, the sounds becoming more and more muffled.

No sooner had the young woodpeckers flown from this nest than a pair of starlings took over the hole, and when their young hatched I was able to take a series of photographs of them from the same hide.

After that first pylon I built more than thirty before I obtained my own materials, sufficient to build a hide sixty feet high. A builder friend, who had helped me erect some of these hides, saw an advertisement of an auction sale near Torquay, Devon. All the effects of a bankrupt film company were being sold, including a mass of tubular duralumin complete with fixing clips. As my friend required some of this material for scaffolding he suggested that we should go down in his lorry and make a bid. Fortunately nearly all the buyers were film photographic people and no one else seemed to want the tubes. We bid only twenty pounds for the lot and as there were no other bidders it was knocked down to us. The builder had about two-thirds of it. My share has been to Spain and in many places in this country. It is easy and quick to use, comparatively light, yet rigid and strong.

However, because the main poles are ten feet long it is impossible to transport them in a private car, so on those occasions when only a small pylon is required, say up to ten feet, I use a Dexion, a sort of giant Meccano.

I have found this ideal for photographing water birds. A hide on a boat is not altogether to be recommended because it is so difficult to keep a boat still, and any movement at the moment of exposure can cause camera shake. With Dexion it is possible to construct the platform on land and then transport it by boat to the site, there lowering it into position.

Some people have extraordinary ideas about hides. I was once photographing a long-eared owl's nest from a hide twenty feet from the ground. Below me several people gazed upward at the queer contraption.

'Don't you know,' an authoritative male voice was saying, 'that in the spring keepers put up these contraptions for pheasants?' He went on to explain that the pheasants take up their young (he did not say how) to give them flying lessons: the young are jostled to the edge of the platform and then shoved off, so that they are forced to use their wings. How expert can you get!

People sometimes ask: 'Aren't birds afraid of hides?' The question is akin to the old tag: 'How high is up?' It depends on the bird—and the hide. Some birds are decidedly more nervous than others. A poorly constructed hide, unskilfully erected, would almost certainly cause a nervous bird to desert. But when used near any nest the hide should first be erected a fair distance away, and moved only gradually at twenty-four-hour intervals to its final position.

Yet I have photographed birds that did not seem to realise a hide was there. Once, on the Gorple Moors near Halifax, I erected a hide at a twite's nest, fixed up the camera and looked through the view-finder: I could see nothing, nothing at all. Had I left the lens cap on? No. I looked out through the peep-hole and there, sitting on the hood with its tail completely covering the lens, was the twite! And whenever I was there, that twite used the lens hood as a perch before descending to its nest.

It is important to be constantly alert in a hide; a few moments' inattention and the chance may be lost of a rare observation or photograph. I have referred in Chapter 7 (Finland) to a colleague missing a rare photograph because he was asleep at the vital moment. Once on the Little Eye at Hilbre another photographer and I were in nearby hides. Suddenly a peregrine falcon stooped and neatly picked off a dunlin from the edge of the flock. It alighted with its prey just by the other hide—the shot of a lifetime! How I envied him for I only saw it, the angle was too acute for my camera. When we emerged from our hides I congratulated my companion on his luck. He looked at me a bit strangely and asked why. He had missed it . . .

Several times my hides have been destroyed. A hide seems to have a strong fascination for cows, who rub against it, ripping the covering with their horns. I once found a cow careering round a field with my precious hide wrapped round it head. Now, whenever working in a field where there are cattle, I erect a barbed-wire fence round the hide and the nest. The nest is included because in trying to get at the hide cattle are likely to trample on it.

A hide I had erected on an island at Walthamstow Reservoir was badly damaged by hooligans. I so much wanted to photograph the reservoir's heronry that, with the help of George Edwards, I transported a pile of tubular duralumin. During the next three weeks we made over a dozen journeys by boat, taking a few tubes at a time. Eventually the scaffolding was in position and the hide completed. Then, as usual, we left the herons in peace for a few days.

When we returned, I could see as we approached the island that something was wrong. Some of the tubes were bent, and the guy-ropes that anchored the scaffolding were adrift. The place was in confusion. Only a gang of irresponsible youngsters could have carried out such a mad exercise and they must have gone to the trouble of swimming out to the island—the boat was locked up—just to commit this act of wanton destruction. So we had to start all over again.

Charles Rose once built a hide at Mistley, Essex, from which to photograph a green woodpecker's nest. It was a pylon hide about eighteen feet high, covered with hessian. Stuart Smith saw me settled in with my cameras, complicated flash gear and heavy batteries, and then left. It was a beautiful sunny day and the hessian was dry as tinder. Thinking a pipe would be pleasant, I lit up, dropped the match on the floor of the hide and stubbed it out with my boot—so I thought. But, with one of those million-to-one chances, the nails on my boot spanned the match and before I knew what was happening the hessian was ablaze.

I poked my head out and yelled desperately to Stuart: 'I'm on fire!'

'Hope you fry!' he retorted, without turning round, obviously thinking I was joking.

I yelled even louder. 'Stuart!'

Recognising the urgency in my voice he rushed back, shouting: 'Your hair's on fire—bale out!' The next minute or so is a blur in my memory. Stuart shinned up the pylon, in spite of a danger that the fire might short-circuit the electrical apparatus and add shocks to scorching, and helped me down with the equipment. Somehow, I still don't know how, I got down relatively unharmed with cameras and apparatus intact, but the hide was burnt to a cinder and the woodpeckers reared their young without further bother from photographers.

Bird photography can indeed be a hazardous occupation; it can even cause political complications. In preparation for our 1957 Coto Doñana Expedition (see Chapter 14) we had the problem of exporting several tons of tubular duralumin and other heavy gear. This was essential for the pylon hide we should need to erect near to the nest of the Spanish Imperial eagle—one of the world's rarest birds and the main photographic object of the expedition. The previous year we had used the only scaffolding available—eucalyptus poles—but they were too short and it was impossible to join them together because the hard wood bent the nails. We put our problem to Lord Alanbrooke, who was to come with us, and he, in turn, promised to ask Lord Mountbatten—the First Sea Lord—to help. Wheels turned smoothly, and eventually a supply ship of the Royal Navy took on a slight extra cargo on a trip to Gibraltar.

When the first photographs of the expedition were published we mentioned, as a matter of courtesy, that the Royal Navy had helped to make them possible by transporting our heavy gear to Gibraltar. Innocent enough? Not on your life. Here is an extract from *Hansard* (30 April, 1958):

ROYAL NAVY

Bird-watching Expedition (Transport)

17. Mr. Shinwell asked the Parliamentary Secretary to the Admiralty what facilities were provided by his Department for the transport of equipment and stores for a private bird-watching expedition conducted by Mr. Guy Mountfort; what Admiralty vessel was used for this purpose; what was the amount paid for these services; and whether his consent was obtained to this transaction.

The Parliamentary and Financial Secretary to the Admiralty (Mr. Robert Allan): Royal Fleet Auxiliaries sail frequently to the Mediterranean. Inquiries were received as to whether any such ship might have space available to carry some of this expedition's equipment.

There was available in the RFA 'Fort Dunvegan' the very small space required: this space would otherwise have been empty. A charge of £2 was made to cover handling. This arrangement was made with due Admiralty approval.

Mr. Shinwell: Is the hon. Member aware that Mr. Mountfort in his book—which, by the way, is a profit-making venture—stated that Lord Mountbatten, the First Sea Lord, used his influence in order to obtain these facilities? Is it customary for the Admiralty to provide facilities of this character for a private venture of this kind?

Mr. Allan: Yes, Sir. It is customary to provide Service facilities in certain circumstances. This was a serious expedition of an international character, the reports of which will be of value. The Admiralty has always had what it is pleased to call an indulgence rate at which freight can be carried, provided that it does not inconvenience or displace any official freight. This request was originally made by Field Marshal Lord Alanbrooke, and it was perfectly in accordance with custom to accede to it.

Mr. Shinwell: What does the hon. Member mean by 'an expedition of an international character'? Are we to understand that if a number of people gather together and decide to proceed on a bird-watching expedition in Spain, that has international implications?

Mr. Allan: I merely meant that it was international in character. There were other nationalities in the expedition.

Mr. Chetwynd: Are we to understand that the birds in question were wrens?

Mr. Wigg: Would the hon. Member be good enough to circulate in the OFFICIAL REPORT the conditions under which these facilities are available to all sections of the community? Or are they the exclusive right of the personal friends of Lord Mountbatten?

Mr. Allan: I said that this authority was given with due Admiralty approval.

Mr. Callaghan: Is this not a perfectly normal and good piece of public relations?

We heard no more.

This was not the first time I had been associated with Lord Alanbrooke and a hide. In the spring of 1945 Tony Wootton, a keen bird-watcher who lived at Camberley, Surrey, located the nest of a hobby, one of our rarer birds of prey of which, up to that time, few good photographs had been taken. Hobbies do not build nests, but use old ones built by other birds. And usually they select a nest near the top of a tall tree. Our hobbies were no exception, their nest being in a tree fifty-nine feet high on the Surrey–Hampshire border. I had never worked on a hobby before and was extremely keen to try, but there was one snag: Tony had not only trespassed to find the nest, he had done so on ground belonging to the Water Board—a serious offence, for the Government was concerned about the possible contamination of water supplies.

I recalled that Lord Alanbrooke lived nearby, and although I had met him only once before, I knew that he was very keen on photographing birds. Although he was then the Chief of the Imperial General Staff, I banked on his overlooking Tony's peccadillo in his excitement about the hobby.

We drove to Lord Alanbrooke's house and, with some trepidation, knocked at the front door. It was answered by a man wearing an old, open-necked shirt, vivid red braces and old khaki trousers. I was just about to ask for the great man himself when I realised this was he. He looked at us with that penetrating, non-smiling gaze that so many found disconcerting. I briefly introduced Tony and recalled that we had met before, told him about the hobby and explained our problem to him. Lord Alanbrooke said that he would see what he could do. He was leaving next day for the Potsdam Conference and promised to ring me before he left.

'If I get you permission,' he added, 'are you going to let me use that hide?' Would we not! The following morning he telephoned—a permit was on its way.

When the second volume of Lord Alanbrooke's diaries was published—*Triumph in the West* edited by Sir Arthur Bryant (Collins, 1959)—I was interested to read this entry for July 1945.

'It was one Sunday afternoon at this time that the great bird photographer, Eric Hosking, then a stranger, called at his house to ask his help in obtaining leave from the local Water Board to put up a hide to photograph a hobby's nest. When permission had been secured Hosking offered him the use of the hide: "This" Brooke recalled afterwards, "was the beginning of many happy days bird photographing with Eric Hosking to whom I owe a great debt." '

When the Field Marshal's diaries were published he sent me inscribed copies. In the first volume he wrote:

'To Eric from Alanbrooke with deep gratitude for much help and assistance in the art of bird photography, but especially in memory of the many hours we have spent with our hides in close proximity and surrounded by waders of all kind. Feb. 1957.'

We had to work fast, yet I knew this hide, sixty-four feet high, was going to be difficult to build. At first I thought a contraption I had seen used at the nearby Wellington College might do—a huge cradle affair used to reach lights suspended from the high roof of the main hall. We hired a lorry and with the College's permission transported the cradle to the hobby's site. But the lorry could get no nearer than the edge of the wood. With many willing hands helping us, we manhandled the cradle half a mile to the site—only to find that it was not high enough!

It was obvious there was going to be no easy way: we should have to build a metal pylon hide. I estimated that several tons of tubular steel would be required—a formidable difficulty when all available steel was needed for essential industries. (This was, of course, before I had my duralumin tubes.)

Then we had a stroke of luck. There was a building site about three miles away with plenty of steel scaffolding. We saw the builder and told him our problem. He agreed to help.

Operation Hobby was planned like a military manœuvre. First the builder surveyed the site, decided that five tons of scaffolding would be needed, then dumped it from a lorry about 100 yards from the tree. Building the pylon was quite a long job, and since it is always important not to disturb any nesting bird more than is absolutely necessary—and how much more so with a rare falcon such as the hobby!—we decided to limit each building session to one hour in every forty-eight. It took ten men ten sessions to complete the job. A lorry collected the men from the building site, rushed them to the tree where they worked like fury, and the moment my stop-watch ticked sixty minutes it was down tools and away from the site as quickly as possible. None of this seemed to ruffle the hobby, which peered unconcernedly over the side of the nest at the feverish activity below.

Everything was eventually in position and, after leaving it for forty-eight hours, I entered the hide. A mistle thrush mobbing nearby gave warning of the cock's approach, and almost at once he alighted near the nest with a small decapitated bird in his talons.

My first vision of the cock is indelibly imprinted on my mind—the dark piercing eyes; the hooked blue-grey bill; the slate-blue head with the dark moustachial streaks drooping down on either side of the throat, and the whitish feathers of the chin and cheeks. The bold flecking of dark brown feathers on his otherwise cream-coloured breast, his firm rusty-coloured thighs and bright yellow legs added a bright touch of colour. When he moved, his blue-grey back and wings glinted with a pearly lustre. As he stood there perched on a bough only a few feet in front of me I was fascinated by his beauty.

The hen took the food and he was gone. She fed the young for a few minutes, then settled to brood.

Suddenly the cock called as he swiftly flew past. The hen shot off the nest and chased the cock like a rocket. There was a breathtaking moment when the birds converged so rapidly that a collision seemed inevitable. Then they rolled over, swung up their feet and passed food from one to the other. It is the speed and precise flight control which makes the hobby's food-pass so exhilarating to watch.

One evening the phone rang—a personal call from Potsdam. Lord Alanbrooke was on the line. 'How's the hobby hide? I'm coming over tomorrow—when can I occupy it?'

Thus it was that a lone bird photographer was on the tarmac of the Blackbushe military aerodrome, surrounded by top army brass, all waiting to welcome home the CIGS after one of the world's historic conferences. I drove him to his home at Hartley Wintney, and within a few hours of landing he was in the hide filming the hobby.

From the moment it was first used, the hide was occupied almost continuously during daylight. At least twelve people spent some time in it—the oldest the sixty-two-year-old Field Marshal, the youngest an enthusiast of fifteen.

One day I was in the hide when a thunderstorm raged overhead. When the storm was as its height and the light at its worst, the cock hobby flew to the nest with food for the hen and young. The shot of a lifetime. And conditions were impossible for photography. I fumed in helpless impatience. The meal was nearing its end when the gods relented. A sudden bright patch broke the overcast for a second or two. I let fly and caught what was almost certainly the only photograph in existence of a pair of hobbies together at the nest.

Photographing the hobbies so absorbed my attention that I never thought of my danger at the top of a steel tower, taller than the surrounding trees, with lightning flashing all around. But I dare not leave for fear of scaring the hobby and causing her to desert. My hair was literally standing on end. Was it the electricity? I don't know. I do know that all the scheming, worrying, work and fear were forgotten in the wonder of watching and photographing such a rare falcon.

Stone curlews just after the change-over at the nest

Left: An early pylon hide at Eyke, Willy Bilham at foot. The hide was erected to photograph a green woodpecker's nest in a hole twenty-three feet up the tree

Above right: Green woodpecker

Below right: When the woodpeckers left, the hole was appropriated by starlings

12 | *Flash*

To me, the greatest technical development in bird photography has been the electronic high-speed flash. Coupled with improved cameras, lenses and fast film, it has enabled photographs to be taken of the fastest avian movements, even 'freezing' the insect-fast beat of a humming-bird's wings. As a result, problems have been solved which had puzzled ornithologists for centuries, because they concerned movements too fast for the eye to analyse.

Yet, surprising as it sounds, high-speed flash is almost as old as photography itself. William Henry Fox Talbot, the first British photographer, patented a method of 'instantaneous photography' in 1851. He attached a clipping from *The Times* to a rapidly revolving disk. Then, in a darkened room, he focused his camera on the disk and took a photograph by the light of an electric spark produced by the discharge of a Leyden battery. The result was an unblurred picture of newsprint which, when enlarged, could be read easily.

Then in 1881 Ernst Mach took shadow, or silhouette, photographs of bullets in flight, using such extremely short flashes that the results are comparable with much of the high-speed work of today.

The early British bird photographers used chemical, as opposed to electrical, flash. Lord Alanbrooke told me that when he was in India early this century he made his own high-speed equipment. A small metal box was filled with two pounds of magnesium and when electrically fired the lid burst open, tripped the shutter and the photograph was taken. There were two drawbacks: the almighty flash sometimes set fire to the surrounding vegetation, and only one photograph could be taken each night because the explosion frightened away all the wildlife, and probably the smell of the burnt magnesium hindered their return.

Then in the late 1920's Joseph A. Speed of Preston, who was fascinated by bird flight, constructed apparatus which was capable of

M

taking a photograph in 1/5,000th second—a remarkable achievement for a man whose profession was industrial insurance. He arranged two shutters so that their synchronised opening was much shorter than that of any single mechanical shutter then available.

As intense light would be necessary to take a photograph at such short exposures, Speed used six ounces of 'gingered-up' flash-powder. This was divided into six cups each containing one ounce, and fired electrically. The result was a miniature atomic explosion—on one occasion the police thought the local gasworks had gone up! It was with this ingenious apparatus that Speed took the excellent photograph of a swallow in flight which won its place in *Masterpieces of Bird Photography* (Collins, 1947), edited by Harold Lowes and myself.

However, the light from flash-powder and flash-bulbs lasts too long to stop movement, which is why the early pioneers had to modify their shutters. Because of my life-long interest in owl photography I have tried to keep abreast of all developments in flash technique. Before the war I corresponded with Dr. Harold E. Edgerton of the Electrical Engineering Laboratories at the Massachusetts Institute of Technology. He had produced flashes with a duration of 1/100,000th second which were brilliant enough to 'freeze' a golf ball at the moment of impact with the club, fast-revolving machinery and a bullet speeding from a revolver.

The principle of the high-speed flash is an electrical discharge, in a fraction of a second, through a glass or quartz tube filled with gas— usually krypton or xenon, or a mixture of both. The current causes these gases to glow with a brightness far exceeding that of the most brilliant sunlight. The duration can be as short as a ten-millionth of a second, but flashes of the order of 1/5,000th second are quite adequate for my purposes.

I use the flash in conjunction with the fastest possible shutter speed, and with a lens aperture so small that daylight does not register on the plate or film during the split second that the shutter is open. During that split second the daylight is 'swamped' by the ultra brightness of the electronic flash, and the photograph is taken.

During the autumn of 1945 Dawe Instruments marketed a portable high-speed flash set giving an exposure of 1/5,000th second. I bought a set at once—but soon discovered the snags. It was built for the press photographer, who switched it on, took his photographs and switched off again. As I never knew exactly when the bird would arrive at the spot where I wanted to photograph it I had to leave the set switched on, and within an hour the battery was exhausted. There was no provision for the set to switch itself off when it was charged, or to switch itself on again when it needed recharging.

Notable species of the kingflasher (*Ericus electronicus superbus*):
cartoon by Leslie Baker

Stuart Smith, who helped me so much, mentioned my difficulties to Dr. Philip S. H. Henry, of the British Cotton Research Association at Didsbury, Manchester. Philip is an experienced and resourceful physicist and electrical engineer, and he built into my Dawe set several novel ideas, including a cut-out device which ensured that power flowed only when required.

It worked beautifully but was not sufficiently powerful for bird photography, where the light source has always to be several feet distant from the object to be photographed. So Philip then built a set especially for me. It consisted of two condenser packs, one power pack, a twenty-four-volt battery, lamps, reflectors and the inevitable cables. It had an output of 670 joules, weighed one hundredweight and stored enough energy to electrocute me! I sometimes saved space in the hide by using part of the equipment in place of my stool, but it was akin to sitting on a bomb, a condition not calculated to improve my concentration on bird photography.

The first time I tried out this new set in the field was in the spring of 1948 at Staverton Park, Suffolk. Philip Henry was with me. Here I was attempting to photograph birds in flight, but all I achieved was the discovery of another snag about high-speed photography—not a mechanical one this time but a human one. A small bird flying about four feet in front of the camera at 15 m.p.h. is in the field of view of the lens for only about 1/10th second. And in that fraction of time I had to decide if the bird was in focus, and press the shutter release at the precise moment when it would be in the centre of the plate. Co-ordination of eye, brain and finger were just not swift enough. Consequently, my first results were a fine crop of disappearing tails, half heads, empty bushes and clear skies.

Again Philip came to the rescue. The birds must photograph themselves. Anyone who has walked through a self-opening door has experienced the principle—he has broken a light beam which interrupts an electrical circuit which, in turn, actuates the machinery to open the door. The bird does the same thing, except that instead of opening the door, it actuates the flash and takes its own picture.

It was this photo-electric eye, suitably adapted, that Philip used to solve my flash problems with flying birds. The photo-electric cell and lamp unit were erected on tripods, so that the beam ran diagonally in front of the hide along the bird's flight path. Great care had to be taken to see that the light from the lamp pointed exactly at the cell. In the hide the camera was adjusted and aimed on to a spot halfway between cell and lamp. To aid critical focusing a piece of string was temporarily tied between the two, and halfway along this was a card to simulate the bird. Finally, the two high-speed flash-lamps were directed on to the card.

The above may sound very complicated, but it was surprising how quickly it could all be assembled after a little practice. With the help of a friend I used to get everything erected and would be ready in the hide within ten minutes of our arriving at the site.

It was very exciting sitting in the hide waiting for the bird to photograph itself. Immediately it cut across the beam it interrupted the electrical circuit, and through a solenoid (acting as an electro-magnet) fired the camera shutter and with it the two flash-lamps. When using the outfit at night an infra-red filter was placed across the lamp unit so that it was not visible to owls or other nocturnal birds.

The resulting photographs were spectacular. I was delighted; so were the editors who reproduced so many of them.

In 1949 Collins published the cream of the photographs in *Birds in Action*, for which Cyril Newberry wrote the text.

I was happy thus to pioneer this development in bird photography in Britain. I thought many of my colleagues would buy high-speed flash-sets of their own and the countryside would soon be lit up by miniature flashes of lightning. Not at all. Most of our leading bird photographers were hostile to the whole idea. It was almost as if I had introduced something indecent into bird photography.

As bird photographers are highly vocal, I was soon aware of what they thought of Eric Hosking and his newfangled works. My friend John Markham—a first-class nature photographer—went so far as to declaim: 'I will never in my life use high-speed flash.'

Why all this violent opposition to a new technique which, to me, opened up such exciting possibilities for bird photography? There were a number of objections but I think the following sum up the strongest. Many of the photographs obtained by this means showed birds in poses, and unaesthetic ones at that, which no bird-watcher ever saw. Often the photograph had a pitch-black background giving it an unnatural effect as if diurnal birds were in full flight in the middle of the night. Some people maintained that it turned bird photography from an art requiring skill and patience into a technique of engineering and electronics. As flash was used for bird flight, some photographs showed extraordinary wing positions which some people found 'unnatural'. Finally, I think that some bird photographers, who still used the large format cameras, found that they were already carrying across mountain or moor so much equipment that the thought of being weighed down by still more apparatus was too much for them. After all it must be remembered that nearly all of them are amateurs, to whom photography is a hobby and recreation, and they therefore do not want to make too much labour of it.

But as well try to halt the waves as try to stop inevitable technical advances. First one, then another—maybe surreptitiously at first—tried out the new technique, were pleased with the results and became converts. John certainly held out a long time but one season he went with Walter Higham to photograph birds in Scotland. There he saw Walter's high-speed flash apparatus in action and was so impressed that —yes, he broke his vow.

I shall never forget the first time I took the high-speed equipment abroad; on an expedition to Holland with George Edwards in the early summer of 1952. I was working on the only known nesting pair of hoopoes in the country and was thrilled with the results. I had taken six exposures when I noticed something that worried me. The set had two lights: red for charging, green when charged and ready to flash. But now the red just stayed on, indicating that the set was being heavily overcharged. I am no electrician and had not a clue what to do. Suddenly there was a tremendous bang and the set went dead. Coming in the middle of my first nesting season abroad this was grim.

George and I thought that the best plan would be to ask the famous Philips electrical firm at Eindhoven to help. We had the wiring diagram, but they said that the symbols which Philip Henry used for the electrical circuit were so different from those used in Holland that they could not understand them, and consequently could not repair the set.

At all costs I had to get the equipment working again, so I telephoned Philip in Manchester and asked him to fly out at my expense as soon as he could. In two days he came and in about a quarter of an hour he had traced the fault, a broken resistance.

The next morning I tried it out again at a blue-headed wagtail's nest, as the young hoopoes had flown by now. After a couple of flashes the set went dead. My mood just then is well expressed in this extract from a letter I wrote to Dorothy:

'I honestly felt like throwing the whole lot in the nearest dyke! I had only got two exposures. I put the handkerchief out and soon Philip and George arrived and we had to lug the whole lot back to the car and came back home here. Philip soon located the trouble—it was the same as before and it appears that he has got hold of a dud lot of resistances. Anyway we decided to cut the whole lot out and do away with all the improvements he fitted into the set last winter. Unfortunately he is unable to put it back as it was last year so I am now back to where I was in 1946!'

Even that was not the end of the troubles. After thirty minutes with the now somewhat emasculated apparatus, there was another bang— this time one of the tubes had burst. Fortunately I had a spare and after that was fitted the set worked reasonably well.

I suppose it was the failures and the anxiety they brought that cause me to remember these teething troubles so vividly, but I should hate to give the impression that the set was always breaking down. Once the initial difficulties were ironed out the set operated excellently for many years.

Since those days developments have taken place, especially in Dr. Harold Edgerton's laboratory, which enable high-speed flash-sets to be much simpler and lighter than my original apparatus. But because these new sets have a longer flash duration (on account of the lower voltages employed) it is still necessary to build special sets for bird photography. Philip Henry tells me that one is now (1969) under construction which 'will probably consist of a central combined power and control unit weighing not more than eight or ten pounds, perhaps fitted into a leather case, together with three rather bulky flash-heads weighing about six pounds each, connected to it by domestic three-core cable—total weight around twenty-eight pounds'.

Now, when high-speed photography is commonplace, it is difficult to think back to the late 1940's and realise fully what it meant. The title of Cyril Newberry's first chapter in our book on the subject was no exaggeration: 'A Revolution in Bird Photography.' Anybody with a high-speed flash-set is now independent of natural lighting conditions —indoors or out—and, moreover, can be sure of a uniform light source without recourse to meters when working within a few feet of the subject.

Whereas photographs in the pre-high-speed era were primarily of birds at rest or moving slowly, now the fastest movement could be recorded. For the first time it was possible to see what a bird looked like when it was performing actions too fast for the human eye to register.

One unexpected 'bonus' of high-speed photography is of great interest to entomologists: the pin-sharp definition of birds bringing food to the young enables the insect prey—sometimes even its sex—to be identified.

But it is probably in the study of avian wing-movements in take-off, flight and landing that the most remarkable and interesting results of high-speed flash have been obtained. Not only is the wing frozen, but every feather, every barbule is stopped to show its beauty of line and function.

One series which especially pleased me was of a sand martin approaching its nesting hole in the side of a sand-pit. Like other ornithologists, I have often marvelled at the way this graceful bird comes swooping back to its hole at some 20 m.p.h. and, when within a few *inches* of dashing itself to death against the wall of the pit, decelerates with apparently miraculous disregard of all the laws of motion, to glide safely through the four-inch-wide hole in the bank of sand. Perhaps the high-speed flash could reveal the secret of the sand martin's flight. It did. In the last split-second of flight the martin spreads its wings to their limit and drops its tail so that its body hangs vertically. Then the wings beat sharply *forward* and the tail is spread and arched upward. The bird is then a virtual parachute, braking horizontally.

The Air Ministry invited me to show them some of my more remarkable flight photographs. They were very interested but one of the photographs was so unusual that they virtually accused me of faking it. The high-speed flash had caught a redstart in flight with one wing fully spread, the other almost folded to the body; an impossible position for flight—the equivalent of an aeroplane flying with one wing! A small group of scientists under Dr. R. H. J. Brown at the Zoological Laboratories at Cambridge undertook experimental high-speed work not only into bird flight and aerodynamics but also into animal movement generally. Who knows, maybe aeroplanes fly a little better and safer today because of the lessons learnt from the birds.

Right: It took a hundred man-hours to build this five-ton sixty-four-foot high steel pylon near the hobbies' nest

Below: The view from the top

Above: 'Look, it's got a rat in its bill!'
Such was my excited outburst to my mother on developing the negative of this
early flashlight photograph of a barn owl at the entrance to its nesting hole

Below: Hoopoe, caught by high-speed flash, feeding a mole cricket to its young

THE MAGIC OF BIRD FLIGHT CAUGHT BY HIGH-SPEED FLASH

Above: Redstart, with rat-tailed maggot in bill, photographed as it comes in to land

Below: Sand martin turns its body into a parachute as it brakes hard a split-second before landing

This high-speed photograph of a hovering cock nightjar reveals the surprising fact that the farther wing has bent round so far that the primary feathers are pointing forwards

I 3 | *Experiments*

One evening in May 1946 Stuart Smith, George Edwards and I were sitting round the old open fireplace in the little thatched cottage in Staverton Park. We were discussing various ornithological problems and how best to photograph various aspects of bird behaviour. The fire started to smoke, so Stuart opened the door and just outside, on a low branch, was a cuckoo. This took Stuart's mind back a few years and he told us this story. He and his young son, David, were sitting one day beneath a tree when a cuckoo called, and Stuart had imitated the call by blowing through his clasped hands.

Then something strange happened. A willow warbler that had been singing on a nearby bush stopped immediately, flew towards him, alighted on a twig above his head and started an aggressive display. It spread its wings and moved them slowly up and down, at the same time making a curious chittering *chee-chee-chee*, a call Stuart had never heard before. The warbler became more and more excited as the human cuckoo continued to call until Stuart thought it was going to attack his face. But after a while the reaction died down and the warbler returned to its bush.

This behaviour fascinated us and we wondered how such displays could be photographed. But how could we get birds to display at will—our will—and how could we entice them to do so within range of the camera? However willing, we could not expect Stuart to put on his cuckoo act every time. If only we could get birds near the camera the new high-speed flash-set, operating at 1/5,oooth second, would freeze any rapid movement they might make. If only.

Then an idea came to me. If a willow warbler reacted so violently to the imitation of a cuckoo call, how would it behave when confronted with a stuffed cuckoo? We recalled that other ornithologists had used dummies, generally stuffed and mounted bird-skins, to stimulate reaction. One idea led to another and soon we were making plans to use mirrors, painted cardboard cut-outs, carved wooden models and even stuffed birds of prey and mammalian predators. Thoughts flooded our minds—do small birds react the same way towards a cuckoo as they do to a bird of prey, or a stoat; how do birds react when a cuckoo comes to lay an egg in their nest: and do they all react in the same way? Here was a fascinating line of research with Stuart, the scientist, interpreting the behaviour; George, the artist, preparing the models, making the cut-outs and painting them to look as lifelike as possible; and me, the photographer, to record it all.

It was too late in the season for us to start work immediately so the following winter we collected a fair-sized aviary of stuffed birds as well as a moth-eaten but ferocious-looking stoat. We were fortunate in finding a retiring taxidermist who had four ancient cuckoo skins for sale and, at our request, he stuffed them tight with peat and inserted stout wires to make them easy to handle. We all looked forward to the spring with keen anticipation.

We began our experiments at Staverton Park with the same species which had aroused Stuart's interest. George found a willow warbler's nest in the cottage garden with newly hatched young. As the cock was singing in a nearby tree, Stuart approached the nest holding the dummy cuckoo in his hand. He was fully twenty yards from the nest when the cock stopped singing and showed obvious signs of agitation. He flicked his wings rapidly and began calling with the same high-pitched *chee-chee-chee* that Stuart had heard from his first warbler. Immediately the hen heard this call she left the nest and joined the cock.

Stuart moved nearer and, kneeling down, held the stuffed cuckoo over the nest. Immediately the cock attacked, hitting the stuffed bird on the crown of its head. He attacked again and again, concentrating on the cuckoo's crown, eyes and neck. Feathers began to fly as they were ripped out of the dummy. The hen joined in but far less vigorously, and after a few minutes she retired to a nearby fence, where she continued to chitter and flick her wings. But the cock kept up his non-stop attack for eight minutes, had a short rest, then came back for a second round of three and a half minutes before joining the hen. They continued to heckle until we retired.

The attacks made by the cock had been so quick that it had been difficult to photograph him. My line of vision was very restricted as I sat in the hide and peered through the small peep-hole. I could see that Stuart was wondering why I did not fire the flash more frequently. I had to press the camera shutter release while the warbler was at least three feet distant and then sometimes he veered away without completing the attack. However I obtained a reasonable series of the experiment.

The warblers quietened down and the hen returned to brood the young again, so we left them in peace for a while. I then returned to the hide and the birds reacted quite differently, showing the normal reaction to man, calling with the familiar anxiety note—*hewie*. Stuart wondered what would happen if the warblers again saw the cuckoo. Had the previous bout of tremendous emotional activity temporarily exhausted their anti-cuckoo feelings? Or would the sight of the enemy inspire a further furious outburst?

Stuart approached the nest again, hiding the stuffed cuckoo under his jacket. The warblers sounded the *hewie* note up to the the moment that Stuart pulled out the cuckoo, then immediately the chittering, wing-flicking and 'approach for attack' routine began.

The intensity of the attack was as great as before. During its height the hen attempted to join in but to our astonishment the cock attacked her, forced her to the ground and savaged her. His high-pitched calls attracted other birds to the scene and when a cock tree pipit attacked the cuckoo, the warbler furiously drove him away. Once the warbler caught a reflection of himself in one of the flash reflectors and attacked that. He was obviously berserk.

Stuart hid the cuckoo under his coat and stood by the hide as I packed up the camera. The cock warbler was still attacking—this time *the place* where the cuckoo had been. It seemed as if its image was still imprinted on his eye and that he was still trying to drive it away.

We retired to the cottage where Stuart pointed out that it would be unscientific to base any general conclusions on experiments with a single pair of willow warblers. Birds are individuals, and one series of experiments with one pair of willow warblers was inconclusive. We realised the size of the problem facing us, for not only was it our intention to carry out many more trials with these warblers, but also with several other species as well.

We wanted to find out how reactions varied according to the stage reached in the breeding cycle—during nest-building, egg-laying, incubation and when there were young. Were parts of the cuckoo of special significance—was it the head, the eye, or the bill that caused such violent reaction? Did birds recognise our stuffed model as a cuckoo or could they tell the difference between one dummy species and another? It was a formidable task and obviously we had years of work before us. Eventually we carried out hundreds of experiments and the results were published in 1955 in our book *Birds Fighting* (Faber & Faber). I shall mention here only a few of the highlights.

One generalisation we felt safe in making as the result of the dummy cuckoo experiments was that the presence of the detested object aroused emotions of the utmost violence. These were so intense that the normal fear of man was completely swamped by hate of the cuckoo. We found it impossible to avoid anthropomorphic language in discussing this work.

We had a striking example of this abhorrence when working at Minsmere with Ludwig Koch. He wanted to record the nightingale's distinctive alarm note—a harsh churring note—which it seemed could not come from the same throat that pours forth the melody that touches the midnight wood with magic.

A microphone was fitted near a nightingale's nest and I carried the stuffed cuckoo at arm's length towards it. As soon as the birds spotted the dummy they seemed to go crazy. As I was the nearest object to the cuckoo, the cock alighted on my head and then dive-bombed the enemy. He struck it with all the force of his tiny body, nearly knocking it out of my hand. Then he swung round in mid-air and alighted on my head again. A moment's hesitation and then the manœuvre was repeated—again and again. Sometimes the hen joined in and my hand became quite sore from the buffeting of wing, bill and claw. And always the alarm note was sounding, greatly to Ludwig's delight. When I eventually retired and the raucous sound ceased, he threw up his hands and shouted: '*Wunderbar.*' I did not need to understand German to know what that meant.

At another nest a pair of nightingales were furiously attacking the stuffed cuckoo, sometimes banging into each other, and once the hen, like the willow warbler, fell to the ground on her back. Furiously the cock attacked her instead of the cuckoo. Either Wordsworth was a better ornithologist than he is given credit for, or he wrote better than he knew, when he exclaimed: 'O Nightingale! thou surely art a creature of a "fiery heart".'

Such family strife was not confined to nightingales. We erected a cuckoo near a stonechat's nest containing young. When the hen returned she immediately attacked. Seconds later the cock arrived, rushed to the cuckoo and tried to attack its head. But the hen was already in full combat and when the cock joined in she turned viciously on him. He retaliated and there was a wild mid-air free-for-all, until the two birds fell to the ground locked together. The shock of the fall jerked them apart and, as soon as they were separated, they both returned to fight the cuckoo.

We observed such mutual fighting three times in fifteen minutes. Once the cock seized the hen's left foot in his bill and appeared to be trying to wrench it off. As I was trying to remove the cuckoo they both continued to attack it, completely ignoring my presence. Even when the dummy was out of sight they continued for some minutes to dive-bomb the place where it had been.

George made a sectional cuckoo, giving it a wooden body on which we could attach the head, breast feathers, wings and tail. We found another willow warbler's nest and placed alongside it the wooden body only. The adults returned to feed the young and ignored the piece of wood. We then fixed the tail, and still there was no reaction. Next we added the wings, and now the willow warblers took some notice but not sufficient to stop them feeding their young. But when we attached the head and breast feathers immediately there was the full violent reaction with vicious attacks on the head, crown and eyes.

We then placed the wooden body near another warbler's nest, and although the birds took some notice of it, they were obviously not greatly alarmed. Then we put just the head on. The cock was singing but after a moment or two he left his perch, collected some food and made his usual approach to the nest, alighting by the dummy. He either swallowed or dropped the food, pecked the cuckoo's head, then launched a full-blooded attack on it accompanied by chittering cries.

We were now convinced that the head was the point of valence so we decided to make the final test. George found yet another willow warbler's nest in an unworked area—we did not want these warblers to be in any way conditioned by previous experiments. We fixed the head alone to a stick and placed it above the nest. I got into the hide, while Stuart and George hid themselves nearby and watched through binoculars.

The warbler approached carrying food in its bill and had almost reached the nest before it saw the head. It dropped the food and launched a furious attack. Then its mate appeared and joined in. There was no doubt that they recognised the head as a cuckoo and were determined to drive it away from their nest. At two other willow warbler nests we had almost identical reactions.

Very different were the reactions to other dummies. Birds showed intense fear of a sparrow hawk, although some small birds attacked it. But the stoat seemed to terrify them even more and they all kept well out of its way.

During the nesting season most birds stake out an area or territory which they look upon as their own. It ensures that there will be sufficient food for them and their young. If any other bird of the same species trespasses, it is driven away. Perhaps the intruder has what might be called a 'guilty conscience' because, as soon as the owner approaches, it will usually leave the territory. Early in the season cock birds sing to advertise their presence and to warn others that the ground from which they sing is theirs. While they are establishing these territories there are often aggressive displays, and sometimes brief fights, but generally threats alone are sufficient.

We wanted to photograph some of these aggressive displays so we again decided to use dummies, but this time of the same species as the ones we were to study.

On a heath in Staverton Park, George found a ringed plover's nest and I erected a hide nearby. We decided to put a stuffed ringed plover four feet from this nest to see what would happen. The cock was the first to return and instead of going to the nest he walked round the dummy, eyeing it curiously in a humped-up attitude. He ran a few yards and then false brooded in a slight hollow. After a few seconds he gave this up and incubated the eggs. He sat almost motionless for half an hour and then the hen arrived to take her turn. As she approached, the cock ran from the eggs but stopped when a few yards away. The hen seemed to weigh up the situation immediately and attacked the dummy, stamping on its back and pecking its crown. The cock joined in but there was never a simultaneous attack.

After almost every attack the plovers jumped back as though expecting the dummy to retaliate. Attacks were often followed by the threat displays, the birds running towards the dummy with the black and white pectoral bands puffed out as much as possible. They also attacked from the air—kicking viciously as they flashed over the model. The hen was always much more aggressive than the cock. After some twelve minutes reaction died down and both birds went through a form of 'displacement activity', picking up small stones or pieces of grass and casting them to one side or over their backs. The hen then went to the nest and settled to incubate the eggs with the dummy still in position but badly battered.

We then erected a mirror about six feet from the nest. Unfortunately the bird approached from an angle which meant that, as it was getting interested, its image disappeared off the other end of the mirror. I could hardly contain my laughter as I watched the bird approach its image, start to display to it and, as its reflection disappeared, jump and begin a search round the back of the mirror trying to find the intruder!

In 1947 Stuart, George and I stayed among the high Cairngorms and tried some experiments with oystercatchers. We found a nest containing two eggs by a burn so we placed a stuffed oystercatcher nearby. When the hen saw it she first clucked, then gave a loud call note. This brought the cock and both birds ran towards the dummy with lowered heads, bills open, wings partly raised, and with varied calls, especially a prolonged trill which was indistinguishable from the so-called piping note associated with the nuptial display. As they neared the dummy they momentarily hesitated, then the hen attacked violently. In a minute or so the dummy was very battered and there seemed to be a victorious glint in the hen's bright red eye.

Throughout all this the cock stood by, never attacking but calling and showing such signs of nervous tension as throwing grass and stones, and 'pseudo-sleeping', tucking his bill into the scapular feathers while his eyes remained wide open.

Such was the reaction to the dummy when it was placed on the ground. The next day we nailed it on top of a post about two feet above and just behind the nest. As soon as she returned to the nest the hen attacked, sinking her long orange bill into its neck, then tearing the breast. It took George most of the night to repair it.

Next day we suspended the model from a wire frame-work so that it swung just clear of the ground. The cock returned first and mooched around calling for about three-quarters of an hour. Then the hen arrived, and went through all the previous types of display before attacking. As the dummy swung back after each buffet the hen sprang away nervously, but quickly recovered to launch another attack.

While we were carrying out these experiments Ludwig Koch came to make sound recordings of the oystercatcher's piping displays. He decided that during the day there was too much extraneous noise and more satisfactory results could be obtained if he recorded at night. Oystercatchers often pipe at night, especially around the time of the full moon. Just as these lovely trills were coming through loud and clear some engines started shunting waggons in nearby Aviemore station, thus completely ruining the recording. Ludwig stayed out until morning without success. He tried unsuccessfully again the following night, and the next, this time going to a different place farther away from the station, but the oystercatchers remained silent. Ludwig was getting desperate by the time we met him as that night he had to travel back to London.

He poured out his sad story to us and was quite mystified when we calmly asked him if he would like us to arrange everything for him, guaranteeing that if he did as we told him he would obtain all the recordings he wanted. He agreed. We loaded his gear on to a tractor and we all went off to the oystercatcher's nest. While Stuart fixed the microphone into position we helped Ludwig set up his recording apparatus in one of my hides. All the time we kept our stuffed oyster-catcher out of sight. When all was ready I placed the dummy in position, but hid it from Ludwig's view. We retired to watch from a short distance, out of sight of the oystercatchers. The adults returned and within ten minutes my hide was going in and out like a concertina and we could hear Ludwig exclaiming: 'It ees *wunderbar*—I do not know hows they doos it!' We told him and he went back to London a happy man.

During the years in which we were conducting these experiments we made many other observations, as can be seen from our book. One of the simplest of all our experiments could be duplicated by anyone prepared to take a little trouble to set the scene and exercise patience to watch the results.

We made an artificial pool deep in a wood, using an eighteen-inch-diameter tin receptacle sunk into the ground in a small clearing. We filled it with water and then erected hides close by. None of us approached for several days so that the birds could become accustomed to the sudden change in the local scenery and amenities.

Then, one sunny day in early June, when the wood was alive with bird-song, we entered the hides. It was soon obvious that the pool was already well known. About a dozen blue tits were bathing, drinking, squabbling and jostling in and around the small oasis. A family of hawfinches arrived and drank deeply—hawfinches are particularly thirsty birds. Then came some young mistle thrushes. It was then that the fun began, for the area of water was small, the competition great.

A mistle thrush approached at the same time as an adult hawfinch which is a naturally aggressive bird. For a moment they stood glaring at each other with open bills. Then the hawfinch lunged and the thrush sprang away. The birds squared up again, the hawfinch snapping its large nut-cracking mandibles; the thrush screaming at the top of its considerable voice. Neither would give way. Suddenly the hawfinch sprang at the thrush, snapping its mandibles with the sound of a small explosion. The thrush, not in the least intimidated, leapt into the air and kicked the hawfinch in the face with its claws.

During the next few days we witnessed several such aggressive displays during sessions we spent in the hides. The hawfinches were always the attackers and when they were at the pool the smaller birds, such as tits and small finches, kept a respectful distance. We saw many threat displays, even sparrings, but few fights.

One afternoon I watched a fascinating charade played around the hide by an adult and four young stoats. They jumped, fell over, pirouetted and performed various antics for about two hours. Why? I believe the idea is to make birds curious; they come closer and closer and as soon as one is within range, the stoat springs. It did not work this time: all the birds watched the circus from the safety of nearby trees.

What had our experiments accomplished? Had we done anything more, to quote the gibe of one unsympathetic ornithologist, than 'torment small birds with stuffed cuckoos'? Scientists, and ornithologists are scientists, carry out a lot of experiments because they think such work will help them to find out the truth about something. Our 'something' was bird behaviour, and we think our experiments did

Above: Willow warbler dives furiously at the head of a cuckoo. Experiments proved that the head alone was sufficient to rouse birds' antipathy

Below: left to right: Attacking willow warbler, stuffed cuckoo, dedicated scientist (Stuart Smith)

Above: The stuffed cuckoo, erected near a nest, often provoked the parent birds into a frenzied attack. Here the hen stonechat was already attacking when the cock joined in—her mate then turned his fury on her

Below: Hawfinch and mistle thrush spar beside a man-made pool in a wood

enable us to understand a little better the brain that lies behind a bird's bright eye.

They enabled us to study more displays of various kinds than we could have seen in a lifetime of normal bird-watching. We learnt that: the stage reached in the breeding cycle has an important effect on both the manner and intensity of reaction to a cuckoo; a full aggressive response is engendered by showing only a cuckoo's head; responses vary with individuals and their situation; reaction to danger is clear-cut and specific according to the nature of the predator; some birds have special cries for special situations (e.g. the little-heard 'croak' of the nightingale and the *chee-chee-chee* of the willow warbler); the displays for love (breeding) and hate (aggression) are sometimes indistinguishable; and that birds are, above all, 'eye-minded'—visual stimuli are all-important. And a valuable by-product to us was that walking about with a dummy cuckoo was an easy way of finding nests. It worked on the hot-and-cold principle—the nearer we approached to a nest, the fiercer the reaction.

In one way our experiments showed that a vital problem of the bird world finds its counterpart with man. A bird is at its fiercest when it thinks its living space is threatened. Is it too much to hope that man might learn something from this?

N

14 | *Spain*

'I think it unlikely that I shall do much travelling abroad until I have the majority of our British species in my bag.' When I said this to George Yeates on 14 March 1954 I sincerely believed it to be true. Within a matter of hours I was practically eating my words.

I had been to Bristol to join with George Yeates in a broadcast discussion on bird photography. James Fisher had invited us both to one of his famous *Birds in Britain* series and in the same programme was Guy Mountfort, who spoke about his favourite bird, the hawfinch.

There could not have been two men less alike in their approach to bird photography than George and I. Although we used similar types of apparatus, George concentrated on photographing one rare species at a time and would travel far to do so. I loved *every* bird, and although owls have always been my favourites, I get a thrill from photographing even the most common species. If George could come out of a hide with one superb photograph he was happy: I wanted the whole story.

At that time, apart from one visit to Holland, all my work had been done in Great Britain, but George had visited many European countries. To him the spice of life was the planning, the reading about wild places, the travelling, living close to nature and actually tracking down his quarry. To me the essence was an intimate study of a bird at close quarters using whatever equipment—light or heavy, simple or technical —that was necessary.

George had no time for backdoor-step photography, neither could he be bothered with high-speed flash. Just imagine transporting such complicated heavy apparatus to remote parts of Iceland! I said that there were 426 birds on the British list, and up to that time I had photographed only 182 of them. 'The British Isles are beautiful, with beautiful birds; and I think it unlikely that I shall do much travelling abroad until I have the majority of our British species in my bag.' I was absolutely sincere, but, ironically, the man who was instrumental in making a mockery of my assertion was there as I said it.

After the broadcast Guy Mountfort drove me back to London, entertaining me with wonderful stories about a place called the Coto Doñana in the south-west of Spain. He was thinking of organising an expedition to go there to make a detailed study of the bird-life. 'Would you consider joining such an expedition and taking complete responsibility for all the photographic work?' I promised to think about it and the more I thought the more attractive the whole idea appeared to me, and my broadcast vow faded into the background. Soon after I told Guy that I would accept his invitation.

Guy Mountfort is one of Europe's outstanding ornithologists with a special gift for leadership and organisation. His expeditions into the wilds of various countries not only bring back new and valuable information but, perhaps more important, alert the people themselves to the value of their own wild-life and the need to conserve it. Guy is a tall, lean, bespectacled man, with a forceful enthusiastic personality, a gift for lucid expression in both speech and writing, a talent for sketching and a keen sense of humour, gifts which are apparent to all readers of his various books.

Until his retirement he was managing director of a large firm of advertising agents, a high-powered and exacting job, but he still found time for much valuable work for the world's wild-life. He played an active rôle in the founding of the World Wild-life Fund, is one of its International Trustees, and serves on some of the committees. For ten years he was Honorary Secretary of the British Ornithologists' Union, during which time the membership doubled, and is now (1970) President. But of all his activities I think he will be best remembered as co-author with Roger Peterson and Philip Hollom of *A Field Guide to the Birds of Britain and Europe* (Collins, 1954)—a book that has done more than any other to help people find enjoyment in bird-watching.*

The Coto Doñana and the Marismas in south-west Spain is the greatest and richest wild-life sanctuary in Western Europe. Then administered by enlightened landowners, the Coto comprises some 350 square miles of desert, scrubland and water. It is bounded on the south and west by the Atlantic Ocean, with a twenty-five-mile sweep of dazzling white sandy beach. To the north and east are the Marismas— hundreds of square miles of grass, mud, marsh and water.

The other members of the party were Dr. Roger Tory Peterson; Lord Alanbrooke, whom I recommended to help with the cine-photography; James Ferguson-Lees, executive editor of *British Birds*, who has a vast knowledge of birds and their identification; James Fisher, renowned for his bird books as well as his hundreds of radio

---

* Guy received a well-deserved O.B.E. in the Queen's Birthday Honours in 1970.

and television appearances; E. R. (John) Parrinder, a quantity surveyor with a great enthusiasm for birds; George Shannon, dental surgeon by calling, ardent ornithologist and cine-photographer by choice; Jerry Jamieson, a banker whose hobby was bird photography; and the Hon. Mariegold Fitzalan-Howard, who helped Jerry drive all our heavy equipment across Europe. They fell in love on this trip and were married the following year.

The expedition was made possible by the exceptional kindness and generosity of Don Mauricio González Díez, his father and his family. A keen and experienced ornithologist, Don Mauricio fully approved of our expedition, and put himself, his staff and his home at our disposal. It was he who later translated the *Field Guide* into Spanish.

We assembled at London Airport on the night of 27 April 1956, and were in Gibraltar about three the next morning. While some of my companions snatched a few hours' sleep, I and several other energetic spirits explored the Rock. By breakfast-time we had seen many different species of birds, as well as the famous Barbary apes.

Having cleared the British and Spanish Customs, we were greeted by the welcome sight of Jerry and Mariegold with a large bus marked 'Coto Doñana Expedition', thoughtfully provided by Don Mauricio. We piled in and by noon were at Jerez, where we were warmly greeted by our host. We were now in the original home of sherry and liberal portions were imbibed by my companions—I equally enjoyed several cups of tea.

Our thirst quenched, we drove the few miles to Bonanza to board Don Mauricio's launch in which we travelled for two hours up the broad Guadalquivir River. After a picnic lunch on board we landed on the opposite bank, where a motley assortment of mules and horses was awaiting us, then the only practical transport across the eighteen miles of scrub, marsh and soft sand separating the Palacio de Doñana—the expedition's headquarters—from the outside world.

My previous experience of horse-riding was limited to a docile beach pony. I had never even sat on a mule, but Guy had assured me that it was much more surefooted than a horse, and with all the equipment I carried round my neck would be safer.

I could not help but recall George Yeates's account of his ride to the Palacio in 1935 which he described in his book *Bird Life in Two Deltas* (Faber & Faber, 1946). Like me he, too, was a novice on a horse. When he was in wooded country a wasp suddenly stung his horse on the hindquarters. The rope reins were torn from George's hands and his nag took off like a Derby winner. As branches whistled over his head George thought his skull would be cracked open at any moment so he tucked his head into the horse's neck and clung to its mane. After a hectic half-mile it stopped and George dismounted quickly before another wasp took offensive action.

Our journey took six hours, the last part being in rain and darkness. I was so stiff and sore that I had to be lifted off my mule, and when lowered to the ground I could not straighten my legs for some minutes. It was painful to sit down for the next forty-eight hours!

Although Guy had given me a glowing description of the great white Palacio it was even more impressive than I had imagined. In the 15th century the Coto Doñana was the hunting reserve of the Dukes of Medina Sidonia, one of whom later commanded the Armada. For 300 years Spanish kings stayed there periodically to hunt deer and boar, the last to do so being Alfonso XIII. Each time a Royal party descended with its horde of retainers, it became a man-sized job to accommodate them. Thus a hunting-lodge—Palacio—was built in the wilderness, and through the centuries enlarged, refurbished and modernised. The latest addition, I am pleased to say, was the installation of modern plumbing, including two bathrooms.

The Palacio is an immense square building able to accommodate at least 100 people, its four sides enclosing a large cobbled courtyard. The exterior plainly shows its medieval origin: a massive outer wall, heavy iron-bound doors, and barred windows ten feet from the ground. The ground floor of the main building, which extends along three sides of the courtyard, houses the servants' quarters, kitchens and store-rooms. A stone stairway leads to the living quarters, the many bedrooms being on either side of the echoing stone corridors.

The great hall is the main living-room. Its timbered ceiling arches high overhead, and on chill days sweet-smelling logs of stone pine burn in the massive fireplace. A hundred stag-heads decorate the walls and the framework of the magnificent central chandelier is fashioned from antlers.

This was to be my home for the four weeks of this expedition, and again during the four weeks of the second. I have travelled far and stayed in many strange and beautiful places—hovels to palaces—but the Palacio stays longest in my memory. This (apart from the modern plumbing) is how Spanish aristocrats and their retainers lived for hundreds of years.

We arrived in drenching rain; we awoke to brilliant sunshine—and a typical British breakfast of fried eggs, but cooked in olive oil.

The first day on the Coto Doñana is one that lives vividly in my memory. I had come straight from the bricks and mortar of London to a bird paradise. On the eucalyptus trees that partly sheltered the Palacio perched dozens of woodchat shrikes, a species I had seen only once before in my life. Occasionally one would dart to the ground, capture a lizard, grasshopper or beetle, and batter it against the branches in the manner of a kingfisher killing a fish. Scores of swallows hawked winged insects, frequently diving to catch those stirred up by the horses' hooves. A green woodpecker called but with a very different note from the laughing yaffle I knew in Britain. Two white storks flew over, a score of cattle egrets in train, a squacco heron bringing up the rear.

Avocets, so rare at home, paddled in the shallows, while many Kentish plovers and black-winged stilts stalked on their long legs in deeper water. A pratincole leapt up in front of me revealing a flash of red beneath its wings. Almost from beneath my feet a short-toed lark flew up to expose its nest, as yet with only one egg. A bittern boomed, little egrets fed along the water's edge, sometimes dancing in a most peculiar fashion—I realised afterwards that this was to stir up fish or water-life. Turnstones, ringed and little ringed plovers, and curlew sandpipers strutted and preened and fed.

Everywhere there were photographs to be taken, but the horses arrived and we set off to visit a heronry. Bee-eaters darted about us through the still air, their courtship displays in full swing, the males catching dragonflies and offering them to their mates. Others dug vigorously in the ground to make nesting holes. Generally, bee-eaters nest in sand-pits but on the Coto, since there are no banks of sand, they have to dig into the flat soil. So anxious was each bird to take its turn that it was smothered by the debris excavated and kicked out backwards by its mate.

There were birds all the way to the heronry, some well known in Britain, others I knew only from books. We spotted a hoopoe diving into the apex of the thatched roof of a *choza* (small hut) and, as we watched, almost full-grown young emerged to peer at us. At the heronry Roger Peterson, while focusing his camera, suddenly remarked: 'I can hear an Imperial eagle calling.' This extraordinary man never ceases to astound me. Here was an American, in Europe, correctly identifying a bird circling in the sky at least half a mile away, by its call-note alone.

The heronry was very different from anything I had expected. From afar hundreds of white wings were silhouetted against a clear blue sky. Near at hand every bush blossomed with little and cattle egrets, all squawking and bickering. The noise was deafening. Hides were erected and occupied by Guy, Roger and me while the others rode away. In a surprisingly short time the heronry returned to normal and it was possible to see that, apart from the large numbers of egrets, there were a number of night and squacco herons. The little and cattle egrets mainly occupied the centre of the colony, while the night and squacco herons occupied the perimeter and appeared to be less advanced in their nesting activities.

I was fascinated by a squacco heron nesting right in front of my hide. Every time a bird came anywhere near, it protested vigorously, spreading its neck and breast feathers, until it seemed twice its normal size. Nearby a male cattle egret displayed, raising his crest and spreading his buff throat feathers. He then started to 'blush', his yellow bill flushing blood red as he tried to attract his mate's attention.

As I sat watching and photographing these cattle egrets I thought of how widely this bird had spread. Until about 1930 it was known to breed in only some areas of southern Asia, Africa and south-west Europe, but in that year a number flew the Atlantic and landed in British Guiana. Apparently finding the climate and food to their liking, they bred and have since colonised much of both North and South America. Other cattle egrets flew eastwards until, by 1948, they were breeding in Australia: quite a success story in a world where the numbers of most animals are declining.

After we had been on the Coto about a week we were joined by Lord and Lady Alanbrooke. With typical modesty he had agreed to join the expedition on one condition: that he should take his full share of the organised work. Incidentally, the Alanbrookes were the only two members of the expedition who completed the strenuous ride from the river to the Palacio in five hours without a halt; both were more accustomed to horseback than the rest of us.

We soon found that *mañana*, and all that it implies in contempt for time, is a built-in characteristic of the Spaniard. In the whole of the Palacio there was one clock—ours. A picnic meal promised for noon would arrive, without apology, at three-thirty. But such inconveniences were small indeed compared with the lavish help and hospitality we received: this despite the fact that some of the staff considered we were quite crazy to go to such immense pains just to *look* at birds. And any lingering doubts they may have had of our lunacy were dispelled when one day they caught a group of us solemnly searching for, and then dissecting, the regurgitated pellets of fur, bones and other indigestible debris found beneath an Imperial eagle's eyrie.

This expedition, fruitful though it was, still left much to be done, especially the photographing and filming of the Spanish Imperial eagle. I was, therefore, eager to go on the next expedition in spring 1957. This was to be a larger party of fifteen members. Four of the original expedition were missing—Mariegold Fitzalan-Howard, Roger Peterson, Jerry Jamieson and James Fisher—but seven others joined us.

It was good to learn that two of these were to be Sir Julian and Lady Huxley. Having worked with Julian for many years I knew his great abilities and energy, while Juliette, apart from being a most charming person, has a considerable knowledge of botany and was to take charge of this side of the expedition. E. M. (Max) Nicholson, then Director-General of the Nature Conservancy and an outstanding ecologist, was to be in charge of this important part of our work, namely the elucidation of the complicated interrelationships of all forms of life.

We also welcomed the company of Philip Hollom, another of the editors of *British Birds* and co-author of *A Field Guide to the Birds of Britain and Europe*. He is one of those quiet unassuming folk who are content to stay in the background, but are always there when help is needed. Tony Miller, another excellent ornithologist, could turn his hand to almost any job and was especially helpful in the construction of the pylon hides. Dr. John Raines came with us primarily for his knowledge of European birds, but also in case anyone needed medical treatment. Finally, there was Don José Antonio Valverde Gomez— Tono to all of us—who had an excellent all-round knowledge of natural history, and was almost as familiar with the Coto Doñana as Don Mauricio himself.

With a small advance party I flew ahead and worked in the magnificently rugged country around Arcos. Alas, instead of the hygienic comfort of the Palacio we had to endure the primitive conditions of a village inn. The warmth of our bodies as we climbed between the none-too-clean sheets summoned up several regiments of voracious bed bugs who promptly set to work. Fortunately, we had only three nights at Arcos, and spent the remainder of the time in Jerez.

So much happened during those two unforgettable expeditions that I can pick out only the highlights. Those who want to know more should consult Guy Mountfort's *Portrait of a Wilderness* (first published in 1958). The number and variety of birds were fantastic. On one memorable day the expedition listed no fewer than 113 species, and altogether on the expedition 193 species were recorded.

One of our objectives on the first expedition was to photograph the kites—the common or red, and the black—which have a special interest for British ornithologists. In Shakespeare's day, kites were the scavengers of our streets and, in London especially, were very common. Today, in the whole of Britain there remain under twenty-five pairs of red kites in a small area of Wales. It was very different on the Coto; kites were everywhere. Our only problem was to find a suitable nest; young chicks, right position relative to the sun, and accessible without too much gardening.

We eventually chose a red kite's nest thirty-seven feet up a cork oak. It was a true scavenger's nest, consisting mainly of rags, paper, bones, dried cow-pats and other unsavoury refuse. By cutting away only two small branches and a few twigs, which did little harm, I could photograph the nest clearly and with maximum benefit from the angle of the sun.

So far so good. But the height of the nest meant that we had to erect a pylon thirty-five feet high and we had insufficient equipment. At the Palacio, however, were some slender eucalyptus poles, and we decided to use these plus some old sherry cases for a platform. As our first consideration was not to disturb the birds unduly we worked in easy stages, about forty-five minutes each morning.

But we soon ran into snags. The pylon had to be constructed against the slender outer branches of the oak tree which would not support a man's weight. I think we should have had to abandon the attempt had it not been for Pepe, one of the more remarkable members of the Palacio staff. He juggled his body between poles and branches as though the laws of gravity did not exist. He was quickly nicknamed El Mono, the monkey. But even with all his enthusiastic help and the pylon-building know-how of the rest of us, it was a decidedly rickety thirty-five feet of eucalyptus and sherry cases that I was invited to climb to have the first photographic session.

My colleagues had barely left when the hen arrived, and to my great relief did not even glance at the hide. She was not in the least suspicious and started to tear morsels from the sun-dried body of a rabbit. Without warning the cock arrived with a black and yellow lizard-like creature—probably a salamander—dangling from his bill. Gently he offered it to one of the chicks who grabbed it and swallowed it whole. The cock left and the hen and chicks went to sleep.

The wind played through the cork oak, swaying the hide, and I felt very drowsy. But to sleep at such a time would be unforgivable. Apart from the danger, it was my duty to obtain a complete series of photographs. Fortunately the cock returned and all thoughts of sleep were banished. The hen took the rabbit he brought, tore it to pieces and fed the ravenous chicks which soon became satiated and huddled pown to sleep. The cock departed and the hen took her fill of what was left.

Although the kite is generally regarded as a scavenger, it also catches live prey, and during the next few hours the young were fed on an ocellated lizard, and a water snake which was still writhing. During the middle of the day as the wind rose, the hide creaked and groaned, and the sherry-boxes moved ominously. But all was well.

Nine hours later my companions came to relieve me. I stuck my head out of the hide and my face, although crimson from the steam bath I had endured inside (96°F), clearly showed that the session had been successful. They told me afterwards that as I slithered down the pylon I kept up an almost incoherent commentary from which could be distinguished, 'Simply terrific . . . couldn't have been better . . . absolute peach of a bird . . . both parents at the nest!'

In a hide time means nothing. During the whole of that nine hours I had forgotten to eat my lunch—all I had was a large flask of tea.

On this first expedition the flask had figured in an amusing altercation with Roger Peterson. In an adjoining hide Roger was trying his luck with a night heron. At one point he had the heron sharply focused but two cattle egrets in the background spoilt the composition of the picture. So Roger uttered a low 'moo-oo-oo' which had the desired effect of frightening away the egrets without disturbing the heron. He got his photograph.

I teased: 'It's not cricket to disturb the birds with strange noises.'

To which Roger replied: 'Every day at 4 p.m. I hear from the direction of your blind [American for hide] the pop of a cork and the *glug-glug-glug* of tea being poured from a Thermos. Is that cricket?'

Roger says that my only answer was a snort.

From a photographic point of view the main objective of the second expedition was the Spanish Imperial eagle, now so rare that there are probably no more than fifty pairs left in the world. It is a sub-species of the Imperial eagle, which is found in parts of eastern Europe and occasionally as far east as Japan. The exciting thing to me was that it had never before been photographed. During the 1956 expedition no suitable nest had been found, so before we left for home we urged the local keepers to do their utmost to locate a nest for us before we arrived in 1957. Often such a request goes unheeded, so I was not optimistic.

One great problem we have on our expeditions is time: there is never enough of it. Days, even weeks, are sometimes spent finding a nest and by then it may be too late, either because the young are too big or because our time has expired. We were, therefore, most excited when, in April, Guy received a letter from Mauricio González saying that his keepers had found the ideal nest on the top of a stone pine tree. On arrival at the Palacio I could scarcely wait to be taken to the site and could hardly believe my eyes when I saw it.

We had brought half a ton of tubular duralumin scaffolding (see pages 151 and 153), and with this erected a pylon hide nineteen feet from the nest. We worked very carefully, since I would never have forgiven myself if anything happened to the chick, now nearly a month old.

Each morning Guy arranged for all the expedition members to lend a hand, and we worked furiously for an hour, hoisting the tubes into position and securing them with strong clamps. Then we abandoned everything and hurried away. Thus the pylon hide slowly grew, and the adult Spanish Imperial eagles had plenty of time to become accustomed to the peculiar tower growing near their nest. The work was completed in six shifts, with the platform in position and the canvas hide erected. Then I insisted that no one should go near the nest for forty-eight hours to give the birds ample time to become thoroughly accustomed to the hide.

Anxiously I looked forward to the end of the waiting period, and then entered the hide and quickly fixed the camera in position. The sun beat down from a clear blue sky; the chick panted and sweat dripped off my nose. But I forgot my discomfort in the absolute absorption of watching the eaglet. It was still covered in white down except for the first traces of feathers on the extreme edges of the wings, and its crop was so distended that it must have had a fairly large meal just before I arrived.

Nearly five hours elapsed before the hen returned and words cannot convey my tremendous excitement as this magnificent eagle glided down to the eyrie, so close to the hide that I could almost touch her. I am sure my heart missed a beat.

As always with a new bird, I did not attempt photography until I was certain that the adult was relaxed and occupied with a chore about the nest. It was fully twenty minutes before she picked up a rabbit and started to feed the young. I studied her reactions carefully as I released the camera shutter but she appeared not even to hear it. I had obtained the first-ever photograph of this very rare eagle.

I had many thrilling sessions in that hide, but that first view of the hen Spanish Imperial eagle alighting on the nest is the most vivid of all.

When George Shannon occupied the hide he excelled himself, taking some of the finest sequences of his distinguished career as a bird cinematographer. One sequence in particular is a classic. It shows the eaglet trying to swallow a young rabbit whole, failing to do so and then trying to pull it to pieces. But not having learned how to grasp the prey beneath its talons, every time it tried to pull off a piece of meat, it pulled the whole rabbit instead. Then, purely by accident, it put its foot on the prey—and succeeded in feeding itself.

Lord Alanbrooke also filmed at the nest. Although in his seventies, he agilely climbed the thirty-foot pylon with its three-foot 'steps' and made light of the gruelling heat of the hide. Back at the Palacio after his triumphant session he appeared less tired than any of us, and kept us enthralled with his after-dinner conversation.

I was particularly glad to receive a letter from Don Mauricio on our return home, saying that the young eagle was now flying strongly.

Although birds were the main object of these two expeditions, they were not our sole interest. The Coto has some thirty species of mammals, and over twenty of reptiles and amphibians. And, of course, there is an abundance of plants, trees and flowers.

However, some of the locals were among the most interesting of the mammals. The staff of the Palacio was an enclosed community, shut off almost completely from the outside world, living much as people lived in the Middle Ages, with Don Mauricio as the benevolent feudal lord. The amenities of modern medicine were a day's mule or horse ride and a river crossing distant, and were called upon only in dire emergencies.

One of the expedition's favourites was Pepe, a small wiry man about thirty years old, whom I mentioned earlier as helping with the pylon for the kite's nest. We were told that he had come to the Palacio to escape his demon—drink—which, in his youth, had come near to wrecking his life. The hard outdoor work and Spartan existence saved him. He seemed a very happy man, utterly content with a life as near to nature as he could get. He scorned a bed, preferring to sleep in the open, and he rarely wore anything on his feet; his calloused soles were so thick that he could slide down a tree as though it were a greasy pole and stamp out the embers of a fire without the slightest sign of discomfort.

Pepe was immensely strong. At Gibraltar it took two hefty dock hands to lift my case of pylon clips. When we were unloading at the river bank, Pepe slung the case on to his back and carried it through thick mud to the waiting mules. We were told that he had several times thrown an adult Andalucian bull. His technique was to run alongside, put his hand underneath its throat and grab the offside horn, then with an almighty tug jerk its head round to throw it off balance. Fantastic as it sounds, I am sure this was no fairy tale; Pepe offered to give us a demonstration but, despite our interest, we declined.

One day when we were exploring scrubland on a tractor we witnessed another of his feats. Pepe, with his faithful one-eared greyhound, was riding with us when he suddenly spotted a hare. Immediately dog and master gave chase, dashing through gorse and bramble—barefoot, of course. Ten minutes later they reappeared, the hare dangling from Pepe's belt. He vaulted over the tailboard and sat down. The greyhound was panting. Pepe breathed normally.

I had two experiences with non-avian species—one large, one small—both of which could have been disastrous.

Guy had suggested to me that sometime during our stay I should photograph the varied types of habitat on the Coto Doñana. The most important of these were the Marismas which attracted so many of the birds. Then there were the sand-dunes which support a very varied vegetation, the cork oak woods, the scrub-land and heath-lands.

Apart from these areas, there were large stretches of featureless plain which were not pictorially inspiring. I therefore sought view-points from which to photograph where the direction of the light, foreground and perspective would give the most pleasing result. I felt that the right spot could more easily be found on foot so one day, when we were returning to the Palacio, I decided to walk the four or five miles across the flat open plain, rather than ride the horse that had been provided for me. I tried to explain this to the guide accompanying me but, not speaking a common tongue, I doubt if he understood my sign language. He seemed reluctant to leave me and I soon realised why.

After walking fewer than 100 yards I noticed one of the many bulls, which more or less run wild in these parts, taking an interest in me. These animals are reared for the bull-ring and are very different from British bulls. In place of the fat lethargic beast with a ring through its nose, in Spain the bulls are lithe and nimble, and never seem happier than when bashing their heads against the beast on the adjoining territory. Instead of the cows being brought to them in their own comfortable stalls as in Britain, the Spanish bulls have to fight for their harem and, therefore, constantly patrol the perimeter of their domain. These bulls are accustomed to seeing horses wandering about, and take no notice of them, even when carrying a rider. And on the Coto no one in his right senses ever walks.

When the frisky bull that had taken such an interest in me started to make a detour round me I tried to kid myself that I did not look in the least like a cow. Anyway, there must be no panic, for there is nothing that makes a bull more likely to charge than the sight of something running away. But the bull seemed to lose interest in me and I breathed again. But not for long. I was now approaching another bull which was pawing the ground and snorting ominously. I decided that there was a far better picture at right angles, so headed in that direction. The ruse worked, but it was not long before I was on the territory of another bull. My only protection was a heavy wood and metal tripod which I opened up to its fullest extent. Fortunately there was no need to use it. No wonder my guide had not wanted to leave me.

The other adventure occurred when I was photographing from a hide. Through forty years and countless thousands of hours spent in hides, it has become second nature to me to remain quite still, except for the inevitable movements needed to operate my camera. One afternoon while quiet and engrossed at the peep-hole, a Lataste's viper, the most poisonous snake in the area, slid into the hide, curled up between my boots and went to sleep. And there it stayed for four

hours, fortunately undisturbed and therefore unaggressive. The slight
noises and movements I made had no effect and it eventually slithered
out of the hide.

Snakes were fairly common, and we were warned not to put our
hands in nesting holes in trees, or down rabbit burrows—the occupants
might well be vipers. Evidently through the centuries there have been
many fatalities from snakes—the peasants are so superstitious about
them that even to mention the word snake is considered unlucky If one
has to be mentioned the euphemism 'lizard' is used.

Snakes form a sizable part of the food of some predacious birds on
the Coto, especially of short-toed eagles which are also called serpent
or snake eagles. The way eaglets cope with several feet of sometimes
still writhing snake is remarkable. I was in the hide when a short-toed
eagle alighted on the nest with a two-foot snake dangling from its bill.
At once the chick seized the snake by its tail and pulled vigorously.
With quick backward movements of its head it began to swallow the
snake. But something went wrong, and the chick regurgitated it and
began all over again, this time tackling it head first. In an astonishingly
short time the snake disappeared—all two feet of it into a chick about
ten inches long.

Even this performance was eclipsed when a still larger snake
nearly three feet long and one and a half inches across the middle was
delivered by the male. The female started to tear off tiny pieces for the
chick but such dainty feeding was too slow for the rapacious youngster
who, at the first opportunity, grabbed the relatively huge snake and
started to swallow it. Eight inches quickly disappeared, but then the
chick began to choke and had to disgorge. But not for long. Again the
snake was attacked, section by section disappearing at the steady rate
of four seconds per gulp.

When the thickest part of the snake was reached the chick's small
gape was stretched to the utmost, and the weight of the snake was so
great that the youngster keeled over on its side. Righting itself the
chick continued its gargantuan meal, but had to pause every few
minutes from sheer exhaustion. When the tip of the snake's tail finally
disappeared down the chick's throat and it could at last close its bill,
the struggle (I can hardly call it a meal) had lasted thirty-seven minutes.
By then the chick was in a state of collapse and its crop was blown up
like a miniature football. Yet three and a half hours later, it ate another
snake! The rapidity of the digestive processes of young eagles is one
of the wonders of creation. I was using my cine-camera so managed to
obtain sequences of all the highlights of the feast, showing how a ten-
inch chick can swallow prey nearly four times its own length.

During the expeditions the cine-photographers exposed five and a half miles of colour film to produce the highly successful *Wild Spain*. Apart from several television performances both on BBC and ITV, it was shown to two full houses at the Royal Festival Hall as well as in most of the large halls throughout the British Isles.

All the claims that Guy had made about the Coto Doñana were fully justified. The birds, the weather and the generous co-operation I received from everyone enabled me to take some of the best photographs of my life. I made enlargements of a selection of these—some 40 in. ×30 in.—and shipped them to Spain, where they now decorate the walls of the Palacio. Guy's book, and I like to think my photographs, stirred public opinion when it seemed possible that part of this wonderful sanctuary might be taken over by international speculators and 'developed' with, for example, a vast holiday camp stretching the length of the Coto Doñana beaches. The World Wild-life Fund went into action and after a hard struggle, and with the full co-operation of the Spanish Government, saved the main area of the Coto, which is now a permanent wild-life sanctuary. Guy, who worked as hard as anybody to achieve this result, tells the full story in the preface to the revised edition (1968) of *Portrait of a Wilderness* (David & Charles).

15 | *Bone-breaker*

Lammergeier, flying dragon, ossifrage, golden-headed eagle, bearded vulture, bone-breaker: such are the names which have been applied to this magnificent bird—half vulture, half eagle. Having studied and photographed it in the air and at the nest in the high sierras of southern Spain, watched it at close range in Pakistan and East Africa, and observed it dropping bones in Jordan, I can only echo the words of that veteran ornithologist, the late Dick Meinertzhagen: 'Seen at close quarters I know no bird so impressive.'

The lammergeier is primarily a gliding bird—an albatross of the land. With its huge angled wings spreading nine feet, the great bird glides effortlessly for mile after mile, sometimes sweeping a few yards above the ground, sometimes soaring until it is invisible. Just how high it soars no one knows, but it has been seen at about 25,000 ft. on Mount Everest.

However like an eagle in appearance, the lammergeier is more like a vulture in character. It rarely makes an overt attack on any mammal or bird capable of defending itself, although it occasionally attacks a wounded one. It is a scavenger, living largely on carrion, offal and bones. If it finds other vultures at a feast it stands by until the carcass is picked clean, making no attempt to join the squabbling. Only when the others have departed does the lammergeier descend upon the skeleton.

But it is a master of the sneak attack, when it can do the maximum of damage with the minimum of risk. One habit, according to Dick Meinertzhagen, is to swoop on an animal—such as chamois or wild goat—when it is in a precarious position on a cliff-face, strike it with the tip of a powerful wing or with its talons, and send it hurtling to its death. There are even a few records of attacks on humans, but they are decidedly exceptions to its general behaviour.

The lammergeier is a bone-breaker. Bones and even skulls of

GLASS AND ITS REFLECTING PROPERTIES ARE UNKNOWN IN NATURE
When, therefore, a bird is faced with its own reflection it behaves as though
it were facing a rival. A ringed plover displays aggressively to itself, (above) by
fanning its tail, and (below) by stretching upward

THE COTO DOÑANA PARTY

Above: Formal. *Left to right standing:* George Shannon, Tono Valverde, James Ferguson-Lees, Mauricio González, Tony Miller, Phil Hollom. *Sitting:* Max Nicholson, Guy Mountfort, Lady Huxley, Lord Alanbrooke, Lady Alanbrooke, Sir Julian Huxley, E.H.

Below: Informal. *Left to right:* Guy Mountfort, E.H., Lord Alanbrooke, Lady Alanbrooke (half hidden), the Hon. Mariegold Fitzalan-Howard, James Ferguson-Lees

SPAIN

Above: Spanish Imperial eagle and month-old young

Below: Griffon vulture at red deer carcass

IN QUEST OF THE BONE-BREAKER

Above left: The hide (circled), perched on a rock jutting out over a valley 200 feet below, was blown away during a violent storm. *Above right:* Expedition members below the nest in the cave. *Below left:* Bundled into a sack, the young lammergeier is carefully lowered for inspection and photography. *Below right:* As Antonio Cano grasps its huge wings, it displays formidable bill and talons

carcasses are taken aloft and dropped on rocks. Heaps of splintered bones are sometimes found near outcrops of rock, the bone-breaker's anvil. Writing of such an ossuary in Kenya, R. E. Moreau says: 'Over an area of some forty yards each way the bare rock was littered with white splinters of bone. In hollows they lay in drifts. I could have collected a dozen pailfuls.' The purpose of this exercise is to get at the marrow and brains from the bones and skull. The lammergeier's stiff, gouge-shaped tongue is adapted for extracting such succulent fare.

While in Wadi Rum with Guy Mountfort and John Wightman in 1963 we watched a lammergeier dropping an object on to the top of Jebel Um Ishrin. One of the best-known natural history legends tells how the Greek dramatist, Aeschylus, died when an 'eagle' (almost certainly a lammergeier) dropped a tortoise, mistaking his bald pate for a rock.

Lammergeiers nest in mountains, usually in a cave or a recess in a cliff, the foundation of the nests being sticks and branches, but various adornments are added. E. H. N. Lowther says of a nest built on a precipitous crag 6,000 ft. high in the Himalayas near Simla:

'My first impression was that the lammergeier must be the King of the Rag and Bone merchants, for the nest was a huge collection of soiled sticks and dirty old rags and pieces of wool, with a large piece of sacking billowing in the breeze; this the bird must have had considerable difficulty in carrying. On these reposed pieces of green bottles, old bones—real veterans these—and horns. The far wall was white with droppings, possibly of years.'

One to three eggs are laid, but generally only one young is reared. Incubation lasts for an average of fifty-three days, and after hatching the fledgling remains in the nest for between 105 and 117 days.

Such is a brief account of the lammergeier, the bird that lured me to Spain in the early summer of 1959. But to photograph this magnificent bird at the nest is no light undertaking, so I decided to lead an expedition of my own, 'Operation Bone-breaker'.

For months I read every word I could find about it, wrote scores of letters and planned everything down to the last detail. The other members of the expedition were Dr. John Ash, a professional ornithologist; James Ferguson-Lees, John Parrinder and George Shannon (all of whom had been in the Coto Doñana and Finland with me); Mrs. Eileen Parrinder, who came as botanist; Johnnie and Gwen Johnson, who not only took out all our equipment and brought it back, but also did all the sound recording; Bob Spencer, an excellent field ornithologist who wished to do some ringing, especially of young lammergeiers; and Dr. John Stafford, medical officer and naturalist.

The Spanish ornithologists, Antonio Cano and Antonio Valverde, joined us in the high sierras of south-eastern Spain. During the spring

o

of 1958 they had found a lammergeier's nest but it was not, unfortu
nately, occupied in 1959. Like many other birds of prey, the lammergeier
often has several nesting sites, sometimes using one for two or three
years in succession, then abandoning it for another, only to return to
it later.

We were probably the first party of Englishmen to visit the area for
many years, because we were received by the Mayor and the whole
town came to greet us. We were interviewed by the local newspaper
men and I had to give an impromptu radio talk.

Unfortunately a landslide had completely blocked the mountain
road so, to while away the time, we went for a walk accompanied by
at least forty of the local children, who, by their chatter and laughter,
made certain that we saw few birds. We were amused to see a boy
goat-herd carrying an umbrella—it seemed so completely out of place—
until without much warning the heavens opened and we realised how
sensible he was. Later we discovered that it was the general practice,
not only to keep off the rain but also to shelter from the blistering sun.

Bulldozers were unknown in this part of Spain and the landslide
had to be cleared by an army of men with shovels and wheelbarrows.
Next morning we got through and were soon admiring the spectacular
scenery.

Once settled in, our first task was to find a lammergeier and hope
that it would lead us to a nest. Each day we went to different parts of
the sierra, watching with binoculars and telescope. Sections of cliff-face
were carefully examined for white droppings, hours were spent in
positions that had commanding views, in the hope that a lammergeier
would show up. Sometimes the weather was gorgeous, sometimes it
poured with rain, and on at least one occasion it snowed and was
freezing cold.

Then suddenly one day a huge bird flew overhead. It looked like
an outsize falcon with long diamond-shaped tail and long narrow
wings. My first sight of a lammergeier. What a view, what a bird!
Breast and throat were bright orange, head cream, the back was brown,
eye a vivid orange-red. We watched it for an hour or more, hardly
daring to lower our binoculars lest we lost sight of it. Eventually it
flew into a small cave on the side of a steep limestone cliff, 1,500 ft.
above the valley floor.

The next day we set out to examine the cave. As we climbed, the
scenery became more and more fantastic; jagged limestone peaks
towered above us, streams in the distant valleys glinted in the sun,
forests of pine trees threw long, cool shadows, and all around us the
ground was carpeted with a variegated pattern of wild flowers, especially peonies and saxifrages.

We eventually reached a narrow grassy ledge about thirty feet below the cave. The two Spaniards were determined to get to the cave but when halfway Tono Valverde slipped and crashed back on to the ledge, narrowly missing the edge and a sheer fall of 150 to 200 ft. We feared he was seriously hurt but he picked himself up as though he had just tripped over his bootlace. Eventually, with the aid of pitons and rope, Antonio Cano scaled the vertical cliff-face and disappeared inside the cave. He found a nest about three feet across, made of pine, oak and juniper branches with a thick lining of sheep's wool. Scattered about were two legs of sheep, several hooves and bones of sheep and goats, a dog's skull—and an old rope sandal! There was one huge chick.

Antonio let down a rope and Tono climbed up it followed by George. They put the youngster into a sack and lowered it to us. It was by far the largest chick I had ever seen, as big as a medium-sized turkey. Wearing leather gloves James made a careful examination—it had enormous talons, a three-inch hooked bill and a gape big enough to take a man's fist.

Never have I wanted to photograph anything more than those lammergeiers—but never have I seen a more difficult site. We had to erect a hide inside the cave no more than a couple of feet from the nest, or across a gully 150 ft. away. The first site was too close, the second too distant for successful photography.

We finally put up two hides, one for me at the 150 ft. site, the other just over 200 ft. for George to make the film. My hide was on a rock jutting out over a valley with a sheer drop of about 200 ft. When I entered the hide my companions roped me to a nearby rock, for fear I might make a false move and fall into the valley.

Early on the morning of 2 June I left with two keepers for the first attempt at photography. As we approached the hide we saw a lammergeier circling overhead. Then it closed its wings and dived headlong, swinging up at the last moment before disappearing into the cave. It stayed for only a moment or two, then flew out of sight. We arrived at eight o'clock and the keepers saw me into the hide.

The young lammergeier was two months old and I had imagined that the adults would bring in food only once or twice every twenty-four hours. But within half an hour I saw an adult fly into the cave carrying what appeared to be a piece of wool a foot long. The parent stayed only forty seconds.

As the sun began to warm the air, thousands of flies appeared, and at times I wondered whether they would make photography impossible as there were clouds of them between the camera and the nest.

Soon after ten-thirty I heard the young bird chittering and a moment later an adult alighted by its side. It did not bring any food but picked up bits of fur and bone and offered these to the chick, which pecked at them but made no effort to swallow any. The adult stayed for twenty minutes and, after photographing it with the 600 mm lens, I studied it carefully through my ×8 Zeiss binoculars. Seeing it thus at only fifty yards range was a wonderful experience and its beauty left an indelible impression on my mind. As it left the cave it leaned forward, opened its great wings and, without a flap, sailed away.

Shortly before 1 p.m. I heard an adult call, and from the side peep-hole which overlooked the valley, saw the bird fly towards the hide. Closer and closer it came and sailed by with one wing no more than two feet away. It was the most incredible view imaginable—for seconds my eye seemed fixed on the lammergeier's and I am sure my heart missed a beat or two. I also realised why the lammergeier is so often called the bearded vulture: two black tufts of long stiff bristles stood out prominently from its chin. It turned and swept round towards the nest and I could see that it carried food in its talons. It flew well below the cave and then soared up to it. The chick nearly fell out of the cave as it dived for the food and swallowed great hunks of it. This was surprising, because I had watched the feeding process at the nest of a griffon vulture and there the adult had regurgitated all the food. Vultures do not, as a rule, carry food in their talons but this lammergeier certainly did.

The temperature inside the hide at 4 p.m. was 92°F and when the lammergeier again visited the nest so much perspiration dripped from my forehead I could not see clearly. I stayed in the hide till 7 p.m.—eleven hours of superb bird-watching.

After the first session we left the hide for two days. When we returned the whole outfit had disappeared. Three of the support poles were found in the valley but the fourth and the hide itself were never recovered. A tremendous gale had swept down the valley carrying all before it. I had a nightmare vision of a bird photographer dangling from a rope, buffeted by an angry wind, swinging to and fro over the deep valley!

Having photographed the lammergeier at the nest I now wanted to photograph it on its own. I bought a sick lamb, had it painlessly put to death, and then we pegged it down near the top of a mountain where we hoped the lammergeiers would see it. We erected two hides thirty feet away so that George could film from one while I took stills from the other.

Before long clouds of flies descended on the carcass. A raven tore at the entrails, carrying some away. An Egyptian vulture inspected it but after twenty minutes decided it was not ripe enough to be seasonable and went away. We stayed for eight hours in those hides, getting hotter and hotter, but no lammergeiers obliged.

The next day I decided to make another attempt. The smell from the carcass nearly knocked me over but, somehow, once settled in the hide I did not find the odour so offensive. I had not been waiting long when I realised that great shadows were sweeping across my hide—griffon vultures. Out of the corner of my eye I saw an Egyptian vulture alight and move towards the carcass, then a raven flew on to the lamb's head and pecked at its eyes. As the raven flew away, a black kite alighted but this was chased away by the Egyptian vulture. Some griffons came down in the distance but seemed in no hurry to start their feast. Was this because they were not hungry or the carcass was not ripe enough, or because they were suspicious?

Four hours elapsed before things really started to happen but once they did it was a free-for-all with no holds barred. With its wings widespread a griffon waddled and, growling gruffly, jumped towards the carcass. Others alighted some yards away and bounded forward—let battle commence! For a time they seemed more intent on fighting each other than in feeding but there soon developed a 'pecking order'. One huge griffon sank its head into the carcass, tore a lump off, swallowed it and at the same time viciously struck out with its feet in an attempt to drive off competitors.

I made a quick count: there were thirty-four griffons at or near the lamb, four Egyptians, two black kites and two ravens, with another seventeen griffons waiting on rocks or pine trees.

But there was no sign of a lammergeier. Although we tried again and again we never saw one come down to take food. But to my dying day I shall never forget that view of the bone-breaker as it swept by my hide, our eyes fixed on each other.

16 | *Bulgaria*

Bulgaria was the first Iron Curtain country I visited, again on an expedition organised by Guy Mountfort. Less was known of Bulgarian wild-life than of almost any other European country, and since Bulgaria is at the junction of four different climatic and faunistic zones—boreal, steppe, temperate and Mediterranean—the expedition presented an exciting prospect. The formidable difficulties in mounting an expedition from the West to a communist country were eventually overcome and we flew to Sofia on 15 May 1960. The other members of the expedition were James Ferguson-Lees, Philip Hollom, Jerry Jamieson and George Shannon—all of whom had been to the Coto Doñana in Spain with us—and E. D. H. (Johnnie) Johnson, Bob Spencer and Dr. John Stafford who had accompanied me on the 1959 Bone-breaker Expedition.

I was indirectly responsible for one alarming incident that happened to Johnnie Johnson, who had undertaken to drive nearly 2,000 miles across Europe with half a ton of our photographic and recording apparatus. At the Bulgarian frontier Johnnie used all the phrases which had worked so well before and the Customs officials were respectful and well disposed. Certainly, a scientific study by British naturalists and photographers at the invitation of the Bulgarian Government? Welcome! Welcome! No formalities, just an inspection of one case—any will do.

That did it. As soon as the lid was lifted there was a hiss of indrawn breath—sub-machine-guns! This was the gun-butt which I attach to my 35 mm cameras when photographing birds in flight. How Johnnie talked himself out of that one I do not know, but somehow he did.

But that was not the end of our troubles. Our heavy baggage containing essential stores had disappeared. It was sent from England by rail and could be traced to Frankfurt but no farther. Neither was there any sign of the vehicles we had been promised. All enquiries were parried. We began to wonder why we had come at all and whether we should just turn round and go home. Then we learned the reason for all this evasiveness. The Summit Conference of the Big Four in Paris had collapsed in acrimony over the notorious U-2 spy plane incident. Had it not been for the intervention of the Minister at the British Legation, Mr. Anthony Lambert (later Sir Anthony Lambert, British Ambassador in Portugal), and his diplomatic skill, we would probably have abandoned the expedition. As it was, the vehicles were ready the next morning, and since we had enough stores to make a start we got away without further mishap. But it was not until a fortnight later, when we had reached the Black Sea coast, that our main baggage caught up with us.

We soon discovered that Bulgaria was no Coto Doñana: there appeared to be a singular lack of birds. Peasants take wild birds' eggs to augment their meagre protein ration. That anyone could have an aesthetic and scientific interest in birds seemed beyond their comprehension. And there are swarms of magpies which rob many of the nests that the peasants miss. Moreover, we found that we had been misled about the time of the nesting season: in Bulgaria it is several weeks later than in Western Europe. The country is roughly in the same latitude as the French Camargue, but the nesting season in Bulgaria has not even started when in the Camargue it is almost over.

One of the main objects of the expedition was to study the pelicans on the Danube: the white and the Dalmatian. The latter is slightly the larger of the two species, and represents about a third of the total pelican population. Owing to severe persecution by the peasants, who object to anything that takes their fish, the Dalmatian pelican is in danger of extermination as a European species. In flight the lower surface of the wings are greyish white with black edges, whereas in the white pelican the primaries are black.

Accordingly we spent our first day in the wild-life sanctuary at Lake Sreburna near the Danube in north-east Bulgaria. Our punts glided over the sparkling water surrounded by a forest of reeds, some ten feet high. A flight of Dalmatian pelicans, in V-formation, circled above us, their greyish-white under-surfaces gleaming against the sky. We hoped they would drop on their nests among the reeds, but they flew off to the Danube.

We met with better luck at Lake Burgas in the south near the Black Sea coast. While we were photographing a white stork at its nest in a farmyard someone shouted: 'Pelicans overhead!' and there, approaching on stiffly held wings, were wave after wave of white pelicans looking like squadrons of bombers. As I watched, they found a thermal and wheeled even higher, rising in the warm air currents without a single wing-beat. Some circled clockwise, some anti-clockwise, their paths crossing and re-crossing in complicated manœuvres against the vast arc of the sky. Then, with no apparent signal, the leaders headed towards Lake Burgas and the rest followed—and so did we.

Half a mile from the lake we began to stalk the pelicans across the water-meadows to the shore, wallowing knee-deep in muddy water until we were within 100 yards of where they stood preening in the shallows. Quickly we erected a hide on a muddy promontory and the other members of the party left me in it.

Fortunately the pelicans gradually drifted towards me, some actually standing round the hide. I shot dozens of stills and several hundred feet of film. Some of the birds seemed overcome by the intense heat, and lay down in the shallows with beaks wide open and heads half submerged in an effort to keep cool.

While filming at Lake Burgas I witnessed the most peculiar behaviour of a little egret. First it ran in one direction, then in another, turned about and repeated the performance, all the time vigorously flapping its wings. It looked as if it were having a fit. Actually it was fishing; the vigorous movements stirred up the fish, and several were snapped up while I watched.

Having obtained our records of pelicans we now wanted to photograph one of Europe's most beautiful birds, the wall creeper. We were told that one nested in the wall of an Alpine hut near the Rila Monastery, ten miles distant in the highest mountain range in Bulgaria. We decided to spend a night at the monastery and try our luck the following day.

The mountain road to the monastery from the Sofia Basin is magnificent. Following the valley of the Rilska River we turned upwards through densely wooded foothills, warm with the fragrance of lowland trees. As we climbed, the air became crisp and cool, scented with the tang of conifers. In the far distance were the snow-capped peaks of the Rila massif. Torrents of snow water cascaded down deep rocky gorges far below us. At about 4,000 ft. we saw grey wagtails and dippers disporting themselves at the waterfalls. Lowland birds had almost disappeared but we now saw and heard nutcrackers among the pines.

The monastery itself was a fitting climax to the journey. Nestling in a valley among snow-capped peaks, it shelters behind massive fortress walls designed in medieval times to withstand the longest siege. The monks treated us with traditional hospitality—they have 173 rooms—and we looked forward eagerly to the next morning. However, our companion, Nikolai Boeff, a Bulgarian ornithologist, told us that the climb was so difficult and strenuous that we should need an alpine guide, and that we could take nothing with us. Only a string of experienced alpine porters would be adequate to transport all our photographic gear. So we decided to take only one small cine and two 35 mm cameras.

Early next morning we set out, our guide equipped with ice-axe, ropes and pitons. No lives were to be lost if he could possibly help it! Dressed as we were for no more than a stiff hike, we felt at a distinct disadvantage, and decidedly apprehensive.

Our way led up a fairly steep track skirting the snow-fields. Pines and junipers were soon left behind and we entered real climbers' country. Ahead, no doubt, lay the suicidal rock-faces and other hazards of the high mountains—the Bulgarian equivalent of the north face of the Eiger. We braced ourselves and wondered how our prentice hands and feet would cope with the ropes—alas, we had no ice-axes and pitons of our own.

Hours went by, the scenery became ever more majestic, the climb, so far, well within our modest capabilities. Then, some five hours after leaving the monastery, and 6,300 modest feet above sea-level, the guide pointed to a small stone building on the other side of a lake. We were there!

The ludicrous contrast between the dire warnings of exhausting mountaineering and the exhilarating ramble it had turned out to be (it was no more than that to fit men) made us laugh out loud. Why Boeff thought it so difficult was beyond our comprehension.

A flash of crimson silhouetted against the distant building showed that our quarry was at home. The cock wall creeper brought food to the incubating hen. He looked beautiful in flight, similar to a hoopoe but coloured red and black. And to think I had, quite unnecessarily, left behind the right equipment to photograph such rare and spectacular birds—and so tame! As it was, the only mementos we brought back were a few cine-shots of the male bird taken by Jerry—who had the foresight to slip a telephoto lens in his pocket—and some stills of him taking them.

There is no greater thrill for a bird photographer than watching and photographing an eagle from a hide. Bulgaria is pre-eminently eagle country: all Europe's nine species have been recorded and six still nest there. One of these is the lesser spotted eagle, a bird I had never photographed. This species is a very dark brown, and about two feet long—nearly a foot shorter than the golden eagle.

While exploring in the Baltata Forest near Varna we flushed a lesser spotted eagle from its eyrie, which was heavily overhung with dense foliage, some forty-five feet up a white elm tree. A local forester, using climbing irons, inspected the nest for us and said that it contained a single egg. Should we erect a pylon or not? We did, after more than the usual difficulties. We worked in intense humidity, attacked ceaselessly by clouds of mosquitos, and with our near-naked bodies torn and bloody from the scratches of a thorny vine which rambled over every branch.

But when, eventually, I entered the hide I had my reward—my first glimpse of one tiny eaglet, dressed in white down but so weak that it could scarcely lift its head. Although the nest was so well protected, I decided not to garden for fear of revealing the helpless mite to the hooded crows and other predators in the vicinity. Photography would be difficult but, with reasonable weather, just possible.

Then our luck ran out. It rained virtually the whole of the day following the erection of the hide. The Batova River burst its banks and the path to the forest was an impassable morass. Rain continued for yet another day and we were in despair. Two weeks had been spent erecting the hide and we all dreaded to think that, after all, we might fail to get either film or photographs of the eagle.

We decided that, whatever the weather, we would try to reach the forest on the next (third) day, if only to recover the hide. It had stopped raining and we sloshed, ankle-deep in mud and water, along the forest tracks. I climbed to the hide, then hauled up the equipment and cameras. Only then did I glance at the nest. It was empty. There was no sign of either parent or eaglet. It was the most bitter moment of the expedition for me.

Suddenly I heard a shout. Someone had seen a flash of white on the ground—the chick. The heavy gales had evidently blown it out of the nest. I hastily climbed down, only to be told that the chick was dead. It was cold and covered with flies.

But, ever the optimist, I removed the flies, carefully dried the white down, and nestled the chick inside my shirt next to my skin. And, to the amazement of all of us, the life-giving warmth soon began to take effect. The chick opened its eyes—then gave me a kick in the chest with a sharp talon. I was sure that it had fallen out only a few hours previously, so we decided to put it back in the nest, and hope that the parents would return to feed it.

Johnnie Johnson volunteered to go in search of the forester, for he was the only one capable of making the difficult climb. Within two hours he was up the tree, let down a light rope and to this we attached a handkerchief in which the chick was hauled up and gently lowered into the nest, where it settled down as if nothing untoward had happened.

I decided to have one more brief session in the hide, and asked my companions to return within an hour. If the eagles were not back by then we would dismantle it. There seemed little likelihood of the eagles returning, the light was poor and the wind was buffeting the hide. But I had not been there for more than a quarter of an hour before the female dropped soundlessly on to the nest, fluffed out her feathers and started to brood.

Immediately the others returned I told them the good news. Could I still obtain photographs? Quickly I prepared both for still and movies, asked everybody to pray for better light and, while they moved off into the forest, I attempted my task in the worst conditions I have ever known. Rain fell intermittently, and in spite of an occasional bright period, my light meter registered zero, so effectively did the foliage blanket the nest. To add to my misery, nest and hide were swaying wildly, often in different directions. But I was determined to get those pictures: and get them I did. By synchronising the swing of hide and nest, using the brief bright periods, and varying shutter speed and lens aperture, I eventually succeeded. (See plate facing page 207).

On this expedition I was more than ordinarily interested in the people and their ways. We found that the general rule for visitors from the West was not to allow them to travel about the country unless accompanied by an interpreter, who is told where to go. This sometimes raised difficulties for us: we wanted to see birds, not inspect Bulgarian ancient monuments. And our difficulties were not eased by the Bulgarian habit of nodding the head for 'No', and shaking it for 'Yes'.

In some of the towns accommodation is allocated by a central clearing house where all visitors must report—a kind of lucky dip. All the *modern* houses and hotels were built to the same specification, each one being the same as its neighbour, without variety in style or interior design. Even the equipment was standardised: sideboards, mirrors, chairs, beds, carpets—even the towels—were all alike. Of course such standardisation makes manufacture and replacement easy, but how dull!

One omnipresent reminder of Big Brother was the State Radio. It boomed from radios in cafés, restaurants and hotels; from loudspeakers on all public buildings; from the open windows of private houses; and from transistor radios of cars and pedestrians. Broadcasting was continuous, and was particularly annoying in cafés and restaurants as it made conversation almost impossible. In addition to all this broadcast propaganda, most public buildings were festooned with huge red banners carrying slogans or production targets.

Judging by the efficiency standards of the 'hotels' in country districts, Bulgarian workmen needed all the encouragement and exhortation they undoubtedly receive. I use the inverted commas advisedly. Our hotel in Silistra, an important Danube shipping centre, was little more than a tiny foyer, an office and a few bedrooms. No meals were served; the toilet was literally nothing more than a hole in the floor;

and the taps over the bedroom basin gave no water. We washed from a stand-pipe in the street. But, to be fair, the hotels in the large towns were very good, some quite luxurious.

During the first evening in Silistra the electric light failed four times. The telephone was equally inefficient. Guy tried to telephone the British Legation in Sofia to report our progress. Sometimes he got through to Sofia, sometimes to the Legation, but always the line went dead before he could speak. It took him a couple of hours of continuous perseverence before he was connected long enough to speak, and then he was only able to leave a message with the night watchman.

On all expeditions writing up the daily diary is an important but wearisome business; never more so than on this trip. It sometimes took two hours to get dinner. Consequently it was often ten or eleven at night before we began to write, and after that I had to clean and re-load my cameras.

If our experience is an adequate guide, most Bulgarian hotels had neither cloak- nor baggage-rooms. This was a far greater hardship to us than to most travellers, for we had a great deal of luggage. Several times we had to rent a separate room solely to store equipment; once this added £11 to our bill for six days.

We appeared to be unwelcome in some hotels, which is not surprising, for after a day in the field we must have looked a disreputable bunch as we straggled homewards, wet and muddy, our apparatus round our necks, under our arms, on our backs, and in our hands. In Varna a woman cleaner was specially deputed to follow us upstairs with dustpan and brush to remove our trail of mud. The next time we stayed at that hotel we were given villas in the grounds—like a holiday camp.

One of my most vivid memories of that particular stay is not of the birds, nor the mud, nor the food, but of a swarm of tiny beetles which flew across our path, their 'tail lights' flashing vividly in the darkness.

Driving was a motorist's nightmare. Only the main highways were in reasonable condition, the others were made of earth—dust when dry, mud when wet. Except in the environs of the big towns the roads were practically deserted, and the Bulgarians had become so used to this dearth of traffic that they stepped into the road without a look.

Garages were few and far between and to obtain petrol was a complicated undertaking. Only after passport inspection, completion of two forms and, finally, payment at eight shillings a gallon, was the petrol poured into the tank from a pump marked SUPER. But judging by the way our engines knocked on the hills the octane content was very far from super. And to try to obtain another grade was useless because all the grades were the same.

Food was more than ordinarily important on this expedition as we rarely got more than one good meal a day, but the food we did get was in itself a new experience. Several times we ate strawberries as large as medium-sized apples. These were delicious, but I did not relish the thick, black, sweet Turkish coffee we were occasionally offered. *Chàen*, 'tea'—the first word I learn in *any* foreign language—was scarce and was often served without milk. I drank gallons of the fizzy fruit juice called Gazikan Plodov Suk, which is the favourite Bulgarian beverage.

Yoghurt in Bulgaria is a national food. There are three grades: sheep's milk makes the first grade, buffalo milk the next, and the third is made from cows' or goats' milk. High claims are made for the health and longevity of those whose diet includes a high proportion of yoghurt.

Bulgaria is largely an agricultural land, and vast fields stretched as far as the eye could see, sown with corn and other cereals. Sunflowers were a common crop. Much of the work was done by hand and there seemed to be virtually no machinery. In one field fifty men were scything corn. The standard of agriculture seemed high, and little ground lay fallow. Frequently notices were displayed along the road-sides indicating the agricultural target for the area.

In many places we appeared to be the first Englishmen—and often the first West Europeans—the Bulgarians had ever met. In Sreburna the last English visitors had been soldiers in the 1914–18 war. But they left an enduring memorial: football was unknown in Bulgaria until the Tommies introduced it. Now it is the national game.

In view of the 'rarity value' of an Englishman, it is not surprising that wherever we went we attracted attention. At any café or restaurant where we ate regularly, the Union Jack was placed on our table. In some restaurants a forest of flags, many of them strange to me, appeared on different tables. Evidently Bulgaria attracts tourists from many lands. Often people came to our table and conversed eagerly with us, sometimes directly in English, but more often through Georgi Petrov, our interpreter. They were extremely friendly and keen to know about life in distant England. Some of them seemed surprised to learn that Britain was a welfare state with a National Health Service.

It was the same in the field. Our cars and equipment rarely failed to attract attention. I remember especially the little village of Sreburna which was our headquarters for four days: each time our cavalcade returned from an expedition, the entire village turned out to greet us. Johnnie's Vauxhall was the star turn, as it was the first British car they had seen. Men and boys poked about under the bonnet inspecting the engine, then rocked the car violently to test the springs. They seemed to agree it was a roadworthy effort, but decidedly on the slow side.

The speedometer recorded only up to 110. Why, the small Russian Volga went up to 180—kilometres, of course (110 m.p.h.)!

The most disturbing experience I had with the authorities was when I was filming a pair of brilliantly coloured rollers from a hide in a flower-filled valley of the Batova River. A slight noise disturbed me and as I swung round twelve inches of steel appeared through the peep-hole—a soldier's bayonet! And he was having difficulty in restraining a fierce guard dog which seemed set on tearing the hide and me to pieces.

What in the world . . . ? I launched myself into another of those Bulgarian 'conversations' in which neither party understood the other. Then I had an inspiration. Guy had once placated a sentry by showing him an official-looking document (in English) and out of my pockets I fished the only piece of printed paper I could find—a telegram from England asking me to take various photographs. It did the trick. The soldier studied it gravely, saluted, and left.

These are some miscellaneous memories of Bulgaria: the enormous range of temperature—50°F one day, 90°F the next; the extreme youth of some of the parents—the marriage age is as low as fifteen; the dense thunder-clouds reflected in the Black Sea which told us immediately where its name originated; banks opening at 7 a.m.; the strangeness of the trade-name '9th September' over some shop doorways—until we realised that this was the date on which the 1946 referendum was ratified, thus changing Bulgaria from a monarchy to a republic.

But of all my memories I think the most poignant is of a child's speech so well described by Guy in *Portrait of a River*. We had been shown over a school at Sreburna where Guy spoke through an interpreter. As we were about to leave the entire staff appeared, accompanied by a twelve-year-old girl with dark eyes and the face of an angel, who presented Guy with a bouquet of flowers and made a short speech. As our visit was unexpected, she had little time to prepare. It was perfect. With complete composure she said how much pleasure our visit had given to the school, which was proud to have met such distinguished Englishmen. She gravely wished us well in our studies of Bulgarian wild-life, and hoped that we would visit her country again.

Guy thanked her, obviously moved, and then, to the wild delight of the school, bent and kissed the child on both cheeks. He wanted to give her a small gift, but all he had that was suitable was a newly minted sixpence. She received it graciously and said: 'This portrait of your beautiful Queen will be a treasured souvenir and will be given a place of honour in our school museum.'

17 | *Hungary*

Bulgaria had whetted my appetite for photographic exploration in Eastern Europe, so when Guy Mountfort suggested that we should go to Hungary I agreed at once. But first we had to get permission. Guy applied in October 1960: permission was not granted until March 1961—memories of the 1956 revolution died hard. In the meantime other tempting tours had been accepted by some who had come with us to Bulgaria. However, we were fortunate in assembling the following party: Andrew Burnett, Guy's nephew, who took over all the sound recordings; Erik Hansen, a well-known Danish ornithologist who was mainly interested in the raptorial birds; John Wightman, a seasoned traveller with a wide knowledge of the birds of many lands; and George Shannon, veteran of many expeditions with me, who was to help with the filming.

We flew on the morning of 14 May 1961. As we passed over the Rhineland the Rhine twisted and turned like a tortured snake and despite the height—23,000 ft.—we could pick out the autobahns running ruler-straight across Germany. At Budapest we were given VIP treatment. A representative from the Institute of Cultural Relations greeted us, as well as two famous Hungarian naturalists and an interpreter. We were quickly ushered through the Customs and taken to the Astoria Hotel in a huge Russian limousine. The car belonged to the diplomatic service and people stared to see who the VIPs were. The numerous pockmarks on many buildings bore mute witness to the hail of bullets this beautiful city had endured in the recent past.

The Astoria is regarded as the Savoy of Hungary, but its standards were not high. My room was small and shabby, and the bed had a solid hair mattress with a worn covering.

When we went down for dinner we were shown to a reserved corner table adorned with a Union Jack. A *tzigane* orchestra was playing Hungarian gypsy music and when the leader saw us he immediately came over and played a medley of traditional English airs—some of it uncomfortably near Guy's left ear!

Our meal consisted of a steak with an egg on top, with oranges to follow. Then we had two shocks; the oranges cost two shillings and sixpence each, and we learnt that the communist view of human stomachs accords with Leninist principles—they are all equal! All tourists are issued with meal vouchers of fixed values—forty forints for lunch, sixty forints for dinner (about 14s. and £1). But such money covered only the middle range of the menu and the set number of courses, and if hunger was still not satisfied, tomorrow's coupon had to make up the difference. On the other hand, if you ate less than a voucher's worth, no change was given.

Next morning, in the hotel lobby, we awaited the cars to take us on our first Hungarian field trip. Our appearance caused some astonishment to the hotel staff who were accustomed to more orthodox guests. In addition to our rough dress we were draped with cameras, tripods, hides, binoculars, etc., and carried sound-recording equipment, electronic apparatus and ruck-sacks on our backs.

The cars drove us to the Telki Hills a few miles outside Budapest. Where the road ended in the foothills, we bumped for a while along a rutted track, then got out and began to climb the slopes.

The timbered hills were cool and green, and the air throbbed with the songs of nightingales, wood warblers, chiffchaffs and golden orioles. Black woodpeckers drummed occasionally, cuckoos called continuously in the background. Incongruously amid such an idyllic scene, we suddenly came across a horse-drawn trap carrying two enormous dead wild boars armed with ugly curved tusks. Apparently boars are a nuisance in these parts and are shot freely.

Before the day was over we had seen an eagle owl's nest from which, sadly, the young had been taken—the pungent odour still clinging to the nest showed that the predator was a fox; two species of buzzard; a red-footed falcon; an Imperial eagle and its nest seventy feet up a tree; a host of small birds and a red deer. It augured well for the rest of the expedition.

One of our targets was another eagle owl's nest in a disused quarry at Sirok. We first called on the director of the local museum, a giant of a man, bubbling with energy and good humour, over six feet tall, who talked non-stop in a fascinating mixture of English and Hungarian. To his delight we christened him Big John. He poured drinks of home-brewed spirit and afterwards I was warned not to strike a light near him—Guy said that the spirit tasted like petrol!

Eventually we set off, Big John promising us 'a jolly fine *Uhu*, with youngs'. The nest was in a small cave near the top of an almost vertical

Left: Photographed from the hide 150 feet across the valley, an adult lammergeier stands in the entrance to the nesting cave

Below: With diamond-shaped tail and huge wings, a lammergeier soars overhead

BULGARIA

Above: Like a squadron of bombers, a flock of white pelicans drifts on stiffly held pinions over Lake Burgas

Below: In the Baltata forest, feathers bedraggled from the rain, a lesser spotted eagle stands over the eaglet that was rescued after being blown out of the eyrie

cliff, and I decided to wait on one side of the quarry with the cine-camera focused on the spot. Even so I missed the hen when she suddenly took off well to the right. But eventually we reached the cave and saw the owlet. It had crawled about twenty yards from the nest and its enormous golden-orange eyes glared straight at me. I wrote home to Dorothy:

'Boy, oh boy, what a chick it was! But to our great disappointment we cannot put a hide up as the chick just wanders around and it is quite certain that it would not stay near. However, it was a thrilling experience just to see it and the old bird. We found three dead hedge-hogs, a mole, a partridge, a hare and a roe deer fawn all within twenty yards of the nest so the young looks as though it is being well fed. I only left it with regret—I have never seen such a fabulous youngster.'

Unfortunately we never did succeed in taking a series of photographs of an adult eagle owl—until I went to Norway in 1964.

We witnessed a memorable aerial duel between two Saker falcons and two Imperial eagles: fighters *versus* bombers. First we saw the eagles soaring in a thermal when suddenly a Saker stooped with half-closed wings. The eagle saw it coming and jinked so that the Saker missed. The other Saker then stooped, with the same result. For the next ten minutes we had a ringside seat at some fantastic aerobatics. The Sakers dived at an incredible speed; the eagles dodged with split-second timing. Several times the eagles rolled over and snatched at their attackers with their large yellow talons. The Sakers won, for the eagles were forced farther and farther away.

For me, the most outstanding period of the whole expedition was the fortnight we spent on Lake Velence, eleven square miles of reed-covered water in the centre of the country—the Norfolk Broads of Hungary. We made several sorties from Budapest but later made our headquarters in a tiny lakeside inn at Gárdony. The front door opened directly into the kitchen. We had three small bedrooms and our pile of equipment was stored on the landing. My bed was a child's cot from which my feet projected fully six inches!

The wooden verandah was a tracery of grape vines, the yellow flowers of the oleaster trees perfumed the air, and before us lay the lake teeming with the widest variety of bird-life. Our presence there quickly became known and we received letters from various Hungarian ornithologists, some merely addressed: 'Angol Ornitólogiai Expedició, Gárdony'.

We had a great stroke of luck when Stefán Müller—the Jim Vincent of these Broads—offered all the help he could. His father had helped R. B. Lodge—a pioneer of bird photography—when he visited the lake in 1906. Stefán had worked with the leading Hungarian bird photo-

P

graphers and was the finest assistant we could wish for. Guy paid him this well-deserved tribute in *Portrait of a River* (Hutchinson, 1962).

'He knew all there was to know about siting a hide in relation to the sun's position and about tying back the vegetation instead of cutting it. When he took down a hide and replaced the foliage it was almost impossible to see any sign of disturbance. His skill with a punt was fascinating to watch. Long periods of solitude under the blazing sun or drenching rain had made him impervious to the weaknesses of the flesh to which lesser mortals are heir. He was immensely strong and could pole a heavily laden punt through almost impenetrable reeds rising far above his head. But it was as a nest-finder that he most excelled and in this he had an uncanny knack of anticipating our needs. Conversations with him had, of course, to be conducted through Paul Ambrus [our interpreter], but he knew the Latin scientific names of most of the birds and could pick out the species quickly from the illustrations in the *Field Guide to the Birds of Europe*. We had only to mention the notion of photographing a certain species, and he would be out on the lake before five in the morning, ready to offer us the choice of half a dozen nests by the time we arrived two hours later.

'I remember a remarkable occasion when we were setting off in our punts one morning and I said casually that I hoped before long we should be able to find the nest of a little crake. This secretive, starling-size bird has a positively fiendish skill in hiding its nest among the litter of dead vegetation at the foot of reed-clumps; moreover, once on the nest it covers itself with foliage and sits so tightly that one can be within two feet of it before it will suddenly streak away, running like a rat through the reeds. Müller said nothing, he was a silent man who spoke only when he had something important to say; but as we moved slowly down the long avenues of reeds he stopped from time to time for a few seconds to peer among them. Presently he stooped and parted the vegetation with his hands and, with a slow smile, pointed. There, immobile on its nest, sat a little crake!'

I particularly wanted to film spoonbills and great white egrets, both of which bred on the lake. We visited the Kisbalaton colony of spoonbills and found fifty or so pairs, mostly with young learning to fly. A few birds were sitting on fresh eggs, their first clutches probably having been lost. I made my acquaintance with the spoonbills during a seven-hour session in the hide. At close quarters they are ungainly birds but their colouring is beautiful; the dazzling white plumage and long mane of silky feathers extending halfway down the graceful neck contrasting with the huge shining black bill often tipped with brilliant yellow.

My other quarry, the great white egret, is the rarest and most majestic of European egrets. It stands four feet tall, has snow-white plumage, black and yellow legs, and a dagger-like bill that is black, yellow and pale green in the summer, but entirely yellow during the rest of the year. Its crowning glory nearly brought about its destruction. During the breeding season the egrets grow greatly elongated scapulars which form magnificent delicately flowing plumes on the back.

About the turn of the century it was considered highly fashionable to wear these—and those of the little egret—as hat decorations. Consequently, 'plume-hunting' became a profitable trade and there was a barbarous slaughter of these handsome birds in their breeding colonies. Fortunately, nature-lovers, forerunners of today's conservationists, protested loudly enough to stop the slaughter. The little egrets recovered quickly but even today the great white egret is on the danger list.

This bird is, of course, strictly protected in Hungary—so much so that we nearly failed to get permission to photograph. What happened was this. About a year before our arrival, a Hungarian commercial film unit had worked at the colony on Lake Velence and caused so much disturbance that several pairs deserted. Accordingly, the Council for Nature Protection ruled that no more photographic permits should be issued. The Council thought that we were another film company and refused a permit. Fortunately, all was resolved when we met Dr. Zoltán Tildy, the Vice-President of the Council. He possessed most of my books and we had a long talk on bird photography. Permission was granted. George Shannon and I spent several days there while the others continued to work on different parts of the lake. George concentrated on filming, I on stills.

The colony is at the western end of the lake amid a forest of ten-foot-high reeds stretching for half a mile, and growing so close together that our punt had to be *forced* through them. I have punted on the Broads and know something about quanting, but I would never have reached the egrets had it not been for Stefán Müller.

The going was fairly easy until we turned into a dyke leading to the colony. Then we had to use all our strength to move the punt at all, so thick and strong was the growth of reeds. We literally moved only inches with each pole-thrust.

Then suddenly we came upon the colony and the exhausting journey was forgotten in the thrill of witnessing a sight few ornithologists in Europe are privileged to see. Overhead several of the beautiful birds wheeled and turned above nests containing snow-white young. At a suitable nest we erected a hide using piles of reeds for a foundation, and placed a large board on these to form a floor. Müller stipulated that we should not approach closer to the nest than thirty-five feet, which was right for cine but rather distant for still cameras.

The time I spent in that hide was fascinating. Part of a tape-recording I made while there captured the thrill of those hours.

'At this moment, I am sitting in a hide some thirty-five feet from the great white egret's nest so I can only whisper into the microphone. Müller, the keeper, left me here about five minutes ago and already the adult has alighted just at the back of the nest. What a really glorious bird she is, standing quite four feet with her neck fully stretched up. She is very alert and obviously just a bit suspicious of the hide. In the nest are three young about ten days of age, almost completely white like the adult. They pant a bit in the heat. The hen flaps forward and has now reached the nest, standing like a statue. The young call for food but she ignores them. She leans forward and moves a bit of reed from one place to another. As she lowers her bill so the young grab hold of it and pull trying to stimulate her to regurgitate food. She retched and down her bill comes a small fish. One chick swallows this in a flash. Every few moments she stands alert.

'We had been told by Dr. Tildy that the great white egret is an exceptionally shy bird. Having photographed all the other European herons I rather doubted this but he is right. The least sound from a shutter and up goes her long, snaky neck and she stands motionless.

'The hen is grunting and overhead the cock bird circles and lands with a crash on the nest. They display to each other, by raising crest and spreading their beautiful white plumes. Then both fly away.'

Although I concentrated on the herons there was plenty of other activity around. I wrote home:

'A young moorhen came and fed just in front of my hide, a queer little thing with black body and bright red bill. Water rail belched all round, little crakes "craked", bearded tit pinged, Savi's warblers reeled, bitterns boomed and there was a procession of purple and grey herons flying by all the time. A dragonfly used the alley-way between the hide and the nest to fly backwards and forwards as though it was on guard duty!'

And once, while I was filming in these marshes, an inquisitive little crake tried to enter the hide.

Great thunderstorms are an unnerving feature on Lake Velence, and nowhere else have I experienced such atmospheric violence as here. In some storms lightning is continuous for minutes together, and there is one long earth-trembling roll of thunder. I was not surprised to learn that the lake is the storm centre of Hungary.

I shall never forget one of these storms. One minute the lake was still, the next it was whipped by a hurricane-like wind that roared through the reeds, lashing their fronds almost to water-level. Then came the rain. Driven by the violent wind it lashed us like whips.

George Shannon was marooned in the aluminium Dexion hide, and Guy and Andrew Burnett punted over to rescue him. They did—just in time. As they made for shelter on the leeward side of a reed-bed there was a tremendous flash and a violent explosion. Lightning had struck the aluminium hide. Less than thirty seconds before they had all been clinging to the metal uprights.

Away from the lake and the marshes our chief quarry was the great bustard, the second heaviest bird in Europe, with a maximum weight of about forty-five pounds—only mute swans are heavier, some weighing fifty pounds. It is a vastly impressive bird; four feet tall with chestnut brown, white and grey body on very long sturdy legs. The slow powerful beat of its wings drives it through the air at up to a mile a minute. Well into the last century this magnificent bird bred in the flat countryside of East Anglia and is still seen there occasionally as a very rare vagrant.

In Hungary, the bustard's home is on the great plains of the middle Danube; flat country extending in all directions as far as the eye can see—and then beyond for mile after featureless mile.

On the Csákvár plain, west of Budapest, half a dozen of us spread out at intervals of about twenty yards, walking slowly forward in what seemed the pretty forlorn hope of finding a bustard's nest. We were told that the hen would sit motionless until we were almost on top of her, relying on her dun colouring to make her invisible as she flattened against the brown earth. She nearly succeeded. Guy said that only when she sprang into flight a few yards away did he see her. She was a magnificent sight, her slow powerful brown and white wings stroking the air as she made for the horizon. There was no nest, just a scrape in the sun-cracked earth amid scanty vegetation about five inches tall, in which lay two big olive-green eggs blotched with black.

I was eagerly looking forward to fulfilling a long-standing ambition to photograph a great bustard at the nest. We put up a hide about 250 yards away. Alas for my hopes. When we arrived there the next day, only the broken shells of the eggs remained. A fox had beaten us to it.

Eight times altogether our hopes of photographing the bustard were raised but always something happened to the eggs. Two clutches were eaten by foxes, two taken by humans, four destroyed by combine harvesters or mowers. Stealing eggs is rampant; several people boasted to us of the long *series* of clutches they had. And there is good reason to believe that great bustard eggs from Hungary are sent to augment collections abroad.

This was my second visit to a communist country in successive years. There was a gaiety about the Hungarians which was not so apparent in the Bulgarians. But then the Hungarians are famous for their high spirits.

Some of them at times betrayed a sensitivity that bordered on the pathological. We were filming in Budapest one day and an onlooker seemed to be especially interested. Thinking to pay a graceful compliment, Guy said that we wanted to show British audiences what a beautiful city Budapest was. The onlooker was intensely offended. Why? It was insulting to suggest that the British did not already recognise that Budapest was the world's most beautiful city.

We had numerous reminders that we were in a police state, euphemistically called a People's Democracy. Whenever we went to a new area we had to report to the local police. At Gyöngyöspata, Andrew Burnett and Erik Hansen were sitting in the back of the cars adjusting the recording apparatus when a plain-clothes policeman sharply ordered them out. He said that he was confiscating the equipment and taking them into custody. Fortunately, Paul Ambrus intervened and eventually managed to persuade the police that we were not spies.

We all felt that the expedition was most successful. By working in the field eighty hours a week for a month we managed to see 166 different species of birds and photographed thirty, some of them very rare.

It was a great pleasure to meet Hungarian ornithologists whose work we admired but whom we had known only as names. The kindness and generosity we received were unforgettable, nothing was too much trouble for the 'Angol Ornitológiai Expedició'.

18 | *Jordan*

By now (1962) the Mountfort Expeditions had become well known and enquiries were received by Guy from a number of countries which were concerned about the status of their fauna and flora. Among these was one from King Hussein of Jordan, who was alarmed by the dwindling wild-life in his country and realised the urgency of the problem.

Many of the animals that once thrived in Jordan have disappeared; in this century roe and fallow deer, Arabian oryx, Addax antelope, wild ass and Syrian bear, crocodile and ostrich have been exterminated. The cheetah, almost certainly, has also gone, although a female was shot as recently as 1962 and her cub taken by a Bedouin. Other mammals, such as the ibex, Arabian and Dorcas gazelles, and the wolf, are declining rapidly.

It used to be a sign of virility for a man to go out alone into the desert, track down an oryx or gazelle and kill it with a spear. But modern cars and rifles have changed all that. Unless drastic action is taken even the remnants of Jordan's large mammals will very soon be lost for ever.

Because Jordan is nearly all desert we knew that a reconnaissance would be involved and difficult, but the tougher the task, the better Guy likes it. So complex were the preparations that it took him six months to work out all the details before the British Jordan Expedition left London on the morning of 11 April 1963, arriving in Amman in the evening.

The other members were Sir Julian Huxley, who already knew parts of Jordan and had written a stimulating book about the Near East, *From an Antique Land* (Max Parrish, 1956); Max Nicholson, George Shannon, James Ferguson-Lees, Philip Hollom and John Wightman, who had all previously been on expeditions with us; Dr. Duncan Poore, then a professor in the University of Kuala Lumpur (now

Director of the Nature Conservancy) who already knew Jordan well and is an excellent plant ecologist; Jan Gillett, Principal Scientific Officer at the Royal Botanic Gardens, Kew; Sdeuard Biss.rôt, a cinematographer with a special interest in entomology, amphibians and reptiles; and Ian Wallace, a fine field ornithologist and artist.

One of the fascinations of going to a new country is that everything is unexpected—living conditions, food, people, transport facilities, the subjects to be photographed. People have criticised the amount of equipment I take but I do my homework thoroughly and assess the conditions; whether I shall require telephoto lenses and, especially in Jordan, whether pictures will have to be taken in confined spaces necessitating a wide-angle lens; what flash equipment (just a small set for taking close-ups or a much more powerful one for taking night portraits of animals at long range); what sort of film, slow as well as fast emulsions, colour as well as black and white and what quantity of each; a heavy tripod or only a light one; how many hides, bearing in mind that I must cater for George and probably Guy and Sdeuard as well as myself—if I take only four, that is eighty pounds for one item alone. And so on. There is nothing more infuriating than being in a foreign land, with wonderful photographic possibilities, and minus the proper apparatus.

After spending two days in and around Amman we left for the Azraq oasis on 14 April. Instead of the primitive living conditions we had anticipated we were pleasantly surprised on our arrival to find that our quarters were not in tents, but in a building known as the Hunting Lodge built by Glubb Pasha during the First World War. It was extremely hot and settling in was a slow process. We had just unloaded the last of the three cars when we received a radio message from King Hussein, asking Guy, Julian, Max and me to see him in Amman, where we had spent the previous two days. Julian was too exhausted and asked to be excused, but the rest of us piled into a Land Rover and were there in two hours.

King Hussein was charming and most interested in what we proposed to do. He plied us with many searching questions, stressing again his concern about the future of his country's wild-life, urging us to find ways and means of saving it. He asked for copies of all our reports to be sent to him and promised every assistance. Finally, he graciously autographed three copies of his book, *Uneasy Lies the Head* (Bernard Geis, 1962), which I had brought with me.

Back in Azraq we quickly got down to work and our first trip was to an ancient hunters' castle Qasr al Amra. It was deep in the desert, and although built about AD 700, when probably much of the surrounding land was forest, was still in remarkably fine condition, owing to the

HUNGARY

Above: Perilous beauty
Such was the demand for the feathers of the great white egret for decorating hats in Edwardian times, that the birds nearly became extinct

Below: Ungainly beauty
Although lacking the graceful beauty of the egret, the dazzling white plumage, silky neck feathers and shining black bill, often tipped with brilliant yellow, give the spoonbill a striking appearance

Above: Duncan Read makes a rare find. There is only one previous record of the finding of a nest of a Sinai rosefinch

Below: The oasis at Qasr al Amra where we suddenly landed beside James Ferguson-Lees and Ian Wallace. Their Land Rover stands to the left of the castle

BIRDS OF JORDAN

Above left: Pin-tailed sandgrouse in the desert near Azraq

Above right: The wryneck, ringed by Guy Mountfort, that was picked up dead sixteen days later in Russia, 1,330 miles away

Below: Tristram's grackles near the Dead Sea

Above left : The poisonous black widow spider that ran over my hand

Above right : White-crowned black chat with grasshopper for young, pauses momentarily at the entrance to its rocky nesting hole

Below : 'It was now nearly mid-day and the metal parts of the cameras were so hot that I could hardly touch them.' Sdeuard Bisserôt took the photograph

hot dry atmosphere. Inside the lodge were splendid murals of the game animals which once inhabited the region. Our interpreter, Abdullah Bushnaq, led us to a nearby tree-lined wadi where he told us that only four years ago he had seen a herd of fifty Arabian gazelles. Now there remained no trace of them.

But there was plenty of other wild-life. In a *Retama raetum* bush Sdeuard found a lovely green mantis, *Blepharopsis mendica*, and while I was trying to take colour photographs of it Sdeuard caught a lizard, *Acanthodactylus grandis*, which was sheltering under the same bush. (Many of the small creatures we found in Jordan have no English name.) Almost every stone hid spiders, ants or beetles. James discovered a cream-coloured courser's nest with two eggs, and George spotted a little owl peering down from the roof of the castle. James found five thick-billed larks, a species which has developed a massive bill for crushing the very hard fruits of the desert shrubs. Then Phil flushed a hoopoe lark from its nest and later, as we watched it feeding, we observed how wonderfully its long downward-curved bill was adapted to its particular method of collecting insects hiding between stones. Many lesser short-toed and some short-toed larks were seen, as well as bar-tailed desert and desert larks. There are two forms of desert larks in Jordan, a pale sandy-coloured race found on limestone hills, and a very dark brown one among the almost black basalt boulders. I was fascinated by the astonishing way these creatures had evolved for such specialised living.

Because Azraq is an oasis, it attracts many birds. Some are temporary inhabitants, such as migrants passing through, others stay only to breed, while many more are permanent residents. To photograph many of these, hides were erected at their nests, while red-backed shrikes, ortolan and black-headed buntings, pied flycatchers, rufous bush chats, masked shrikes, turtle doves and several other species were photographed by stalking. We were surrounded by animal and plant life and the days were too short to do all the photography we wanted.

At Azraq Druz we saw the castle where Lawrence of Arabia recovered after his brutal beating by the Turks in the First World War. It was gloomy and dim, the rooms floored only with earth. It was a forbidding place, yet its coolness and its spring of fresh water were extremely welcome in the searing heat of this arid land.

This was to be a bus-stop tour and our work had barely begun before we had to move on. We spent a day at Wadi Zarqa, where George found the nest of a pair of Palestine sunbirds, tiny creatures, the cock glistening with iridescent greens and blues. They feed on the nectar of oleanders and pomegranates, sometimes almost disappearing inside the flowers. While there I saw several 'lifers'—including blackstarts, fan-tailed ravens, graceful warblers and a lappet-faced vulture.

Our next stop was Karak, where we stayed three nights in an Italian hospital-cum-guest house. Here was the largest castle ruin I saw in Jordan, and it was still in process of excavation. It had been a bastion of the Crusaders, who tethered their horses right beside their living quarters so that they could mount and be away in a moment. The Mayor of Karak received and entertained us, informing us with great pride that he had four wives and forty-three children—our muster was twenty-four children among the twelve of us! A mansef, or Bedouin banquet, was given in our honour and while speeches of welcome were exchanged we sat cross-legged on colourful tribal carpets, sipping sweet coffee from tiny china bowls.

The open-air meal was stewed lamb surrounded by rice served in a dish a yard across, embellished with a sheep's head complete with lolling tongue.

The dish was set down and a kettle of boiling fat poured over it. Tactfully I watched to see the correct manner of eating. A piece of meat was pulled off and rolled into a ball with rice, everything being done with the right hand—the left is considered unclean. Having studied the procedure I tried my hand and all went well until the final act—flicking the mixture into the mouth with the thumb—I missed the target and the messy substance burst on my spectacles and dribbled down my face. Practice helped but I never became perfect. Afterwards our hands were rubbed in sand, washed with water and dried on a communal towel. Apples, bananas and oranges followed, with glasses of mint-flavoured tea.

From Karak, at 3,000 ft., we journeyed to the shore of the Dead Sea, nearly 1,300 ft. below sea-level—the lowest place on earth. When we arrived at 6 a.m. it was blissfully cool, but by eleven o'clock the heat was burning our skins, and by noon it was intolerable. During our six-hour stay we worked endlessly. For me there were abundant opportunities for photography. A flock of Tristram's grackles, birds I had never seen before, perched on the top of a bush and waited for me to stalk them; fan-tailed ravens circled overhead, their tails looking exactly like fans; swallows, red-rumped swallows and sand martins sat side by side on a telegraph wire making a splendid comparison; four see-sees, or sand partridges, ran from bush to bush, seeking cover, reluctant to fly.

Sdeuard found several giant grasshoppers, three or more inches in length, feeding on the leaves of Sodom-apples (*Calotropis procera*) and, as it happened, Julian remarked that we were probably standing near the spot where Sodom was before 'the Lord rained upon Sodom and upon Gomorrah brimstone and fire'—almost certainly the results of volcanic eruptions that occurred about 2000 BC.

Jan asked me to photograph a number of plants he had found, especially a fine specimen of a zizyphus tree—Christ's thorn—which had needle-like spines three inches long. Guy drew my attention to a great herd of camels among whose feet darted blue-headed wagtails, catching the disturbed insects.

It was now nearly midday and the metal parts of the cameras were so hot that I could hardly touch them. Even so I would have carried on working but it was time to leave. The cars climbed along the steep road winding round innumerable hairpin bends amid spectacular, even frightening, scenery. The great barren mountains, without a vestige of vegetation, are all part of the gigantic Rift Valley, the 4,000-mile-long fracture in the earth's crust, which stretches from the Taurus Mountains in Asia Minor to Mozambique in East Africa.

Then there was Petra—the rose-red city. So many words have been expended on this fabulous place that I will add few more. Known to the ancient world, it somehow slipped into oblivion during the Middle Ages, and for 600 years no Western eye lit upon its haunting beauty. Then, during a journey from Cairo to Damascus in 1812, the Anglo-Swiss explorer, Johann Burckhardt, stopped at Petra, but was forced by hostile tribesmen to leave almost immediately. The account of his travels was published in 1822. In the meantime, however, two English naval officers, Irby and Mangles, managed to spend several days there in 1818, and in 1823 published privately a detailed account of their experiences.

It was awe-inspiring to walk the length of the Siq—the narrow, mile-long sandstone gorge that local tradition claims was formed by Moses when he struck the rock. Only eight feet wide in places, flanked by towering 300 ft. high cliffs, it is agleam with a kaleidoscope of colour—rose red, brown, yellow, blue, white and black and many intermediate shades. The canyon was carved by water and only ten days before our visit it had again shown its terrifying power. After a long period of drought, a torrential storm had burst upon the land. On the surrounding hills the hard dry earth channelled the waters down to Wadi Musa and straight into the Siq, where twenty-three French tourists and their driver and guide were drowned. A car, badly smashed, told the story.

Suddenly we came upon one of the most remarkable architectural sights in the world. Framed between the tall, narrow cliff-faces were the great rose-red pillars of the majestic El Khazna—Pharaoh's Treasury, not built but sculptured out of the solid rock.

Julian was in his element and I marvelled at his knowledge, energy and enthusiasm at seventy-five. He was the one member of the expedition who had been to Petra before and was anxious that we should see everything, and that I should photograph as much as possible. He almost exhausted me, climbing up, scrambling down and all the time asking me to photograph this and that—a close-up here, a distant view there. But what an education—Julian was full of information and keen to share his knowledge. We climbed to the High Place of Sacrifice, the centre of the city's religious life, where he pointed out two stone altars, one of which was used for sacrificial purposes, channels having been cut to drain away the blood of the victims.

We descended by a different path and photographed the exquisite red and gold Tomb of the Roman Soldier, then on to the elaborate Palace Tomb, the Snake Monument and Qasr al Bint—the Roman temple. At each, Julian showed me points of interest, such as a particularly fine column, a well-preserved façade, a viaduct, or a god-box (a rock-imprisoned god). He told me that there was some evidence that Jehovah was originally a god-box from this area.

On one occasion we focused our cameras on a picturesquely dressed Bedouin riding a beautifully caparisoned camel, but he quickly made it clear that he was a professional model and, since the place was besieged by American tourists, he probably made a living in this way. So—no pay, no portrait. While he tried to make a deal, he kept his camel fidgeting about to make photography as difficult as possible. So we offered him a 100-fils coin (about two shillings). This, he made plain, was so far below his usual fee that he would have nothing to do with us, and disdainfully threw the coin on to the ground, riding off in a huff. What he did not know was that the bright light and our fast-shutter cameras had enabled us to take all the photographs we wanted, despite the camel's movements. What *we* did not know until afterwards was that he had cleverly palmed our 100 fils and had flung down five fils instead.

With so much to portray I hardly had a moment to look at the birds, but a gorgeous cock Sinai rosefinch alighted on a balustrade right in front of me, bringing me back to earth and making me realise that I was primarily in this fascinating land as a bird photographer.

During part of this expedition I shared sleeping quarters with Sdeuard, which meant that I sometimes slept in company with a small zoo. One night we bedded down with several dozen lizards, numerous insects and other small livestock, while Palestine mole rats wandered about the room. The mole rat is a most intriguing creature. About three times the size of our mole, it is shaped like a fat sausage and has only vestigial eyes which are hidden deep within thick fur. It has two pairs of powerful, permanently growing incisors which meet *outside* its mouth. When Sdeuard released one on rocky ground, I saw the reason for these anatomical peculiarities. It literally *chewed* itself into the ground. The four long powerful teeth attacked the earth like miniature pneumatic drills. I was amazed at the speed with which it disappeared.

It is normal practice in the desert to inspect your boots every morning, since they are a favourite overnight lodging for scorpions. But it was another arthropod which figured in an incident I shall long remember. Sdeuard found a large black spider on a bush, resting beside its web containing two beetles. As it was not in a good position for photography I urged it on to my hand and off again in a better spot. I did this several times before we were satisfied. Only later did I discover that it was a black widow spider (*Lactrodectus mactens*) whose bite can cause death by neurotoxic poisoning. I thought I knew well enough the diagnostic marking of this spider—bright red spots on the abdomen —but what I did *not* know was that these distinguishing marks are absent from the Jordan species.

And so to Rum, about fifty miles south of Petra. As vista after breathtaking vista of mountain scenery unfolded itself, I thought nothing could be more spectacular. Even Julian ran out of superlatives, saying that he had never seen anything like it in his life, long and varied as that had been.

From the tawny desert, stretching away to the far horizon, rose enormous natural skyscrapers of multi-hued rock 2,000 ft. high, with cliff-like faces. As the evening light caught the jebels, as these rock formations are called, their pastel stripes and swirls of red, blue and mauve appeared breathtakingly beautiful.

Our destination was the fort at Rum which is now used as a police post. As we arrived, a camel patrol, dressed overall, appeared.

We had looked forward to this visit ever since our arrival, but the anticipation had been somewhat marred by an accident to our advance party when the steering of their car collapsed, putting the driver in hospital with a broken collar-bone and cutting Max and Duncan about the head and hands.

But that was not all. No sooner had we arrived at the police post, which was to be our headquarters, than we received word that the vehicle carrying our domestic gear had crashed. Abu Saif, a most conscientious and lovable old Arab, who thought we should be without food and bedding, decided, against orders, to drive across the desert after dark. Most of the route was as flat as a billiard table but unfortunately, owing to the exceptionally dry weather, large cracks had appeared in the mud-flat. It was one of these, eleven feet wide and five feet deep, that was Abu Saif's undoing. Driving at speed he did not see it. The front wheels hit the farther edge, the lorry somersaulted four or five times and ended upside down, a complete wreck, forty-five yards from the fissure. It was a miracle he was not killed.

The fort at Rum was 3,000 ft. above sea-level, so, although it was hot during the day, it was beautifully cool at night. It was manned by ten Arab soldiers and they told us that they had not seen a single European or American since part of the film *Lawrence of Arabia* had been made there eighteen months previously.

A police post in the middle of a desert seems an unlikely place to yield much bird-life, but I had reckoned without camel droppings, a rich source of bird food because of the large number of insects that feed on them. We photographed Sinai rosefinches, Cretzschmar's buntings, white-crowned black chats, pale rock sparrows, masked shrikes, and, far better known to us, spotted flycatchers, redstarts and lesser white-throats. While George and I were thus engaged, John and Sdeuard returned with a twenty-inch-long Palestine viper. I am sure the Arabs thought we were quite mad to bring in such a venomous snake, photograph it, return it to its original haunt and release it.

One evening John drew our attention to a lammergeier which was repeatedly dropping a skull or tortoise—it was too far away to be sure —on to the great jebel which towered above the fort. The nest was about 1,500 ft. up one of the sheer cliff-sides which the soldiers said was unclimbable.

Guy's target on this visit was a pair of white-crowned black chats nesting in a cleft on a steep slope. There was barely space for the hide, and when Guy entered he found it was about twelve inches too close to the nest for his 200 mm lens. He had to move the hide back until the back legs were dangling in space, and even then he only just obtained his photographs.

Afterwards he was kind enough to write in *Portrait of a Desert* (Collins, 1965): 'I reflected that the difference between Eric Hosking and me was that he would never be caught out with the wrong lens. We constantly teased him about the enormous load of equipment he insisted on carrying. It would now be his turn to laugh.'

Apart from the scenery and the birds there was much else to portray. Sdeuard caught a fine specimen of the long-legged, bright blue Sinai lizard, and a fan-footed gecko, which has toes beautifully adapted to enable it to run up smooth walls and across ceilings.

The survey of Wadi Rum complete, we returned to Amman and then to the King Hussein Bridge over the River Jordan, now alas ruined during the Israeli-Arab war. Here we watched the behaviour of the Dead Sea sparrows, surely one of the most beautiful of that wide-spread and numerous family. The cock has a pale grey crown, a whitish stripe over the eye becoming chestnut farther back, dark grey ear coverts separated from a jet-black throat by a white band, and a conspicuous yellow patch on the head. The mantle is pale chestnut streaked with black.

This large colony of sparrows was so tame that we could study, film and photograph them at fairly close quarters. The nuptial display is particularly interesting. The cock builds the foundation of the nest and then displays to attract the hen. Occasionally, he carries a twig much longer than himself and, after weaving it into the nest, gives an almost frenzied display, flapping his wings, bobbing and singing at the top of his voice. When he has won a mate, the pair complete the large oval nest, made of sharp sticks and tamarisk needles with the entrance near the top. Some of the nests are eighteen inches high and seven inches in diameter.

All too soon our time was up and we set out for home, having observed 217 species of birds, collected some 400 varieties of plants for Kew Gardens, and secured a sizable collection of insects for the Natural History Museum in London. We took 11,000 ft. of film and 4,500 photographs.

Then came the hard work. Every member had to prepare a report of his activities, and Guy and Max had the major job of preparing the recommendations to be made to King Hussein and his government. Briefly these were that there should be established three national parks: (a) 1,500 square miles of desert tract surrounding the Azraq oasis; (b) 800 square miles surrounding Petra; (c) 750 square miles centred on Wadi Rum.

Guy pointed out that a further aim of the expedition was to help people discover the real Jordan, which extends far beyond the few cities at present known to tourists. When they do they will find a country 'more rich in historical heritage than Egypt of the Pharaohs, with more archaeological treasures than Greece and scenic magnificence rivalling the Grand Canyon or Yosemite'.*

He suggested that the United States Government might provide a suitable specialist adviser on national parks. Subsequently Mr. Joseph Jaeger, formerly Director of State Parks in Missouri, was appointed to assist the Jordan Government. In addition, as a result of our reconnaissance, the International Biological Programme published *An Approach to the Rapid Description and Mapping of Biological Habitats* by M. E. Duncan Poore and V. C. Robertson (1964), a valuable book in view of the intolerable way man seeks to exploit nature.

It soon became apparent that a detailed survey must be made of the proposed Azraq National Park, so Guy set about organising another expedition for 1965. The plan was to extend and broaden the previous biological reconnaissance, to appraise the possibilities of the Azraq

* *Portrait of a Desert.*

oasis for major hydro-biological studies, to reach conclusions on the feasibility and implications of a possible International Biological Station at Azraq, to make a survey of the vulnerable forms of wild-life, such as gazelles and the Houbara bustard, and to prepare plans for their conservation.

As far as possible Guy selected the same team, although inevitably there were some who could not manage the second trip. These were Sir Julian Huxley, Dr. Duncan Poore, Philip Hollom, Jan Gillett and John Wightman. In their place Dr. Julian Rzoska came as hydro-biologist, and Clifford Townsend as botanist. We left on 13 April. The 14th was spent attending various functions in Amman but we also managed a car tour, first to the place on the River Jordan where Jesus was baptised by John the Baptist, then to Jericho, allegedly the oldest city in the world, where we were shown pottery made 10,000 years ago. Here our guide explained that the fall of Jericho as recorded in The Book of Joshua was perfectly feasible.

'And seven priests shall bear before the ark seven trumpets of rams' horns: and the seventh day ye shall compass the city seven times, and the priests shall blow with the trumpets. And it shall come to pass, that when they make a long blast with the ram's horn, and when ye hear the sound of the trumpet, all the people shall shout with a great shout; and the wall of the city shall fall down flat.'

The vibrations set up by the trumpets and shouts echoing against the dry, hard-baked, mud walls could, we were told, cause them to crack and collapse.

Finally, on to Qumran to see the cave where the Dead Sea Scrolls were found and the area that is still being excavated. The surrounding escarpment harbours hundreds of caves, most of them not yet examined because they are in sheer cliff-faces impossible for any but skilled cragsmen to scale. One wonders what stories lie buried in these rock fortresses.

Next morning we set off for Azraq, where we were to work for the next three weeks. After twenty miles we turned off the fast tarmac road into the desert and almost immediately were struck by the difference from our visit in 1963. Then everything was parched. Now heavy rains had worked their magic, and there were areas of lush green.

We stayed in the Hunting Lodge, which had been greatly improved since our last visit. The whole place had been repainted, electric wiring and furniture renewed, and our beds made up with white linen. Our cook wore a tall white hat in the best tradition, and the kitchen was equipped with a refrigerator and a laundry. Luxury indeed! And all this came from having Joe Jaeger—with his sophisticated American ideas—working on the spot.

Above: Kingfisher

Below: Great frigate birds, photographed on Tower Island in the Galapagos

Above: Aerial view of Azraq

Below: Aerial view of Wadi Rum

We quickly settled to work, starting with a visit to Qasr al Amra, where we were dismayed to find that the beautiful murals we had admired so much two years ago had been still further disfigured. The iron gate protecting the castle had been broken down and these exquisite relics of Arabic art, which had lasted more than 1,200 years, had been mutilated by the modern Bedouin. Everywhere was spattered with green paint, empty oil drums littered the floors, the beautiful painted ceilings were smoke-blackened, Arabic scribbles were scratched over the walls, and other surfaces were pitted by rifle fire. Jordan is like a gigantic archaeological museum with few specialists and wardens to guard its treasures.

Here Julian Rzoska found that the water in the oasis at Shishan contained Foraminifera, normally marine organisms, yet we were over 120 miles from the nearest sea. He also found fairy shrimps, catfish and some small cichlids (*Tilapia*). The latter fish, which live in both salt and fresh water, weigh up to twenty pounds, and are a valuable source of protein in parts of Africa.

Guy erected mist nets and caught migrant and resident birds, which were ringed, weighed and measured and then released, among them a fine cock Persian robin, the first recorded for Jordan. It was about the size of a chaffinch and was mainly blue-grey above and chestnut below, with black on the sides of the head and a black tail. It had white over the eyes, on the throat and under the tail. But his *pièce de résistance* was the wryneck he trapped on 18 April. This was re-trapped by James Ferguson-Lees and Ian Wallace five days later. By that time its weight had increased by over twenty-five per cent, which shows how rapidly a migrant recovers when a rich food supply is available. Then it must have continued its journey without delay, for it was found dead seventy-five miles north of Kiev in Russia on 9 May, having travelled 1,330 miles in only sixteen days.

James and Ian spent every day exploring different types of desert to discover what species of birds lived there; the limestone flint known as *hammada*; the basalt lava of black stones; *ghors* or areas of temporary flooding; the wadis, dry now but raging torrents during the rainy seasons; and an oasis, where so much of the bird-life was concentrated and which varied from fresh-water pools to salt-flats, from fourteen-foot-high reed-beds to water-meadows. James and Ian recorded no fewer than 231 species of birds, of which nearly sixty were breeding. They identified twenty-eight species of birds of prey, thirty-two waders and thirty warblers, eleven larks and nine wheatears, as well as herons, storks, ducks, gulls and terns—and all this wealth of bird-life in a desert!

The migrant population in this wilderness was unbelievable—on

Q

one day we estimated that there were between 10,000 and 20,000 swallows, while red-throated pipits, yellow wagtails, and lesser white-throats were also numbered in thousands. While at the Hunting Lodge, James called to us on one occasion to see the birds of prey circling above. We counted 165, mainly buzzards but also a few honey buzzards, short-toed eagles, black kites and Egyptian vultures. They were on migration and just drifting northwards in thermals—an easy way of travelling which conserves energy.

Cliff and Sdeuard usually went off together, the former collecting plants, the latter insects, reptiles and amphibians. It fell to these two non-ornithologists to find the nest of a pin-tailed sandgrouse with three eggs, which was exciting news as this was one of the typical desert species we particularly wanted to photograph. So that there would be no difficulty in finding the nest again, three rocks were marked with bright red paint: a necessity in a desert where everything looks alike.

George and I set out on the fifty-mile rough, bumpy drive, chauffeured by the same driver who had accompanied Sdeuard and Cliff. Near the site we mounted long telephoto lenses on our cameras, ready to stalk on foot the sitting bird. We made a slow, careful approach, stopping to examine the ground every few yards through binoculars. No bird was visible but this was hardly surprising because a sandgrouse harmonises perfectly with its surroundings. We approached to within ten feet of where the nest should be—the bird was gone, the nest empty. A Bedouin probably watched when the nest was found and later took the eggs. It was a bitter disappointment.

We let it be known among as many Bedouin as possible that we offered a reward for a sandgrouse's nest. News in the desert spreads rapidly. A Bedouin walked twelve miles across rough country to tell us of a nest with three eggs. Our hopes rose again, for the finding of a nest in such a vast desert is worse than looking for the proverbial needle. As I was the only ornithologist available I set off with a driver and the Bedouin. Crashing and bouncing along, my head twice hitting the roof of the Land Rover and nearly splitting my scalp, we drove up to the nest but—yet another disappointment—a camel had trodden on it just when the young were on the point of hatching. I could have wept.

The next day the same Bedouin appeared at the Lodge at breakfast-time; he had found another sandgrouse's nest and had again walked twelve miles to tell us. He shared our breakfast, then George and I set off with him, half-expecting yet another disappointment and accordingly less enthusiastic. However, we took our cameras, to show willing.

When we got to the spot the Bedouin got out of the car, carefully crept forwards, beckoning us to follow and putting a finger to his mouth to warn us to keep quiet. But when he got within about ten yards of the nest he could contain himself no longer and leapt into the air and waved his arms about. We drew level with him as he excitedly pointed and gesticulated. We could see nothing but stones. Then, as he indicated a spot between two unusually shaped pebbles with a clump of vegetation just in front, we gradually became aware that what we were looking at through our binoculars was indeed a bird, but the cryptic coloration was so perfect that it took us a long time to make it out. That Bedouin certainly earned his reward.

Two hides were erected fifty feet away and George and I entered. We dared not go closer for fear of frightening the bird. I used the 600 mm lens. With all the fuss the sandgrouse ran from the nest and flew away, but very soon after we were left in the hides she came back and gave us plenty of opportunities for photography. A dream had certainly come true, but only just—the following day we had to pack all our equipment in preparation for the journey home.

Another expedition had been completed, thousands more photographs had been taken, miles of cine-film exposed. The ever enthusiastic Guy was impatient to have the results quickly to show to influential people and thus preach the gospel of conservation. One day in New York he met Duncan Read, a retired banker, who was deeply impressed by the message. He asked whether there was anyone who would be prepared to go with him to Jordan to take photographs and make a film which he could show to his fellow countrymen, and help to rouse them to aid in the work of conservation. Guy mentioned my name and Duncan Read telephoned me. I said at once that while I would love to accompany him I could not undertake to do both still and movie photography, and suggested that George be asked to make the film, thus leaving me free to concentrate on the stills.

George and I took off from London Airport on 16 April 1966—a dreary, drizzly Saturday morning. But the VC10 soon rose six miles above the clouds and into brilliant sunshine. With a strong tail-wind our effective speed was 650 m.p.h. and by 4.20 p.m. local time we were in Amman, enveloped in a heat blanket of 86°F compared with the 46°F we had left in London. Duncan was there to greet us.

Soon after 6 a.m. next morning we were on our way in a Land Rover to Wadi Rum, 170 miles to the south. An American Scout car and heavy lorry followed, laden with our gear: tents and beds, a table and chairs, cooking-pots and food sufficient, it seemed to me, to feed the 5,000, a great tank of purified water, and two enormous insulated boxes packed with ice to act as refrigerators.

We finally reached our destination at 6.30 p.m., having stopped several times to take pictures and admire the scenery, and in the gathering darkness it was a tedious business erecting tents and sorting out our gear. The oppressive heat of the day rapidly turned into intense cold and this, coupled with the fact that we were starving—I had eaten only two sandwiches since breakfast—left us in such a state of exhaustion that when we fell into bed at ten-thirty we slept immediately.

By five-thirty next morning the sun was shining brilliantly from a cloudless sky, although it was still very cold. But the temperature rose quickly and we soon wore only the minimum of clothing. I shall never forget breakfast that morning. There cannot be many Westerners who have breakfasted in the open air, in the middle of the desert, and watched lammergeiers flying overhead, with a host of other birds flying around: buzzards, brown-necked ravens, crag and house martins, swallows (both common and red-rumped), white-crowned black and hooded chats and several species of larks. It was quite a job to get a mouthful of egg and bacon in the short intervals when our hands were free from putting up the binoculars to identify yet another bird.

Later that morning we left for the police post, a Beau Geste fort. Although only five miles away, it took us over three hours, for the scenery was so spectacularly beautiful that we kept stopping to record it with our cameras. What thrilled us most was watching at least three pairs of lammergeiers between our camp and the fort, one bird coming so close that we could clearly see its beard.

That night, back at camp, Duncan erected his telescope and through the clear desert air we distinctly saw Jupiter's four moons.

In 1963, while staying in Wadi Rum, George and I had visited Desaa, a Bedouin encampment. On this return visit we were welcomed like long-lost brothers, photographs I had taken and sent to them being produced and proudly displayed to Duncan. We were surprised to see how much the encampment had grown. In addition to many more tents, there was now a brick-built school and village hall. We were invited into one of the tents and coffee was brought, Bedouin style— one mouthful per cup, which is swallowed in a gulp. The cup was then replenished with another mouthful, then another, and so on. The accepted signal for 'enough' is to waggle the empty cup but it is polite to have at least two.

The standard of hygiene was fairly good here. Several times I have shuddered when taking coffee with the Bedouin, the cup having been merely rinsed in very dirty water, then wiped with a filthy thumb and first finger. I presume that hot coffee kills off the many bugs that must have been skipping about.

Somehow Duncan managed to get all the local Howeitat tribes to bring their camels to Desaa; there were at least seventy camels, dressed overall in their colourful regalia. While George and I filmed and photographed them, Duncan thought that it would make a favourable impression if he took a photograph with his Polaroid camera, which produces a print in half a minute. It certainly made an impression but not the one Duncan intended. All the Bedouins wanted a print of themselves—there was nearly a riot.

That night I decided to take a shower. The 'bathroom' was a small bell-tent with a slatted floor. Slung on the pole was a gallon bottle of water equipped with a hand pump and nozzle. The idea was to spray oneself with water, soap all over, then spray again. But alas! the water supply was exhausted before stage three was even attempted. There was no way to get more except from the lorry and I did not fancy walking naked across razor-sharp flint-stone chips. It was only then that I realised how difficult it is to clear a well-lathered body of soapsuds without benefit of water!

Our next stop was Petra. We looked forward to this visit for, however many times one sees it, the beauty never palls. That night we slept in caves like the inhabitants of Petra a thousand years ago, except that we had electric light and wash-basins.

We ate supper in a restaurant and, as I entered, I saw a man reading *Portrait of a Desert*. I introduced myself and found that he was an archaeologist, Victor Wolfgang von Hagen, who was making a study of Roman roads, of which there were once 58,000 miles.

As I was trying to photograph a starred agamid, a lizard, it was brought home to me how much still remains to be done on the educational side of wild-life conservation. A party of some forty student teachers came by and immediately started stoning the creature. When I protested they became nasty and I was very glad there was a soldier within call. As soon as the students saw him they ran off. But what hope is there for an understanding of the value to Jordan of its wild-life if *students*—the country's intellectuals and teachers of tomorrow—behave like that?

Before we left for Amman, Duncan made a discovery which surprised and pleased us all. In a small hole in a sandstone rock he found the nest and four eggs of a Sinai rosefinch—only the second time the finding of a nest has been recorded.

We spent many of the daylight hours of the next two days in the air. On previous visits to Jordan, Guy had tried hard to obtain the use of a helicopter to make an aerial survey of the places we were visiting. Yet, despite the fact that on both expeditions one had been promised, it never materialised. Where Guy failed, Duncan succeeded.

A new six-seater French helicopter was put at our disposal complete with RAF-trained pilot and navigator. We flew first to Wadi Rum at about 90 m.p.h. and 9,000 ft. The ground looked parched and bare, a patch of vegetation showing up prominently. At Jebel Ishrin we came down just below the summit of the great rock formation and for a moment looked into the cavern where the lammergeier had its nest; the outside was completely white from its droppings.

In a shade temperature of 108°F we landed to refuel at Aqaba on the Red Sea, Jordan's only port, then followed Wadi Araba and the edge of the Rift Valley until we were over Petra. We hovered over some of the tombs and temples, filming and photographing; looked down at Aaron's tomb on the summit of Jebel Harun; were fascinated to see the whole length of the twisting Siq; came in close to the huge Temple of El Deir, the Monastery; admired the fine Roman amphitheatre; had the most impressive view of the massive Qasr al Bint, a temple built in the reign of the African-born Emperor Septimius Severus (AD 193–211); saw the sheer cliff-face where the King of Judah is reported to have thrown 10,000 Edomite captives to their death; and then we returned to Amman.

James Ferguson-Lees and Ian Wallace were working at Azraq on the International Biological Programme and, knowing how keen they were to make an aerial survey of the oasis, I persuaded Duncan to take them for a trip in the helicopter. We telegraphed to say that we hoped to land at the Hunting Lodge about nine-fifteen next morning. We did, but they were not there; the message had not arrived.

We decided to fly over the desert and look for them. This was more difficult than it sounds; not only had we no idea in which direction or how far they had gone, but they were riding in a camouflaged army Land Rover.

But find them we did. By sheer good fortune I spotted their Land Rover near Qasr al Amra and the helicopter landed within a few yards of James. If we had descended in a parachute direct from the heavens his face could not have registered greater astonishment. He did not even know we were in Jordan, let alone that we had miraculously borrowed a helicopter—and then we had found him in a vast expanse of desert! His jaw dropped but suddenly his whole face broke into a smile as he recognised us. He told me afterwards that he thought he was about to be attacked, even machine-gunned, by some marauding pilots who thought he was an enemy. Duncan took him and Ian up and gave them an entirely new impression of the oasis, then they went back to their field-work.

Since the aircraft tank held only 150 gallons of high-octane petrol—enough for three hours' flying—we had to return to Amman for a refill before taking off for Jericho. It was easy to see from the air what a small part of the whole area was occupied by the ancient walled city.

As we flew parallel to an old monastery built into a cliff-face, we saw part of yet another old city which recent excavations had revealed.

We wanted to see Qumran, Jerusalem, Bethlehem and the Sea of Galilee but they were in military areas and over-flights were forbidden. So Duncan suggested that George and I should drive to Jerusalem and Bethlehem to film and photograph.

As we drove into Jerusalem we noticed the streets were gaily decorated and crowds of people were milling about. We waved and the crowds cheered back. We certainly had not expected quite such a welcome—then we found that King Hussein and Sheik Shakhbout were also expected! The Sheik had given a handsome donation for the relief of the recent terrible Ma'an floods.

But we were saddened by the rampant commercialism of the holy places of Jerusalem. It was moving, as it must be for any Christian, to visit the Mount of Olives, the Garden of Gethsemane and other places which are the heart of the Gospel story. In the Church of the Holy Sepulchre a priest greeted us, not with a blessing as one would expect, but with: 'Money for the church, money for the church, money for the church.' I thought of Christ and the money-changers.

We were gladdened by the quiet peace of the Garden Tomb, which was just as I had pictured it from the New Testament account. The area was beautifully kept and we enjoyed its cool shade and isolation. At the far end of the garden we had an impressive view of Golgotha.

There was time only for a brief excursion to Bethlehem before returning to Amman to prepare to visit the H4 Pumping Station on the Iraq–Syria oil pipeline. The station lies in the eastern desert on the main Baghdad road to the north-east of Azraq, and a community has grown up round it. It is a man-made area of trees, other vegetation and buildings and, like the other pumping stations, such as H3 and H5, it forms an artificial oasis. Along the road we frequently saw lesser grey shrikes sitting on telegraph wires and decided to count them: 234 in 160 miles. They were on migration, resting and refuelling after a long flight across the desert, before continuing their way, probably to Eastern Europe. There was certainly a readily available supply of food —insects killed or injured by the fast traffic.

We stayed at the Rest House at H4 which offered every comfort, including very thick walls to keep the interior cool. The trees surrounding the building were alive with a wonderful variety of birds, among them many redstarts, turtle doves, spotted flycatchers, hoopoes, kestrels and nightingales. During the intense heat of the day they hid in the densest, coolest part of the trees. But towards evening they came out to feed and we saw a gorgeous cock rock thrush with blue head and bright orange breast and tail, accompanied by a brown hen with heavily barred breast. A cock golden oriole was almost as resplendent with his vivid yellow body and contrasting black wings and tail. Then, just as dusk was falling at five-thirty, a flock of at least fifty bee-eaters suddenly flew in from the desert, all calling with a loud, liquid constantly repeated *prruip*. They circled overhead, trying to find a suitable roosting place, and as the sun set they dived into a tree and became silent. This oasis was an ideal stop-over during migration.

The next day we drove to Qasr Burqu, a water catchment area some fifteen miles away. As we travelled across the wild desert we noticed that on every shrub that stood slightly above average height rested a red-backed shrike. It perched, motionless, waiting for an insect or lizard to move, then a rapid glide earned another meal.

At Burqu some Bedouin were using modern petrol pumps to fill water tanks on ancient lorries. Their sheep and goats had already eaten every scrap of vegetation and had moved on, so now water had to be collected and taken to them.

Round the lake we stalked six greater sand plovers, wood, green and marsh sandpipers and red-throated pipits, while hundreds of swallows skimmed the surface, making rippled 'v's' as they capture floating insects. Nearby George found the nest of a Temminck's horned lark and we took photographs of the adults feeding the tiny young. They were too busy to bother about us standing within a few feet.

On our drive back across the desert a soldier, who was accompanying us, shouted: 'Houbara! Houbara!' The driver braked so suddenly that I almost shot through the windscreen. It was so sudden, so unexpected, that we did not, at first, take it in. But there, thirty feet in front of us, was a Houbara bustard. We could hardly believe our eyes— this was the bird that we had longed, but so far failed, to see on all our visits to Jordan. It was a magnificent bird, appearing even larger than it was when compared with the much smaller birds we had seen recently.

As it ran away, we drove cautiously after it, stopping as soon as we got within photographic range. But each time it was too quick for us. Six times we did this until finally it took off and with slow powerful beats of its great wings disappeared from sight. But it had made our day.

Having visited Azraq briefly by helicopter, we now drove there to spend a few days, staying in the British Embassy hut—the Hunting Lodge was already occupied by the members of the International Biological Programme under the leadership of Dr. John Morton Boyd. Part of their programme was to catch and ring birds. Bob Spencer, Dr. John Ash and James Ferguson-Lees were carrying out this work and we were impressed by their devotion to the task. They were up each morning at four-thirty, were at their thirty mist nets by sunrise, and did not leave until it was dark at about seven. Meals were taken to them. In all, over 2,500 birds of fifty-five species were caught, ringed, weighed, measured and released. These included 650 sand martins, 350 swallows, and more than 100 each of red-throated pipits, yellow wagtails, lesser whitethroats, blackcaps, and garden and willow warblers.

Bob and John Ash had learnt a useful tip from a local boy; this was to set fire to a small patch of rushes to make insects, especially small moths, fly out. These, in turn, attracted swallows and sand martins which circled overhead catching the insects. Sometimes 700 to 800 birds were thus brought within range of the nets, a small proportion of them being caught.

A Bedouin told us that he had seen a pair of Houbara bustards together and thought they were nesting at a spot only some ten miles away. We decided to look for them. It was extremely hot but the Bedouin was wearing what looked like woollen combinations reaching from neck to ankles. Over this he had a heavy cloak and then—believe it or not—just before he got into the car he pulled on a thick greatcoat! And we were perspiring in the absolute minimum of clothing. Bedouin rarely wash (water is needed for more important purposes) and it was very obvious that our bustard-spotter was no exception. He stank. We failed to find the bustards although we drove around for fifty to sixty miles, the Bedouin meanwhile enjoying himself—he had never been in a car before.

Another day we drove across the desert to Faidhat edh Dhahikiya, about twenty miles south-east from Azraq, to photograph the spectacular chalk cliffs which stretch for some ten miles, almost to Saudi Arabia. At nearby Umari, shepherds were watering their sheep and goats exactly as, I imagine, they did in Biblical times, even using a goatskin as a container. But some of the more modern Bedouin were actually using petrol cans to draw their water.

I was cheerfully shooting away with the camera when a soldier warned me that women were about and that the men might be angry. The lens of the camera is looked upon as an evil eye, especially if turned towards a woman, so I had to wait until all the women—and that included even little girls—had been sent away.

The lot of the woman in the desert is hard. When quite young her face is tattooed, so that if she runs away other Bedouin tribes will know where she has come from and can send her back. Guy asked our driver one day if he had a family and he replied: 'One and a half children.' I thought that he had one child and another was expected but what he meant was that he had a son and a daughter—who counted as only half a child.

The women do most of the hard work. On the rare occasions when a man decides to wash a woman pours the water over him. I saw one woman, who looked at least sixty, breast-feeding a baby, but I was assured that she was not more than thirty and that this was her twelfth child. In this strange country you dare not even admire a young girl. It is believed that admiration encourages the Devil to visit her and cause serious illness.

The Bedouin own nothing except the rags they wear, their tents, a few home-made cooking utensils, their animals and their womenfolk. They are always on the move, staying in one place only as long as it takes their animals to clear the surrounding vegetation. Shoes would soon be cut to pieces in the flinty desert, but the Bedouin dispense with footgear—the soles of their feet are hard as horn. The Bedouin go to bed when it gets dark and get up as soon as it is light—they have no light but the sun. Thus life is stripped to the barest essentials, a life virtually unchanged for thousands of years.

It is gratifying to know that as a result of our expeditions the country now has an excellent programme of wild-life conservation, which is being vigorously applied by the Government. The Azraq Desert National Park has become an important international research centre, in which the University of Amman is taking a prominent part.

It was on my return from the 1965 Jordan Expedition that I went down with a bad form of dysentery which reacted on me rather like malaria. Approximately every four weeks for six months I developed a temperature, became delirious for twenty-four to forty-eight hours, then quite quickly recovered. I was coming round from one of these bouts at ten-thirty in the morning and was about to light a cigarette. I had been an inveterate smoker since I was fifteen, thoroughly enjoying both pipe and cigarette, and had never even thought of giving it up. Now I hesitated and decided to see whether I could go till lunch without smoking. After lunch I thought of going till tea-time, then to dinner, then to next morning. Since that day I have never smoked, yet still, five years later, greatly miss it. But my health is definitely better; I can now climb again without puffing too much and enjoy my food more—although I always seem to be hungry and I have to watch my weight carefully. My 'smoker's cough' has disappeared completely—and ash no longer falls on my best negatives!

19 | *Pakistan*

In 1966 Guy Mountfort was asked by the Pakistan Government to advise on nature conservation, and the setting up of national parks and nature reserves. He invited me to go and on 20 October we set off from London Airport in a Boeing of the Pakistan International Airlines. The other members of the expedition were Dr. Duncan Poore, Director-General of the Nature Conservancy; Jimmy Hancock, an ornithologist with special knowledge of Pakistani birds; and George Shannon.

With an intermediate stop at Frankfurt we reached Moscow at midnight. Soldiers came aboard, and kept us firmly closeted in the plane during refuelling. This irked me, since this was the first time I had landed in Russia. I spoke to one of them who understood English, and he relented and allowed me to walk down the gangway—after I had handed him my passport.

I need not have bothered; shortly afterwards fog came down and prevented us from leaving. We were all shepherded to the airport lounge, which was already crowded with Russians. Since take-off would not be until dawn, we endeavoured to snatch some sleep, my bed being three wooden chairs, my pillow a camera-filled ruck-sack.

We awoke, unrefreshed and hungry, at 6 a.m. With no roubles, it looked as if we should remain breakfastless, but an official of Pakistan Airlines led us to a restaurant where, an hour later, we were given bread and cheese. After this large bowls of boiled eggs arrived—three each—with copious supplies of black acorn coffee.

At ten-thirty we were still grounded. Could we telephone the British Embassy asking for a cable to be sent to Karachi explaining the delay? No, there are no telephones.

'But look,' we insisted, 'there are at least six here in this room.'

'Ah yes, but they are for internal use only.'

'All right then, give us the number of the British Embassy. Or lend us a directory and we will find it ourselves.'

'No directory!' Check—and, it would appear, Mate. But when we finally left the airport at 1.40 p.m. we had the satisfaction of knowing that Guy had eventually won, and the cable was on its way.

There was, however, one valuable by-product of this frustrating hold-up. In a showcase in the airport lounge I saw a 1,000 mm MTO mirror lens. The normal length of such a lens is about thirty-five inches; this mirror lens was under ten. I bought one of these lenses when I returned to England and it has proved to be most valuable.

Later that same day we arrived at Karachi in West Pakistan and were met by Chris Savage, who had done much of the local organising of the expedition, and our Pakistan hosts led by Mr. G. M. M. E. Karim, Deputy Director of the Department of Tourism. We were soon catching up on our lost sleep in the air-conditioned bedroom of the Intercontinental Hotel.

After lunch we flew to Multan and thence by car to the Commissioner's house at Bahawalpur, sixty miles away. The farther we drove, the hotter we became. Guy took off his jacket, then his tie, then his collar, then—he hastily put them all on again as the car drew up alongside a red carpet. Two gorgeously decorated elephants trumpeted a ceremonial welcome and, as he stepped from the car, a glistening garland of tinsel, sequins and imitation pearls was draped round his neck, the traditional Eastern welcome for distinguished visitors. Then, to my astonishment, I too, was decorated and all the other members in turn.

The fifty yards of red carpet led us to a marquee where we were showered with rose petals. Here we met the Commissioner, took tea and inspected an exhibition of local wares including delicate filigree silverware. Alongside were large glass jars containing snakes and lizards, and one of the attendants—a snake-charmer—lured the snakes head-high from the jars so that I could photograph them. But what I really wanted was a picture of one of the leopard geckos *outside* its jar. Consternation. This gecko, I was assured, could kill a man just with its breath. This I would not believe and, to prove it, held my hand out and allowed the 'poison-breathing monster' to crawl on it from there to the ground.

We left at 7.30 p.m. to drive to Fort Abbas to spend the night there, but the drivers took a short cut across the desert and we got lost. Guy and Duncan took over, navigating by compass, map and stars, and we eventually arrived above five hours late. We were still dressed in our best after the Commissioner's reception but were completely smothered in yellow dust. Even our cameras and binoculars, although they were wrapped in plastic bags, were coated with this ultra-fine powder which plagued us wherever we went. We dined at 2.45 a.m. and went to bed.

Later that day, however, we were rewarded with some fine views of the desert avifauna, including a flock of forty-four Imperial sandgrouse and a Houbara bustard. Here our party was joined by Tom Roberts, who has an outstanding knowledge of Pakistan birds, and Jerry Wood-Anderson, who is equally expert on mammals, amphibians, reptiles and insects.

We left early next morning by car to explore the banks of a canal, hoping to see much wild-life, especially birds which lie up in the shade during the heat of the day. We were well rewarded. Dozens of bright rose-ringed parakeets embroidered the trees, a Lagger falcon came by, and the tawny eagles were so tame that they flew only when we were almost on them. By the canal white-breasted kingfishers perched on slender pampas grasses and trees, making colour transparencies of their reflections in the water below. But what impressed me most was a pair of Indian rollers feeding their young. The male gave a magnificent display flight, his wings in vivid shades of blue shining brightly as he soared vertically. Then, calling discordantly, he spiralled down and alighted on a tree.

Our hopes of further discoveries were sadly dashed, however, when, after about two miles of a rough narrow track through the jungle, the car slid off the road into a ditch. It was so firmly stuck that we decided to abandon it and crowd into another car to take us to keep a luncheon appointment with the Amir. We presented ourselves at his gleaming white Sadiq garh Palace, one and a half hours late, travel-stained and in our rough field clothes. But the Amir and his three princely brothers put us completely at our ease and we enjoyed a delicious seven-course meal. We were then joined by General J. H. Marden, nearly eighty years old but very active, who made all the arrangements for our stay.

We spent the night at the Palace, Guy and I sharing a luxurious bedroom, with our personal bodyguard stationed outside the door. Presumably he was there to see that we did not get our cameras stolen— but since his snores disturbed the warm night air, it was as well no felons were about.

The next morning, I explored the garden. A blaze of flowers flamed before the dazzling Palace; pelicans and geese swam on an artificial pool, large Indian parakeets with brilliant green feathers and scarlet bills swooped from tree to tree. It was like a fairy-tale come true.

Our next stop, after a drive across the desert, could not have been in greater contrast. After the lush comfort and green beauty of the Palace, Fort Derawar was barren and grey. The huge desert fortress stood on a high mound near an old caravan route, its large courtyard dotted with ancient cannons and balls, chain-shot and other engines of war. From the great towers the desert could be seen stretching into the far distance, and an approaching enemy stood little chance of arriving unnoticed. Deep below the tower were well-ventilated cellars with an adequate water supply. Thus the soldiers defending the fortress could take cool comfort in the heat of day, while the enemy sweltered in the desert sun.

Conditions in the nearby village of Firoza were shocking. Mud huts huddled along the banks of a canal which appeared to be a communal sewer. Drainage consisted of a hole cut through the wall of each hut and the effluent discharged straight into the street and thus into the canal. The stench was appalling. Scraggy, sickly-looking children stood about in a state of bored apathy, and altogether conditions were such that we decided not to linger.

Wherever there was water in this parched land, birds were abundant. Swallows and martins hawked over the surface of roadside pools, and greenshanks, redshanks, little stints and black-winged stilts waded in the shallow water.

We slept that night at the pleasant hunting lodge at Jhajjia Abbasian, and after breakfast set off for the jheels of Gagri. Here we were greeted —or rather stared at—by what appeared to be the entire male population. Two ancient punts were to transport us, and all the onlookers seemed anxious to act as boatmen. After the dust and heat of the desert, the smooth stillness of the water was a delight. We threaded our way through a carpet of lotus pads, embroidered with exotic waterfowl, while on a reed frond swayed several blue-cheeked bee-eaters.

Some of the lotus leaves were eighteen inches in diameter and only when I pushed on one with all my strength did I manage to submerge it. No wonder the pheasant-tailed jacanas and coots run on them so easily.

During the night we travelled by train to Renala Khurd where we breakfasted next morning with the late Colonel J. H. Taylor, an Irish horse-breeder, who told us that his horses had won the Derby three times. How, we wondered, did we come to be enjoying a delicious breakfast with this particular host? He had been asked by one of our earlier contacts to give us breakfast. It was the accepted custom. You look through the telephone directory until you find someone in the district where your party is going, ring him up and ask for food to be laid on. Colonel Taylor showed us round his stud—I regret to say that I was more interested in the Indian mynas and golden-backed woodpeckers in the trees above.

We visited Chhanga Manga, a supposed national park, but were disappointed to find that the only wild mammals which were protected were a few deer, and those mainly in cages. All birds of prey were shot freely. Eagle-shooting is quite common sport in Pakistan.

During the forty-mile car journey, we passed many ancient, ram-shackle vehicles—privately owned buses, which are a feature of Pakistan. They trundle along the highways, packed with passengers, the overflow festooning the steps, and piles of luggage perched pre-cariously on the roof. The buses are decorated with colourful and elaborate paintings and are driven with complete recklessness. During our hour-long journey we passed two overturned buses by the side of the road; one squashed tonga (a passenger-carrying tricycle); one donkey and four dogs—all recently killed.

Life in the Orient is said to be held more cheaply than in the West. One little pastime of Pakistan drivers was a good illustration of this sad truth. Many of the roads in the Pakistan outback are single track, with soft mud edges. Cars approach from opposite directions, each endeavouring to force the other off the track and on to the mud. Last-second, and often last-split-second, decisions are made, and thus the driver with the strongest nerve wins—or maybe both lose if his opponent also persists.

We had another vivid example of Pakistan road manners at a level-crossing. Our driver, belting along at 60 m.p.h. and suddenly con-fronted with the closing gates, screeched to a halt; at least we were first in line. That is what we thought. But following cars and lorries, instead of lining up behind us, spread themselves, side by side, right across the road. The drivers and passengers—between two and three hundred of them—all piled out and stood around chattering and enjoying the scenery, including the cause of the hold-up: a seventy-five-waggon goods train that took an unconscionable time to clatter past.

As soon as it had gone there was a massed rush back to the cars; a good imitation of a Le Mans start at a Grand Prix race. The engines were already warming up and the moment the gates opened everybody was off—on both sides of the line!

The night train from Lahore took us to Kalabagh where we were to be guests of the Nawab. Although we had first-class tickets, the compartments were dirty and grimed with desert dust. The train jogged up and down, swayed from side to side, ground to a halt and jerked into motion again. Only a roller-coaster could have given us a rougher ride—but not much.

At the Nawab's Palace we were surprised to see a guard mounted by soldiers armed not only with rifles but sub-machine-guns as well. Wild country this, and the Nawab was taking no chances.

Wild the country may have been, but there was nothing in the guest-house that was less than luxurious. My air-conditioned bedroom was *en suite* with its own bathroom, but Guy's room was even grander. His bed was three times the size of an ordinary double bed, and sunk into the floor of the room was a green-tiled bath, seven or eight feet long.

On our arrival, and before we were shown to our rooms, we had left our mountain of photographic equipment strewn around the porch. The servants had obviously seen nothing like it before, and from their excited chatter we gathered that they imagined it might be a battery of modern armaments—certainly my long telephoto lens complete with pistol grip and shoulder brace was reminiscent of a sub-machine-gun.

In the grounds of this guest-house was the most fantastic tree I have ever seen—a banyan tree whose roots grow downward from dozens of heavy branches. At first, bundles of fine shoots sprout from the branches, and descend until eventually they root into the soil. Then they thicken and harden until they can support the heaviest branch. This tree, which was hundreds of years old, looked more like a miniature forest than a single tree; it had spread itself over about half an acre. Some banyan trees are said to have a circumference of 2,000 ft. and to be supported by 3,000 roots. Legend has it that Alexander the Great camped 7,000 men under such a tree.

At dinner that evening, for the first time in my life, I ate silver. Over the rice lay a fine coating of what I thought was tin foil. But it was silver, hammered to a tissue one thousandth of an inch thick, which was claimed to be good for the digestion. Delicate finger bowls, with floating rose petals, decorated each place, and overall lay the sweet heavy scent of the Queen of the Night—a flower that blooms only after sunset.

The next morning I saw two Indian honey buzzards in a tree in the garden. I snatched a couple of cameras and started to stalk them. But each time I nearly got within range they flew on. I gradually got farther and farther from the guest-house. Then a guard came up to me, took my arm and gently but firmly led me back. Apparently I was getting nearer and nearer to the Nawab's private quarters.

The Nawab particularly wanted us to photograph the Punjab urial, a very rare mammal akin to a sheep, which is believed to be nearly extinct. The ram is a handsome animal with a reddish brown coat, white on the inside of the legs, and a long black beard. The Nawab has established a reserve in the 120-mile-long Salt Range—the S-shaped boundary extending southward from the sub-Himalayas—in which urial are rarely shot.

We took off for the reserve at 4.30 a.m. in brilliant moonlight. Cars

Above : Leopard

Below : Cheetah

and jeeps rattled over the long iron bridge spanning the Indus, through villages still asleep, and once our headlights picked out a scene unchanged since Biblical times—a camel train meandering along with the cloaked drover asleep on the foremost beast.

We arrived at the reserve as dawn broke over the distant mountains. We divided into groups, each with a guide, hardy hawk-nosed tribesmen with henna-dyed beards and moustachios. Their green tunics were wound with bandoliers of cartridges for their long rifles, which they carried, not to slaughter the urial, but for our protection. Taking pot-shots at strangers was a pastime of some hill tribesmen, who also 'earned' ransom money for occasional kidnapping. Shortly before our visit, six of the Nawab's men had been ambushed.

Guy, Jerry and I set off first, our gear on our backs, and were soon panting and puffing. The final clamber to the rocky summit of the first ridge finished us completely and once there, Guy and I collapsed, exhausted, on the ground, while our guide—who looked older than either of us and was festooned with rifle, bandolier and heavy ruck-sack —was not even out of breath and stood grinning down at us.

It is an exhilarating experience to sit on a mountain ridge with the sun rising and gradually touching the peaks with golden light. The valley, still unlit, lay far below. We crept along the ridge until we had a good view across the valley. About six-thirty, through our binoculars we glimpsed our quarry—a fine ram urial with several ewes; and soon after a herd of seventeen in the charge of a male with massive horns. One ram, his ewe and a year-old kid stood on a crag, the sunlight full on his splendid black beard. He was a magnificent sight but at least a mile away. We climbed a small cliff which seemed almost as vertical as the wall of a house, and had an excellent view of an immense herd of between seventy and eighty urial in the valley below. Unfortunately they saw us as soon as we saw them, and turned to climb an almost sheer rock-face.

As the sun climbed, the heat in our exposed position became unbearable. Everything quivered in the heat haze. The rock was scorching. Nothing moved. Only when we reached the guard hut where we had left the vehicles did I find relief in the delicious coolness. The thick mud walls of the hut gave complete insulation from the furnace without.

Next day we went again to the reserve and this time beaters drove the urial toward us. The animals' agility and sure-footedness were amazing. We saw parties of them running across what appeared to be an almost perpendicular rock-face.

From Kalabagh we drove to Khabbaki Lake where we saw huge rafts of coots and flocks of pochards, tufted and white-headed ducks,

R

Opposite: grey heron

pintails, wigeon, teal, bar-headed geese, little and black-necked grebes and great white egrets. Flamingos stalked gracefully in the shallows. At a rough estimate I should say that there were between five and six thousand birds of various species on this lake.

Leaving this enchanting scene we drove to Rawalpindi where we stayed in a fine modern hotel. Despite the fact that fewer than a quarter of the people can read, various slogans were prominently displayed in the towns. 'Family planning means prosperity', 'Planned families are happy families', 'Only a fool shares his house with bugs!', etc. English was the main language for public displays, and the influence of the British Raj remained even in Pakistan street names—Sir Hugh Rose Road, Great West Road, The Mall and Queen Victoria Street—but there the resemblance to their British equivalents ended.

After dinner at the hotel I held court in my room which soon looked like an Oriental bazaar. Local merchants brought shawls, carpets, precious stones and other products of the region, some very beautiful. But it was fatal to show interest; this was the East, where hard bargaining is a game with rules of its own.

'Too much! Too much!' Three or four times we dismissed them. 'Still too much!'

'The Sahib is a hard man,' they muttered, only to return a few minutes later with yet a lower offer. Eventually, after much conspiring and a promise not to tell anyone of these special concessions, we bought some of their treasures—at less than half the original price.

Next morning we were airborne for Lahore. We had a splendid aerial view of Nanga Parbat, one of the six highest mountains in the world, its snow-covered peak glinting in the brilliant sun against the purest blue sky.

A short stop at Lahore, then we were off to Dacca, 1,200 miles distant in East Pakistan. Fortunately we had reserved seats, for the plane was crammed with passengers and children crouched on the floor, while cooking pots, bedding and assorted bundles were crammed into every available space. Only the gangway was clear. We were impressed by the unobtrusive efficiency of the pretty little stewardesses who wore the most attractive uniform I have seen—long emerald green jacket and flowing white trousers.

Several Muslim families were aboard and at sunset their menfolk laid prayer mats in the gangway and quite unselfconsciously prayed to Allah. We all kept silent until their devotions were done—we could not but admire their piety.

As we stepped from the aircraft at Dacca the humid heat enveloped us. It was like entering the tropical house at Kew Gardens. That night, for the first time, I slept beneath a mosquito net.

Back again at the airport next morning, we flew to Chittagong in a Fokker turbo-prop aircraft. These machines have the wings above the fuselage, thus allowing an uninterrupted view through the port-holes. It was most disappointing that aerial photography is forbidden in both East and West Pakistan.

East Pakistan is very different from the West, where the prevailing impression was of sand and dust; here it was of water and vegetation. On the flooded land below we could see hundreds of canoes and sampans plying between isolated homesteads.

Chittagong airport was crowded and a kaleidoscope of colour; the men and women all in brilliantly coloured costumes. Many of the younger women were unveiled and talkative, the elder ones mostly veiled and silent.

We were certainly at Chittagong, but most of our luggage had been left behind at Dacca and was not due to arrive until the next plane, about three and a half hours later. So we visited the Bayazid Bustami shrine, passing down narrow alleys jammed with stalls selling a repulsive array of raw offal. Kites and crows hovered overhead, waiting their chance to pounce. When we reached the shrine we understood; the offal was fodder for the sacred black mud turtles. Visitors sat beside a fetid pool feeding the beasts.

And as if this were not enough, outside the café where we lunched was a dead flying fox—one of the world's largest bats—electrocuted by the overhead high-tension wires from which it hung by its feet.

Public transport has its own idiosyncrasies. In addition to the decorated buses most taxis display elaborate designs, each driver trying to outshine his rivals in pattern and colour. The taxis are mostly three-wheelers with a maximum passenger load of two. Here in Chittagong the petrol engine is replaced by tongas.

Smoking seemed to be an almost universal habit, even among children, but instead of cigarettes and pipes, the hookah was smoked— a hubble-bubble pipe like a miniature bassoon filled with home-grown tobacco.

We collected our luggage at the airport and drove off to Rangamati, where we lodged in a rest house beside an enormous lake. The place was alive with insects; it seemed that there were billions rather than millions! Geckos scoured the walls and ceilings, while toads banqueted on the floor inside the house, all devouring insects.

Next morning—4 November—I awoke at dawn and looked across the lake. It was a magical moment. The first rays of sunlight dissolved the mist, casting an enchantment over the whole scene reminiscent of mist-enshrouded mountain-tops in a Chinese painting.

By motor-boat we made our way to Pablakhali where we were to stay at a lake-side bungalow built on stilts sunk into the hillside. Thick plastic covered the floors, to keep out damp and insects, but it failed miserably in one regard, for here, if it were possible, the insects were even more numerous that at Rangamati. They got in our hair, our shirts, our trousers, our boots, in our noses and our ears. The chirping of the crickets and grasshoppers made the air vibrate. Enormous rhinoceros beetles crashed into the paraffin lamps and if we attempted to pick them up they hissed at us—a most unnerving experience.

But next morning even the memory of these horrors could not spoil the boat journey over the lake, and the sight of the bijou blue-eared and the sturdy stork-billed kingfishers with brilliant blue wings and massive red bill, as well as Pallas's fishing eagles, herons, egrets, bee-eaters and parakeets.

The following day it was 92°F in the shade and over 125° in the sun—my thermometer scale goes no farther and the mercury was over the top. Guy and I, with four local guides, tramped for miles along a jungle path. Suddenly, with a great crash and a rending of the under-growth, two enormous bull gayals confronted us. I took one quick picture, then shot off the path while they charged by at an alarming pace, passing me no more than ten feet away. On our way back we saw three species of birds which I shall never forget for their sheer beauty: a party of scarlet minivets, a purple sunbird and a scarlet-backed flowerpecker.

One memorable day Guy and I travelled by motor-boat up the River Kassalog to Gonacheri, a small settlement where all the houses were built on bamboo stilts. Ospreys fished, purple gallinules flew within a few feet of us, and a black-winged kite circled over our heads. Guy casually remarked to the villagers that we would like to see a python.

'There, there,' they said, 'one has just swum across the stream. We catch it.' They jumped into a dug-out canoe, Guy joining them, and paddled quickly to the opposite bank.

With a loud cry three men grabbed the snake's body, while a fourth seized its head, and out came a fourteen-foot-long, seven-inch-diameter python which writhed and struggled in the four-man vice. They brought it back and Guy and I photographed it, and then suggested that they free it so that we could take more pictures of it on the ground. But we were too slow. With one quicksilver movement the python flung itself into the river and was gone. From the photographs it was identified as a reticulated python, the first time it had been recorded in Pakistan.

Our journey home was no less memorable, for it was as if the river flowed through an endless tropical aviary. We saw red-breasted parakeets, racket-tailed drongos, pigmy woodpeckers and little green bitterns; flocks of blue-tailed and green bee-eaters, gorgeous king-fishers and a small flock of Indian pied hornbills feeding on wild figs in company with rhesus Macaque monkeys.

That night the sky caught fire as the most glorious sunset I have ever seen swept across the heavens and was reflected in the lake. Sky and water were one vivid red. Slowly the fires banked down and I pre-pared for the sudden tropical nightfall. But a quarter of an hour later the heavens glowed again, softer yet infinitely varied colours patterning the evening sky. Then at last the final blush of colour faded and all was dark. One of the colour photographs I took was used on the jacket of Guy's excellent book of our Pakistan expeditions, *The Vanishing Jungle* (Collins, 1969).

The next day was mostly spent looking for a herd of Indian ele-phants which we never found, although we got near enough to see their still-steaming droppings.

Our next journey took us to Chit-Morong, a village I remember chiefly for its pipe-smoking women and blood-sucking leeches. The women were camera-shy, giggled and turned away. The leeches dropped on to us from the banana trees. Once attached to bare skin the victim feels nothing. Even when they have sucked their fill and dropped to the ground, the wound continues to bleed. The anti-coagulant injected to facilitate their own bloody meal continues to operate, and the first indication the victim has is a sticky red patch oozing through his shirt.

Now we had to return to Chittagong and after the peaceful river journeys of the past few days jeep travel on rough roads was grim. From Chittagong we flew to Comilla, and thence to Dacca. Guy and Duncan continued their journey to Karachi to see Ayub Khan (then President), while George and I remained to have the best day's photog-raphy of the whole expedition in the company of Colonel Angus Hume, a keen local ornithologist. Near a main road we discovered 100 or so white-backed vultures feeding on the carcass of a water buffalo, and we just went trigger happy. A Pallas's fishing eagle obliged by feeding farther along the road. Beside the river, fishermen and birds lived in happy tolerance. Little green bee-eaters perched on fishing rods, sometimes three to a rod. A pied kingfisher clung to another, and a lovely Brahminy kite posed on the pole of a large fishing net. To complete the bag we photographed black kites and house crows feeding on scraps in the grounds of our hotel.

From Dacca we flew to Karachi, and after an exciting visit to a snake farm, where we watched the venom being milked from black cobra and Russell's viper, boarded an aircraft for home. We took off on 12 November at 2.15 a.m. and I fell asleep. An hour and a half later a voice urged us to fasten our seat-belts, we were about to land—at Karachi! We were back where we started—air-conditioning trouble this time. We breakfasted at the KLM hotel, eventually leaving at 8.45 a.m. and, travelling via Teheran, Moscow and Frankfurt, landed at London Airport at 5 p.m.

Guy and Duncan submitted a detailed report of the expedition to the Pakistan Government but made it clear that we had been unable to cover more than a fraction of the great variety of habitats that are found in both West and East Pakistan. It was suggested that there should be a second expedition. We had seen nothing of the Western Himalayas, nothing of the vast mangrove swamps of the Indus Delta, nor the tidal jungles of the Sunderbans in the Bay of Bengal—all quite different with their own wild-life. Worthwhile visits could also be made to the Kirthar Mountain range and the forestal region of Sylhet near the Assam border. Chris Savage and Tom Roberts dealt with these proposals with the Pakistan authorities who said that they would welcome a further expedition.

Thus, during November 1967, I made my second visit to Pakistan. Because of other commitments, I was unable to go on part of the expedition—to Gilgit in the Western Himalayas and later to Sylhet—but a full account of these can be found in Guy's book. He was accompanied by Dr. Duncan Poore and Lord Fermoy, who came as liaison officer and sound recordist. A week after they left, George Shannon, John Buxton, who helped with the production of a documentary film, and I flew out via Turkey and Persia. Fortunately there was no repetition of the Moscow delays we experienced on the previous journey, but there was a frightening ten minutes near Istanbul where we encountered a violent thunderstorm: vivid streaks of lightning seemed to strike the plane, disappearing inside the jet engines.

We landed at Karachi about 5 a.m. and were met by officials of the Tourism Department. Dawn broke at six-fifteen but we were able to snatch a few hours' sleep. Then off on a local trip to view the large concourse of birds on a low-lying refuse dump. Some 300 black kites glided above us, using thermals, and feeding along the edge of some small pools were wood, green and marsh sandpipers, grey plovers, little stints, greenshanks, little egrets, and pond herons, while on the waste ground yellow-headed wagtails, mynas and crested larks chased insects, and gull-billed terns dived for fish in the water. It was a good welcome back to Pakistan!

One of our objectives was to film and photograph the Sind ibex, or Persian wild goat, of which it was estimated that there were approximately 2,000 spread over the extensive Kirthar Range. Soon after leaving Karachi our jeep turned off into the desert and for the next sixty miles we drove along a narrow track at little more than 10 m.p.h., arriving at Thana Bola Khan at dusk. Here we picked up two local guides and continued our journey. Soon it was dark, our guides had lost the way, and the car was bogged down in soft sand miles from anywhere. I thought we might still be there at dawn. Then, in the blackness and solitude, voices were heard. Help had arrived. This happened several times until we were eventually located by a search party sent out from our base at Karchat. It took us exactly ten hours to drive 120 miles.

We slept in tents on beds made of straw rope surmounted by a two-inch-thick hair mattress; hardly sleep-inducing. But worse was to come. I shared a tent with our interpreter, who possessed the loudest snore in Pakistan! The air vibrated, and even George, in another tent yards away, was awakened by the stertorous reverberations.

We had been assured that beaters would go out well before dawn to drive the ibex toward the positions we were to take up. We were up early and ready to leave, but there were no signs of the jeeps. The sun rose higher, the heat became more intense—it was infuriating. We discovered that the beaters had not left until well after dawn and the cars had not yet returned. But finally we were in position by late morning, with our backs to a rock wall which would help to make us inconspicuous. In the distance we heard the beaters shouting and hurling rocks over precipices as they drove the ibex. A herd of twenty-three, with a magnificent bearded male bringing up the rear, came into view a mile or more away. But by the time they came down to the place where we had hoped to photograph them, the mountain was in shadow and their cryptic colouring made them almost invisible. If only we had arrived earlier . . .

Another day, another area. We took up positions on the mountain-side, George below, myself halfway up and the intrepid John almost at the top. From my vantage point I had excellent views of the magnificent scenery, immense cliffs separated by narrow gorges whose sides were clothed with scattered bushes and dwarf trees, whose rugged tops were covered with lichen. White-backed vultures soared overhead, crag martins captured insects on the wing, a flock of blue rock pigeons was silhouetted against the rugged landscape, two Bonelli's eagles drifted by. A kestrel spotted John and screamed its annoyance for a couple of minutes before flying off. Lower down the valley squadrons of dragonflies rustled along. The 1,000 mm lens was on the tripod waiting for the ibex, and for want of something else to do I focused it on some larger birds that were now rising in the thermals. I was, of course, using the lens as a telescope when to my great surprise a lammergeier sailed into the picture, so near that I could easily see its beard.

The Sind ibex were seen again but the beaters failed to drive these elusive goats near enough for successful photography. We returned to our camp, packed and made our way back to Karachi, where repairs were needed to my tripod, torch and trousers. The Karachi Iron Foundry Company Limited—a man sitting on the street kerb with a welding outfit—attended to the tripod, which was as good as new in ten minutes. Trouser repairs took longer, but the torch was subjected to one hefty bang in an electrical shop and has worked perfectly ever since. And if I had wanted secretarial service, that also could have been provided, for dotted about the streets were professional letter-writers. They sat on stools with a board across their knees, quill pen in hand, and took down in beautiful copperplate the missives of their illiterate customers who sat cross-legged on the pavement.

Guy, Edmund Fermoy and Tom Roberts now joined us from Gilgit, where they had been working at altitudes up to 12,000 ft. in the Himalayas. They made many interesting records and had a fascinating time.

On the 14th we were off on the second part of the expedition, a journey to the mouth of the Indus, on a sixty-foot-long motor-launch. I was surprised to find part of our cargo was live chickens—for us. Keeping food fresh on a launch in a hot climate without a refrigerator is a problem. One solution was the chickens, but there was a snag. Once killed they would keep only a few hours, and therefore they had to be cooked immediately, which made them tough and stringy. But we had plenty of freshly caught fish which were delicious.

Next morning we lounged on the upper deck, rejoicing in the cooling breeze and the rich panorama of bird-life which unfolded before us. Overhead flew ospreys, brown-headed gulls, lesser-crested, gull-billed and Caspian terns—the latter easily recognised by their enormous bright red bills. Great white egrets stalked in the shallows; there were at least 1,000 cormorants, and curlews were everywhere. So were reef herons with every gradation of plumage from pure white to near black. Tom pointed out a dozen crab plovers, a species not before recorded from this area, and as a strange bird with a snake-like neck whipped past, he shouted: 'Darter.'

The curtains fell on this open-air aviary, as so often in Pakistan, with a glorious multi-hued sunset, followed by an almost full moon which shone brilliantly in the clear cold air, turning the Kodachrome pageant to monochrome.

The next day followed a similar pattern and I took hundreds of photographs. Then, unfortunately, since we were behind schedule, we

PAKISTAN

Above: Widespread wings of a white-backed vulture soaring near Dacca

Below: A 'squabble' of white-backed vultures surround the carcass of a water buffalo. As vultures quarter the air, they watch their companions and as soon as one descends to a carcass the rest quickly follow

Above: In the Salt Range Reserve, a Punjab urial ram warily eyes the photographer a quarter of a mile away

Below: Wings at full stretch, feet not yet retracted, a white-bellied sea eagle at the moment of take-off

EAST AFRICA

Above: View across the eleven-mile wide Ngorongoro Crater taken with an 18 mm. super wide-angle lens

Below: Dorothy pays silent homage at Michael Grzimek's grave on the Crater's rim

Above left: Like relics of a prehistoric age, a black rhinoceros with young lumbers across the Ngorongoro Crater

Above right: Half way between a giraffe and an antelope, the tree-grazing gerenuk is one of the most elusive mammals in Africa

Below: An elephant family out for a stroll in the Amboseli Game Reserve

had to turn back, although we had not reached the mouth of the Indus as we had hoped. However, there was still plenty to see. For a time we were followed by Brahminy kites, beautiful birds with pure white head and red-brown body, which dived and wallowed in our wake to rescue scraps of food we had thrown as a lure.

At one stage in our journey a school of plumbeous dolphins played around the launch. We tried to film and photograph them but this was an almost impossible task since they rarely surfaced for more than a few seconds at a time. An equally difficult subject was a banded sea snake—very poisonous—which Guy spotted wriggling along the surface.

We finally docked at Korangi Creek after an idyllic few days. I particularly appreciated this journey for the absence of the dust which blankets almost the whole of West Pakistan, and which is the bane of a photographer's life.

The third part of our expedition started with a flight to Dacca in East Pakistan. As we flew across India, large areas of it looked dry and parched, with not a vestige of green. Yet two months before, during the monsoons, we were told that torrential rain fell for days on end causing widespread devastation and drowning tens of thousands of people when flood-water surged across the countryside, leaving appalling havoc in its wake.

From Dacca we flew to Jessore, and thence by jeep to Khulna where boats were to take us to the Sunderbans—tiger country. We realised, of course, that our trip might be dangerous, but our immediate concern was with the danger from our driver, whose one ambition appeared to be to complete the journey in record time. With continuous blasts of the hooter, he tore at maximum speed along the single track road, leaving any oncoming traffic to look after itself.

Before we left we had been given Tahawar Ali Khan's book, *Maneaters of the Sunderbans* (International Publishers, Pakistan, 1961). It was not calculated to reassure us. One illustration showed half a human corpse—a tiger had eaten the other half.

A strange assortment of craft awaited us at Khulna, the main vessel being *The Harrier*, diesel-driven and about 100 ft. long. Roped to it was a kind of houseboat, complete with dining-room and cabins, and attached to this another diesel-powered launch. Behind rode two speed-boats, a dinghy with an outboard motor, and a cabin cruiser at the rear.

This flotilla was to be our home during the nine days we explored the island-dotted waterways of the Sunderbans, a tract of country stretching about 160 miles along the coast of the Bay of Bengal. The whole area is a labyrinth of creeks and estuaries enclosing flat marshy islands. Many of these are clothed with trees, and dense undergrowth which thrive in the soft mud. The islands' chief inhabitants are chital, or spotted deer and, at one time, leopard and tiger.

When we awoke next morning we were deep in jungle country. Perhaps this was the place Ian Grimble had in mind when, in a radio discussion on Guy's book on the expedition, he said:

> 'Deep in the forest something stirred,
> It was Eric Hosking photographing a bird.'

Along the shore were forests of pneumatophores, large air-breathing root-like spikes four to twelve inches high. Overhead soared a white-bellied sea eagle, and following in our wake were Brahminy kites, gull-billed and lesser crested terns. Ashore we caught glimpses of the beautiful chital.

As our chief objective in this area was tiger, we had several discussions about them with the accompanying Forestry Officers. Tigers are surprisingly aquatic, sometimes swimming six miles between islands. Occasionally one will leap from the shore on to a boat, seize a man and leap back again. So far during the year of our visit, tigers had killed twenty-six people in the Sunderbans alone. The main, probably the sole, reason why these tigers have turned man-eaters is because man has destroyed their natural food supply, especially the barasingha, or swamp deer.

We were heading for the worst-hit island of all—Mandarbaria—known locally as the 'Island of No Return'. The illustration in that tiger book flashed through my mind. I never thought bird photography would lead to this!

As we dropped anchor, we were greeted by the two local shikaris, who were brothers and came aboard for more tiger talk. The elder was reputed to have shot fifty man-eaters, and their father's bag was fifty-five before he fell victim to a tiger himself. One of their grandfathers had met his death in the same way. I looked with dismay at one of the renowned tiger-hunter's weapons—a twelve-bore shot-gun dated 1892!

Next day we set off after lunch for Mandarbaria Island and our first tiger hunt. The quarry was not far away, for immediately we landed we saw pug marks in the mud. It was safest to walk in single file, Karim in front, the shikari bringing up the rear—both carrying guns. Man-eaters habitually attack from the rear and pick off the last man in the line—my favourite position, since that is best for photography. This time I chose the middle, darting to one side every now and again to take a photograph, hoping a tiger would not pounce before I got back in line again.

After a mile we reached a big keora tree in which a machan, or platform, had been built. The two cinematographers took station here while Guy, the two shikaris and I walked on a mile to another tree. A goat was tethered to a stake about fifty feet away. I hated this until I remembered that swift death by a tiger was preferable to the alternative of a cut throat and a slow death from bleeding as required by Muslim ritual. With one shikari we climbed into the machan which was built twelve feet up the tree—but this was cold comfort since tigers can leap fifteen feet. But I need not have worried. We sat motionless for two hours without seeing a single tiger.

John and I boarded the houseboat next morning with the intention of exploring some of the mysterious-looking creeks between the islands. John was look-out and suddenly from his post on the roof he shouted: 'Crocodile ahead!' and what I had previously thought to be a broken piece of wood became the snout of a twelve-foot-long estuarine crocodile. The Sunderbans once had an enormous crocodile population, but so many have been killed to provide skins for ladies' shoes and handbags that we were lucky to have seen one at all.

Back at base again, it was decided that we must mount an all-night vigil for tiger in the twelve-foot machan. I did not fancy this job at all, and Guy, sensing this, sportingly offered to take my place. That is one of the many things I admire about Guy; he never expects any of us to do anything he is not prepared to do himself. However, I could not accept his offer since he did not understand my high-speed flash-gear.

Eventually Edmund, a shikari and I settled into the machan, at about 5 p.m. Two flash-lamps, well camouflaged, were in position, and the goat was bleating so loudly that any tiger in the vicinity must surely have heard it. But by six o'clock it was dark and the goat decided that it was bedtime, stopped bleating and settled down for the night. Chital wandered near us and we felt that this itself was not propitious; if a tiger had been nearby they would have scented it and kept their distance.

We settled down to a long vigil and I learned what silence really is—deep and profound. There were no bird sounds, not even an owl hooted. At first there was an occasional rasp from a cicada or grasshopper, but by nine o'clock even they were still. I wrote in my letter to Dorothy:

'As a Londoner I had forgotten what it was like to sit in complete quiet, for at home the night sounds of traffic could always be heard. I only wish that I had the ability to describe the scene as vividly as I felt it. What an experience, sitting in the jungle, up in a tree, in total darkness, in the awful silence, waiting for the tiger to take the bait! This is the sort of thing that some people might enjoy. I was not scared because the shikari who was with us had his gun and I felt quite certain that no tiger could leap up our tree without our first having some knowledge of its presence. Time went very slowly. If only that tiger knew that we were waiting there just for him to come and take the goat!

'At eleven-thirty the moon rose, only half now and completely upside down as we never see it in Britain. It was quite brilliant and I could easily see to read the time on my watch. We saw three satellites crossing the sky quite rapidly, but, of course, at nothing like the speed of a shooting star. For once in my life I wished I knew the names of the stars as they shone so brightly. The Plough, for example, was upside down and I found the North Star, not that that was any use to me!

'You would have laughed at my dress! It started to get quite cold so, quietly, I pulled on my thick woolly. Then I wrapped my black focusing cloth round my middle so that it hung down like a skirt. Next I wound my second woolly over my knees and finally put a hat on in an effort to keep my head warm.'

The first trace of dawn lit the eastern sky at five-thirty and by six it was deep red. Twenty minutes later the sun looked over the horizon, climbing quickly into the heavens, and we decided to leave. For thirteen hours we had been in the tree, almost noiseless, not daring to move. Neither dare we drink, for we could not relieve ourselves, an action which would assuredly warn any tiger nearby of our where-abouts. I was most disappointed not to have seen a tiger but proud to learn later that the shikari reported: 'The old man [that was me!] sat like a rock all night and did not move a muscle. He would make a fine shikari.'

In the morning we left for Kotka, a wild-life sanctuary in the Bay of Bengal, arriving about 8 a.m. the next day. We went out at once in a speed-boat, watched rhesus Macaques leaping from tree to tree, saw two chital sunning themselves about 200 yards ahead—ideal for photography if only we could get near enough. The outboard motor was stopped, and while the boat drifted I took two or three pictures before the deer heard the shutter click—at a distance of over 100 yards—and bounded off into the jungle. A golden-backed woodpecker called close to me and I had an excellent view of it perched on the side of a dead tree.

So we started on the long journey back, Khulna, Dacca, Karachi and home.

During the two expeditions to West and East Pakistan we recorded 423 species of birds, and made notes or observations on ninety-nine mammals and forty-five species of reptiles.

Various recommendations were made to the Pakistan Government to help them save their country's wild-life for future generations to see and enjoy. As I write, most of our recommendations have been implemented.

For ourselves, we brought home not only thousands of photographs but also memories of a wealth of experiences of this wonderful sub-continent: sometimes frustrating, often beautiful, always interesting.

20 | *Africa*

The very name of Africa has always held a kind of magic for me. As a boy I heard my father tell the story of David Livingstone, and in my teens read with almost breathless excitement the accounts of big game by Frederick Courtney Selous, Radcliffe Dugmore, Marcuswell Maxwell and Cherry Kearton.* I never imagined how touched with modern magic my first visit to that continent would be.

Along with my friends Ian MacPhail and Jimmy Hancock I was invited to join the party of eighty on the British United Airways VC10 proving flight to East Africa and Rhodesia, on 13 September 1964. Included were four girls to model British fashions, their own photographer, and a Rolls-Royce to demonstrate that BUA can handle cargo just as easily as it can handle passengers.

Soon after take-off I was vaguely aware that this flight was somehow different. It was not just the luxury of everything connected with a proving flight. It was the silence. The four jet engines were at the rear of the aircraft, and as we flew at about 600 m.p.h. we literally left the sound behind. It was uncanny at first; like flying in an unusually long drawing-room.

At 9.35 a.m. we landed at Entebbe, Uganda, in a temperature of 90°F, having flown 4,000 miles in eight hours. Bill Cowen, a friend of Hilbre days now living in Africa, met us and soon Jimmy, Ian and I were whisked off to the northern end of Lake Victoria.

There were so many birds, comparatively tame and mostly new to me, that it was like touring a miraculously enlarged aviary. Pied kingfishers hovered over the water, suddenly plummeting down to catch fish; huge black and white-casqued hornbills wheeled overhead; a fish eagle stood in full view, its snow-white head silhouetted against

---

* Little did I think in my young days that this great explorer's memorial medal would be awarded to me in 1968 by the Royal Geographical Society.

the clear blue sky; and drying its wings beside the lake sat a snake-bird or darter, a cormorant-like bird with an elongated neck and rapier bill.

A group of crowned cranes was just beyond camera range. A lily trotter—jacana—tittupped across the water-lily pads on its immensely long toes. There was a host of smaller birds quite unknown to me, but it was pleasant to see some British species—common and wood sandpipers fed along the edge of the lake, swallows hawked insects overhead, and in the distance a greenshank called. Everywhere flowers grew in profusion: jacaranda trees covered with blue blossoms, bougainvillaea aflame with purple and red bracts, and banana trees with their giant leaves and purple flowers.

The next day we flew to Nairobi, where the High Commissioner, the Rt. Hon. Malcolm MacDonald, had invited us to stay with him. John Williams, author of *A Field Guide to the Birds of East and Central Africa* (Collins, 1963) and *A Field Guide to the National Parks of East Africa* (Collins, 1967) and one of the greatest field ornithologists in Africa, greeted us and drove us to State House to leave our luggage before taking us on an avian sightseeing tour. It was a fascinating experience. Any bird that was glimpsed was instantly identified; the briefest snatch of bird-song was sufficient for John to name the singer.

A lake just outside Nairobi presented a profusion of birds: fish eagles, pelicans, Goliath herons, yellow-billed egrets, red-knobbed coots, wood ibis and many other species. I just could not take it all in. Once we saw a pair of lammergeiers perched high up on a rocky ledge each preening the other's head. To me, there is no more spectacular bird than the lammergeier, and I was thrilled to see it again. Although the range was extreme, with the help of Big Bertha—my 600 mm lens —I managed to obtain a reasonable photograph. Later Rena Fennessy, a fine artist of African wild-life, painted the scene for me.

Being so fascinated by what was happening overhead, I did not realise what was going on around my feet. Then John casually remarked that we were standing in an area infested with puff adders, and leopards often slept in the thick undergrowth!

Dawn on the 16th found us in a Land Rover visiting Nairobi National Park. In the first fifteen minutes we saw Thomson's and Grant's gazelles, warthogs, kongoni, common zebras, wildebeest and an ostrich. Then we spotted a lion and lioness. With my head and shoulders through the circular roof-hatch I took pictures to my heart's content and soon the lioness stalked towards the car. This was fine; as she came nearer and nearer I envisaged a fine series until suddenly John jerked me back inside. Lions dislike trespassers and a photographer had already been mauled when one sprang on top of his Land Rover.

The lioness was within three feet of us when the lion roared—the car windows rattled and so did our eardrums. Having thus rent the air, he rose lazily to his feet and sauntered off.

Since breakfast was at State House at eight-thirty we reluctantly had to leave. But later in the morning we drove 100 miles to Lake Nakuru. Throughout the journey the profusion and variety of bird-life was so great that I can only call it a bewilderment of birds.

Lake Nakuru is nearly 6,000 ft. above sea-level and we caught a first glimpse through a gap in the craggy hills enclosing its thirty square miles. I blinked. The lake was pink! Then through binoculars I realised this was not a geographical freak but a breathtaking avian miracle—the lake was alive with flamingos. Our first sight from four miles away was fantastic enough; as we got nearer I ran out of adjectives.

The best part of a million flamingos, both lesser and greater, stood in the bitter soda lake, their half-submerged bills filtering out their algal food with a soft muttering sound borne on the air like a multitudinous whisper. As we approached, the nearer birds rose in a pinkish flock and wheeled over the water; I do not wonder that Roger Tory Peterson said that it was one of the great ornithological sights of the world.

During our ninety-minute stay I took over 400 photographs, resulting in a sizable blister on my right forefinger. I learnt later that, apart from the flamingos, over 370 different species of birds are found in the Lake Nakuru area.

My companions had almost to force me back to the car and then it was a mile-a-minute dash to Nairobi. Only when I arrived back at State House did I realise what all the panic was about. Malcolm MacDonald was giving a cocktail party to celebrate my first visit to Africa. I was the guest of honour! What a delightful gesture from this eminent man who, like many before him, has found relaxation in ornithology.

After the party a private dinner. I have never seen a table more exquisitely arranged, lit only by six large candles surrounding a huge bowl of red roses. To complete my contentment an Abyssinian nightjar called through the warm African night.

Before turning in I spent fully two hours cleaning my cameras and equipment. My mind was awhirl with the experiences of the day and it was gone two o'clock before I fell into bed. In thirty-six hours with John Williams I had seen 136 species of birds, nearly all of them 'lifers' for me.

How I wished we could have stayed longer, but next morning we were due at the airport by eight-forty-five on the last leg of our journey —to Salisbury, Rhodesia, 1,270 miles distant.

Rolf Chenon-Repond, a local ornithologist, took Jimmy Hancock and me to the Umfuli River about forty miles from Salisbury. Again I was impressed with the wealth of African bird-life: red-breasted swallows, Namaqua doves, fiscal and magpie shrikes, blue waxbills, drongos, and brown-hooded kingfishers (which feed on insects a long way from water and do not catch fish). These I particularly remember, but many more species were seen.

Our journey to the Umfuli River was primarily to see the great colony of carmine bee-eaters which hack out twisting six-foot-long tunnels to make a nest chamber in the sandstone cliff forming one of the river-banks.

When we arrived about twelve-thirty not a bird was in sight but we were told they would start returning about two-thirty. The bee-eaters arrived on time in a long procession, and by five about 800 perched around us. One carmine bee-eater is a splendid sight, 800 are superb. There was a constant calling, a wave of anticipation seemed to surge through the colony and suddenly they all took off in a flurry of wings. They wheeled round, chattering excitedly, then dived down to land at nesting hole or tree perch.

We talked to Desmond Jackson and Hilary Fry who were making a special study of the bee-eaters by using a technique, devised by Peter Ward, of attaching tiny radio-active leg-rings to some of the birds. The radiation is of such low intensity that the rings can safely be handled and are believed to be harmless to the birds. The signals are picked up by a counter and transmitted to a recorder which makes a permanent trace. A counter was also lowered down a shaft near a nest deep inside the bank.

And the purpose of all this sophisticated technology applied to the nesting habits of a bird? To obtain an accurate round-the-clock record, without human supervision, of the frequency and duration of the bee-eater's visits to the nest.

We stayed as long as there was enough light, but by six photography was impossible and we turned for home. As the sun dipped below the horizon the sky flamed a vivid red, then, suddenly, all was dark. As we drove back to Salisbury the car's headlights picked out fiery-necked nightjars as they sat on the road, their eyes shining like tiny balls of fire.

Next morning, after half an hour's hectic shopping, a car whisked Jimmy and me away for further sightseeing at the Lake McIlwaine Game Park where we saw African and lesser jacanas, swallow-tailed bee-eaters, Jameson's firefinches and red-billed queleas, and a painted snipe, as well as such familiars as marsh harriers, ruffs and common sandpipers.

Here I saw and photographed a cuckoo which seemed exhausted,

S

as if it had just ended its migration flight. I reflected wryly that in Great Britain I had spent many hours during the past thirty years trying unsuccessfully to photograph an adult cuckoo, yet here, halfway round the world, one sits on a branch and almost asks to be photographed.

Reay Smithers, author of *A Check-list of the Birds of Southern Rhodesia* (1957), took me for a drive after dark, when we caught a pennant-winged nightjar in the car headlights, where it stayed until we were within four feet—and this was the first time during the whole trip that I had not brought a camera with me! Its brilliant yellow-red eyes reflected the headlights, and as it flew off we held it in the light of a powerful torch and I saw the reason for its name. Very long attenuated feathers trailed from the wings, floating gracefully up and down as the nightjar disappeared into the darkness. As we tried to follow it in the torchlight, two deep red eyes peered at us from the top of a tree—a bush-baby.

After my nightly camera chore, and packing for home, it was two-thirty before I turned in. But by seven I was out in the cool and cloudless morning taking photographs of Salisbury—further mementos of this memorable trip.

During this wonderful week I saw one of the greatest concentrations of birds in the world, and over 100 species I had never seen before, took about 4,000 photographs and averaged four hours' sleep a night.

On the homeward flight I looked down, from 40,000 ft., at the Murchison Falls and the Nile, little thinking that within four years I should see this great cascade from ground-level.

In 1968, Nigel Sitwell invited me to lead an *Animals*-Lindblad safari, visiting some of the finest national parks and nature reserves in East Africa. Dorothy accompanied me on that September day when we landed at the primitive airfield; no runway, no control building, no other planes—just grass, thatched huts and a windsock. This was the airport for the Murchison Falls National Park, an area extending for 1,500 square miles. Towards the end of the last century sleeping sickness, spread by the tsetse fly, almost destroyed the population. The survivors were evacuated, thus leaving a tract of fertile land to become a wild-life paradise. It is to be hoped that the 20th century will not see this sanctuary destroyed by man's return.

Cars took us the fourteen miles to Paraa Lodge—a luxury hotel with a superb view of the Nile. We had a ground-floor room and while we unpacked, an elephant with its young passed close by our windows just beyond the boundary wall. This wall, which surrounded the grounds, was about thirty inches high and twelve inches wide, and was to exclude elephants, who will not step over even so small a barricade.

As we watched we saw a man sitting with his back close to the wall with a large mug of beer in his hand. The elephant put its trunk neatly into the tankard and drained it at a gulp.

After a long tiring day with little sleep the night before, we went out like lights as soon as we hit the sheets. Well before dawn next morning we were awakened by a grunting snuffling sound and, from the window, a hippopotamus was clearly visible in the moonlight, cropping grass not ten feet away from the wall. Now we understood why, at all the lodges, we were not permitted to walk outside the compound. This was not Whipsnade but the heart of Africa, where animals are wild and free.

Our first excursion was a cruise up the Nile to the Falls. The river teemed with wild-life; this stretch is famous for its crocodiles, and scores lay on the banks or in the shallows. The nervous ones slipped away at our approach, others did not budge until we were within snapping distance. It certainly did not surprise us to learn that the Murchison Falls has the greatest concentration of crocodiles in the world.

Hippos were everywhere, generally only their snouts and their eyes, which are on top of their head, breaking the surface. These huge animals rarely leave the water during the day, submerging their bulk to keep cool; they even mate under water and the young are born there. But at night there is a general exodus to the land to feed; sometimes a hippo will travel thirty miles between darkness and dawn before its hunger is satisfied.

Then there were elephants, Rothschild's giraffes, buffaloes, monkeys —and everywhere birds! The majestic fish eagle whose echoing cry is so typical of wild Africa; grotesque storks—saddle-billed, openbill and marabou—vultures soaring overhead, skimmers with elongated lower mandible which skims the surface of the water to pick up food, and gorgeous kingfishers—all were there.

We had a thrilling moment when our boat drifted slowly towards the shore where a herd of elephants was feeding and drinking, and we came within five feet of a great tusker.

The climax of the excursion was the fantastic sight of the Nile erupting through a narrow twenty-foot gorge to become the Murchison Falls. They were discovered in 1864 by Sir Samuel Baker, the great African explorer, who named them after Sir Roderick Murchison, then President of the Royal Geographical Society. The noise was deafening; the water boiled and churned, making a foaming white spray which rose higher than the rocks through which it thundered. Over all lay a rainbow created by the sun's rays on the spray. Any creature falling into this maelstrom is killed instantly, making a feast for the crocodiles in the calmer waters below. This fact probably accounts for their large numbers at this spot.

Back on land we drove round the Lake Albert Reserve, rich in wild-life of many species. We were especially excited to see six white rhinoceroses, some of the original twelve introduced from the Sudan, which have now increased to eighteen. Incidentally, there is nothing white about this rhino. The 'white' is derived from the Dutch 'weit' meaning 'wide' and refers to the mouth. Another difference is that whereas black rhinos usually browse on plants, white rhinos more often graze at ground-level.

That night we were disturbed again, this time by the elements as the fury of an African storm burst upon our slumbers. The blazing sheet lightning, reverberating thunder and torrential rain made us wonder how the animals fared in these raging elements.

Dawn broke bright and sunny and soon we were on our way to the Chobi Game Reserve, seventy-seven miles away. On the way we saw many bright red bishop birds, and widow-birds with long trailing tails. We stayed at the lodge near the Victoria Nile. Baboons ambled about the lawn below our bedroom window, vervet monkeys swung in the trees, and lizards darted about the terraces inquisitively searching for insects. Farther afield we glimpsed buffaloes wallowing in mud at the river's edge; a crocodile, a real leviathan, floating along like a piece of wooden flotsam; yellow-billed egrets patiently stalking fish; snake-birds or darters, with only their heads and necks showing above the water-line, which made them look exactly like snakes; and sixteen hippos fast asleep, each using another's broad back as a monstrous pillow.

In the distance a Rothschild's giraffe strode by, every now and then becoming invisible among the trees, such was the perfection of its camouflage. A movement in the trees revealed long bushy tails, which we recognised through our binoculars as belonging to four handsome black and white colobus monkeys.

Later in the day we were driven around part of the reserve and walked on the banks of the Nile. Amid the wealth of wild-life we were particularly pleased to see a common whitethroat and a reed warbler— we might have been at Minsmere. Back at the lodge that night, powerful floodlights were switched on, illuminating a fascinating panorama of the African night. Two great hippos heaved themselves out of the river and disappeared into the scrub; a serval, a smaller member of the cat family, stealthily crossed a short clearing; a four-foot monitor lizard searched for crocodile eggs; while round the beams of the arc-lights swarmed clouds of insects, a feast for the numerous bats.

Back at the primitive airport next morning we leap-frogged to Entebbe and thence to Nairobi. A short stay, before we descended from its cool height of 5,000 ft. for a long dusty drive across the Rift Valley to Keekorok Lodge. After a night's rest we cruised over the wide plain, leaving the track for the open veldt where vultures circling over a ridge attracted our attention. They usually indicate a kill so we made a wide detour round a rocky, dried-up river-bed. Lionesses! Then followed a cautious exciting approach to within fifteen feet of four lionesses at a fresh zebra kill. Furtively I aimed the camera at this gruesome spectacle, half expecting the great cats to object, but they continued to feed unconcernedly. Eventually, a lioness gripped the remains of the prey in her immensely strong jaws and hauled it into a gully, thus evading the attendant vultures.

Soon afterwards we beheld the greatest congregation of mammals within the experience of any of us. Tens of thousands of wildebeest stretched in lines as far as the eye could see. They were at the end of their migration and would stay on the plains until November—the beginning of the dry season and consequently the end of their food supply.

Two black rhinos lumbered across our path like relics of a pre-historic age. Six replete lionesses dozed in the shade of a tree, not even bothering to flick an eyelid to look at us and, as a superb finale, silhouetted against the setting sun, a magnificent bull elephant made his slow majestic way across the savannah.

Next day we journeyed to the Serengeti National Park, made famous through books, films and television by Bernhard and Michael Grzimek, but in such a short sojourn we could hope to see only a tiny part of the 4,500 square miles of this famous reserve. We lunched on this first day at Seronera Lodge which was to be our base. We slept in tents—but with all the trimmings: comfortable beds, electric lights, showers ingeniously devised from an overhead bucket and separate toilets.

The lodge grounds seemed to be the centre of an open-air aviary, so plentiful was the bird-life. There were Hildebrandt's and superb starlings, black-headed orioles, mosque swallows, masked and black-headed weavers, Madagascar and little bee-eaters, go-away birds and a Gabar goshawk and, right by our tent, a pair of D'Arnaud's barbets, singing the most delightful duet in perfect synchronisation, the cock starting the phrase, the hen completing it. Among the mammals, in an outcrop of boulders, was a large colony of tame rock hyraxes which fed from our hands. With such a wealth of wild-life we had great difficulty in identifying many of the birds, so we particularly appreciated the little museum within the compound, housing a comprehensive collection of skins of most of the local species. The curator was a young enthusiastic Tanzanian with wide knowledge of East Africa's 1,500 species.

Within a couple of minutes of leaving camp by minibus we saw a pregnant lioness, and her companion. A lioness heavy with young is helped by a comrade who kills food for her and is almost an attendant midwife. A little farther on we were excited to see two leopards in a tree with their kill: three Thomson's gazelles and a young topi, carried there to prevent lions from stealing them. One leopard, taking a siesta, made a fine picture and I persuaded our driver to close in. Through the open roof of our car I obtained an excellent clear view for the camera. We were only twelve feet beneath it—fine for photography, but Dorothy had a vision of us ending up in the tree alongside the gazelles!

On the open plain we were lucky to see a pack of hunting dogs, which really do hunt in packs. They pick out one animal from a herd and pursue it remorselessly, often driving it in a wide circle so that some dogs can rest while the others continue the chase. Eventually the victim falls exhausted.

Towards evening we suddenly came upon lions at buffalo kills— eight at the first carcass, five at the second. I was halfway out of the roof, photographing happily, when one of the lions rose, snarled, then growled at me. I dived for cover! How, we wondered, had these lions combined to kill such powerful and dangerous animals as buffaloes?

As dusk approached a splendid black-maned lion, walking in solitary dignity towards the setting sun, passed so close to the car that I could have stroked him.

Our courier throughout the safari was Doortje Bakker, a slip of a girl who took charge of all the details and helped in a thousand ways. Our three minibus drivers—Sam, Edwin and Paul—met us at Nairobi and stayed with us all the time. They were Kikuyus, delightful chaps who were always friendly and seemingly pleased with life. Paul, at nineteen, was the youngest. With his hat at a rakish angle and a devil-may-care attitude, he was never happier than when driving at full speed. His car was supposed to travel behind the other two, which pleased him not at all, and whenever he got the chance he accelerated and took the lead in a cloud of dust.

The hills were partially obscured by heavy black thunder-clouds shattered by vivid lightning flashes as we drove towards Ngorongoro, one of the largest craters in the world, twelve miles long with walls 2,000 ft. high. The higher we drove the cooler and clearer the air became and, as we mounted the rim, we had a spectacular view across this immense volcanic bowl. We were too distant to be able to pick out any wild-life, but the silvery lake at its heart excited our imagination and we wondered what animals might frequent it.

We spent the night in a log cabin near the rim of the crater at about 8,000 ft. Although it was the coolest night we experienced in Africa, we slept well, awakening to find everywhere shrouded in a dense mist which quickly dispersed as the sun rose higher and gained strength.

For our trip down to the floor of the crater Dorothy and I had a Land Rover to ourselves. There are no roads and each time we bumped harder than usual our driver invariably said: 'So sorry, *madam.*' He evidently thought I could take it. But I wondered if my cameras could.

The amount of wild-life in this gigantic crater is amazing. Along the water's edge was a wealth of bird-life: hundreds of pelicans, storks, spoonbills, egrets and waders, while numerous swallows and martins skimmed the surface. Wildebeest and zebras came to drink. But even in this Garden of Eden the eternal triangle was in evidence— two enormous black rhinos were contesting for the favours of a female.

I had long wanted to see the largest of all the antelopes, the giant eland, which stands six feet at the shoulders. We searched all morning without success, but just as we were about to leave the crater our driver's keen eyes saw one in the far distance. We bumped and crashed towards it in a cloud of dust only to discover that there were three: two nonchalantly chewing the cud, the third lying down, its majestic head crowned with spiralled horns held high.

As we regretfully left Ngorongoro we stopped by Michael Grzimek's grave on the crater's rim and silently paid homage, in deep gratitude for men such as he, who have given their all that future generations may also see Africa's wonderful wild-life. Michael was killed in 1959 when his small survey aircraft collided with a vulture. He was twenty-five.

Our courier asked me whether there was any particular animal I wished to see. On the spur of the moment, the rarest mammal I could think of was the elusive gerenuk. She shook me by stating quite confidently that we should see them soon after entering Amboseli Game Reserve. Sure enough, there among the shrubs we glimpsed these enchanting long-necked gazelles standing on their hind legs to reach vegetation that is out of reach of most other ungulates.

For some time a large cloud mass had been looming ahead of us, and gradually we realised that hidden in its depths was Kilimanjaro, Africa's highest mountain. The clouds thinned and rolled away as we came into camp and the 19,000 ft. snow-capped summit was revealed in all its splendour.

At the Amboseli Camp we slept in tents, all so arranged that the first view in the morning was of the sun striking the pure white peak.

And to make sure we saw it at dawn we had the most original of alarm clocks—a troupe of vervet monkeys inhabiting the tree above our tent. The first thing we knew was *wham, wham, wham* as the monkeys broke their jump to the ground by first landing on our tent. They were entrancing little creatures, mischievous as the devil. Four nipped into a tent when the occupants were out, and seized the first-aid bag. Soon plasters, bandages, bottles, tubes and other impedimenta were scattered everywhere, bandages flying like streamers from the trees overhead. Thereafter all tents remained zipped up.

An attractive feature of the camp was the bird-table. Left-over food was collected in the kitchen throughout the day and after breakfast mixed into a paste in a large bowl the size of an old-fashioned preserving pan. From first light birds arrived by the score, gradually weighing down the branches of surrounding trees, filling the air with their shrill chattering until it reached a deafening crescendo as the bowl was emptied on to an enormous flat stone. With a whoosh of wings a multitude of excited birds descended on this open-air banquet. So great was the crush while we were there that birds stood on each other's backs fighting for the food below.

Amboseli has been made famous for its elephants by the great wild-life painter David Shepherd, and one day we came across a scene he might have painted—a gigantic bull with his harem and their young. One little chap was enchanting; he kept swinging his trunk with all the motions of having a dust-bath. Our ranger told us that the bull was a great age and the little one, who was usually kept between two big females, was no more than three months old.

No visit to East Africa's game reserves would be complete without visiting Lake Manyara and seeing the famous tree-resting lions. In this area they are plagued by tsetse-flies at ground-level so they seek peace among the branches, as these pests do not rise much above the ground. After a search we came across three somnolent lionesses spreadeagled, dozing and panting among the branches some twelve feet above us. As we watched this peaceful scene we were delighted to see a lorry-load of African school children out to enjoy their own wild animals. The younger generation need to be made aware of their wonderful natural heritage. Its future lies in their hands. It made us realise the tremendous importance of conservation, for surely our descendants, whatever their colour, will never forgive us if we bequeath to them a world in which children ask: 'What was a lion?'

21 | *Owls*

In a lifetime of bird photography owls have brought me the greatest pleasure. I first made their acquaintance in the playing-fields near my boyhood home, where two pairs of tawny owls nested in holes in trees. They fascinated me, and whenever I was missing from home at dusk during the nesting season—and often at other times of the year—my parents knew where to find me. Despite frequent scoldings, the tawnies mesmerised me. Time meant nothing. The owls' territorial hootings, echoing across the fields at dusk, was glorious music to my young ears and lured me as surely as the Pied Piper of Hamelin.

I had a camera at this time (1918), and dearly wanted to photograph the owls. But this was impossible for a long time. Flash-bulbs and electronic flash were unheard of, the only 'flash' material being magnesium powder. And no owl would stay immobile long enough to be photographed by that crude illumination, as the flash duration was about half a second.

The breakthrough came in 1936 when the General Electric Company brought out the Sashalite bulb, which was as revolutionary in its day as the electronic flash was ten years later. The Sashalite looked like a 100-watt electric light bulb and was about the same size, compared with its modern equivalent which is about the size of a torch-bulb. The Sashalite was filled with magnesium foil and could be fitted into an ordinary torch and flashed for about 1/50th of a second. This was an immense improvement over magnesium powder: no noise, no flame, no smoke, no risk of setting fire to the tree or vegetation, and a fairly short exposure.

Night photography of owls was now possible! In great excitement I wrote to the General Electric Company for full particulars, and enclosed some photographs I had taken of a variety of birds. Back came a helpful letter, together with ten complimentary Sashalite bulbs.

Now all I wanted was an opportunity to try them out. It came in the spring of 1936 when I was staying at Eyke, in Suffolk, with Willy

Bilham and his wife. Willy was a first-class gamekeeper but, like all his brethren in those days, regarded any bird with a hooked bill and talons as vermin and a menace to his beloved game chicks. Owls, of course, were ruthlessly destroyed, and nothing I said in their favour made the slightest difference.

It was therefore a surprise when he announced one day that he had found a barn owl's nest containing four eggs and asked if I would like to photograph them. I was all enthusiasm, for here was a chance to try out the new flash-bulbs. I quickly inspected the site, which was ideal, a hole in a tree only six feet above the ground.

We erected a small pylon hide seven feet away from the nest, and arranged the holder and reflector for the bulbs on the left-hand pole looking slightly downwards on to the hole.

We waited until the beginning of June, when the young ranged from nine to eighteen days of age and had healthy appetites. This was important, as the hungrier they were, the harder the parent birds would have to work to keep the larder supplied, thus giving me more opportunities for photographs. Willy saw me into the hide about 9 p.m. with a flask of tea, food, extra clothing and a blanket, and I prepared to spend the whole night watching—the first of many hundred such nights watching owls.

As soon as I was alone, I noticed a low but persistent hum coming from the nesting hole. Could there be a swarm of bees in there as well? I soon discovered it was the owlets calling for food.

In the fading light I peered through the peep-hole in the hide and was lucky enough to see an adult hunting at a height of about fifteen feet along the edge of a wood. First it would hover, then dip for a closer look, rise again and continue its slow flight, hovering and dipping, hovering and dipping. As long as I watched it caught nothing, then darkness fell and my long vigil began.

Never before having spent all night at one nest I soon found that my imagination was working overtime, seeing parent owls approaching from every direction! When the bee-like buzzing from the ravenous youngsters in the nest reached a crescendo, I became even more alert. Once, although I could see nothing, I was convinced that an owl was sitting in the mouth of the hole. So I opened the shutter with one hand and fired the flash with the other. Momentarily the whole scene was light as day, but . . . no owls. . . .

Owls, of course, fly silently. Their wing and tail feathers are covered with a soft down and this, coupled with the slow wing-beat, enables them to fly, wraithlike, over the ground—detecting the faintest rustle, but themselves unheard.

I began to realise that photographing owls in pitch darkness has its peculiar problems. How could I know when there was a bird to photograph, and even if I resolved this problem, how could I tell whether or not it was facing the camera? Anyway I screwed in another bulb and hoped for better luck.

Shortly after this I distinctly heard the scratch of claws on wood, followed immediately by high-pitched calls from the expectant young. Instantly I drew breath between my almost closed lips, making a slight squealing sound to attract the owl's attention, opened the shutter and fired the flash. No mistake this time. My 'miniature lightning' clearly revealed the parent owl at the entrance to the nest. I was intensely excited.

I waited about ten minutes, then quietly unscrewed the spent bulb and inserted a new one. In the utter silence and darkness, these simple operations seemed to make a tremendous noise and, I felt, must have frightened the parent birds away for the rest of the night. But no, about twenty minutes after the first visit, the owl came back again—and yet again, just before midnight. Each time I fired, and in the light of the flash saw the owl.

After midnight all was quiet, and I felt sure that the owl was brooding the young, who were probably sleeping off the effects of their meal. Just after dawn—about five o'clock—the female emerged, but she was too quick for me. So I packed up and went back to the cottage. Had there been running water, I would have developed the negatives then and there. Instead, about six o'clock I had breakfast and started back to London.

I went immediately to my dark-room, developed and fixed the negatives and then, almost trembling with excitement, I examined them one by one. The first was an excellent portrait of a hole in a tree—no owl. But the next . . . I could hardly believe my eyes. There was the barn owl, bang in the middle of the negative, sharp as a needle—*with a young rat in her bill*.

Belting down the stairs two at a time I yelled: 'Look, it's got a rat in its bill!' My mother had no idea what I was talking about, and it took me a minute or so to calm down sufficiently to explain why all the excitement. But I had some justification, for that picture has proved to be one of my most successful shots. As far as I know, it was the first flashlight photograph of an owl with its prey. It was quickly published by numerous newspapers and magazines throughout the world and later appeared in over 100 books. After nearly thirty-five years it is still selling about twenty-five to thirty copies a year, and at a rough estimate has been reproduced 1,000 times.

Owls again featured in one of my most interesting photographic tasks, which arose from the Little Owl Food Inquiry of 1936-7, organised by Miss Alice Hibbert-Ware for the British Trust for Ornithology. There had been a great deal of controversy about the prey of the little owl, gamekeepers especially maintaining that its principal food was small game chicks. Most ornithologists, however, contended that it was primarily an insect-eater, taking birds and small rodents only on rare occasions.

The inquiry was conducted on three main lines: gizzard contents, nest material and pellet analysis. Owls regurgitate the indigestible parts of their meal and experts can tell from these pellets—an insect's wing-case, a mammal's bone—what the bird has eaten. Miss Hibbert-Ware did a fine job of analysing 2,460 pellets from thirty-four counties. The Report of the Inquiry showed that throughout the year, small mammals and insects comprised nearly ninety per cent of the little owl's total food, birds accounting for fewer than five per cent. Although there was occasionally a 'rogue' owl, on the whole the number of game chicks taken was a small fraction of one per cent. But, as every psychologist knows, opinions held on strong emotional grounds are virtually impervious to fact and argument, and so it was with the game chick fraternity.

It was here that I thought I might be able to make an original contribution. Statistics based on laboratory findings and taken on trust may be arguable, but personal evidence—the evidence of your own eyes—*must* be believed. And this is just what I intended to do: to take as many photographs as possible of little owls with food in their bills. I made a private resolution that, whatever the photographs showed, I would reveal them.

So in the spring of 1938 I went to Doldowlod in central Wales. Several people promised to keep a look-out for nests and eventually eleven were found: three in ruined buildings, three in holes in trees, and five down rabbit holes. It was obviously impossible for me to make a detailed study of the food brought to the young at each nest, so I decided to concentrate on two in rabbit holes and one in a derelict building. It was essential, of course, in every photograph to catch the owl with the prey and also to obtain sufficient detail to enable it to be identified.

I started with the nest in the derelict building, but soon struck a major snag. The cock settled on the apex of the roof with a cockchafer in its bill, glared at the hide, then disappeared under the roof by a hole I had no idea existed. One good photograph missed! I then discovered there were half a dozen or so of these boltholes although, after feeding the young, the parent birds always left by the main exit on which my camera was focused. There was only one thing to do: stop up all but the main entrance.

An ash tree near the nest proved invaluable. The owls bringing food rested on this tree before flying down to the nest, and often the bird called from the tree, thus alerting me. As this was before the days of flash synchronisation I developed a routine: bird alights, open shutter, make slight sound, bird turns and faces camera, fire flash-bulb, close shutter, remain quiet until owl feeds young and flies away, replace flash-bulb, wait for next visit. It worked.

There was an intensive period of feeding about dusk when the owls visited the nest every few minutes, and since most of the prey was only cockchafers it had to be little and often. Soon after darkness fell, visits became approximately hourly. Then, as dawn approached, there was a veritable shuttle-service, birds coming and going every few minutes, sometimes as often as ten times in thirty minutes. Once the sun had fully risen, visits usually ceased. Although it was impossible to mount a twenty-four-hour vigil, as far as my observations went the young were fed only once during the day and that was after a very wet night.

During one night of continuous heavy rain, no food whatever was brought to the nest, but when the rain ceased soon after dawn, seven visits were made in fifty-three minutes. Evening feeds coincided with the beginning of flight activity of the larger beetles, especially the cockchafers, and *their* first flights varied with the weather. On a fine clear evening in June the first chafer was heard within a minute or so of 10 p.m., but when it was dull and misty the characteristic drone could be heard by about nine-forty.

Conditions at the rabbit holes were somewhat different. Obviously there was only one entrance, but the birds went straight in without an intermediate stop. So I drove a stake into the ground near the hole which the owls immediately used as a perch, and this enabled me to follow the same routine as before.

A number of photographs were taken of the owls at the nest entrance, and it was through switching from hole to stake that I missed a unique shot. The camera had just been focused on the stake when there appeared what, in the poor light, looked like a rabbit making slowly towards the hole. I watched fascinated as it approached and then, as it reached the entrance, stopped. A chick had been out for an evening stroll! At that moment one of the parent owls flew down and fed the little wanderer. Never, before or since, have I seen such a sight, but I dare not move the camera for fear of disturbing them.

And the results of my efforts? They varied considerably from the official report and were as follows:

1 ground beetle
2 earthworms

3 dor beetles
4 yellow underwing moths
43 cockchafers
1 unidentified but probably a rainsoaked earthworm

Surprising, isn't it? No rodents, no frogs, no birds, no chicks—not even a game chick.

To describe all my experiences with owls over more than forty years of study and photography would be tedious, except to the most ardent student of the order. But I feel that some observations have an interest beyond the realm of the specialist and should be recounted.

I had an unforgettable experience in Norfolk, when I saw two barn owls performing their ritual courtship display. It was just before sunset when the cock returned to the barn, sailing in, a silent ghostly figure in the half-light, landing with barely a scratch on one of the beams between nest and hide. The hen followed almost at once and settled beside him. Neither bird brought prey. They stood looking round for a few moments, until the cock flew down to the nest and glanced at the young. It was a brief visit, however, and almost immediately he rejoined the hen on the beam, settling about a foot away from her, both facing me.

After a moment of stillness, both birds engaged in a twittering 'conversation' accompanied by bill-snapping, after which the cock slowly stretched his head and neck upwards, his feathers puffed into a downy ball. He looked grotesque with his head thrown well back and his bill wide open.

Beside him the hen quivered a little. The cock began to sway his head from side to side, and presently to wave it with a sort of circular motion. The hen swayed in sympathy, uttering a snuffling note as she did so, at the same time edging along the beam until she was close to him. As she approached, he retracted his neck and lowered his head, and the two birds caressed, rubbing cheeks and clicking bills. The cock soon ended this performance, however, by abruptly seizing the hen by the neck feathers and shaking her head roughly from side to side—which treatment she appeared to enjoy, judging from the way she purred.

Gradually the activity subsided and the two birds returned to their original positions, standing side by side. Thus they remained for a while until both flew from the barn.

It was another pair of barn owls that provided me with my most famous photograph. On this occasion they were nesting in a grain hopper in a large barn in Suffolk, and as the birds' entry was restricted to one broken window there was an opportunity to take a large number of flight shots.

This was made possible by using the photo-electric shutter release with the infra-red filter over the lamp unit, in conjunction with the high-speed flash set described in the Flash chapter. The flight path of the barn owl was very similar whenever the bird made an entry, so, by arranging the automatic trip device in a series of slightly different positions, I was able to obtain records of all phases of the wing action. Shortly after the bird had taken off from the window ledge I took the photograph between pages 150–1, showing the middle part of the upstroke.

The barn owl is almost certainly the basis of a number of ghost stories. The ancient trees often found in graveyards provide the holes which are ideal nesting places for these owls. A villager walks near a graveyard at night; an utterly silent white body glides by; a long wild shriek from the 'apparition'—and another ghost story is born.

In the spring of 1940 Nat Tracey invited Dorothy and me to stay with him at his home outside King's Lynn. Nat was a wonderful character. At one time a rabid egg-collector, he became a fanatical protectionist, founding The Association of Bird Watchers and Wardens and going to war against egg-collecting. He told me this story of his unregenerate days. He took the eggs of a barn owl as she laid them, each time replacing the egg with one from a domestic hen. The owl hatched the hen's eggs but the active young were very different from owlets, which are quite helpless at birth. She promptly ate them!

As he knew that we should like to come and go as we wished, Nat accommodated us in his garage which he had converted into an excellent bed-sitter. Nat was a poor sleeper and he used to get up each morning about dawn and go out to watch birds, especially his favourites, woodpeckers. I said that I would like to go out with him one morning if he would wake me. Just as it was getting light, Dorothy and I heard the loud drumming of a great spotted woodpecker so close that it sounded as if the bird were hammering at the garage itself. I leapt out of bed, cautiously crept to a window and slowly opened it. There was Nat with an alarm clock the hammer of which was imitating almost exactly the woodpecker's drumming!

I wanted to photograph a pair of long-eared owls, which had their nest in one originally built by carrion crows in a spruce fir tree about twenty-three feet above the ground. Nat had already constructed a hide nine feet from the nest.

To my mind the long-eared is the most nocturnal of all the British breeding owls, and as little seemed to be known about its breeding activities I decided to spend several whole nights in the hide. But first we thought it advisable to watch during daylight to note the birds' reactions to the hide and to study the method of approach. No sooner was I alone in the hide than the owl returned. She flew from tree to tree and at each stop peered intently towards the hide. She bowed so low that her chin almost rested along the branch, then swayed upwards to her full height without taking her eyes from the hide. As she perched by the side of the nest I had a remarkably good view of the facial disc, and saw how it was brought forward to enhance its frightening effect.

There were five eggs in the nest and she settled to incubate. She hardly moved a muscle during the eight hours I was in the hide. Boring? Not really as there was so much going on elsewhere—once a sparrow hawk perched nearby completely unaware of the close proximity of the owls or me sitting in the hide; two jays were courting and went through elaborate poses and attitudes towards each other, finally flying almost vertically together as if fighting. Frequently cock pheasants called, vigorously flapping their wings; by the edge of the wood a nightingale sang gloriously. To those who say bird photographers must be extremely patient, I would answer that I would never have the patience to teach children, or push a pen over paper all day, or add up accounts; but give me a hide, a camera and a notebook and I am as happy as can be.

Throughout my day and night observations the cock did not take any share in incubation, nor did he appear at the nest during the day. Soon after dark he usually called from a nearby tree, then the hen left to feed. No food was brought to the nest prior to the hatching of the eggs.

There was a short nuptial display one evening while it was still light enough to see. The hen was away from the nest, perched on a tree a short distance from the hide. She called and the cock answered immediately. He flew towards her, keeping well below the tops of the trees, dipping and rising, and circling round the trunk of the tree on which she was perched. Generally he glided but every now and again loudly clapped his wings. Finally, he alighted by her side and called. The hen then left the perch and returned to the nest.

The first chick hatched during the early morning of 2 May. During that night the cock made his first appearance at the nest and brought in food. In all, three visits were made, and although it was too dark for me to see what the food was, I found on the nest after dawn two voles and one rat, all of which were decapitated. This was most interesting because the cock must have realised that the first chick was about to hatch.

Owls in general lay their eggs on alternate days; sometimes three or four may elapse between each egg. As a rule incubation starts with the laying of the first or second egg. However in this instance all five eggs hatched in a little over two days, which suggests that incubation started with the laying of the penultimate egg.

Above: Glaring aggressively, a short-eared owl, with vole in bill, spreads her wings protectively around her young

Below: Dotterel, photographed in the Cairngorms in 1939 with a 35 mm camera. At that time it was considered more as a toy than as a camera for serious bird photography *(see page 280)*

What bird photography is all about.
Shots such as this portrait of a long-eared owl gripping a young rat make the
long night vigils in a hide well worth while

During the darkest hours of the night there was less activity at the nest and as far as I could tell no attempt was made to feed any of the owlets. With the approach of dawn, however, a change took place. Suddenly, quite close to the nest, there came a long-drawn-out hooting *ooo-oo-o* which was answered by the brooding hen. An exchange of calls followed, in the course of which the hen became very excited and started to quiver and vibrate her wings. The cock alighted with a young rat dangling from his bill. Both birds now became very excited, the hen's wings quivering as she reached up to the cock, while he slowly flapped his wings and rolled his body from side to side, clutching and unclutching the branch on which he was perched. The hen took the food and the cock left.

Without rising from her brooding position, she stretched out her foot, firmly gripped the prey and, also gripping part of the nest, she leant forward and ripped off a piece of the rat with her bill. Tiny morsels of meat were passed to the young sheltering below her. The food had to touch the chick's bill before it would open its mouth, and usually the hen gave a low call at the same time. Each of the young were fed and the meal concluded by the hen swallowing all that remained. This method of feeding the young differs from that adopted by eagles, falcons and hawks, which usually stand by the side of the young.

So far as I could ascertain, the cock's hunting territory was restricted to a small area. The nest was in the middle of a plantation surrounded by an area of heather and bracken intermixed with silver birch trees. There were small stacks of dead bracken at various points round the plantation. The cock hunted in and around the wood, particularly among the bracken stacks where rats appeared to congregate. Throughout the night it was possible to hear him calling at intervals of about ten minutes, and generally the hen answered.

Only once did I see the hen bring food to the nest. It was just after dawn and she had left after spending the night brooding the young. She was away for sixteen minutes and just before her return I heard the two birds exchanging calls. A moment later there was a thud on the ground, followed by a rustling of leaves. Apparently the male dropped the prey he had brought and the hen retrieved it. The food was the remains of a full-grown rat, the first to be seen at the nest, all the others being young of various sizes.

At this time (1940) there was considerable doubt whether the long-eared owl hunted during the darkest hours of the night. Without doubt I can say that it does and very successfully too, as on occasions I have shone a torch on to the nest immediately after the cock had left and seen fresh prey. What is equally remarkable is that in the dark this owl is able to fly safely through dense forests, with intertwining

T

branches. I have seen an owl alight on the branch immediately behind the nest without hesitation, or losing his balance, when I could not see the slightest reflection of light from the sky.

Ornithology is full of surprises but an owl's night vision is one of the most astonishing.

It is true that owls cannot see in absolute darkness, but laboratory experiments by Dr. Lee R. Dice, of the University of Michigan, have proved that their eyesight is fantastically acute. The following considerations are based upon Dr. Dice's findings. Imagine an absolutely pitch-black night: no stars, moon or light of any kind. A solitary candle is then lit a quarter of a mile away. From the illumination of this candle alone some owls can see and swoop unerringly on a mouse scurrying across the ground. And the illumination on the earth on a cloudy moonless night is over fifty times brighter than that of the light given by a candle a quarter of a mile away!

Strange as it may sound, my night work with owls was greatly helped by an invention to help warships in night manœuvres. During the war the Admiralty lent me an 'infra-red image converter tube'. This consisted of a brilliant light behind an infra-red screen which stopped it from being seen, but another screen in the tube re-converted the light so that any object at which it was pointed could be seen in a sort of greenish haze.

For night work with owls such a tube is invaluable. It had always been a problem when watching a nest to know when to fire the flash. I was entirely dependent on the sounds I heard and, especially in the early days, sometimes my ears deceived me, as I have related on page 264. Although I used the trick of making a slight noise just before the flash, and this generally ensured that the owl was looking at the camera, there was still a big element of chance about it. This infra-red tube changed all that and I was able to pick my moment as easily as with daylight photography.

Somehow this story got into the world's press, albeit some of the news stories were somewhat distorted. The *New York Herald Tribune* said: 'The British Admiralty has loaned a bird watcher, Eric Hosking, special equipment to enable him to find out what kind of face an owl makes when it hoots.' This prompted H. J. Gottlieb to break into rhyme:

Operation Owl

Weighed down with camera, telescope,
Black searchlight, climbing irons, rope,
And sundry gadgets, furnished free
By an obliging Admiralty,

A brave, perspiring Briton prowls
The Sussex woods in quest of owls.

God speed him! May he carry on
For Country, King and Audubon!
May he define, beyond disputing,
An owl's expression when it's hooting,
And be undaunted if its eyes,
Like mine, regard him with surprise.

H. J. GOTTLIEB

Unlike most of the other British owls, the short-eared shuns the woodlands and is found in open country: marshes, heaths and moorland. Its greatest stronghold is the Orkneys and Outer Hebrides but it is nowhere plentiful. During the winter the population is regularly augmented by visitors from the Continent.

The short-eared owl is nomadic and is one of the most widely distributed land birds in the world, but its numbers in any particular place vary considerably from time to time according to the food supply. It lives almost entirely on small mammals, particularly voles and lemmings and their near relatives, which have an almost world-wide range. Rodents are subject to recurrent periods of excessive breeding, and at such times short-eared owls congregate in large numbers in the affected districts. The rodents are then piled high on and around the nest, the numbers caught being far in excess of the birds' requirements. During these periods the owl becomes much more prolific than usual and instead of the normal four or five eggs, it may lay as many as thirteen or fourteen, and sometimes all this large family is reared.

The nest is a roughly made hollow among coarse grass; the short-eared is the only one of our owls that attempts any construction. The other owls merely use existing nests of other birds—as with the long-eared—or lay their eggs direct in the bottom of a hole without any attempt at lining it.

In May 1942 I was at Hickling, and on the 18th we found a short-eared owl's nest sheltering under a tuft of tangled grasses on the open marsh, only a few hundred yards inland from the sandhills that fringe the coast of Norfolk.

The nest contained three eggs, one of which was on the point of hatching. Two days later I erected a hide about forty feet away so that the owls would have a chance to get used to it from a distance. The following evening I moved it much closer to the nest without disturbing the hen. Two days later the hide was moved into position for photography. The hen left during this operation and I noticed that all three young had now hatched.

Watching the slow rhythmic wing-beat, interrupted every now and then by a wheeling glide on outstretched wings, I was impressed with the beautiful flight of the short-eared owl. Soon she was wheeling some fifty feet above me, her blunt head turned downwards as she scrutinised the ground below. Her great expanse of wing was beautifully marked in various shades of fawn set off by darker crescent markings near the tips, and as she turned and banked close overhead she revealed the golden sandy colour of the upper wing surfaces.

My first spell of detailed observation was in the morning after we had completed our preparations. It was soon after nine o'clock, and she must have been brooding the young at the time, for she left the nest and flew away. First she alighted on a dead tree stump then, after a short pause, flew down to an earthy mound, where she stood looking about her.

The young were so huddled together it was difficult to count them, they seemed just a mass of greyish-white down. The hen soon alighted in the rushes a few feet behind the nest and cautiously made her way forward, stopping every now and then to peer over the herbage at the hide. It was intensely exciting to watch her approach and to see her walk on to the nest, tuck the young under her, and begin to brood.

Her plumage was beautiful. The general colouring was lighter than that of other short-eared owls I had watched, and the brownish feathers on her back and wings were tinged with gold. Her buff-coloured facial disc was edged with a distinct light grey rim, and her golden-yellow eyes were set in small circles of black feathers.

After brooding for one and a half hours, the hen began to preen. She carefully combed her back feathers; then her wings, working from the undersides; and finally her breast. She paid particular attention to some feathers, probably because they had been soiled. The whole of the toilet took about twenty minutes.

When I next visited the hide, the sun was sinking towards the blue-grey mists shrouding the distant horizon. There was a chill in the air that comes with the passing of an early summer day. The owlets were calling vigorously with a wheezy hunger note, and the smallest was trying to crawl under its larger brothers for warmth. The cock alighted on a nearby perch with a vole in his talons. The hen flew towards him, and within two minutes was back at the nest with the decapitated vole in her bill. She dropped it in the nest and started to feed, standing astride the young and tearing off pieces which she dangled in front of the chicks' mouths. The meal lasted about three minutes and concluded with the hen swallowing the scraps that remained. She tidied the nest, then crouched over the young and began to brood. She was still in this posture when the light faded and I left.

My last sight of these birds was on 12 June when the young were about three weeks old. As I dismantled the hide I saw the hen nearby looking very worn and bedraggled and minus several feathers from her wings. She looked very different from the sleek and beautiful bird I first saw.

As the short-eared owls are ground-nesting birds the young are able to wander from the nest at an earlier age than their tree-nesting relatives. I searched around and found one chick resting under a thick tussock of rushes sixty-four paces away from the nest. The chick was almost fully feathered although it still had plenty of down; it was not yet able to fly and was still dependent on its parents for food. The young must have flown soon after, however, for I did not see them again, and presumed they had begun their characteristic wanderings.

None of my work on owls has given me a greater thrill than photographing the snowy owl. Although they have been seen in the Shetlands at irregular intervals since 1811, there had been no definite record of their breeding until 1967. In June of that year, Bobby Tulloch, the representative of the RSPB, was visiting the island of Fetlar with a party of Swiss ornithologists when they saw a male snowy perched on a rock. While this excited them it was not a particular thrill to Bobby because he had seen the all-white males every year since 1963. But, as the party approached, instead of flying away as was customary, the male flew towards them and started an aggressive display. Bobby realised immediately what this meant—there must be a nesting female nearby.

The party quickly left, but the next day Bobby returned and after a cautious reconnaissance found the nest which then contained three eggs. This was the first officially recorded nesting of the snowy owl in the British Isles—just fifteen miles within the northernmost limit. The latitude is equal to that of central Siberia, and in midsummer it never gets really dark.

The snowy owl is, of course, primarily a bird of the far north, often nesting above the tree-line in both the New and Old Worlds. It ranges from the Arctic Circle to Bermuda, from Mongolia to Alaska. In this country it has been recorded as far south as Cornwall and the Scilly Isles.

The snowy is a magnificent owl: a large female stands two feet high and has a five-foot wing-span. The lovely penetrating eyes are golden yellow, and the black bill and claws are almost hidden in a mass of white feathers.

This was the bird the RSPB gave me permission to photograph. The nest was among the rocky hummocks of Stakkaberg—a tundra-like area of Fetlar, very similar to the snowy owl's nesting habitats in more northerly regions.

In July, Dorothy and I flew to Sumburgh airport, skimming so low over the cliffs that the sheep and gulls scattered before us. By bus and boat we eventually arrived at Mid Yell, where we were met at the landing stage by a short, stocky, bearded Shetlander—Bobby Tulloch.

After spending a night on Mid Yell, Bobby took us over to Fetlar in his boat, and there at the tiny slipway we boarded a car which transported us and our gear to the bothy which was to be our head-quarters. A quick cup of tea and we were off on the mile walk to the observation hut, perched on a rocky ridge overlooking the nesting site.

With binoculars I surveyed the barren landscape through one of the peep-holes but, at first, could not see the owl. Only when I had been told exactly where to look did I see the male 'on guard' on a rock overlooking the nest. His pure white figure matched almost exactly the white rocky outcrops. To me this was the most beautiful and romantic bird that ever came out of the Arctic.

Plans had been made by George Waterston, the Society's Scottish Director, for Dennis Coutts, a professional photographer from Ler-wick, to make a cine-film, while I was to take the still photographs. Dennis had already erected his hide thirty feet from the nest, and because of the gale-force winds that frequently spring up in this area, had lashed it securely to the ground. Within two hours of landing on Fetlar I was left alone in the hide to watch the bird return.

Within a few minutes I saw the hen flying slowly towards the nest. She alighted without hesitation, waddled on to the nest and brooded the young. She had laid seven eggs, six of which hatched, the seventh being infertile. Once settled, she turned her head round and glared straight at the camera lens. She must have seen her reflection, for she started to turn her head—farther and farther round it went until it was almost upside down, then very slowly she relaxed. For some time she could not understand the lens and kept trying to stare it out. I hardly dared to breathe.

Being the first to occupy the hide was a great responsibility. If anything went wrong the blame would rest on my shoulders and I should never forgive myself. I realised only too well that this could be the first occasion of regular breeding and that if the young survived they, in turn, might breed either on Fetlar or on one of the neighbouring islands, and if successful, the adults would probably breed again next year. I therefore allowed the hen to become thoroughly accustomed to the lens and refrained from taking any photographs until she was preoccupied with other things. This was one of the most nerve-racking experiences of my life. But I need not have worried. When I started photography she took not the slightest notice of the noises coming from the hide. As I have noticed so often before with birds, sound is not nearly so important as sight.

There was no food available, so she started ferreting about in the black mud in the cup of the nest and before long her lovely white face was dirty. She found a pellet, which she must have cast sometime previously, picked it up and seemed to play with it for a while, then actually offered it to the largest of the young. To my amazement it was taken and swallowed. As it contained only a mass of fur, bone and other indigestible matter the chick could not have got much sustenance from it.

Late in the afternoon I saw the cock alight on a crag where it was vigorously mobbed by a pair of Arctic skuas and a common gull. Each time they dived he ducked his head but refused to be dislodged from his perch.

I spent five hours in the hide but returned the next morning and spent the whole day there. The hen sat facing the hide, and I felt the penetrating stare of her brilliant yellow eyes as she started once more to study her reflection in the camera lens. But she soon lost interest in this and picked up an immature oystercatcher which the cock had left. She ripped it to pieces and fed each of the young. One chick was given a leg and had some difficulty in swallowing it; for five minutes it could not bend its neck. When each of the young seemed full, the hen fed herself, then all slept, the hen's head nodding, until it almost touched the ground.

More than anything else I now wanted to see the cock at the nest. He was almost pure white whereas the hen was heavily marked with dark brown streaks. But although I had seen him go to the nest either before or after I had been in the hide, I seemed to be unlucky. During my last period in the hide before leaving Fetlar, the hen sat brooding for some hours, then left and appeared to go hunting on her own. She had been away nearly twenty minutes when, without warning, the cock suddenly alighted by the side of the young with a rabbit in his talons. And he stood there when the hen alighted by his side!

I must pay tribute to the way the RSPB conducted 'Operation Snowy Owl'. When Bobby discovered the nest he at once realised that great care must be taken to ensure the safety of eggs and young. A premature leakage of such exciting news could bring hordes of sightseers— and possibly egg-collectors. Yet it was impossible to keep the secret for long; already other islanders had noticed the aggressive behaviour of the owls when anybody approached the nesting area. Peter Conder, Stanley Cramp and George Waterston, of the RSPB, decided that a round-the-clock watch should be mounted on the nesting area, a task made easier by the continuous daylight of the region. An observation hut was erected, bothy accommodation provided for the watchers, and sufficient officials and volunteers were mustered to ensure that the snowy owls would have adequate protection. One of the volunteers was Jeremy Woodward, who in 1970 became engaged to my daughter Margaret.

One of the owlets even made use of the National Health Service! A wing was badly cut when it flew into a barbed-wire fence. Dr. Jeffrey Harrison repaired the damage, putting twenty-three stitches into the wing of what he called 'my most famous patient'—an opinion, no doubt, shared by nearly 500 people who made the journey to Fetlar to view these spectacular birds.

In 1968 the snowy owls reared three more young but the following year only one survived from the six eggs laid. The reason for this is difficult to understand because four young were hatched and three reached the flying stage. An observer, Tony Mainwood, provided a clue. He watched the hen take a rabbit to one of the young, now well away from the nest, but, the moment she left, two hooded crows flew down and snatched it away. Could it be that the hoodies were feeding at the expense of the young snowys?

22 | *Photography*

Bird photography is to me the finest of all field sports; a combination of technical skill and sporting endeavour to obtain a successful photograph of a bird without harming it. Even after half a century I still feel an excited tingle in my finger whenever I press the shutter release. It is no wonder that bird photography has proved an absorbing hobby for men from all walks of life.

The fundamentals of bird photography have remained virtually unchanged since the days of the pioneers at the turn of the century. What has changed so dramatically is the apparatus. R. B. Lodge was awarded the Royal Photographic Society's first medal for natural history in 1895. His brother George, the famous bird artist, told me that they used to tramp miles across rough country pushing a huge 12 in. × 10 in. plate camera on a wheelbarrow. Today, 35 mm ($1\frac{3}{8}$ in. × 1 in.) is the favourite format.

Other pioneers such as the Kearton brothers, Pike, Kirk, Ferguson and Macpherson, relied on one camera, possibly two lenses, and probably no more than two or three plate-holders, journeying everywhere by train and on foot. Now, most bird photographers travel by car, carry several cameras, a battery of lenses and a pocketful of 35 mm film, sufficient for hundreds of exposures.

Several other inventions have transformed bird photography in my lifetime. Fine-grain black-and-white film enables big enlargements to be made from small negatives; greatly improved colour emulsions ensure correct rendering of multi-hued feather textures; and, particularly for bird-table and nest photography, high-speed flash makes the photographer virtually independent of lighting conditions. Very long focus lenses make it possible to photograph birds at a distance of 200 ft. or more. Zoom lenses enable the photographer to frame the subject to his liking; through-the-lens metering ensures correct exposure.

For the enthusiast with plenty of money there is an outsize magazine containing 500 exposures, and clockwork mechanisms which can be fitted to the camera to take several photographs per second as long as the button is depressed. Some of these mechanisms take two per second, others up to five and there are sophisticated laboratory cameras which will take up to forty-eight photographs per second. Such rapid-exposure mechanisms are invaluable for recording quick series of actions, and animal movement in general. There is no doubt that by the time this book is published technicians and manufacturers will have added yet more items to the armoury of bird photography—an art that is constantly changing and improving, both in results and in the apparatus to achieve them.

There are three principal ways of obtaining bird photographs: at the nest, bait or drinking pool; by the wait-and-see method at sewage farm, estuary or tide-line; and by stalking. The first two demand a hide, since the bird comes to the photographer; in the third method the photographer goes to the bird.

My first 35 mm camera—a Leica—was bought in 1935 and it was useful for photographing bird habitats, nest and eggs but, because lenses and films were inferior by today's standards, it was not often used for photographing birds. However, in 1939 I took some 35 mm photographs of dotterels in the Cairngorms. The cock was so tame as he incubated the eggs that I worked from four feet. A 10 in. × 8 in. print was made and circulated in the Zoological Photographic Club's folio (see page 287). The members' comments were enthusiastic, which was particularly gratifying as, until then, the 35 mm format had been considered more as a toy than as a camera for serious natural history photography.

One great advantage of 35 mm was that Kodachrome, the only really satisfactory colour film made at that time, was available in this size only. I well remember the excitement of showing friends some of the results, and the gasps of admiration when they were projected on to a large screen.

But it was not until many years later that I went over entirely to 35 mm. There were several reasons for this. In 1958 I had trouble with the eye-cups of my Zeiss binoculars and wrote to the importers, Degenhardt and Company, for advice. The managing director, A. H. (Bill) Degenhardt, sent me two new eye-cups and invited me to lunch with him. I accepted and we have been great friends ever since. In 1963 the company became agents for Zeiss Ikon photographic equipment and Bill suggested that I should try out the Contarex, a single lens reflex that had recently come on the market.

At this time Guy Mountfort was preparing for the first Jordan expedition, and because of the vast amount of equipment to be transported by air he urged me to reduce my photographic gear to the minimum. Since we were to survey as much of Jordan as possible in a month, he felt that there would be little opportunity for using hides, and advised me to be prepared to shoot from the shoulder. After careful deliberation I finally decided to leave my faithful quarter-plate camera at home and rely completely on the Contarex.

This decision was amply justified, for photographs were obtained which would have been impossible with the large camera. For example, by using a 600 mm telephoto lens I was able to stalk close enough to obtain useful records of Sinai rosefinches, masked shrikes, cream-coloured coursers, Cretzschmar's buntings, Tristram's grackles (not photographed before, I believe), the courtship of the Dead Sea sparrows —and many others.

In addition, there were photogenic but agile lizards which could be photographed successfully only with a hand-held miniature camera. And it was also ideal for the everyday jobs such as recording scenery and expedition members at work.

But there was a price to pay. Generally, a bigger and better enlargement can be made from a large negative than from a tiny one, and when I compare some of the bird photographs taken with my large format camera with those I am taking today, it is clear that the exquisite definition is just not there. So I comfort myself with the thought that an inferior photograph is perhaps better than no photograph at all.

In 1963, when I made the change-over, there was a general trend towards 35 mm. Before making the final decision I had long discussions with fellow photographers, publishers, art editors and block-makers. The consensus of opinion was that almost all the camera and lens manufacturers were concentrating on 35 mm, and that film-makers were developing finer grain emulsions in black and white, and better tone balance in colour films. So I took the plunge.

Looking back now after only seven years, I believe I made a mistake, and that it would have been wiser to have gone over to $2\frac{1}{4}$ in. square, even though the equipment then available was limited. I say this because many art editors do not seem to bother to look carefully at 35 mm transparencies—they should be viewed under a magnifying glass against a good white light or, better still, projected on to a screen. Often magazines use indifferent reproductions made from a large transparency when a far better picture is available in 35 mm. But not all the blame must be attached to art editors. Block-makers in this country make a surcharge for colour work made from 35 mm to compensate for the alleged extra time and care in working from the smaller size. Moreover, the cost of retouching is higher for this size.

A considerable part of my life has been spent in the dark-room. I develop all my own black and white negatives and make the enlargements. Each successful day in the field means at least three days in the dark-room; and that is apart from the time spent indexing, cross-indexing, captioning and filing prints—which explains the paradox I sometimes propound to friends: 'The work only starts when I get back home.'

People sometimes ask me how many photographs I have taken. A careful calculation shows that by May 1969 there were 113,000 black and white negatives and 37,000 colour transparencies in my files. (I underestimated my collection when I said elsewhere that it was much smaller than this.) I have taken many more—these are what were kept. Some ten miles of 16 mm cine-film have also been taken.

These figures are largely accounted for by my motto: 'If in doubt, shoot.' I never believe in missing a shot for fear of wasting film—35 mm film is the cheapest commodity in the photographic world. Frequently, several photographs are taken of the same subject in rapid succession.

Always one or two photographs stand out above the rest. There is just one moment—often only a split second—when everything is right: the posture of the bird, angle of its head, highlight in the eye, relative position to its mate and young, and so on. Of the 580 photographs I took while working on the snowy owl in the Shetlands in 1967, only two came sufficiently near this standard to differentiate them clearly from the rest.

With such a large collection of negatives and prints it is vital to have an efficient filing system; one that works not only for me, but for anyone else when I am away. Prints and transparencies are filed in alphabetical order of the bird, mammal, etc., each category being sub-divided into years. Larger-sized negatives are filed similarly, but this is impracticable with 35 mm; several subjects may be on one strip of film, and, since it is necessary to keep the whole strip for ease of handling in the enlarger, every spool is indexed. The negatives, cut into strips of six, are filed in loose-leaf books of transparent sheets (thirty-six to a page) and all the worthwhile results are card-indexed, e.g. Sd/2/47/10 meaning Shetland, second visit, spool number, negative number on spool.

Whole plate enlargements are made of such negatives and at least three enlargements of the most saleable ones are kept in the files. These are, of course, replenished periodically, a task which occupies the greater part of all my time in the dark-room.

I am constantly asked for prints for private use. Naturally a charge must be made, but there are exceptions. During the war I had a letter from a lady in America saying how much she admired my photograph of a barn owl and asking if it would be possible to buy a copy. I sent one, with my compliments. Soon after, a food parcel arrived and subsequently one came almost every month, even continuing into the post-war rationing period. She still sends parcels every Christmas and we open them with great excitement since they contain a wide variety of gifts, from sweets to model owls.

Then there was the little old lady, poorly dressed, who came up to me at an exhibition at the Royal Photographic Society and timidly asked if one of my photographs was for sale. If so, would it be *very* expensive? I replied that if she would leave her name and address I would send the photograph after the exhibition closed. She said: 'I don't want to put you to all that trouble on top of your kindness. I'll send someone to collect it.' She did—her chauffeur in a Daimler!

And now for some grouses. Today, there is considerable money to be made from selling natural history photographs. It is obviously easier to work with animals in controlled conditions—zoos, parks, laboratories, etc.—and many photographs are taken in this way.

There is, of course, no objection to the photography of animals in zoos, or of tame creatures, or those under controlled conditions. I have often taken such photographs myself. Most snakes need to be placed where they can be photographed without extraneous herbage spoiling the result; butterflies and moths can be reared and then photographed when they emerge from their chrysalids in immaculate condition; bats can be photographed flying about a studio by using an automatic shutter release; and I have photographed pet harvest mice, a species which I do not think has ever been photographed in the wild. And it is probably impossible to photograph some of the nocturnal, tropical animals in natural conditions. There is nothing wrong in all this but such results should never be passed off as 'wild and free'.

What is so objectionable is the use of unscrupulous methods. Stuffed animals, or those recently killed, are set up against natural—and sometimes not so natural—backgrounds, photographed and the results sold as genuine pictures. Sometimes injured animals are used in this way. I have seen photographs of shot birds propped against a branch of a tree, and birds tethered to the ground—all passed off as 'wild and free'. Such dishonest photographs are, I suppose, more obvious to me as an ornithologist and professional photographer than they are to most people, otherwise they would be spotted more often. The strongest action should be taken to discourage photography that causes pain and suffering. I wish there were a way of disbarring peccant photographers as with erring members of the professions!

Some years ago I told the editor of a pamphlet that the photograph of a stoat he had reproduced was of a dead mammal set up in a natural position. He expressed surprise at the suggestion because the picture had been taken by a reputable photographer whom he thought would never do such a thing. A few days later the editor received a letter from a student who was making a special study of stoats, saying that he could not understand how the mammal had managed to get its hind legs into the position shown in the photograph. The editor therefore wrote to the photographer and asked him directly how it had been taken. The photographer said that in trying to secure the photograph the stoat had become obstreperous, and in attempting to calm it he had unfortunately and unintentionally killed it, but it was only *just* dead when he took the picture. . . .

Then there was the photograph used on the cover of a famous weekly magazine which showed a fox sitting at the mouth of its den. At first sight it looked a wonderful picture, but somehow it did not ring true to me, it looked *too* good. When the photographer was questioned he confessed that the fox was stuffed and that he had set it up by an earth used by a live fox, to see the reaction when it returned. But although he waited a long time, no fox came. He therefore took some photographs of the stuffed one and they looked so natural that he submitted one for fun to the magazine, never thinking it would be used.

Once at an ornithological congress a film was being shown, the chairman stressing the fact that it was taken in the wild under natural conditions. I was so sure, however, that one sequence was taken under artificial conditions that I exclaimed: 'Fake!'

A prominent ornithologist—but no photographer—sitting nearby turned round and suggested that I should keep quiet and speak about it afterwards. When the session ended we both went to the cameraman and it was intimated to him that I thought one sequence in his admittedly superb film was a fake. He asked me why I thought so.

'Because,' I replied, 'you never get shadows like that in nature—the sun shines from only one direction—but in some of the close-ups there were clearly more than one shadow.' He then admitted that these sequences, unlike the rest of the film, had been taken in a studio using artificial lights.

On another occasion I saw a film showing a fine close-up of a bird silhouetted against the sky. I maintained that the shot was artificial because the bird does not naturally hold its wings in the position shown in the film. The cameraman admitted that the bird was being held by its legs.

Many people regard me as a photographic purist. To some this is a criticism, to me it is an accolade. Whenever a photograph I have taken under controlled conditions is published I ask for this fact to be stated in the caption, but, understandably, editors sometimes refuse.

When such photographs are taken, the surroundings must be as natural as possible. Yet I have seen caterpillars of moths and butterflies photographed on the wrong food plant, marine life photographed against inaccurate backgrounds, and fresh-water fish swimming among salt-water shells or seaweed.

The photography of birds at the nest needs careful thought. The nest is the bird's home and generally the parents construct it to harmonise with the surroundings. Usually the photographer has to tie back foliage that will be out of focus or spoil the general composition. Such gardening needs to be carefully done—just before entering the hide— and it is a code of honour among bird photographers that, after work has finished for the day, the surroundings of the nest are returned as nearly as possible to their original condition. Not every nest that is found is ideal for photography. With common birds it is far more satisfactory to search for another nest than try to make a difficult site suitable.

The birds have to be disturbed when you go to the hide and for most birds there should be no further interruptions for at least three hours—and longer for shy birds, especially some of the predators. Constant disturbances can play havoc with birds, and even if they do not desert their nest altogether they sometimes neglect the eggs or young, thus reducing their chance of survival.

A bird photographer, who had recently returned from a trip abroad, proudly told me that on one day he had occupied no fewer than nine hides. Some had been erected close to the nests and occupied without giving the bird a chance to become accustomed to them.

Some months later I heard the other side of the story. In chasing round from one hide to another with no thought for the welfare of the birds, he had left a trail of deserted nests and bitter feelings among the local ornithologists. Such thoughtlessness and selfishness causes untold harm to bird photography, and is one reason why it is now necessary to obtain a licence before rare birds on Schedule 1 of the Protection of Birds Act 1967 can be photographed in this country.

There is a wide-spread practice which often causes great harm, namely taking fledglings from the nest and posing them on a nearby branch. No doubt those who do this believe that by replacing the young in the nest immediately after photographing them no harm is done. The trouble is that once having tasted the delights of the outside world the young, more often than not, are thereafter reluctant to stay within the confines of the nest. By such thoughtless acts countless fledglings have made premature excursions and, thus deprived of parental care, have fallen prey to numerous predators.

I have always felt strongly that acknowledgment should be given to the photographer when his work is reproduced. I simply cannot understand the attitude of editors and publishers who do not hesitate to credit the work of artists yet refuse to do the same for photographers. The last thing I want to do is to cross swords with our bird artists; I know many of them and greatly admire their skill. But it is well-known that, to ensure accuracy, some of them make use either of photographs they take themselves or, more frequently, those taken by other photographers. I hope this statement will not be misunderstood. I am not suggesting that all artists base their paintings on photographs; I know they don't. But again, why should the artists get acknowledgment and not the photographer?

Another aspect of the same general attitude is, I feel, apparent in many book reviews. The text receives meticulous attention, but the photographs which enliven and enhance the book's appeal are dismissed in a sentence—if they are referred to at all. And the names of the photographers are rarely, if ever, mentioned in reviews. *British Wild Life* (Paul Hamlyn, 1966) was an album of 250 of the finest photographs in the National Collection of Nature Photographs housed by the Nature Conservancy. Acknowledgments to the photographers, who made it all possible, were confined to one page in small type at the end of the book.

Having voiced a protest on behalf of the photographer, let me now say a word of praise to the four photographic societies that have been of so much help to me.

During the autumn of 1927 I met B. C. Woodcock, an enthusiastic and talented amateur photographer, and he persuaded me to join the North Middlesex Photographic Society. I had no formal training as a photographer but learnt as I went along, picking up hints wherever possible. My first lesson—a salutary one I have never forgotten—resulted from entering the Society's competition for lantern slides, although I had never made one before. The results were rather 'soot and whitewash' so I sepia-toned them, using a sulphide solution—an evil-smelling chemical which soon permeated the house with the odour of rotten eggs. The slides looked good to me when viewed in the hand by daylight. With all the confidence of my seventeen years I just waited to be announced the winner, but was sadly disillusioned when they were projected and greatly enlarged on the screen. The toning and the artificial light made them look a ghastly ginger!

At that time some of the finest lantern slide workers in the country were members of the North Middlesex, in particular the Finchams

IN 1967, FOR THE FIRST TIME ON RECORD, SNOWY OWLS BRED IN THE BRITISH ISLES

Above: The all-white cock alighting by the side of the grey-coloured owlets

Below: The brown-spotted hen gazes penetratingly at its reflection in the camera lens

E.H. using Contarex Electronic camera with motor drive and $f/2$–180 mm Zeiss Sonnar lens. A recent photograph by Kevin MacDonnell

With His Royal Highness the Duke of Edinburgh at the Royal Photographic Society's Exhibition of my photographs in October 1967. The exhibition followed my election as an Honorary Fellow *(Sdeuard Bisserôt)*

(father and two sons), H. L. Wallis and, of course, B. C. Woodcock. They took a kindly interest in me and I must have been an apt pupil because I fared much better in another competition, which was for the best photograph of a steam train. I went to Hatfield station in Hertfordshire, and by walking along the edge of the track got near a tunnel where trains emerged during an uphill gradient. There I waited for the Flying Scotsman from King's Cross. As it burst out of the tunnel wreathed in smoke from the climb, it made a spectacular picture which won first prize.

In 1932 I was elected to membership of the Zoological Photographic Club and two years later to the Nature Photographic Society.

The Zoological Photographic Club is limited to forty members who comment each month on a folio circulated among them containing members' prints of a zoological subject. A notebook is included containing information about apparatus, members, news, points for discussion, etc. The Nature Photographic Society is run on similar lines but has only six folios a year and botanical subjects are included as well.

When I first joined the ZPC I circulated a series of partridge photographs showing the hatching of the young and with cock and hen together at the nest. I thought they were pretty good, and fully expected the members to be duly impressed. But when they had finished their criticisms I sadly realised there was still a great deal to learn about bird photography.

The Royal is, of course, the senior Photographic Society, not only in Great Britain but in the world. I am very proud that I was elected a Fellow when only twenty-four, and was awarded their medal for natural history photography in 1937, followed thirty years later by their highest accolade, the Honorary Fellowship, probably the greatest photographic honour in the world.

Through membership of these four societies I have come to know the work of most of the leading bird photographers; so well, in fact, that I can recognise their work at a glance. There is a 'jizz', as we say—meaning individuality or personality—about their work which stamps it as theirs as clearly as a painter's brushwork betrays the artist.

The wide appeal of bird photography was especially brought home to me when in April 1957 Kodak had an exhibition of my photographs at their Kingsway showrooms—the most successful exhibition they have ever held there. At times, police had to control the crowds which packed the pavements waiting to get in. Both *The Sunday Times* and *The Observer* ran half-page illustrated features on the exhibition, there were notices in numerous other newspapers, and I was interviewed on both radio and television. Subsequently the photographs were shown in

U

various provincial cities and in several other countries as well, including the United States, South Africa and Australia. The exhibition was especially successful in Singapore.

So my photographs have travelled the world by exhibition, by books, newspapers and magazines, by calendars and postcards, and by television, thus reaching places I shall never visit. What will the future bring? Still active and healthy and as much in love with my craft as ever, I eagerly look forward to future expeditions.

Between delivery of the manuscript and publication of this book, I have been to one of the most zoologically exciting places in the world, the Galapagos Islands, which lie some 1,000 miles south-west of Panama in the Pacific Ocean. Lars Eric Lindblad, of Lindblad Travel, New York, invited me to accompany a party of tourists as photographer-naturalist on a cruise to the islands. Dorothy and David came with me and we had a marvellous time.

It was the Galapagos that first gave Charles Darwin the idea of evolution. Not surprising, for they clearly demonstrate colonisation by natural selection. These small volcanic islands, which rose out of the sea about three million years ago, have a unique fauna, related to but quite distinct from that of the nearest land mass.

The islands are so remote that humans first visited them only some 400 years ago and the animals have little fear of them. Land iguanas ate flowers from my hand, and one day, while bathing, a female sea lion swam between my legs—I really think she wanted to play!

Some of the birds, especially boobies and albatrosses, seemed to be as interested in us as we were in them. When we attempted to touch them, instead of flying away, they 'touched' us back, by pecking. The mocking birds on Hood Island ran after me and pecked at my boot-laces. Never before have I had to run *away* from birds to photograph them.

As naturalist-photographer to the party, I found my duties included those of general handyman. In addition to repairing four pairs of binoculars and one pair of spectacles, I also had to adjust three exposure meters and no fewer than seventeen cameras.

One 82-year-old lady showed me a camera she had borrowed from a friend and, after assuring me that it took wonderful photographs, said: 'How do you use it?' I gave her a lesson and she went off happily on a camera safari of the islands. Two days later she brought the camera back and said: 'Everything's gone fuzzy in the view-finder but I suppose if I point the camera in the right direction and release the shutter I'm bound to get a good result.' On examining the camera I found that the focusing scale registered nine inches and she was taking views at infinity!

Altogether on this wonderful expedition I travelled nearly 15,000 miles and took 6,000 photographs. And now—what next?

Whatever happens, mine has been a very happy life, for I have filled my days doing what I love best, watching and photographing birds. I have travelled far, seen much beauty, made many friends. And always I have returned to a happy home, the greatest blessing a man can have.

Author's note

As a result of a *Desert Island Discs* programme with Roy Plomley I was invited to write my autobiography. I suppose I am among the few who can honestly say that if I had my life to live over again, I would live it in the same way.

But the idea of an autobiography was turned down immediately—I am a photographer, not an author. I put the idea out of my mind, or rather I tried to, for it persisted, and somehow word got around that I was writing the book. Within a year three publishers had contacted me. I thought about it more and more and ideas of how to tackle it began to germinate. But it was not until I discussed it with Frank Lane that concrete plans began to take shape. Without his unstinted help, his enthusiasm and constant encouragement it would never have reached publication stage. He has been my mentor and collaborator all the way through.

In the writing of this book I have been indebted to so many people that if I thanked each one, as perhaps I should, there would be a catalogue of scores of names. I hope that those whose names do not appear will realise that my appreciation is none the less sincere.

To my wife Dorothy I owe much. In addition to allowing me to quote liberally from her diaries and to include some of her photographs, she has been ever ready to help with discussion, ideas and criticism.

But there are others who helped to make my life what it is and have also aided me in the preparation of this book. Had it not been for Guy Mountfort I might have made only three trips abroad, for it was he who took me to Spain, Bulgaria and Hungary, to Jordan and Pakistan. He has written his own record of these expeditions and because we have described shared experiences there has been inevitably some overlapping, but obviously the story of my life would be incomplete without reference to these expeditions. I am grateful to him for readily giving me permission to make use of his books and for helping in many other ways.

George Edwards reminded me of incidents that had occurred on some of our many trips together. Bert Axell, too, helped in various ways, particularly with the Minsmere chapter. Cecily Morrison did Trojan work on the manuscript and improved it beyond measure. Dr. Bruce Campbell, Bruce Coleman, James Fisher, Cherry Kearton and Nigel Sitwell read parts of the text while still in its early stages. James Ferguson-Lees made valuable comments on those parts of the manuscript dealing with expeditions in which he was involved. Stanley Cramp, Norman Ellison, John Gooders, Robert Hudson, Ronnie Pryor, George Shannon, as well as some members of my family, especially my elder brother Stuart, all read the manuscript and have given invaluable advice and criticism, most of which has been incorporated. There have, however, been occasions where I have thought it best to stick to my guns, so I accept full responsibility for everything said.

Gerald Austin of Hutchinson has been most patient, helpful and understanding and I owe a lot to him. Finally, I must thank Kathleen Dennis, Peggy Hadfield and Ruth Kent who did most of the secretarial and typing work involved (some chapters were typed and re-typed four or five times), Jessica Webster who helped with the final preparation of the manuscript, and Gordon Robinson who compiled the index.

Some readers may have expected to find in this book more serious ornithology, more records of observations made from the hide, and perhaps more about actual bird photography. If this is so I am sorry, but it has been almost impossible to know where to draw the line. No one can please everyone all the time!

Whatever the reaction of readers may be, I hope that they will see beyond my story and camera lens to nature itself, and receive the same pleasure and renewal of spirit it has brought to me.

Chronology

1909   Born
1915   Dylla born. Started school
1925   Started work
1927   Accident to foot. Joined North Middlesex Photographic Society
1929   On the dole
1930   Started free-lance photography. First visit to Hickling
1931   Began professional lecturing
1933   *Friends at the Zoo* published. Worked at Staverton Park
1934   Elected Fellow Royal Photographic Society. Staverton
1935   Joined British Ornithologists' Union. Photographed Princesses. Eyke
1936   Eyke
1937   Eye accident in Wales. Awarded RPS's medal for natural history photography
1938   Wales
1939   Married. Honeymoon in Scotland
1940   *Intimate Sketches from Bird Life* published. Scotland
1941   Hickling
1942   Inception of *New Naturalist*. Hickling
1943   Filming for *Tawny Pipit*. Hickling
1944   Margaret born. *Art of Bird Photography* and *Birds of the Day* published. Gorple Moors
1945   Father died. Filming for *Birds of the Village*. *Birds of the Night* published. Eyke
1946   *More Birds of the Day* and *The Swallow* published. High-speed flash at Staverton and the Orkneys. First Hilbre party
1947   Robin born. *Masterpieces of Bird Photography* published. Vice-President of the Royal Society for the Protection of Birds. Scotland. Rockall and seal flights

1948   Staverton

1949   *Birds in Action* published. Staverton

1950   Awarded Country Life International Exhibition of Wildlife Photography medal. Minsmere

1951   London and reservoirs, Hampshire, Gloucestershire and Suffolk

1952   Holland

1953   Chairman Photographic Advisory Committee to the Nature Conservancy. Skomer and Farne Islands

1954   Council of the RPS. Wales

1955   David born. *Birds Fighting* published. Minsmere

1956   Spain and Scotland

1957   Lectured at Royal Festival Hall. Exhibition at Kodak. Spain

1958   Finland

1959   President Zoological Photographic Club. Hon. Vice-President London Natural History Society. Spain

1960   Vice-President Nature Photographic Society. Bulgaria

1961   *Bird Photography as a Hobby* published. Hungary

1962   Hon. Vice-President British Naturalists' Association. International Ornithological Congress, Ithaca, New York

1963   Jordan and Scotland

1964   Norway and Africa

1965   Elected Scientific Fellow Zoological Society. Jordan

1966   Jordan and Pakistan

1967   Exhibition at the RPS and elected Honorary Fellow. *Nesting Birds* published. Norfolk, Shetlands and Pakistan

1968   Awarded the Cherry Kearton memorial medal by the Royal Geographical Society. Shetlands and Africa

1969   Elected Vice-President BOU. Kodak award. Robin and Ann married. Switzerland and Tunisia

1970   Galapagos and Greece. Margaret and Jeremy married. Exhibition at Tryon Gallery

1971   Switzerland. Minsmere. Rhodes

Index